The Task of the Critic

The Task of the Critic

Poetics, Philosophy, and Religion

Henry Sussman

FORDHAM UNIVERSITY PRESS

NEW YORK 2005

Library of Congress Cataloging-in-Publication Data

Sussman, Henry.
   The task of the critic : poetics, philosophy, and religion / Henry Sussman.— 1st ed.
      p. cm.
   Includes bibiliographical references and index.
   ISBN 0-8232-2465-1 (hardcover) — ISBN 0-8232-2466-X (pbk.)
   1. Criticism—History—20th century. 2. Criticism.
3. Criticism (Philosophy) I. Title.
   PN94.S87   2005
   801'.95'0904—dc22
                                         2005006433

Printed in the United States of America
07 06 05 5 4 3 2 1
First edition

For Carol Jacobs and to the memory of Jacques Derrida (1930–2004).

CONTENTS

ACKNOWLEDGMENTS

However my running critical commentary ultimately fares in the exchange house of academic opinion, it has already achieved distinction and notoriety in at least this one respect: in the select corps of humanities editors who have served as my knowing and consensual coconspirators. These include not only the groundbreaking Helen Tartar, whom I follow with gratitude and devotion from Stanford to Fordham University Press and who, to my mind, epitomizes intellectual engagement in the art of producing books. I have also benefited in many ways from collaborative work with William Sisler, currently director at Harvard University Press, and with Eric Halpern, director at the University of Pennsylvania Press. I have had the great pleasure to produce edited volumes with William Germano of Routledge. It is a delight, both professionally and creatively, to coordinate a book series at SUNY Press with James Peltz, who took over from a splendid predecessor, Carola Sautter. Mr. Peltz was recently appointed to the interim directorship at SUNY Press. During his days at the University of Minnesota Press, the redoubtable Lindsay Waters and I worked together on a serial publication.

The publication of *The Task of the Critic* makes me particularly attentive to the partnership between author and editor. It is a fundamental working rapport between different stages and functions of cultural production in the maintenance of whose integrity all cultural programmers—authors, critics, journalists, archivists, scholars—have a vital stake. The relation between author and editor is privileged in the sense that any cultural programmer is privileged to have the good offices, resources, advice, and technical expertise of an editor at his or her disposal. Given how the editor's job is sandwiched between the negotiation of often unforgiving budgetary and technical constraints and a service, often involving self-effacement, to the author's vision, it is fortunate and in many senses miraculous that humanists in the United States can contemplate professional collaboration with such gifted and engaged members of an impossible profession as Helen Tartar, Bill Sisler, Eric Halpern, Lindsay Waters, Doug Armato, Bill Germano, Bill Regier, James Peltz, and so many others. We have an interest in making sure our editors are treated fairly, whether they publish our productions or not, in the same sense in which we have an interest in making sure that there are outlets for our work, in whichever form publication transpires, and that our submissions are reviewed objectively and in view of appropriate criteria.

Since a book focusing on the theoretical conditions and pretexts of my predominantly literary commentary is not an everyday occurrence, this is a time when I think of other long-term commitments that have contributed materially to my work and its possibility. With great joy and longing, I recall the three occasions during which a respite from teaching and some long-standing administrative overcommitments at the Camargo Foundation, in Cassis, France meant the resumption of writing and the completion of projects. Michael Pretina has been a gifted administrator of that focused, but gracious institution, and without his support, the writing wouldn't have gone nearly as well. The last time I was there, in spring 2002, I benefited both from an NEH Humanities grant, my second, and from supplemental funding from my ongoing university, the University at Buffalo. I gratefully acknowledge my career debt to the NEH and wish it the best, under all political conditions, in fulfilling its mission: sustaining work conducive to authentic thinking, situated at the thresholds of the evolving field of knowledge.

I am most grateful to Yale University for the opportunity it affords me to teach there, to share in the stimulating and uplifting responsibility of instructing its amazing students, and to maintain coherence in my family life. Yet the occasion of a theoretical retrospective on the writing I have done as a critic makes me deliberate more on the effect registered by my affiliation, for twenty-seven years, with the comprehensive arm of a large and diffuse state university. I have indeed drawn heavily over these years on the vitality and freewheeling approach to learning and research characterized by the Departments of Comparative Literature, English, Classics, and the Arts at Buffalo. I've received remarkable creative work and affirmation from the graduate students of these departments, who are simply world class. I am resolved at this stage of my career to redouble my efforts to ensure that these students gain the recognition and placement that they amply deserve.

It is a particular challenge to chart developments on the horizons of the field of knowledge in the rough-and-tumble environment of a public university defined in large measure by the access it grants a broad and diverse public. The task of keeping the institution's eye on the intellectual and academic prizes while it perforce responds to a vast range of sociopolitical and economic forces and pressures occupies many minds and hands. I much appreciate the spirit of liberality in which these issues and conflicts have been negotiated over the years at Buffalo. I wish incoming President John B. Simpson the best during his tenure at the institution.

This project has been the beneficiary of the resources and expertise furnished by three great libraries, the Sterling and Beinecke at Yale and the Lockwood at Buffalo. Would that the idealism and sense of purpose so evident at libraries and archives of this caliber extend to other sectors of public space.

I owe a profound debt of gratitude to Chris Mohney and Bud Bynack of Fordham University Press for an editing that allowed the book to speak in its own idiom while consolidating its major points and tightening its transitions.

Chapters 2 and 5 first appeared among the pages of the Comparative Literature number of *Modern Language Notes*. Chapter 4 appeared in *boundary 2*. Brief passages from Chapter 1 were included in my introduction to *Acts of Narrative* (Stanford: Stanford University Press, 2003), co-edited with Carol Jacobs.

The ongoing inspiration and commiseration of my teachers and mentors, Jacques Derrida, whose recent loss is felt by so many of us, J. Hillis Miller, Richard Macksey, and Allan Grossman, has been absolutely indispensable to my continuing at this labor. There simply is no way in which my ongoing annotations could ever live up to their intellectual power, intuition, and ethical resolve and strength. I continue to lurk in the outer precincts of their classrooms, somewhere between the windows and the door, my ballpoint drawn and my notebook open.

The Task of the Critic: A Game of Registers

The task of the critic has never been harder. Since the New Criticism concentrated critical activity within the linguistic and formal parameters of the artifact, drawing on the Wittgensteinian strand of twentieth-century linguistic rigor renewing the focus of the critical calling, there has been a prodigious, perhaps impossible growth in the discourses, activities, and registers of oversight associated with literary and cultural criticism. Even as such writers as I. A. Richards[1] and William Empson[2] sought, with a precision owing to logical analysis, to delimit the field of critical work, Walter Benjamin, for one, invoked anything and anybody in the grand and ultimately tragic endeavor of improving the condition of society through enhanced public attention to the nuances of language and culture.[3] Benjamin, taking his cue from German idealism, confused the task of the critic by dissolving any limits around it. *The Origins of German Tragic Drama* is as much a handbook for a critical practice refusing to determine whether it is literary exegesis, philosophical argumentation, aesthetic appreciation, or cultural history as it is a paean to a certain formation in the history of a single art form—drama—and the rhetorical usages and circumlocutions that it generated.[4]

Thus, historical happenstance, philosophical argument, ideological documents, material products, and remains of specific sociological formations—all these became fodder in the critic's desperate and belated attempt to forestall the banality of evil through the resuscitation and reprogramming of sensibility. The systematic designs of Kant and Hegel, dolls and other toys surviving from the age of Baudelaire, the pronouncements of Marx and Proudhon, Charlie Chaplin's contortions, not to mention any literary work of consequence, this entire Chinese encyclopedia of phenomena, with all the offshoots that its members generated, became the stuff, material, *Stoff*,[5] with which engaged critics and theorists slapped the face of advanced Western culture as it slipped nonetheless into an irreversible cultural and aesthetic coma.

We should not underestimate the extent to which the ferment of the French *sciences humaines* dedicated itself to the continuation of the discourse of the Frankfurt School.[6] The French version of the *Gesamtkritik* initiated by Benjamin, Adorno, and co-workers brought established academic disciplines, above all anthropology, linguistics, economics, psychoanalysis, and history, to bear on the task of cultural criticism, but the array of artifacts and discourses relevant to the endeavor remained as polyglot as it was under the unauthorized, unsanctioned pickup game of cultural uplift. The *sciences humaines* settled on structures precisely because they are iterable, transferable, *between* the multiple disciplines that were now reorienting themselves to semiosis at the basis of their respective systems of meaning and interpretation. Poststructuralism rebelled specifically against the combined field theory that could reduce, if not obliterate the differentiation between conceptual models and *épistèmes*, the easy, self-aggrandizing iterability of discourses, artifacts, and bodies of evidence available to critical articulation. One might indeed argue that in poststructuralism, philosophy achieved a status as a master framework or perspective to gauge the progress of certain arguments or conceptual projects while productions and formulations from virtually all other areas of discourse, "high" art, and popular culture remained "game" in the critic's tragically flawed, frenetic effort to make sense and non-sense of the world of ideas and the events that transpire under their aegis.

Apart from that British attempt in the 1950s to imbue some sense into the critic, an endeavor repeated unconsciously, since by the disciplines' determinations of their professional subspecializations and their weightings, the task of the critic has, in the post–World War II years, only complexified itself, broadened its purview, and proliferated the artifacts and other phenomena for which it takes responsibility and the discourses and other conceptual tools it brings to bear in intellectual work. The contemporary critic of demonstrable theoretical sensibility is, minimally, at once, enough the philosopher to attach her reasonings to broader issues and arguments that have emerged at the level of the conceptual operating system maintained by that discipline, and a poet, in at least two senses: an observer steeped in the history, sensibility, and substantive and formal judgments of modern Western aesthetics, not to mention a writer aiming often, if not in every sentence, at the Baudelairean "miracle . . . of a poetic prose," in this respect continuing the writerly project common, in different ways, to the *Athenaeum*, nineteenth-century French prose poetry, logical analysis, and the Frankfurt School itself.

Yet through the odd conjunction between the New Criticism and deconstruction's implosion of the arguments and practices that they both bear with them through minute attention to the turns of phrase and argument at the core of textual exegesis, the contemporary critic has also become a close reader: a master of spin and nuance who throws overarching concepts and operations to the wind. In brief, the emergence of values and attitudes embodied by the close reader as an interest, if not persona, to stand alongside the poet, the philosopher, and the critic, may well stand as the most significant single intellectual development (if we truck in such units) to have emerged in the post–World War II years.

The benighted *semblable* or contemporary who sets about even a pedestrian work of criticism thus has, at once, something of the poet, the philosopher, and the close reader about her. And these writerly postures may, in important senses, oppose as well as complement one another. And we have not yet dared to diagram the engine room of criticism. It may emerge that criticism, in its occasional setting and thrust, its fabrication of a throwaway framework for the integration of linguistico-cultural phenomena, its circulation back to a magnetic, fatal constellation of consecrated writers, is merely yet another competing script to be set alongside philosophy, poetry, and close reading.

If this is so, we really are in a stew. How is the contemporary worker in the field of cultural reception and dissemination to differentiate and dance between these registers in her own appropriate writerly practice, especially when the multiplicity of registers and the tensions between them may have never been made explicit? And if much of our writing is laden with the overlap between seemingly similar writerly registers nonetheless bearing imperatives and emphases slightly—but tellingly—different, what of the professionalization that, by virtue of its internal needs and momentum, would presume to compartmentalize us and our work in categories far neater than our writing allows? Above the writerly ferment or ragout that passes inexplicitly from philosophizing to poetry, to minute exegesis, to the makeshift design of criticism in its essence, hovers the backdrop of professional categories symptomatic, in part, of the fact that we have lost a considerable share of the reading public we once might have claimed, that the learned professions are what save us from the oblivion we would otherwise experience in our remoteness from a discernible, definable, noninstitutional audience to which we might write. Within the context of professional associations, vast expenditures of time, energy, and verbiage are being made in the promotion and debunking of diverse conceptual models on substantive, procedural, and political grounds. Yet as often as not, it may well be, in these academic broadsides, that the purity and weighting of the writerly register, whether poetic, philosophical, exegetical, or critical, is being contested, rather than the substance of the inferences drawn regarding the artifact, from whatever professionally sanctioned bailiwick it hails.

Explicitness, the rendering explicit of the otherwise understated, may be the telling common denominator uniting the poetic, the philosophical, the exegetical, and the critical registers that might be negotiated by the contemporary intellectual writer demonstrating theoretical sensibility. It is in the name of a relentless critical enterprise of rendering explicit that I will, in these and the following pages, tease apart the different writerly registers of poetry, philosophy, close reading, and criticism, which are all interrelated and coimplicated in contemporary critical work, albeit solely for the purpose of releasing them back to their unmarked and conspiratorial collaboration.

It is already definitively too late to think in terms of separate genres or subgenres of critical discourse essentially defined and deployed in some clear-cut cultural division of labor. Jacques Derrida has performed the necessary task of interrogating these invariably prefabricated categories, interestingly, in relation to literature, which for him is as much of an institution, linking it to religion and law, as a creative or aesthetic venue. His essay "The Law of Genre" arises to embellish a particularly dense and performance-rich prose poem by Maurice Blanchot, *La folie du jour*, but in its wake, it leaves a profoundly disturbing picture of genre as the very principle of categorical thinking and exclusion in Western ontotheology and religion.[7] Derrida's prose dramatizes the extreme exception he takes to "The Law of Genre" by near-systematically violating the discursive conventions to which he would be assumed to adhere. His philosophical argumentation has been known to veer off into associative prose poetry, while his exegeses of particular passages and formulations in the texts he interrogates successfully vie with academic criticism in his historical erudition and preparation, not to mention in their detailed and sustained analyses. Sentence by sentence, his grammar, syntax, diction, and semantics demonstrate a detailed attentiveness to the tangible features of language customarily taking center stage in poetry's variegated performances. Derrida indeed places himself in a line of writers including Poe, Nietzsche, Heidegger, Blanchot, Benjamin, and Borges for whom the true payoff of synthesizing discourse is the nodes of poetic crystallization that emerge along its prosaic trajectory.

From its very outset, then, my project is beset with a formative double bind: In the name of culture's relentless work of making explicit, there is indisputable value in the task of surveying the shock, confluence, and reverberation between different strands of discourse whose cumulative tapestry or text approximates a discursive "division of labor." In certain passages, this work therefore may demand a teasing apart of the textual strata or performances whose colloquy is responsible for a compelling work of discourse. But this analysis must not come at the expense of relapsing into the predetermined law of genre to which Derrida has applied such a far-reaching, profound, and ethical statute of limitations. In one phase of the current project, I therefore would hope to render explicit a differentiated census of discursive tasks that cultural writers can live with, a set of weightings and values emerging from the writerly process itself that do not mobilize or involve transcendental selves or their inherent moral imperatives. I would hope, in this exercise, following Derrida, to defuse the value-laden with the singularity and relentlessness of articulation, to marshal specificity against the law of genre, which acts blindly in the name of a precision it then proceeds to discard at every turn.

1

Romantic poetry is a progressive, universal poetry. Its aim isn't merely to reunite all the separate species of poetry and put poetry in touch with philosophy and rhetoric. It tries to and should mix and fuse poetry and prose, inspiration and criticism, the poetry of art and the poetry of nature; and make poetry lively and sociable and life and society poetical; poeticize wit and fill and saturate the forms of art and poetry with every kind of good, solid matter for instruction, and animate them with the pulsations of humor. . . . It alone can become, like the epic, a mirror of the whole circumambient world, an image of the age. And it can also—more than any other form—hover at the midpoint between the portrayed and the portrayer, free of all real and ideal self-interest, on the wings of poetic reflection, and can raise that reflection again and again to a higher power, can multiply it in an endless succession of mirrors. . . . Romanticism is in the arts what wit is in philosophy, and what society and sociability, friendship and love are in life. . . . The romantic kind of poetry is still in the state of becoming.

(Friedrich Schlegel, Athenaeum, Fragment 116)[8]

The greater the share of the shock factor in particular impressions, the more constantly consciousness has to be alert as a screen against stimuli; the more efficiently it does so, the less do these impressions enter experience [*Erfahrung*], tending to remain in the sphere of a certain hour in one's life [*Erlebnis*]. Perhaps the special achievement of shock defense may be seen in its function of assigning to an incident a precise time in consciousness at the cost of the integrity of its contents. This would be a chief achievement of the intellect. . . . In the dedication of his collection to the editor-in-chief of *La Presse,* Arsène Houssaye, Baudelaire wrote: "Who among us has not dreamt, in his ambitious days, of the miracle of a poetic prose? It would have to be musical without rhythm and rhyme, supple and resistant enough to adapt itself to the lyrical stirrings of the soul, the wave motions of dreaming, the shocks of consciousness. This ideal, which can turn into an *idée fixe,* will grip especially those who are at home in the giant cities and the web of their numberless interconnected relationships."

(Walter Benjamin, "On Some Motifs in Baudelaire")[9]

After closing his pharmacy, Plato went to retire, to get out of the sun. He took a few steps in the darkness toward the back of his reserves, found himself leaning over the *pharmakon,* decided to analyze.

Within the thick, cloudy liquid, trembling deep inside the drug, the whole pharmacy stood reflected, repeating the abyss of he Platonic phantasm.

The analyst cocks his ears, tries to distinguish between two repetitions. . . .

Holding the *pharmakon* in one hand, the calamus in the other, Plato mutters as he transcribes the play of formulas. . . . The walled-in voice strikes against the rafters, the words come apart, bits and pieces of sentences are separated, disarticulated parts . . . become rejoined, bounce off of each other, contradict each other, tell on each other, come back like answers . . . take themselves for a dialogue. Full of meaning. A whole story. An entire history. All of philosophy.

"*hē ēkhē toutōn tōn logōn* . . . the sound of these arguments rings so loudly in my head that I cannot hear the other side."

In this stammering buzz of voices, as some philological sequence or another floats by, one can sort of make this out, but it's hard to hear: *logos* beds itself . . . *pharmakon* means *coup* . . . "so that *pharmakon* will have meant: that which pertains to an act of demoniac possession [*un coup démoniaque*] or is used as a curative *against* such an attack . . . an armed enforcement of order [*un coup de force*] . . . a shot fired [*un coup tiré*] . . . a planned overthrow [*un coup monté*] . . . but to no avail [*un coup pour rien*] . . . like cutting through water [*un coup dans l'eau*] . . . *en udati grapsei* . . . and a stroke of fate [*un coup du sort*] . . . Theuth who invented writing . . . the calendar . . . dice . . . *kubeia* . . . the calendar trick [*le coup du calendrier*] . . . the unsuspected dramatic effect [*le coup du théâtre*] . . . the writing trick [*le coup de l'écriture*] . . . the dice-throw [*le coup de dés*] . . . two in one blow [*le coup double*] . . . *kolaphos* . . . *gluph* . . . *colpus* . . . *coup* . . . glyph . . . scalpel . . . scalp . . . *khrusos* . . . *chrysolite* . . . *chrysology* . . .

Plato gags his ears.[10]

Like the truest secrets, this one lies fully exposed to the public sphere: At its pivotal moments, critical script delivers itself of the *jouissance* of poetic composition. At certain junctures—never haphazard—the memorable critics, whether Plato, Rousseau, Schlegel, Benjamin, or Derrida, abandon their disputations in the name and practice of a poetic reverie. This poesy is surely a benefit of the austere labor of careful exegesis and cracking semiotic codes. It would be a stretch to assert, however, that the poetic moments, or impasses, or cloverleafs of criticism, constitute the discourse's underlying motives or first causes. In criticism, poetry occasionally happens. It is to the credit of a comprehensive discourse such as was synthesized at Jena and Weimar that it could account for the poetic condensation, compression, and detonation in which critical discourse, under specific conditions, gathers itself.

Understated, inhabiting a nether stratum of the work, like the mined silver underwriting all values and activities in Conrad's *Nostromo*, the poetics of criticism remains an ongoing pretext and motive to the otherwise degraded and forbidding work. In specific moments, and by no means in all of them, the critic *delves into poetry*, whether through a near-interlinear intimacy with the poetry crystallized in the artifact under discussion or in the critical dance *between* the artifact and its critical recapitulation, orchestrating a syncopation and counterpoint between the counterdiscourses. There are moments in criticism when the counterpoise and reverberation between commented and commentary are just right, no less pristine, hovering, and freed from the gravity of sense and instrumentality than the well-wrought poetic line. These are the moments in Benjamin's critical discourse that he might associate with shock: the precipitous emergence of an image that magically both coalesces and ties together hitherto proliferating loops of association. They are the occasional passages in Derrida's writing when the philosopher abandons his staging of the play between something metaphysical, or morbid, or otherwise regressive, and what eschews the bounding and simply revels in the play of text detached from this scenario.

In the understandably celebrated fragment from the *Athenaeum* at the head of this section, Friedrich Schlegel evidences that Romantic discourse, as Lessing, beforehand, with a somewhat different hermeneutic ethos, anticipated the problematic of the present essay: the inevitable, but disoriented confluence of the discourses. Whether prosaic or lyrical, Romantic poetry took on the systematic aspirations that philosophy, at that moment of ideological formation and European history, afforded itself. In poetic form, it would fuse poetry to philosophy, rhetoric, the visual, and prose. The poetic art form takes on the lineaments of a system at the same time that it becomes one form of the fragment that is the inevitable remainder and byproduct of the systematic enterprise. We may say even that the system conjures up the fragment, which henceforth opposes it by resisting every principle and category by which the system constitutes itself.

In keeping with the Enlightenment ideology configuring itself through such systematic projects as Kant's and Hegel's, and receiving its aesthetic transformation in Romantic stylistics, Romantic poetry would be "progressive and universal," would proceed immanently and gradually from a human provenance toward a general emancipation. In keeping with the Kantian speculations, society—and sociability—it would be the counterweight to any tendency toward dissolution, anomie, or corruption implicit in this evolution. Even in his fragmentary broadside, Schlegel, like the Kant of the *Critiques*, installs a governor within the machinery progressing toward the release of the intuitive and the synthetic, and this mechanism is the insistence on a societal payoff and assent, enacted by the tribunal of reason.[11]

Under the aura of Romanticism, then, and for many, including Foucault, Romanticism inaugurated the modernity whose paradigms are still, with some modification, in effect: Poetry is at the heart of discursive speculation. Poetry both embodies and opposes the comprehensive frame around discourse that the systematic enterprise imposes. Poetry would furnish the grandeur of systematic dimensionality with the circumspection that thought machines, purely conceptual computers, should profess in an age of universal Enlightenment. It would be the inbuilt soul of discursive systems. Through its sociability, it would ensure a human dimension to systems making, which, left on its own, whether in *Frankenstein* or *Moby-Dick*, may well eventuate in monstrosity.

For Heidegger, poetry would demarcate the only site at which philosophy delivers itself over to thinking, where language achieves a critical mass and density sufficient to release it from the sway of logic.[12] Walter Benjamin surely does not devalue the power of such poetic condensation. But where Heidegger appropriates poetry as an edifying tribute to philosophical inquiry, the very arena or clearing of philosophy, Benjamin marks it as the traumatic disruption to communal life and psychological coherence.

The prosaic under the aesthetic of Romanticism would be poetic, a contract already in effect by Baudelaire's moment. But by the time Benjamin adopted the Baudelairean exhortation to a poetic prose, his interest, at least in this section of "On Some Motifs in Baudelaire," had shifted from the problematic of systematicity to the poetic as a phenomenological category, a place where texts and other artifacts allegorize shocks and other insults to *durée*, cognitive coherence, and psychological equanimity. The inauguration of this modernist phenomenology may well occur in the above-cited Schlegel passage, where poetry will "mirror . . . the whole circumambient world" and be an "image of the age." This is surely a phenomenological extension, as well as a rhetorical one, of the concerted work that the Schlegels, Wordsworth, and Kierkegaard, among others, did on the image. Benjamin has shifted the terms and terrain of the investigators' skill with systematic dimensions. He is at the same time engaged in synthesizing an aesthetics imbued with the particular features of experience (*Erfahrung*) in "advanced" Western societies in the twentieth century with an artistic phenomenology, a politics of experience that has allowed itself to be driven by aesthetic, rather than metaphysical or transcendental categories.

Within this enterprise, the shock that incorporates poetic condensation, but that disrupts the time-space continuum and the field of knowledge, rather than integrating them, is more constitutive of discourse than any systematic overview. The extended images by which Benjamin fulfills the Baudelairean wish for a poetic prose trap the reader in knots of textual inevitability and aesthetic epiphany. In the figure of gambling machines, Benjamin finds both a Marxian expansion of the means of production, the assembly line, into leisure pursuits and the structure of the wish. The poetic inevitability of the roulette wheel to this swath of discourse traps us, shockingly. Yet the social context in which the image and its poetry erupt is already fragmented and shattered. Gone is the calendar of the ritual year, as defined by folklore and religion. The reference frame for the poetic prose that Benjamin himself attained on many occasions is less a system, as it was for the Schlegels and Kierkegaard, than the phenomenology and mass psychology of the yet unacclimated captives of late capitalism, the dominant sociopolitical and ideological formation in its ascendancy. Benjamin has preserved the aura surrounding the Romantic fragment, but he arrays the *Bruchstücke*, fragments of a degenerate enlightened society in a somewhat alien poetic space.

As Derrida waives the assumed generic differences of discourse in a wider inquiry into the status of writing and its freedom, the sociopolitical aspirations still discernible in Benjamin's messianic eulogy give way, or rather resurface at the syllabic and subsyllabic levels in a critique of ideology's torque on language. Derrida takes up the Romantic *Auseinandersetzung* with systematicity at the hinge between the precincts and margins of systems. But the actors in the encounter are rigorously held to a linguistic provenance and status, so that after configuring and assaying the *pharmakon* as both the pith of Western metaphysics and its dissolution and downfall, Derrida's text is free to enter its own reverie, a moment of condensed dissemination, in no simple way retracing the *pharmakon's* sinuous path and stuttering rhythm. The citation from "Plato's Pharmacy" at the head of this section encloses the "stammering buzz of voices" into which Platonic idealism, under very specific stresses and within a marginal purview, degenerates. This writing joins the commentary on Blanchot's *Folie du jour* as a release from the tensions gravitating to the hinges of systems, a moment of deconstructive text allegory projected affirmatively, a reveling (or revelation) in pure textuality, pure in the Kantian sense. Plato becomes almost a character in the textual drama, at least an icon. Marginal to the economies of representation and identity, the *pharmakon* performs itself.

Derrida is no less a poet at this moment than the Mallarmé of "The Double Session" or Benjamin's Baudelaire. Poetry is not inimical to discourse. On the contrary, it erupts there. It adorns the extensive facets of discourse like crystals of stone and metal produced under specific seismic conditions. The poetic nuggets that have formed under the pressures of exposition and rhetoric often steal the show or furnish a vivid sideshow to an elaboration of concepts and topoi less vivid. Yet criticism, whatever that may be, and philosophy furnish an organic compost for poetry. When the moments of poetic condensation exasperate the commentators, this may be less due to the enigma of the images than to the interlacing of discursive registers.

2

Were there to be any *proof* of the intense investigation into modalities and registers of script common to the Romantics and contemporary critical theorists, of the hope to the point of messianism invested in the very medium of inscription, it would need to come out in the *reading*, to be registered in the insight and lucidity that can be furnished by interpretations. It is at this point that we need to return to the textual passages at the head of the first subhead above, which served us as a motive, a starting-off point, and an occasion for our own deliberations.

It took a Benjamin, in the polymorphous writing media that he opened up for contemporary cultural discourse, to follow to the letter what the Germans of the *Frühromantik*, early Romanticism, demonstrate tangibly, the potential that wit, fragmentation, poetic condensation, shock technique, and radical citation (a play of textual fragments, if you will) held for cultural discourse in an age of technological reproducibility, mass media, and unprecedented urban intensity. (I'm suggesting here that Benjamin's different writing genres, from conventional essays of literary scholarship, to his auto-biographical reminiscences, to his fragmentary manifestoes—e.g., from "The Work of Art in the Age of Its Technological Reproducibility" and "Theses on the Philosophy of History" to *The Arcades Project*, which may be described as a massive experiment in radical citation or print-medium Web site formation—actualized, with different degrees of emphasis, the scriptural modalities first systematically envisioned by the early Romantics.) For all that Schlegel and his coterie set the stage for a radical practice of reading, he did not deliver or fill in the meticulous readouts that constitute the basis for cultural reception, critical discernment, and formulations of taste in the contemporary cultural scene.

There were any number of ports or accesses to the terminal of close reading, which as an explicit mode of cultural synthesis did not hit its stride until after World War II. Among these we can recollect at least the follow-ing: the intense scrutiny of sense in assertion and statement accorded by logical analysis, which surely carried over to the New Criticism and its ap-proach to texts; the rise of linguistics as an interstitial social science with close ties to the disciplines overseeing the artifacts that embody language's exemplary and extreme deployments; the formal, semiotic, narratological, and structural analyses introduced into cultural studies by the deployment of linguistic perspectives and procedures; the insistence, emerging from modern phenomenology, that philosophical investigation be driven by the philological and etymological deep roots of the language implicated by the discussion, rather than by predetermined etiquettes of logic; and the insight that the excruciating complexities of reading follow certain of the pivotal figures pursued throughout the history of rhetoric. All of the methodologi-cal platforms for intellectual work abbreviated above imply an exegetical imperative, an ethics of close reading that the likes of the *Frühromantik*, Kierkegaard, and Nietzsche envisioned, but didn't quite arrive at delivering. (Interestingly, Freud may well have been the first overarching figure of modern thought and culture who recognized the parity between psyche and text, the indispensability of a meticulous exegesis of personal and collective dreams to any discipline or clinical protocol that was to rise to the shock and complexity of those phenomena.)

It was, then, left to the ragtag horde of the students of Romantic theory, philology, linguistics, psychoanalysis, phenomenology, and rhetoric to ful-fill the promise of and imperative to close reading that had been first imagined at the apogee of German idealism. The payback to this anticipatory speech act may have been late, but it came furiously. The stage for the invariably performative act of close exegesis was backlit, as we have seen, by a broad range of intellectual traditions. What is common to each of those disciplinary case histories is that close reading, once entertained, is an allegory of its own unfolding, a configuration of meaning simultaneous with itself. That is why we *engage* in close reading, against a backdrop of a delirium of signification by the established cultural codes, long before we organize its history or orchestrate its given place in a division of labor.

To place, characterize, or account for close reading is to *perform* close reading. We are hence thrown back on the fragments of citation that inspired our meditation on the *Frühromantik* and its role in setting the mood and setting for theoretically astute discourse. Yet the reading we have already performed in the course of the present chapter primes us for what we are capable of receiving from the Schlegelian, Benjaminian, and Derridian passages at hand. This cycle, to which Hegel and Kierkegaard imputed the characteristic of infinity, may well characterize all close reading: My prior immanent engagement with texts prepares me for a specific encounter with passages whose selection is by no means haphazard, and the production of this expenditure of exegetical labor can be only further immanent formulations whose only potential realization consists in being directed at further swaths of textual programming, of necessity fragmentary and inconsequential.

We are then, free—free, but under a certain constraint, if not obligation, to go in close. Our close reading of the passages is both an ultimate subjection to the prior decisions constituting the text, a self-effacement while the words themselves speak, and the greatest liberty we could take with the artifact, its radical reprogramming according to predilections and tendencies that have crystallized in our prior reading, according to patterns we've been primed for in our scanning. It is in keeping both with our openness to Schlegel's *Athenaeum* Fragment 116 and the recognitions that have emerged during our readings *around* it that the passage stands out as the Grand Central Terminal in the progressive, multidirectional, porcupinelike accretion of drafts *toward* the synthesis of a hermeneutically intense, self-generative, self-critical writing. It is to the variegated emergence of this synthesis that the collective bodies of the *Fragments* are dedicated. Schlegel has powerfully fitted *Athenaeum* Fragment 116 out with a rhetoric and momentum of infinite growth, development, movement, modification, and possibility that apply both to the Romantic script, which is an updated medium of inscription with vast potential, and to the heady cultural milieu of the moment.

It is the *coordination* between terms, figures, and modalities of expansion and potential endlessness in the fragment that must at some point strike us in our role as close readers. A substantial and careful orchestration of expansive modalities must prevail if we are to heed the announcement of a "progressive, Romantic poetry." This is a major happening, particularly if a new centrality of the likes of poetry, criticism, irony, and wit is going to be achieved by this new scriptural medium. A good measure of the power requisite for such a momentous event emerges from the juxtaposition in a very concentrated space (this is, after all, the dimension of fragments) of different images for freshness, expansion, inclusion, amalgamation, continuity, and progression.

It makes perfect sense indeed, then, that Fragment 116 could effect a poetic synthesis combining the freshness of articulation of the "poetizing child," epic's embrace of the "whole circumambient world," the "endless succession" or hall of mirrors opened by an inherently critical poetry, and the "infinitely increasing" access to the immanent aura of classical texts that such a poetics gains us. This is Romantic poetry gathering itself as an unadulterated interface: "It tries to and should mix and fuse poetry and prose, inspiration and criticism, the poetry of art and the poetry of nature; and make poetry lively and sociable; and life and society poetical; poeticize wit and fill and saturate the forms of art with every kind of good, solid matter for instruction, and animate them with the pulsations of humor."

One fashion in which Romantic poetry fulfills its expansive and assimilative imperative is by a sequence, again potentially endless, of chiasmuses or crossings, as between art poetry and nature poetry, inspiration and criticism, but the absorption of oppositions is in the name of an overall opening. The ultimate product, or rather process, of such a texture or linguistic material is an open-ended becoming, one open in multifarious and overdetermined ways. In this passage, Schlegel ushers in an age in which "Romantic poetry is in the arts what wit is in philosophy." This is an age when the lion lies down with the lamb, when poetry and philosophy are no longer antithetical. Schlegel figures the historically antagonistic discourses as now maintaining the relationship of Chinese twins, joined at the shoulder, where poetry verges into wit. Cultural history remembers this fragment for the parabasis defined and demonstrated by the "endless succession of mirrors." But more important is an imponderably heavy condensation of figures and modes of expansion, incorporation, and the self-sustenance of activity that achieves freedom in its endlessness.

We read the passage closely and find it both to intensify the textual neighborhood that it belongs to and to join that ecology, although not quite perfectly. A similar relation prevails between the passage from "On Some Motifs in Baudelaire," also cited at the outset of the first subhead of this chapter, in which the author appropriates Baudelaire's exhortation for a "poetic prose" as a pretext to his own technique of shock therapy in writing. For Baudelaire to declare the necessity of a poetic prose medium in order for it to be possible to make the interventions requisite to his particular cultural milieu, and for Benjamin to take him up on this suggestion is not a far cry from certain of the possibilities entertained by the *Frühromantik*, as they have been scored in *Critical Fragments* 26, 53, and 100 and of course in the redoubtable *Athenaeum* Fragment 116. Yet shock receives a treatment under Benjamin's imprimatur distinct both from its announcement in section 4 of "On Some Motifs in Baudelaire" and from its orchestration as multifaceted expansion in *Athenaeum* Fragment 116.

It was surely Benjamin's innovation to incorporate within the complex tissue of criticism the density of population and experience, the variegated visual field, the new styles of transportation and physical movement, distinctive cadences and tempos, and outpourings of energy of twentieth-century urban life. Benjamin devoted himself to reading the fabric and energy of the city and to allowing them in turn to color the transcript of criticism like no other writer before or since. It was indeed his intuition of the impact of urbanity upon modern experience, cognition, and aesthetic improvisation that drew him to some of his most revisited authors: Proust, Karl Krauss, and Franz Hessel, along with the likes of Baudelaire and Hugo. So it is that by the end of our citation from "On Some Motifs in Baudelaire," Benjamin can scroll the ideal of a poetic prose directly into "the giant cities and the web of their numberless interconnecting relationships."

Imagistic shock is as contractive amid the miracle of Benjamin's poetic prose as the range of "progressive, universal" Romantic poetry is expansive, virtually endless. It is with the most finely attuned expression in prose that Benjamin can repeatedly arrest, litter with bombshell craters, the otherwise too fluid plane of exposition. The formulation "all great works of literature establish a genre or dissolve one . . . they are in, in other words, special cases"[13] initiates his definitive, if early brief study of Proust. He highlights shortly thereafter "the image of Proust" as "the highest physiognomic expression which the irresistibly growing discrepancy between literature and life was able to assume."[14] "Fairy tales for dialecticians are what Kafka wrote when he went to work on legends. He inserted little tricks into them."[15] Given the tradition of fragmentary writing that Benjamin shares with Kafka, which Kafka's achievement reinforces as an aesthetic parameter of Benjamin's critical prose, it is no accident that the critic should find an auratic object in Kafka's treatment of the gesture. "Each gesture is an event. . . . Like El Greco, Kafka tears open the sky behind every gesture; but as with El Greco—who was the patron saint of the Expressionists—the gesture remains the decisive thing, the center of the event."[16]

"On Some Motifs in Baudelaire" does not content itself with tracing the flow of the nineteenth-century European metropolis into the tempo, rhythm, and affect of discursive writing, it takes upon itself the performance of these jarring influences and infiltrations. Hence it is, in this essay, that "the delight of the urban poet is love—not love at first sight but at last sight. It is a farewell forever that coincides in the poem with the moment of enchantment." It is within a galactic expanse of literary connections, whose graphic depiction in the cartoons of Grandville surely endeared this artist to Benjamin, that the critic repeatedly brings the show to a sudden halt with formulations of drop-dead intensity. It is only through the close reading of Benjamin that we discern the gravitation of his prose, alongside the auratic celebration of handiwork, design, and the rich weave of language, toward the jugular of death in the city. Benjamin's shocking aphorisms, camouflaged within the upbeat journalistic tone and expansiveness of his prose, bring the progression of thinking to a dead halt as often as they move it on. This downtime in the writing is not a literal death. It is, rather, a time-out, a productive interruption, a void that the text configures so that through it, as in the Swiss anthropologist Johann Jakob Bachofen's "hetaeric stage," the forgotten "is actual by virtue of this very oblivion."[17]

It is true that it would be difficult to trump Benjamin or Derrida on the closeness of their encounters with the specificities in the works and passages impelling their exegeses. Yet only through our own close reading of Derrida can those pivotal moments at which elucidation seamlessly morphs into performance become discernible to us. In our quotes from "Plato's Pharmacy," we are literally beset and buffeted in an open-ended gauntlet of blows or *coups*. These are delivered by the *pharmakon*, which, while serving as a basis and facilitator for a whole sequence of basic Western attitudes that Derrida assembles, among them purity, morality, authenticity, and dependability, is also a runaway figure, a rhetorical loose cannon wreaking havoc on the system of values—and way of life—that it seems to predicate.

When he wishes to leave us with an imagistic trace of the *pharmakon*, Derrida engages in a play of genres within philosophy reminiscent of Kierkegaard. For an instant, Derrida narrates an imaginary scene of witnessing Plato in the pharmacy of his philosophical tricks and interventions. But his text, at this interstitial transition between two substantial sections, quickly devolves into the stuff of dense prose poetry. Philosophy, under the administration of Derrida, abandons its argumentation and its refinement of terms and concepts only to enter a complex of loose etymological associates—semantic fragments, if you will—verging on terms for strikes, hits, tricks, ciphers, chance, cutting, and stones, which in turn contours any further assertions to be made about Plato. Philosophy has here dissolved its traditional roles and parameters, as it does in the *Frühromantik*, but instead of assuming the posture of yet another traditional genre, it operates at the level of discourse unsprung from its traditional constraints. Philosophy configures and articulates itself as a composite medium of loosely, but significantly related words and subverbal elements. The cultural heritage of language—Saussure's *langue*—is sufficient to this most energetic exercise. While Derrida could acknowledge a tempering of the tenor and results of writing brought about by modern urban conditions, he would never get to the point that Benjamin reaches, of devising an allegorically urban script.

"Pharmakon means coup," Derrida writes. The report echoing from its sudden concussion includes "a shot fired," "a planned overthrow," "dice," "the unsuspected dramatic effect," "*kolaphos . . . gluph . . . colpus . . . coup . . . glyph . . . scalpel . . . scalp . . . khrusos . . . chrysolite . . . chrysology*." What is being opened up here is not an endless horizon for sociolinguistic intervention, as was the case in the *Athenaeum* fragments. The existing network of signification encompasses all the variants it needs for a critical questioning of historically arranged sequences and formal, generic, stylistic, and grammatical typologies.

Derrida's reading of Plato is not only language-critical, in the sense in which the commentaries of Schlegel and Benjamin are as well. It not only incorporates the "stammering buzz of voices" that is the outer limit of signification, it allows itself to be driven only by the anomalies and accidents of language. The downbeat in Derrida's discourse is squarely on what is incommensurate to the Western tradition and ethos of meaning.

At the point where the essay devolves into a concatenation of *coups*, the subsignifying or presignifying elements of language have more caché in Derrida's project, the disclosure of points of linguistic and ideological fixity in Plato, than the keywords and concepts responsible for supplying the Western way of life with its thrust and direction. Derrida's close reading constitutes an irresistible invitation to witness the productions and assertions of culture at the infrastructural and infrasemantic levels. To read Derrida closely is to follow his signals regarding the location of the significant interfaces, switchboards, and turntables between the signifying shifters that surface in particular texts. In a discernible sequence of transformations, the fragmentary discourse and practices that were initiated in the *Frhüromantik* became a by no means self-sufficient or exclusive pretext for modern criticism. This transpires when the linguistic resources constituting the very possibility of cultural artifacts devolve—and advance, as Derrida powerfully demonstrates—to the subfragmentary level.

As the phenomenon of Derrida indicates, considerable misunderstanding has arisen simply from the need, on the part of more traditional scripts, to *make room* for the close reader, to acknowledge her seemingly misplaced and inverted values. For indeed, the close reader will part ways with an overarching conceptual framework, however edifying and philosophically rigorous, where the text under illumination will not bear it out, will foreclose the situational improvisation of criticism before it blurs and misstates the text's specificities. Close reading—and of course it also can be practiced by individuals publicly identified as poets, philosophers, and critics—has produced some of the most stunning and disoriented cultural discoveries of our epoch. These transpire at a level of detail beyond that traditionally identified with intellectual achievement. The reproach leveled at the close reader is more often a consideration of scale or applicability than a contestation of relevance or accuracy. The close reader embroiders the text in a closed boutique at the margins of the intellectual marketplace, abuzz with hawkers touting the virtues of different intellectual models. She is constrained, at intervals, to name her embroidery, to identify it with some transtextual rubric or movement beyond the work, a phenomenon whose existence alone does not refine its place in culture or justify its being. The preexisting argumentative rubrics to which she may attach her reading are the cultural equivalents to the Lacanian upholstery button that in this case leads from the public sphere of discourse into the vagaries of a text *aufgehoben*, appropriated by the reader through a critical transference always on the verge of explicitness, but never quite explicit.

Close reading is either a genre unto itself, sui generis, or a discursive chameleon taking on the appearance of preexisting formats, of, say, literary criticism or philosophy. When not empowered to declare itself, that is, to perform itself, close reading places itself at the service of discursive genres with, as the marketing department would formulate, greater recognition.

The pressing question for the close reader, which defines her performance, is the following: How long can she justify her precipitation of dense nuance from the text without needing recourse to the preprogrammed cultural rubric, or enterprise, or collective deliberation, or critical contract that would define, frame, package, or represent the sheer play of articulation? Further questions we pose to the close reader, whose answers delimit the scope, scale, and density of her performance, itself an art of suspension: When and where does she pull the trigger that propels the sheer play of sensibility and text into the public sphere of regulatory discourse? How long does she hold off triggering this hairline mechanism? To what extent, and in what fashion does she place reading at the service of ideology, or does she succeed, through smokescreens and mirrors, in preempting this eventuality? There are close readers and close readings, and such considerations, I would argue, define the grain and pitch of their respective labors.

3

Can the philosopher write herself out of the system that has furnished not only a framework and a context, but also a horizon to her notation? Can she release the *Begriff* or conceptual handle that, at least since German idealism, has assured some degree of consistency and objectivity in an investigation constrained by Enlightenment ideology into human provenance and scale, faculties, and materials? Is there a philosophicalness extending from Plato through Nietzsche and even Derrida that does not inflect the discourse of a Benjamin or a Blanchot in quite the same manner, as philosophical as these writers and critics surely are?

I would argue that a subtle borderline separates the broader philosophical enterprise from the philosophical formulations that emerge, often, from the pen of Kafka and Beckett, not to mention of Benjamin and Blanchot. Yet Plato, Kierkegaard, and Nietzsche, to name a few, establish beyond any doubt that philosophy is not a genre. Heidegger, for all the force of Wittgenstein in his day, held it distinct from logical procedure, from the world articulate as a *Gestell* or framework of logical propositions.

The status of the human in Kant's systematic work, which lent a modern cast to all speculations that followed, is double-sided. With the exception of a small amount of hardware, to wit, the Pythagorean proportions, which Kant acknowledges to be hard-wired into an autonomous, objective universe, the human must be sufficient to generate all we know and all we know about knowing. Through synthetic faculties, intuition, and "free disinterested thought," human beings demonstrate the capacity to deduce transcendental constructs and perspectives previously attributed to the objectivity of logic, science, and an autonomous, preexisting deity. By virtue of the "transcendental illusion," the Kantian transcendental, with its all-too-human faculties and philosophico-scientific operations, stares back at the empirical world with a gaze at once uncanny and ironic. Alien as the transcendental Other may seem, its gaze is uncannily human, because ironic.[18] The transcendental supplement to our world becomes the foundation for a perspectivist critique, but it has arisen in an all-too-human cognitive dissonance akin to an optical illusion.

The interconnective hardware that Kant devises in order to sustain the encounter between a speculative subject and an object of reflection, to assure the follow-through of the process linking the faculties of sensibility, understanding, and reason, is by the same token, bionic. Elaborated constructs such as categories, the copula, and the concept itself make up formal philosophy's heritage and contribution to the play of human faculties. They amount to the human-generated tools or implements that facilitate the achievements of understanding and reason. It is not surprising, then, that in an enterprise tracing the highest achievements of, say, science, art, and social justice from their inbuilt human lineaments outward and upward, the hardware of logic should incorporate certain undeniably human features.

Kant, father of original genius, in this fashion anoints the speculative subject as a cyborg or bionic man or woman.

No element of the systemic hardware is more inflected by the humanity and hence by the undecidability installed into putative objectivity than the conceptual handle itself, the Kantian *Begriff*. The concept is the presumably more objective or external of the "two conditions under which alone the cognition of an object is possible."[19] The other is intuition (*Anschauung*), an inbuilt guide to experience of a more immanent provenance. The hardware facilitating the speculative subject's engagement with the object encompasses extremes of greater and lesser alienation. Within this division of labor,

> all experience contains, in addition to the intuition of the senses through which something is given, a *concept* [*Begriff*] of an object that is given in intuition, or appears; Hence concepts of objects in general thus underlie all empirical knowledge as *a priori* conditions; consequently objective validity of the categories, as *a priori* concepts, rests on the fact that through them alone is experience possible.[20]

As one segment of the mind's handle on experience, a substrate and a form, the Kantian concept resides between the immanence of subjectivity and the apriority of the categories. The categories are a priori concepts making experience possible, and imagination, as Kant would elaborate, is the faculty that synthesizes possibility. Concepts and categories are but a single degree of separation from imagination, with all its play and idiosyncrasy. They are suspended between subjectivity and its Other, the lateral boundaries of the single dialectical cell that Kant, on the way to more abstruse considerations of, say, language and the genres of culture, fits out and embellishes in the first *Critique*. Kant names "*sensible intuition*" as "the condition under which . . . the categories, as mere forms of thought, acquire objective reality, i.e., application to objects that can be given to us in intuition."[21] Not only does the hypothetical subject of philosophical speculation waver between the all-too-human and transcendental hardwiring of the universe, so, too, does the conceptual hardware that Kant, drawing on the history of Western logic, retrofits for the momentous occasion. Following the logic or mega-argument, of transcendental deduction, Kant provides for the centrality of a retrofitted battery of philosophical superconstructs within speculation disabused of mechanical formality.

By means of these conceptual instruments or prostheses in the hands of a Kant or his dialectically more dynamic successor, Hegel, philosophical discourse acquired a certain *gravity* from which it has yet entirely to recover. This is a philosophical gravity that, in contrast to Milan Kundera's marvelous title "The Unbearable Lightness of Being," incorporates weight, in part the mass of such durable implements as concepts and categories, density, momentum, atmospheric concentration, and seriousness. There is a tonal gravity to modern philosophy, at least in the wake of Kant and Hegel, a recourse to issues of substance and matters of weight, whether death and memory, being, representation, ethics, or war. (It is perhaps this momentum toward the grave that places Nietzschean laughter, Kierkegaard's inquiry into irony, and the seriousness with which Freud took humor in their full relief.) Derrida's most playful tangents and riffs, as evidenced above, may well be in reaction to this tradition of philosophical gravity or equipment, which he may nonetheless, in other contexts, extend.

Yet the philosophical gravity to which I allude, this attention to a specific discursive infrastructure that never wanes, does not come near to telling the whole story of philosophy's participation in the collective registers of memorable discourse. Through this submission to gravitas, this trucking in the heavy machinery of logic, categories, and conceptual armatures, the philosopher claims a difficult freedom alien to all the other of the exemplary writers in the present prospectus save the poet. The rigorous philosopher exercises the liberty, generally renounced by the close reader and the critic, of expounding directly on basic issues, such as love and death, enmity and friendship, in relative autonomy from the pedagogical function of cultural elucidation. The freedom and responsibility that accrue to this critique not explicitly directed at an object or in the service of cultural dissemination are equal in intensity to the gravity that the philosopher customarily bears. The discourse of philosophy erects a platform at the same time that it conveys the weight of a tradition, and from this platform the philosopher is free to discourse on topoi of putative cultural significance *an Sich*, simply for their own sakes, free not only to range, but on the odd occasion to tell a joke or two. This is one of the things that is meant by thinking, or at least by thinking in a discursive medium and mode. The working philosopher thus pulses in a rhythm between gravity and its release, between custodial care of a tradition and its calculated elision or bracketing, a hovering in the density and play of poetry at which the close reader and the critic, in their constant ministration to the artifact, only occasionally arrive.

It is of nothing less than decisive consequence whether the deployment of philosophical infrastructure eventuates in the questioning and dislocation of systematic parameters or whether it reinstates systematic hardware, whether the metaphysics of the subject, the dialectical tension between the expression and restraint of the drive, or that between the "inside" and "outside" of the system, a heritage of authority and conflict on which it thereby confers indispensability. Although Derrida is quite explicit regarding the facility in the aspiration to attain the systematic "outside," the thrust of his multitudinous exercises is invariably toward the thinking of the limits in the systemic programming of whatever artifacts or situations are at hand. Through the thinking of these limits, a range of ignored possibilities—or unwritten phrases, if you will—come to the fore. It is precisely this compulsive articulation of the limits in a situation that has created a "natural" alliance between deconstructive philosophy and literature, that enables deconstruction to confer upon philosophical discourse a literary sway and ambiguity.

The systolic and diastolic pulse of systems may well lie at the point at which they either submit themselves to the opening of possibility or resign in service to the immutable and inevitable dialectics of authority, repression, desire, revenge, and sublimation. One isolates a downbeat on the open-ended play of possibility in a line of scribed interventions extending from the Schlegels and Nietzsche to Heidegger[22] and Derrida.[23] Psychoanalysis, on the other hand, at least the brand marshaled in contemporary cultural studies–inspired interventions, seems never to overcome its certainty that all cultural artifacts are mediated and brokered by predetermined dialectical conflicts, impasses, and schemata.[24] It increasingly becomes the task of the engaged interlocutor in culture to discern the bearing and tack of systems, what Barthes might have termed their "rustle"[25] and what Anthony Wilden called their "noise."[26] The scope and mechanics of prevailing systems, whether of concepts, government, administration, or domesticity, are of less telling cultural consequence than their rhythm, counterpoint, or drift. This challenge posed by the multiple systems that we inhabit—to discern their subtle underlying rumble and thrust—is one of the most pivotal at stake in contemporary cultural analysis.

At a moment when philosophy's outreach into criticism has even surpassed the critical role of transcendental analysis that Kant envisioned, it behooves us to address this tradition of philosophical stances, to inquire if the wider circle of philosophers, among them Heidegger and Derrida, can ever relinquish their hold on the *Begriff* and break the cycle of gravity and its release. It may well be precisely at this parameter or signpost, slight as it sometimes is, that the essays of Derrida or Agamben part ways with those of Benjamin or Blanchot, however philosophically erudite these latter two critics, and I use the term "critic" advisedly, have proven themselves to be. Is it worthwhile, in this spirit, to posit a distinction between Gilles Deleuze's philosophical works and those that, inflected by psychoanalysis and other social sciences, join the literatures of criticism and radical sociology?

These are some of the considerations that the vast and irreducible play of philosophy within the traditional boundaries of criticism evoke, and like most serious questions, they will not be resolved simply or clearly. But the considerations themselves indicate an overarching play of discursive registers into which we inscribe ourselves and that in turn marks our work, inflects its application, thrust, and reception. The division of labor of which I speak is occupied with units of greater moment and scope than the genres, centuries, and national literatures that preoccupy our professional associations. It engages modalities of writing. To secrete learned writing in utter blindness to this broader array of discursive tasks and postures is tantamount to depriving it of certain degrees of its singularity, to disenfranchising it of a certain measure of its freedom.

The play of discursive registers amid a diversity of cultural idioms makes possible a range of discriminations, and to diverge from the high generality characterizing this piece so far, I will at this point tip my hand as to what some of them might be. I would argue that a certain steadfastness to the ongoing programs and problematics of Western philosophy still informed Derrida's diffuse and multitudinous writing projects, even while, more than any other, he inventively violated the law of genre and marked the bankruptcy of prepackaged discursive conventions and of any institutional division of labor founding itself upon them. Blanchot, by the same token, may be received, first and foremost, as a critic, but he is one who fully claims status as a philosopher in *The Writing of the Disaster*, a work akin in many ways to Adorno's *Minima Moralia*, and who, in his amazing scriptoral polymorphous perversity, has achieved a sustained poetry, with multiple theoretical reverberations, in his novel *Thomas the Obscure*. Close readers, whose fidelity to a text in question is final, nonetheless claim a freedom to situate their readings on the thresholds of different discursive registers: to wit, of systematic philosophy, as Werner Hamacher demonstrates in his *Premises*;[27] of criticism, as Cynthia Chase does in her *Decomposing Figures*,[28] in which she inscribes her meticulous readings of Wordsworth and Kleist, among others, into the debate concerning rhetorical analysis; or of poetry and poetics, as Carol Jacobs does across the board in synthesizing the medium of a highly dense and poetic criticism.[29] And in the sense that their essays arise from contexts and motives that must be termed occasional, and to the degree that these writings repeatedly recur to certain authors and works that have been formative to their sensibilities, Maurice Blanchot and J. Hillis Miller perform, in vital respects, the role of critics.

Pursuing this line of reasoning, it would be possible, even, to argue that the fictive works of theoretically minded authors such as Kafka, Beckett, and Borges, works treating in a sustained fashion such matters as representation and identity, systematicity and fragmentation, may be also read as veiled oeuvres of criticism, rather than of philosophy. The play of occasion, setting, and arbitrary circumstance is simply too decisive to, say, *The Castle* or *Ficciones* to justify their characterization as veiled works of philosophy, although they obviously touch upon profoundly philosophical considerations.

Derrida's later, more socially oriented writings may well furnish one venue, among many, for testing the weight of gravity and the sustained, direct address of issues not entirely text-bound in philosophy as a discursive register. While Derrida's essays have always addressed and drawn their dynamism from the local difference of specific texts, I believe that one can point to some diminishing, over the years, of Derrida's attention to the battery of infrastructural tropes he initially synthesized, which at once highlighted systemic momentum and fragility.

How can this work of surveying and mapping be characterized? I hope without egregious reduction, as an extrapolation of the modalities of ideological repression in Western civilization(s) as they have been conceptually implemented by Western philosophy and culture, as an exploration of language both as the programmed instrument of this repression and the matrix of the supplementarity, *différance*, dissemination, and other figures rendering it the site of an ongoing critique and dismantling of this history and tradition, and as a retrofitting of philosophical discourse as what, in its very composition, delivers and performs this ethical questioning.

One crucial element in this readaptation is a redirection of the primary activity of philosophical discourse away from argumentation and all that it implies toward the minute reading and exegesis of singular texts and artifacts and the occasions in which they arise. In response to a bewildering array of philosophical, other discursive, and cultural works and occasions, *Speech and Phenomena*, *Of Grammatology*, *Margins of Philosophy*, and *Dissemination*, *The Truth in Painting*, and *Glas* establish the ongoing parameters of the critique, the questioning, the enquiry, and the performance. While Derrida's subsequent works, perhaps beginning with *The Post Card*—and this *subsequent* operates in no simple linear fashion—never broke from these parameters, they have manifested some independence from the disseminal putting forth of terms, venues, and scenarios of process.

Yet I would argue that even in later works, whether *Specters of Marx*, *The Gift of Death*, or *On the Name*, Derrida does not relinquish his commitment to and investment in philosophical discourse, in the sense in which it registers itself in the present overview. *The Gift of Death*, on the occasion of Jan Patočka's *Heretical Essays on the Philosophy of History*, may well encrypt and embody Derrida's most comprehensive commentary of that aspect of Western metaphysics that prescribes sacrifice to the transcendent, the ineffable, the future, and the unattainable. The maudlin and generous gesture of giving one's life becomes, through the medium of Patočka's essay, a condensation of Western issues and attitudes surrounding death itself, unselfishness, compassion, sacrifice, and transcendence. The prevalence of this gesture, in history and current events, as well as in an array of canonical texts and artifacts, might seem to place the Derridean work devoted to this phenomenon more in the mainstream of public affairs than, say, such heavy-gauge tracts as *Of Grammatology* or *Glas*. Yet the poetic and readerly, philosophico-cultural composition that delivers the core of this commentary is of a piece with what has always been singular about Derrida. To cite but one example:

> Heidegger doesn't give any examples of sacrifice, but one can imagine all sorts of them . . . (dying for God, dying for the homeland, dying to save one's children or loved one). Giving one's life *for* the other, dying *for* the other, Heidegger insists, does not mean dying in the place of the other. On the contrary, it is only to the extent that dying—insofar as it "is"—remains mine, that I can die for another or give my life to the other. There is no gift of self, it cannot be thought of, except in terms of this irreplaceability. . . .
>
> . . . I can give my whole life for another, I can offer my death to the other, but in doing this I will only be replacing or saving something partial in a particu-

lar situation (there will be a nonexhaustive exchange or sacrifice, an economy of sacrifice). I know on absolute grounds and in an absolutely certain manner that I will never deliver the other from his death, from the death that affects his whole being. For these ideas concerning death are, as one well knows, motivated by Heidegger's analysis of what he calls the *Daseinsganzheit* (the totality of the *Dasein*). That is very much what is involved when to give one's life "for" the other means to give *to* death. Death's dative (dying *for* the other, giving one's life *to* the other) does not signify a substitution (*for* is not *pro* in the sense of "in place of the other"). . . . I can give the other everything except immortality, except this *dying for her* to the extent of dying in place of her and so freeing her from her own death. I can die for the other in a situation where my death gives her a little longer to live, I can save someone by throwing myself in the water or fire in order to temporarily snatch him from the jaws of death, I can give her my heart in the literal or figurative sense in order to assure her of a certain longevity. But I cannot die in her place, I cannot give her my life in exchange for her death. Only a mortal can die.[30]

With an exquisite attentiveness to Heidegger's scenario of Being-to-death in *Being and Time* as well as to Patočka's text, Derrida deconstructs one of the knee-jerk inclinations underlying the monuments of history, the memorials at the heart of religion and nationality, the mentality of sacrifice common to Western societies and well beyond, the notion of *giving one's life for*.

The topic is grave, while the treatment is lightfooted to the point of virtuosity. The attention to Patočka and Heidegger empowers a direct address to the ultimate issues: the meaning of life, death, idealism, and the sacrifices made in its name. Derrida philosophizes in this sense. Patočka's text leads him to pursue the Christian cast that the sacrifice of the here and now in the name of transcendental and ultimate values at the crux of Western idealism has taken on in modern times. Within this context, he also explores the impact of this mentality on a pan-Europeanism gaining increased currency as we speak. The playfulness that Derrida implants, in an essential fashion, into philosophical gravity enables him to deliver showstopping asides to the critical occasion: the uncanny similarity between encryptment, in his sense, and the buried missile silos throughout the U.S. landscape; the godly gaze of the psychoanalyst, within the ethos of the *mysterium tremendum*, who observes the client "from behind my back."[31] But for all its readerly rigor, poetic (and ludic) condensation, and critical occasionality, the performance is, *au fond*, philosophical. Patočka's heretical remarks occasion a deconstruction of the ethos of sacrifice forming part of a wider critique of "incorporation and repression"[32] that has proceeded and meandered since Derrida's first publications. In place of the *Begriff*, a magical tool or instrument, variable while always handy, part idea, part form, that became applicable, since the onset of German idealism, to every conceptual situation or predicament, Derrida has substituted a certain off-center, off-hours, contrapuntal positionality. But in his dedication to this placement (or stage blocking), his bearing up under the weight of the philosophical tradition that his work continues to question and correct, not to mention of his own gargantuan production, he remained, in the sense of the registers of memorable discourse, a philosopher.

4

The preceding, in acknowledging the considerable play and importance in discourse of the poetic, the philosophical, and the exegetical, as this latter term has evolved in the past generation, may well result in a limitation, a scaling down of what we might call the province of "greater criticism," the notion that all "secondary literature" addressing artifacts, cultural phenomena, and discourse belongs to an encompassing, monolithic critical genre. What is the notion of criticism that emerges from the acknowledgment of the play of other discursive designs and registers within its parameters? Can a "lesser criticism" lend some clarity to the contemporary distribution of tasks?

As opposed to the poet, the philosopher, and the close reader, the critic orchestrates, out of the stirrings in the intellectual and cultural worlds, discursive occasions of a homemade nature and of limited scope and application. A relative of Lévi-Strauss's *bricoleur*,[33] the critic fashions a reading of cultural phenomena that may be *close*, but not *only* close, out of the materials at hand: a compelling artifact, the conceptual frameworks that cry out to her, a moment that not only *stands out* but that furnishes a discursive occasion.

Criticism, as it emerges to me in the context of discursive design and registers, is above all an occasional script. It arises to declare, articulate, and bestow an occasion. The occasion may consist in the praise or censure of a development or the marking of a cultural phenomenon. The performative that is inevitably entailed in close reading is of a specific, highly formal nature.[34] The performative of criticism varies with the occasion, itself a creation, or demon, of the critic.

Writing from a series of perspectives that vary, like the perches of a sniper, over the long haul, the critic nonetheless assembles a collection, or manifold, of decisive artists and telling artifacts that have been formative to her sensibility and its occasional script. Like a sociopathic shark, the critic circles back to the scenes of her monumental aesthetic and intellectual feeds. The result of this retrospective circulation is not so much a canon or limited access, a fixed body of authorized artifacts, as it is a constellation of generative modes of thought, each itself in a state of flux or becoming. The sparkling illumination issuing from this constellation is the critic's luster, the contribution resulting from her writing habit, her very identity, albeit shifting and evolving over time.

The critic works out of an occasion and assembles, by varying tools and means, a distinctive landscape. There is a science-fiction dimension to every mature critic's output: Each has founded her own intellectual country. The critic's performance includes tribute. We are drawn to the country the critic founds because the tributes resounding within its borders ring true to our intellectual and cultural needs and aspirations.

From Benjamin and Blanchot to J. Hillis Miller, it is this collectivity of provocative artifacts and artists, whether inspiring or degrading, that presides over the critical obsession. With strangeness and exorbitant fascination, they issue a summons, what Blanchot would term an "exigency."[35] A combination of unresolvable anxiety and warm familiarity, the Freudian uncanny pervades the place to which the critic, ever mindful of this aesthetic aura, hurries with the resolve to stay put as long as possible. Every critic attends to her singular chorus of sirens. From their fateful song, she reads out the occasion that will frame the new project to which a batch of critical script will be consecrated.

The critic will do anything to assure the noteworthiness and coherence of this occasion. The philosophical vocation of correcting and noting the progress and new trigonometry of a conceptual operating system flies out the window where it no longer advances the critical occasion. This is in no way to imply that critics make bad philosophers. On the contrary, the philosophical precisions that one finds in the commentaries of Blanchot or

Miller often shed new illumination, for they have broken free of the operating system's persistent momentum and overarching *Gestalt*. But it is the occasion that prevails in the work of criticism, a pretext conjured silently and enigmatically by a configuration of resonant texts and artifacts comprising the critic's work and signature.

The critic renders herself susceptible to her close encounters with those artifacts that transform everything, to which she relates by the experience of intense reading. The results of these engagements, in which the reader may well "tremble in every fiber of her being,"[36] are by no means categorically triumphant. The poignancy in the critical trajectory pursued by Benjamin, who looms large in the following essays, is precisely the commitment and fatality with which he did not shy away from any significant cultural experience in his path, from the "Notes for a Study of the Beauty of Colored Illustrations in Children's Books"[37] to "Hashish in Marseilles."[38] His purest credo for sustaining critical susceptibility in the face of all historical contingencies and for a quasi-empirical taking in and response to all compelling cultural constellations is to be found in the methodologically intense Convolute N of *The Arcades Project*, whose sequence of twentieth-century "critical fragments" includes:

> To cultivate fields where, until now, only madness has reigned. Forge ahead with the whetted axe of reason, looking neither right nor left so as not to succumb to the horror that beckons from deep inside the primeval forest. Every ground must at some point have been made arable by reason, must have been cleared of the undergrowth of delusion and myth. (N1,4)

> Method of this project: literary montage. I needn't *say* anything. Merely show. I shall purloin no valuables, appropriate no ingenious formulations. But the rags, the refuse—these I will not inventory but allow, in the only way possible, to come into heir own; by making use of them. (N1a,8)

> Barbarism lurks in the very concept of culture—as the concept of a fund of values which is considered independent, not, indeed, of the production process in which these values originated, but of the one in which they survive. (N5a,7)

> On the concept of "rescue": the wind of the absolute in the sails of the concept. (The principle of the wind is cyclical.) The trim of the sails is the relative. (N9,3)

> What matters for the dialectician is to have the wind of world history in his sails. The sails are the concepts. It is not enough, to have sails at one's disposal. What is decisive is knowing the art of setting them. (N9,8)[39]

Arising in a disorienting climate of catastrophe, criticism's course, as Benjamin sets it, is still "full speed ahead." Benjamin establishes a trajectory of successive serial encounters for criticism. The emphasis is on the shock and lucidity of momentary encounters, rather than on the accretion of erudition ("purloin no valuables," the cultural collector's equivalent to "take no prisoners"). There is a bracing momentum to this frontally exposed sequence of critical engagements, which in this section of *The Arcades Project* Benjamin imagistically relates to sailing. (Indeed, the figure of the dialectician's harnessing the concept is but one small tack in Benjamin's ongoing effort to formulate the role of philosophy in cultural criticism. The conceptually oriented critic of Convolute N is nothing less than the urban *flâneur* at sea.) Yet for all the speed and momentum that criticism picks up in its relation to history and in the succession of its significant encounters, Benjamin alternates its progressive resolve with the stunning (and nuanced) standstill achieved by the dialectical image. Indeed, the tempo that Benjamin scores for the rhythm of cultural life in the age of urban shock and technological reproducibility is an alternation between the stunning forward acceleration of pivotal signifiers flagged and charted by criticism, a thrust experienced ethically as well as temporally, and an equally disconcerting arrest instituted by the dialectical image's fascination.

The critic circles back to her motley crew of usual suspects. It makes utter sense for Proust to play a significant role in introducing *Topographies*, a work in which J. Hillis Miller derives inspiration from some of the authors pivotal to his early Victorian and novelistic explorations: Dickens, Tennyson, Hopkins, and Faulkner figure prominently in Miller's project of literary and cultural mapping, along with Kleist, a more recent interest.[40] In large measure, *Topographies* is Miller's excursion into literary space, although on a wider than Blanchottian scale.

> The power of the conventions of mapping and the projection of place names on the place are so great that we see the landscape as though it were already a map, complete with place names and geographical features. The place names seem to be intrinsic to the places they name. The names are motivated. By a species of Cratylism they tell what the places are like. . . . Place names make a site already the product of a virtual writing, a topography, or, since the names are often figures, a "topotropography." With topotropography, the act of mapping, goes topology, the knowledge of places. . . .
>
> This book investigates a cluster of related concepts as they gather around the central question of topography. How do topographical descriptions or terms

function in novels, poems, and philosophical texts? Just what, in a given text, is the topographical component and how does it operate? The other topics in the cluster include the initiating efficacy of speech acts, responsibility, political or legislative power, the translation of theory from one topographical location to another, the way topographical delineations can function as parable or allegory, the relation of personification to landscape, or, as Thomas Hardy puts it, "the figure in the landscape."[41]

The occasion of *Topographies* is a map, at once of certain spatial issues in literature and of Miller's singular aesthetic and methodological sensibilities. The compositional principle of the work introduced in the passage above is one of clustering: The occasion that Miller creates by means of this collection is a coincidence between certain space-critical figures and issues and a cluster of texts in which these tropisms and allegories play themselves out. Miller returns to artifacts and authors whose significance has been deconcealed to him in different contexts. A new framework crystallizes itself out of materials largely familiar. One could indeed argue here that the occasion to which this critical work arises is tantamount and coterminous to the combinatory clusters of texts, tropes, and theoretical themes that it encompasses.

Topographies appeared only four years before a bicolumnar work and joint project that Miller authored with Manuel Asensi, *Black Holes; Or, Boustrophedonic Reading.*[42] Sociopolitical issues, including the role of higher education under late capitalism and the contemporary cultural impact of cybernetics, occupy Miller's substantial contribution. It cannot surprise us that another Proust emerges in the pages of a critical work arising to a somewhat different discursive occasion. This is a virtual Proust, an author not only to whom space was crucial and redolent of literary potential, but whose endlessly contradictory, expansive, and divergent drafts prefigured fractal mathematics and the space of the Internet and the World Wide Web. This revised Proust may well be an extension of the one in *Topographies*, whose place-names constituted "a site already the product of a virtual writing." The freedom that Miller exercises in the later work spins out the implications of this alien, if not entirely unprecedented script.

The form of the *Recherche*, I claim, may be understood by analogy with the graphing of fractals. A fractal is a simple formula that can be represented geometrically, though in a paradoxical or non-Euclidian form. . . . The chief particularity of fractals . . . is their property of "self-similarity." This means that smaller and smaller parts of the whole repeat the pattern of the whole, down to the infinitely small. "A fractal," says Lauwerier, "is a geometrical figure in which an identical motif repeats itself on an ever diminishing scale." Even unimaginably small parts of the whole still repeat the pattern of the whole. . . . This controlled randomness, as Lauwerier shows, is related to what is called "deterministic chaos. . . . A fractal incorporating "deterministic chaos" into the formula it graphs will involve both a high degree of statistical self-similarity and also a high degree of unpredictability and discontinuity. A tiny difference introduced into the numbers setting the parameters of the generating formula will sometimes produce large unexpected differences in the resulting geometrical figure when it is graphed.[43]

When the occasion for Miller's writing becomes the black holes that are at once sublime lacunae opening up in systematic thought and administration and the precondition for writing and knowledge in an age of globalization and flows of enterprise and meaning on a galactic scale, fractals present themselves as a fortuitous figure for the inscription that the situation demands. The fragmentation, synecdoche, and miniaturization that fractals occasion are familiar to us from other contexts and works, for example, from German idealism and Romantic theory, but the particular scale of the "unexpected differences" produced by miniscule changes on the fractal level is singular to this particular trope.

The image of Proust that emerges in a fractal universe is far less familiar and reassuring than the topographer's, who scores the *Recherche* with a map of modernist experimentation and endeavor. What is at stake in Miller's writing here is even grander than the literary production of Proust and its cultural reception: It is no less than the modality of writing and knowledge that comes into being with the reconfiguration of rhetoric, with the emergence of singular and unprecedented tropisms.

How is Proust's *Recherche* organized like a fractal? The *Recherche*, like a fractal, is organized according to a principle of self-similarity. It is, however, self-similarity of the second kind, that is, similarity with a difference, with unexpected and unpredictable irregularities. It might be better to call it "self-dissimilarity." The stories that organize the large-scale patterns of Marcel's life . . . are echoed, though never exactly, in ever-reduced versions . . . down to small-scale episodes like the death of Bergotte followed by Albertine's lie. . . . At a lower level still would be the brilliant metaphorical comparisons that make up so much of the stylistic texture of the *Recherche*. . . . Lower still is the level of word echoing word, beneath that again the level of the letter. At the level of the letter, the reader encounters something similar to Marcel's inability ever to be sure or not whether Albertine is lying.

The comparison of the *Recherche* with stochastic fractals nevertheless gives the reader a way of understanding why an attempt to write about the *Recherche* does not lead to complacency except in those who are able to fool themselves, as Marcel is so inveterately fooled, for example, into assuming that Albertine must be either lesbian or non-lesbian. If you know the *Recherche* at all well, when you are presenting a reading of one episode or passage (and there is no reading of any worth that does not single out individual passages for analysis) you are always uneasily aware that if you had chosen another equally salient passage you would have gotten a significantly different result. . . . The *Recherche* was in principle unfinishable. It would always have been possible to add more material, more short or long interpolations. These would not have repeated anything already said. They would have fitted in with it in the odd, mind-twisting way each part of a stochastic fractal fits the whole. To use the figure of the fractal . . . is, since fractals are part of the new computer space, an example of the way new kinds of telecommunication transform our sense of literature by giving us new models for the formal property of literary works.[44]

A new figure, the fractal, configures a new space and model of spatiality within whose boundaries emerges a relatively new Proust.

The transition from topographical map to fractal mapping signals a sea change in Miller's work, from an academic rhetorical criticism to a still-rhetorical metacritique directing itself at the same sociopolitical configurations that Deleuze and Guattari address in the contrast they draw between various authoritarian formations and the schizo worldview. The fractal Proust of *Black Holes* is a radical mutation that results when a quantitative change, in this case in the degree of fragmentation and miniaturization, transforms itself into a qualitative revolution. This fractal Proust emerges when Miller's customary rhetorical analysis of the past two decades achieves a significantly broader systematic purview and scope. A revolution in the occasion of criticism produces a radical, hitherto unrecognizable Proust.

Maurice Blanchot, by the same token. The occasion of critical writing redefines its literary properties, even when they are so familiar that the critic is on intimate terms with them. As in the case of Miller's reading of Proust, a gravitation toward the purview of systematicity is tantamount to a paradigm shift at the level of occasion. At the same time that Blanchot illuminates his exegeses of a bewildering multiplicity of cultural artifacts with an exquisite philosophical sensibility, he introduces us into a cluster or webwork of telling authors. And as in the case of Miller, the volumes of his critical work may appeal, again and again, to a charmed circle of authors and critics, including Hölderlin, Nietzsche, Kafka, Rilke, Mallarmé, Heidegger, and Beckett, yet what inevitably summons them into being is an occasion marking them as true criticism.

The Space of Literature and *The Gaze of Orpheus* contribute to Blanchot's unprecedented and as yet unequalled phenomenology of writing. In a critical work of marked philosophical sophistication, Blanchot marshals his polymorphous reading in a survey of the possible, spatiotemporal, experiential, epistemological, ontological, pathological, and writerly conditions of writing. Such keywords as "exigency," "solitude," and "death" join a spare, but profound vocabulary of the terms and tropes that condition writing in an aesthetically, rhetorically, and philosophically critical way and trace its weaving and play.

By the moment of *The Infinite Conversation*, many of whose contents were written contemporaneously with the essays in the other two volumes, the critical occasion has shifted slightly. The writers and tropes that Blanchot had traditionally favored reappear in an inquiry addressing writing's engagement with systematicity and the effect of systems and systems theory upon writing. The change in torque upon clustered authors and textual dynamics is slight, but tangible. This kind of readerly adaptation is what marks Blanchot, indelibly, as a critic, however remotely he wanders on occasion from this role.

> To speak of a contemporary writer as a man who went into ecstasy, engaged in irreligion, praised debauchery, replaced Christianity with Nietzscheanism and Nietzscheanism with Hinduism, after having hung around surrealism (I resume some well-intentioned accounts), is to offer thought as a spectacle and create a fictional character with little concern for the niceties of truth. . . . The limit-experience is the response that man encounters when he has decided to put himself radically in question. . . . It is a movement of contestation that traverses all of history, but that at all times closes up into a system, at other times pierces the world to find its end in a beyond where man entrusts himself to an absolute term. . . . Let us note, however, that this passion of negative thought does not merge with skepticism.[45]

The "limit-experience" emerges, early on in the essay of the same title, as a framework for the observation of and participation in writing's asystematic features and implications. There is a slight, but discernible turn away from Blanchot's critical persona as a philosophical aesthete to that of a systematic critic. The Marquis de Sade emerges from this sea change more as the demon and victim of a new social order than as the avatar of modern debauchery. Nietzsche becomes a theoretician of the text rather than the avenging angel of negativity. Mallarmé, within the framework of this occasion, becomes the architect of the work, more than the practitioner par excellence of imagism.[46] In *The Infinite Conversation*, Blanchot matches the philosophical oversight that he attains in *The Writing of the Disaster*:

> The limit-experience is the experience that awaits this ultimate man, the man who one last time is capable of not stopping at the sufficiency he has attained: the desire of he who is without desire, the dissatisfaction of he who is "wholly" satisfied. . . . The limit-experience is the experience of what is outside the whole when the whole excludes every outside; the experience of what is to be attained when all is attained and of what is to be known when all is known: the inaccessible, the unknown itself.[47]

Yet this project is merely one more critical encounter within an infinite conversation. Grand philosophical mind that he is, Blanchot continues in the occasion-centered reconfiguration of cultural resources marking him, indelibly, as a critic, a consummate one. It is the guidance of the Benjamins, Blanchots, and Millers that we who stumble on between the venues of the infinite conversation must seek as we persist in the enervated vocation of criticism.

I have presumed to precipitate out, for the sake of discussion, discursive registers brilliantly coordinated and intercalated in the intellectual works that we remember with greatest vividness. In order to sketch out this rough project of criticism, I've had to delve into the registers of poetics, exegesis, and philosophical disputation, to find myself lost in traversing the unmarked boundary areas between them. My justification has been the status of a certain sensibility and the wish to polish it a bit finer, where possible. We will now, however, perhaps be able in this fashion to separate disagreements of substance from those of register and join together with that much more solidarity in the daunting collective critique of ideology and culture.

Prolegomena to Any Present and Future Language Poetry

> May she become a flourishing hidden tree
> That all her thoughts may like the linnet be,
> And have no business but dispensing round
> Their magnanimities of sound.
>
> —WILLIAM BUTLER YEATS, "A Prayer for My Daughter"

> Call the roller of big cigars,
> The muscular one, and bid him whip
> In kitchen cups consupiscent curds.
>
> —WALLACE STEVENS, "The Emperor of Ice-Cream"

> It Must Be Abstract
> It Must Change
> It Must Give Pleasure.
>
> —WALLACE STEVENS, "Notes Toward a Supreme Fiction"

Nothing could be more paradoxical than a poetry of language, or language poetry. Poetry is, after all, made of the stuff. Starting off from its name, language poetry is a redundancy, the sort of thing we take off for on students' compositions. And nothing could be riskier than discussing a radical and variegated poetic movement in terms of the contributions furnished by a single one of its practitioners, Charles Bernstein, as I will do here. Anything that his poetry and theorizing can say about other splendid poets, including Susan Howe, Ron Silliman, Bruce Andrews, and Steve McCaffery, may be limited, but not in an insignificant or uninteresting way.

Language Is the Stuff of the World

Language poetry, both the term and the enterprise, may acquire additional nuances when placed in context of some of the most significant literary and theoretical developments of the past four decades. Like few other moments in the history of culture—although there are important parallels—the twentieth century, above all its linguistics, literature, graphic art, and music, arose in a vertiginous apprehension of the linguistic constitution of what we think of as "being" or "reality." Over and over again, the linguistics of Saussure, the fiction of Kafka, Proust, and Joyce, and the painting of Picasso and Klee remind us that the world, such as we perceive, "experience," or conceptualize it, is constituted by language, signs, and a rhetoric of tropes by which signs are interconnected, rather than by any entity, essence, structure, or discipline that "precedes" language in sequence or essentiality. The Freud of *Studies on Hysteria*, *The Interpretation of Dreams*, and *Jokes and Their Relation to the Unconscious* essentially knew this, as did, in different ways, Robert Musil, Virginia Woolf, Gustav Mahler, and Charles Ives. The forerunners (or perhaps better "furreigners") of language poetry are as much in prose as in poetry, are as conceptual as they are "aesthetic."

A significant portion of the important conceptual work done in the twentieth century, whether it coincided with or succeeded these aesthetic examples, revised the prevailing wisdom of the scientific and social-scientific disciplines in accordance with this basic apprehension of the linguistic nature and dynamics of reality and its human understanding. Heidegger, for example, demonstrates that if there must be anything so fundamental and general as being, it can only perform the complexity and density of well-written poetic language. Foucault would treat history not as the grand succession of events and concepts, but rather as the fluctuating epistemological horizon in which certain types of statement become possible.

Language predicates and structures the world, such as we are in a position to apprehend, comprehend, or know it. Stein and Joyce were as intensely aware of this as were Paul de Man or Jacques Derrida. This apprehension is crucial. It is the stuff good poems are made of, yet it places the practice of poetry in a slightly uncomfortable position. If poems are "made" of this apprehension, if they are objects in which the linguistic nature of being and reality has already been installed, preprogrammed in an implicit or immanent way, how, then, are poems to register this distinctive twentieth-century "agenbite of inwit" without in some sense relinquishing their poetic nature, without becoming something other than poems as traditionally understood?

This is a predicament in which any poetry of language, any poetry responding to this sort of linguistic apprehension, would place itself. If the linguistic constitution and motive of poetry shuttle from immanence and silence to explicitness, can poetry still be poetry? Or will a mode of poetic discourse have emerged that is somehow poetry and not poetry at the same time, sharing the same bizarre fusion of organic and inorganic, dead and living elements as Kafka's Odradek?[1] Such an uncomfortable but at the same time funny and mold-shattering poetry might well be something new under the sun.

But this wider theoretical meditation is perhaps best reserved for later. When language poetry became aware of itself, in the early 1970s, it celebrated with exuberance the linguistic constitution of the world. Poetry no longer was seen as a rarified form of language, itself the abused handservant of some overarching and prior truth or spirit. The world, such as it exists, is already language, and poetry is the index, the culmination of this linguistic dynamics. The world is already a poem, oftentimes a brutal and sad one, if we are only prepared to read and see the lineaments of its composition.

This is not the spiritually allegorical world-poem that Foucault assigns to the Renaissance.[2] The world is a text already there, under the service of poets, not priests. The world is composed less of discrete works or acts than of poetic substance of the sort initially synthesized by Mallarmé and introduced into the American vein by Stein, Pound, Williams, and the Objectivists.

The poetic stuff of modernity and its implicit successor, whatever it may be called, resides in the heart of the economies of manufacture and waste. Wallace Stevens's dump is a privileged site of its composition. By the time such poets as Susan Howe, Ron Silliman, Bruce Andrews, and Bernstein discovered that they had certain complex poetry games in common, the linguistic material they work had long derived from the repository of exhausted cultural remains whose form is the traditional rhetoric of poetry supplemented by the explosiveness of modern poetic space. The raw material of poetry is signs with considerable circulation to their credit. If there is a certain shopworn quality to material deriving from the repository of exhausted cultural remains, we regard this material with a certain distance, as well. We "leverage" it with the humor that becomes a distinctive mark of this type of poetry.

The poetry of language is hence free to celebrate the poetic composition of a world knowable only as language. It is in this context that Charles Bernstein writes, in an essay entitled "Thought's Measure":

> Language is the material of both thinking and writing. . . . Just as language is something that is not separable from the world, but rather is the means by which the world is constituted, so thinking cannot be said to "accompany" the experiencing of the world in that it informs that experiencing. It is through language that we experience the world, indeed through language that meaning comes into the world and into being. As persons we are born into language and world; they exist before us and after us. Our learning language is learning the terms by which a world gets seen. In talking about language and thinking, I want to establish the material, the stuff of writing, in order, in turn, to base a discussion of writing on its medium rather than on preconceived literary ideas of subject matter or form. And I want to propose "thinking" as a concept that can help to materially ground that discussion.[3]

At the same time that Bernstein's addressing language as the substance of writing and the world is clear, we do not wish, through any theoretical fervor, to exclude the cognitive and sociological dimensions of his critical scenario. Indeed, it is only through misreading that critical theory, with its own grounding in the apprehension that language structures the world, appears indifferent to these dimensions. Bernstein's interest in the relation between language and thought opens poetic thinking to the enterprise of logical analysis, which, I would argue, resides at the spare or anorexic extreme of the distinctive literary styles devised by twentieth-century discourse.

Less important than the formal characteristics of any of these styles is the fact that twentieth-century literary and conceptual discourse has been uncomfortable with residing in the middle ground of moderate prose. It has, rather, gravitated, where possible, to the extremes, illustrated at one end by the precision, spareness, and depression of certain of Kafka's sketches and the prose designed for Wittgenstein's *Tractatus Logico-Philosophicus* and at the opposite end by the florid, endlessly self-qualifying, and fussy stylistic medium common, in different ways, to Proust's *Recherche, Finnegans Wake,* and the philosophical discourses of Martin Heidegger and Jacques Derrida.[4] The play between the anorexic and florid extremes of language is marvelous material for fiction as well as for poetry, and language poetry, in its appeal to Wittgenstein, no more excludes the poetics of expansion explored by Heidegger and Derrida than should contemporary literary criticism. The sociological dimension of the linguistic apprehension evident in Bernstein's "Thought's Measure" is also hardly inimical to the concerns of contemporary theory. Language not only composes reality, such as we know it, it is the encompassing medium of communication between human beings. This poetry, in referring back to the material of which it is made and the manner of the world's composition, only augments the theoretical resources of its readership.

The poetry of language issued its own birth announcement in the exuberance of its apprehension of the linguistic composition of reality, thought, and culture. It is in this sense that the 1980 *LEGEND* collaboration by Bruce Andrews, Charles Bernstein, Ray di Palma, Steve McCaffery, and Ron Silliman[5] incorporated line drawings and cartoons, concrete and geometrical arrangements of syllables and words, as well as recognizable compositions of free verse. As part of a multiform manifesto of the priority of language in poetry and culture, *LEGEND* included compositions of hash marks.

Language, the collection illustrates, can be entirely devoid of substance, whether regarded as content or extension, and still compose itself in interesting ways. A sequence of cartoons develops in a way not entirely alien to a sequence of stanzas or narrative episodes. Every form of writing, *LEGEND* demonstrates, graphics as well as words, the poetry of logical propositions and the poetry of free verse, constitutes the Derridean trace, the rupture in being and knowing that is the site from which writing declares and performs its primordiality, its inevitability.

Within the context of the linguistic composition of the world, the varieties of poetic utterance and discursive form are merely different fruits of the season, to be enjoyed in their time and their difference. Collations of Wittgensteinian propositions are no more authentic than columns and diagonal slashes of inarticulate syllables. Both experiments—and language poetry is a highly experimental mode of writing—have their place. Through all the fashions of literature and intellectual history, poetry has functioned as the preserve of language's exploration of its own parameters and qualities. The poetry of language thus celebrates the variety of modes and forms in which the fundamental linguistic apprehension of the world takes place.

Let It Be Concrete

Arising in an intellectual milieu at least to some extent disabused of its logocentric and ontotheological delusions, language poetry includes among its demonstrations the concrete handling of words, responding to their empirical qualities as things more than to their ideational significations. The treatment of words as things, the transformation of words into things, corresponds to the diversion that takes place when we focus on the soprano's zipper and are deaf to her song. In the case of *LEGEND*, among other examples, we home in on such data as the shape and sound of words, syllables, or letter clusters either in place of, at the expense of, or in supplemental relation to the "idea" that they might "convey."

This field of poetry insists that the materiality of language be accommodated within its register. Language supplies the building blocks of any communicative or cultural production. It in turn incorporates its own materiality. To speak to the materiality of language at once addresses its nonideational, nonmetaphysical dimensions and emphasizes its place within an economy of production and reception, within economy per se. The concrete handling of words and word fragments thus resides at the extreme of language's generative capabilities. It also participates, however, in a slowdown or defamiliarization of referential and logical functions that otherwise becomes too easy.

The syllabic experiments abounding in the *LEGEND* collaboration thus correspond to an exploration of the dual referential surplus and shortfall produced when words are treated in accordance with their thingly facet. The collectively authored "Fantasy on a Hymn Tune" (and collective authorship in poetry already constitutes an important questioning of the sublimity of poetic genius or inspiration) begins with a syllabic matrix or graph whose initial x axis reads horizontally "apl / epl / ipl / oopl / upl / opl" and whose y axis reads down "apl / abl / afl / asl / adl / azl." The matrix goes on to explore, between its axes, the other syllabic variants of these fragments. This constellation amounts to a systematic treatment, a systamatization, of unfulfilled semes, which, although capable of sustaining some meaning, stop short of lexic definition. The poem thus begins in the shadowy world between total nonsense, or a semantic void, and conventional meaning. The following section of the poem, also a matrix, alternates lines consisting of these unmeaning syllables with lines composed of slightly fuller "extensions": "apl / epl / ipel / oopl / upl / opl" becomes "apple eppul ipel oopul opal." We find two recognizable words in the latter line, "apple" and the semiprecious "opal." The poem begins to inhabit the marginal space in which the narrator of Borges' "Tlön, Uqbar, Orbis Tertius" isolates on a map of an imaginary world two or three recognizable places from our own. In gravitating toward concreteness, language poetry has thematized and dramatized the limits of meaning at lexic, semantic, and syntactic levels.

In the concreteness of its demonstration, *LEGEND* gravitates toward the Wittgensteinian extreme of its utterance. In terms of the experiment pursued by the *Tractatus Logico-Philosophicus*, the text of this volume would reproduce a logically constituted world, the world as it would appear were it hypothetically composed according to the propositions of logic. The elements of this world would be logical propositions, and they would be related by mathematics and logical operations. Such an experiment is of course doomed to failure, but it makes for striking poetry as well as interesting reading. In addition to asking us to "say no more than we can know," something harder for academics than for practicing poets, such an enterprise treats propositions (in poetry, we would say "lines") as the tangible components of a world. Wittgenstein's philosophical project is willing to treat the elements of discourse, whether regarded as logical propositions or lines, as building blocks, construction elements, and regards the relations between these elements as the possibilities of a logical or discursive world.

In at least one of its demonstrations, then, this poetry pushes sentences toward the concreteness and rigor of propositions and then explores the possibilities opened up by their juxtaposition and interrelation. This experiment works to the effect of both parodying logical rhetoric and procedures and installing a certain rigor within a situation that might not readily appear to be the case. Wittgenstein is a marvelous context for these particular experiments, both because he explored the claims and possibilities of language in general and because he distilled such a distinctive minimalist style in constructing a picture of the world as a constellation of logical propositions.

The appeal of this poetic state of affairs to Wittgenstein and critical theorists is not anomalous. The vexed schism between "logical analysis" and "Continental philosophy" is one of the decisive optical illusions of the academic world: Both explored the lineaments of language, one in its hyperbolic, the other in its stripped-down articulation. It is in this context that we can appreciate the poetic propositions in such *LEGEND* texts as Bernstein's "My Life as a Monad," Ron Silliman's "It is a five-pointed star," and Ray DiPalma's "Perfect impressions give you lessons." From the first of these we read, "39. Let's buy a box of bandaids," and "89. On Monday I sail for Tunis."

Let It Be Poetry

At the heart of his epoch-making "On Some Motifs in Baudelaire," in which he accounts for the disjunctiveness of modern experience at the same time that he composes a structurally self-deconstructing text, Walter Benjamin cites a captivating question by Baudelaire: "Who among us has not dreamt, in his ambitious days, of the miracle of a poetic prose? It would have to be musical without rhythm and rhyme, supple and resistant enough to adapt itself to the lyrical stirrings of the soul, the wave motions of dreaming, the shocks of consciousness." How curious and touching it is that prose poetry, with its hovering at a discursive watershed, could figure among the factors by which Benjamin would account for the "decline" of modern experience, its structuration by the shocks that, in the Freudian scenario, announce their effect in the penetration of defensive shields, in the invasion of protected fields of energy.[6]

The division of labor between the poetic and the prosaic is an implicitly rich field, made all the more interesting by such equations as the one drawn by Hegel between prose and history. Language poetry does not neglect to include this "demilitarized zone" in its multifaceted exploration of the resources and performances available to poetry. The poets of language are no more reverential toward a prescriptive division of labor here than they are toward the bulk of the metaphysical and aesthetic baggage that poetry making drags with it. Bernstein's "Artifice of Absorption" is in fact a theoretical essay, predominantly set in verse, on the poetics of lucidity, opacity, and performance as it conditions the options currently available to poetry and other discourses. This text furnishes a masterful demonstration to critics of how verse, with the variable length of its lines and its freedom in the spatial arrangement of words, offers certain features particularly suited to the logical turns and delicate qualifications of theoretical discourse. On its side, "Artifice of Absorption" performs many functions that we come to expect from criticism: It pursues ongoing thematic issues such as absorption and opacity in relation to a wide variety of literary and scholarly sources, including Artaud, Bataille, Lévi-Strauss, Veronica Forrest-Thompson, and Jerome McGann. It comes replete with footnotes. And yet, I would argue, for all its receptivity to prose and its questioning of any privileged position assigned to poetry, the poetry of language contributes above all to the body and amplification of poetics.

While Bernstein's work appeals to the prosaic as a defamiliarization away from poetic convention, its insistence on discontinuity as a compositional principle is too strong for it simply to merge into the linear thrusts of conventional prose. Bernstein's writing is hardly insensitive to the sustained linguistic defamiliarization performed by Joyce's *Finnegans Wake*. Bernstein, too, disfigures his words, opens up his syntax, and reduces his signifiers to their subverbal elements. Yet with all its distortion on the microscopic level, *Finnegans Wake* is invested with a certain narrative continuity in the completion of certain structural elements, however "soft" or self-effacing its structure may be. For all its theoretical sophistication and technical receptivity and improvisation, language poetry stops at the marvel of what Baudelaire would call "prosaic poetry" before acceding to the linear momentum of prose itself.

The discourse that Bernstein sets as prose, then, is at all times poetic. In *Controlling Interests*,[7] he elects to explore "The Blue Divide" through the medium of prose. The resulting piece is a dense latticework of superimposed frames, dimensions, and perspectives.

> An almost entire, eerie, silence floats above and between the fixtures that separate me from the doorstep. . . . A table and window frame sit just ahead, to the side of the walls and corners, slat wood flooring, shelves, the tar-backed driveway and terraced approach roads. A person waits in a boat about an hour away, floating in total occasional manner. Stripped of its wood, unparalleled in respect to its riveting and displaced glare, incised by its dimensions, I feel the slight pang of an earlier sensation which rapidly switches in succession to images harder to identify at first, postcard sized shapes, rolling vertices.[8]

While this passage is indeed set in prose, it contains enough material about perspective to explain that its prosaic interest emerges from an exploration of the perspective of prose. The exploration is all. There is a pronounced inconsequentiality about this prose. Where it leads, what it accomplishes, is far less important than the mood it establishes, the jarring juxtapositions (between the window frame and the boat) it effects, and the discontinuities that it incorporates. This language is much plainer than the discourse of *Finnegans Wake*: If poetry is simply the play of language, we would have to think of Joyce's novel as more poetic. Yet Joyce, in order to break and parody the implicit habits of reading, relies heavily on narrative flow, on the promises of conclusiveness made by all types of discourse. Prose occasionally crystallizes within the experimental and theoretical space of language poetry, but only as one additional mode of arrangement. The promises it keeps last only as long as the experiments in which it figures, and even within its scope, continuity is a promise existing largely to be broken.

Let It Be Explicit; Let It Be Theoretical

> Absorptive & antiabsorptive
> works both require artifice, but the former may hide
> this while the latter may flaunt
> it. & absorption may dissolve
> into theater as these distinctions chimerically
> shift & slide.[9]

According to this passage, what Bernstein terms antiabsorptive works "flaunt" their artifice, defined earlier as the "measure of a poem's / intractability to being read as the sum of its / devices & subject matters." "Absorption may dissolve / into theater," he warns us, and a "flaunting" of poetic qualities is manifestly theatrical.[10] The artifice of poetry is the supplement, the unknown quantity beyond the themes and devices, and one of the crucial endeavors of language poetry is to dramatize this artifice in the theatrical space furnished by the blank page. It is in keeping with this dramatic impulse that Bernstein and the poets he writes about synthesize some of its most distinctive styles: a serpentine poetry of dispersion, wandering about the page, demonstrating the silence and emptiness surrounding its far-flung signifiers; a rigid and erect lyric composed of ultrashort lines, initially explored by Williams, emphasizing the mass of individual words and the arbitrariness of line breaks; and conventional lyrics whose seemingly ordinary lines camouflage unmarked deletions or bubbles of introjection.[11]

Language poetry synthesizes such stylistic models, and there are others, not only for the sake of variety, but because each one is particularly suited to dramatize—current psychoanalytical discourse would say "act out"—specific features and activities of poetic composition: the spacing of words on the page, their division into lines and stanzas, the distinction between capital and lowercase letters, the latter tested fully in Bernstein's "Like

DeCLAraTionS in a HymIE CEMetArY." It is at least partially instructive to think of each distinct discursive mode crystallized by language poetry as the poetic equivalent of an elaborate Wittgensteinian language game.

As one of its enterprises, then, the poetry of language aims at a making explicit of the linguistic acts and assumptions responsible for poetry, in part because at other moments in the history of poetry, the very same acts and assumptions have remained implicit, submerged, understated, immanent—sustaining an ideology of poetic magic, genius, wizardry, and inspiration. Poetry was for Kant the highest of the arts, the native habitat for original genius. As Derrida, de Man, Foucault, and others have pointed out, the presumptions of immanence and secrecy that might surround poetic creation have been marshaled innumerable times in support of ideological, political, and conceptual totalization and repression. And if we appreciate the fact that an analogous explicitness, or making explicit, of the ideological, logical, theological, and metaphysical attitudes underlying vast stretches of Western or dominant thought has been one of the ongoing efforts of contemporary critical theory, it seems perfectly reasonable to assert that language poetry, in its flaunting or dramatic dimension, is inherently theoretical, that language poetry and critical theory are engaged, if not married, in a joint endeavor of making explicit.

While such an enterprise as deconstruction has also sought to dramatize or figure, in a "positive" way, the departure of language from systematic thought, the incommensurability and evanescence of language's nonsystematic traces, this figuring has always been founded on a disclosure and release of the points of conceptual fixity or closure in texts, artifacts, and systems. Such a conceptual release or uncoupling absolutely depends on the making explicit of assumptions, biases, orientations—the strong arms by which institutions, whether of state or learning, twist the particulars into conformity with an ideological thrust. Deconstruction thus goes hand in hand with a making explicit, an exposé, an investigative reportage concerning ideology's dirty secrets, its smoke-filled back rooms, where its findings and imperatives collaborate with its concepts.

Language poetry and critical theory thus share a certain commitment to the explicit, to rendering overt and subject to question conceptual and operational underpinnings that in the context of dominant culture are hidden, occulted, sublimated, and a prioritized. Deconstruction is an inherently public posture or set of strategies in a similar sense to the way in which language poetry demands explicitness regarding its production and procedures. At the risk of relinquishing time-honored conventions and techniques, language poetry likewise participates in a poetics of explicitness. Much of what Bernstein says about absorption concerns the relationship between the implicit and the explicit.

This insistence on explicitness gives both deconstruction and language poetry a certain political and ethical dimension. The enterprise of theorizing may be in large measure regarded as an articulation or making explicit of what makes states, systems, and other institutions go. Let's be clear, then, that language poetry's theoretical dimension is not at odds with its political interest or commitment. They are part and parcel of each other. Language poetry doesn't privilege certain "socially oriented" forms of theory over other more "cerebral" or "Continental" varieties. Its theoretical nature is tantamount to its making explicit or its poetic "acting out."

The present point in my own exposition is the moment when one would properly expect a lengthy and weighty digression on the theoretical and philosophical backgrounds of language poetry. Yet for reasons cited above, now is precisely the moment for us to delve into specific texts in a specific way, to read them as closely as possible. The theory of language poetry does not dwell somehow apart from the poems themselves. It is inscribed, imbricated, within the poems.

The poetics of explicitness, for example, does much to account for the remarkably rich assortment of texts and experiments that Bernstein sets out for us in *Controlling Interests*. "The Next Available Place" is a veritable laboratory of associative chainings and thematic displacements. A fragmentary and much-submerged narrative situation suggests problematic travel arrangements to Africa. Difficult as it may be to secure places on this journey, the language of the poem cannot control, cannot resist, digressions and indirections of many orders, if not every possible order. The poem's progress is only too vulnerable to onomatopoeic riffs: "Ether," "Esther," "Erstwhile"; "Orthopsychiatry, opthalometrics, / gastrojejunerology, cryptopsychopathology, oncogenetics"; "Japanese shoe repair. / Iraqi, Iroquois"; and "Mrs. Happenstance had a happy / hysterectomy" (the latter recalling Joyce's "do ptake some ptarmigan" in *Ulysses*).[12] Even in this sampling, the modes of expansion are markedly different: the combination of

Iraqis and Iroquois, although happy, is almost purely assonant; the list of fantastic medical branches begins in the assonance of "o words," and culminates in increasingly outrageous sciences ("gastrojejunerology"). There may indeed be a stroke of happiness in happenstance, but in all likelihood, the fictive character is not all that happy about her hysterectomy: This chain of signifiers is crowned by irony.

"The Next Available Place" is the only destination possible in playful language. Yet the poem not only circumscribes several varieties of indirection, it declares and dramatizes these tendencies, as well. One line exhorts us to "Pattern a once remembered hope that one time. Seepage." "Seepage," like "pattern" is at once a thing and an activity. The poem dramatizes a certain seepage taking place in signification and meaning, the excess and superfluity in words that allows them to take unexpected turns. The speech act performed by the line is demand, exhortation. The line tells us to pattern forgotten hope—and to read: See the pages. The French homonym of "seepage" is *cépages*, the involuted plants of viniculture. In the same gesture, then, the poem thematizes, exemplifies, and critically problematizes the displacement taking place within its own language.

It is hardly out of place, then, within the contours of "The Next Available Place," to come upon a language about twisting and involution:

> Curvacious slurs: misanthropy, cliquishness,
> territoriality, misunderstanding. What is described
> by the patient as 'dizziness'
> has often not even the remotest relation to
> vertigo. Labyrinthine irritation: sensation of
> rocking, sensation of staggering, swimming sensation,
> sensation of weakness, sensation of backward swaying,
> wavy sensation.[13]

Apart from describing, on a discursive level, if you will, a set of spatial and stylistic options available to poetry, this passage pursues an important interrogation into the status of psychological and psychoanalytical categories within a linguistically aware poetic medium. While psychoanalytical situations and terms are as interesting and available as any other subject matter, it is clear that within the domain of this poetics, such issues as vertigo, weakness, or depression, and regression ("backward swaying") must work themselves out poetically, on the page: "Seepage." "Curvacious slurs" and

"Labyrinthine irritation" make for a fine interlude in "The Next Available Space," but these terms also account for one of the major poetic styles or substances that language poetry has synthesized as a medium for its dramatization of the qualities of poetic language and space, what I have termed above the poetry of dispersion or dissemination. In the context of "Curvacious slurs" and "Labyrinthine irritations," it can be no accident that the next poem in *Controlling Interests*, "The Hand Gets Scald but the Heart Grows Colder," begins with precisely such a lyric, whose fragmentary protolines, in order to accentuate their unrelatedness to each other, or at least the tenuousness of the connections between them, are strewn over the page, in "Curvacious slurs."

Maryland has been called a microcosm of America, because within its relatively compact borders thrive most of the environments spread out over the nation at large: mountains, big cities, suburbs, flat farmlands. Within *Controlling Interests*, such poems as "The Hand Gets Scald" and "Standing Target" encompass many of the styles that language poetry has devised for its demonstrations, as I have already noted above: In addition to the labyrinthine poem of dispersion, we find compact columns of ultrashort lines, often themselves subverbal; nuggets of irregular lines that are, through the density of their typesetting, at the edge of prose poetry; and, last, but surely not least, "conventionally" appearing passages of lyric that literally dissolve through their truncations and unannounced bubblings.

This anthologization of different styles is not in itself new: In modern poetry, it goes back at least as far as such Yeatsian medleys as "Upon a Dying Lady." Yet what is striking about these experiments is the extensiveness, and again, explicitness with which each stylistic medium explores its unique linguistic capabilities at the same time that it "processes," poetically more than psychoanalytically, the "material" at hand. Thus, a poem much concerned with mood swings, "The Hand Gets Scald but the Heart Grows Colder," is free to break off into a column of capitalized colors, "Red / Pink / Orange / Pimento," and so on, which themselves "illuminate" different moods or serve as a synesthetic accompaniment, in terms of color, to such moods.

The poem arises, of course, in the confusion nurtured by the English language that the modal (and caloric) opposition between scalding and coldness can be undercut by a certain homonymic similarity. The heart can lose its sympathy regardless of what is taking place physiologically or sexually.

Whether we interpret the hand's getting "scald" in terms of thermodynamic loss or gain, the "heart" can operate on its own wavelength. The poem goes on to play along the rift between activity and affect, to sustain poetically a certain disinterest. Remember that the book is entitled *Controlling Interests*, that Walter Benjamin once appropriated a sterling image for the actor's sensibility from Kafka's description of hammering as "real hammering and at the same time nothing."[14]

By the same token, "Standing Target" is as autobiographical a text as one can imagine belonging to the body of something called "language poetry." The poem incorporates a biography of someone named Ralf D. Caulo, "Deputy Director of the / HBJ School Department," and reports, presumably from summer camp or early school, regarding the progress of someone named "Charlie" in such areas as swimming and arts and crafts. On its internalized bulletin board, "Standing Target" displays corporate biographies and snatches of Proustian recollection (and self-citation) to illustrate the solidity and focus, the sense of meaning, of continuity, and of prevailing that such discourses provide. At the same time, the poem begins precisely nowhere—"Deserted all sudden a all / Or gloves of notion, seriously / Foil sightings, polite society"—and it does not end before it has dissolved this biographical and existential coherence in an unusually disparate lyric of dispersion, beginning,

> fatigue
> of   of
> open for
> to   , sees
> doubles.[15]

The poem duly notes the inevitable fatigue accompanying such intense awareness of self-constitution only in language. It has already accounted for the sadness of lines: "crisscrossing / out the hopes of an undifferentiated / experience, the cold sweeps / past," and it has characterized the end results of an experience whose sudden separations and voids, like going to summer camp, are as empty as the vacuums of the poetic page: "The end result was a gradual / neurosis superimposed upon a pre-existing / borderline character structure."[16]

Within the radically variegated poetic space of "Standing Target," the self, social life, and psychological experience, such as they exist, are functions of poetic potentials and activities. Any coherence that seems to emerge from the losses and separations that structure our experience is subject to the unpredictable chaining and dispersion that prevail within the poetic page. Each of the styles of poetry highlights different aspects of linguistic ambiguity, flow, syntax, and semantic slippage.

Even at the risk of fatigue, which it inventively avoids, Bernstein's more recent work sustains this multifaceted exploration and dramatization of distinct poetic modes in what Derrida would call their local difference. Indeed, as the work proceeds, each different style or poetic utterance seems to gain in resolve, increasing the incommensurability of the "whole." The prose poems are only more unrepentant in their prosaicness, and the ultrashort lines have become, if anything, only more abrupt and leaden. I think of Bernstein's 1987 collection, *The Sophist*,[17] and I close my own initiation into his work and the wider enterprise of those associated with him with the blurred and not unjaundiced eye of "Amblyopia."

Opening with a lyric of lines as stark, final, and blunt as anything that language poetry could imagine, this poem goes on to cast its ambling eye on the current state of cultural illiteracy. Sludge, stunted growth, and the repression of criticism are among the most powerful images by which this extended text articulates the current moment of cultural blindness. "He was a moral dwarf in a body as / solid as ice," "Amblyopia" begins, speaking of a hypothetical cultural subject in an age of "fear and / evasion." We live in a time when "The world grows simpler," the poem complains, "Many people have trouble with everyday / activities, such as speaking, thinking, responding, dreaming, eating, sleeping. A crutch / shares the weight of burden." The state that Bernstein describes is one of enforced cultural mutism, substance devoid of the articulation inseparable from informed deliberation. Amid this darkness, "It is not the eye / but it's the gleam of which we dream." [18]

> There is neither matter nor form, only
> smell, taste, bite—eyes
> hide by their disclosure. There
> is only substance—structure—twin
> fears of an unduplicating repetition. . . .
>
> Keep a curb on your brain. The heart
> beats thrice where the soul has lost
> its foot. . . .

Out of pure sludge . . . and to sludge
shall you—remain.[19]

It should come as little surprise that Bernstein, as he elaborates the sociocultural conditions for this intellectual dimming and regression, ranges
widely in the institutions and rhetorics that he incorporates into the poem.
The poem's ongoing cultural and disciplinary perspectives are psychosexual, economic, biological, and commercial. The "Ministry of Psychological
Science" issues a pronouncement in prose: "Exposure to big businessmen,
right-to-life Christians, military officers, career managers, and *New York
Times* cultural editors causes otherwise healthy young people to become
perverts. . . . Orgasms can only be achieved by this kind of pervert by enacting or fantasizing racist, sexist, ageist, or authoritarian acts."[20] In this passage, the biases of the culture industry are as oppressive as the cultural
wasteland.

Bernstein's critique extends every much to the current truisms put forth
by the publicly sanctioned intellectual world as it does to the sludge or
blindness issuing from continued cultural non-articulation. Hence,

And now . . .
JUST WHEN YOU THOUGHT IT WAS TIME
TO STOP THINKING AGAIN . . .
Yes . . .
. . . the Whipmaster Valorizer™ has arrived,
revolutionizing the psychopoetics industry.
In just seconds, you can turn your sordid dreams
and ambitions into cherished *res intellectiones.*
The Valorizer uses a unique Twofold action.
Negative associations are effaced from habitual
cognitions by a sanitized derealization process.
Simultaneously, positive associations are affixed
to these cognitions by means of thousands of tiny
Idealization Crystals®, a unique adhesion agent.[21]

The sludge of the inarticulate thus invades the institutions of literacy,
courtesy of Textron. What we have here so far in "Amblyopia" corresponds
in many ways to our model for a present and future language poetry: It is
vibrantly open to a wide range of rhetorics and technical models, and its
poetic forms dramatize the subject matter and discourse at hand. Once

again, it incorporates three types of discourse: prose, "conventional lyric," and a starkly abbreviated line. With all this argumentation and social contextualization, "Amblyopia" is nowhere more radical than where it appears most conventional.

Indeed, this field of poetry's most devastating theorizing, its most explosive undermining of conceptual and formal expectations, may well take place in its most conventional-seeming lyrics. The most profound revolution effected by language poetry consists in its refusal to honor venerable lyrical contracts. It is in this refusal that the most devastating, although nearly invisible critique and theory of poetry takes place. The most radical section of "Amblyopia" is hence severed from its polemic, although a complex one, on the state of cultural articulation. It is simply another lyric, potentially like any other:

> Everything external to turn
> out of the last out of accumulated, dig
> slowly, piles trying about, which were
> flaw, fugitive, indeed lights, but when
> mind of stumbles that on accurate
> has to do which become early, say
> at, might just as it is, clash, that
> by mainly intentions, subjected
> as if, were—officious tone—nickel &
> dimed or being given to do
> something that that on our—you
> should, that is, to handle—even
> come up with what amounts to, for
> keeping or setting of respect of lack
> literally trying to prolong, complain
> apparent, is to rather condescended
> correlative as to blind, off, by
> attitude.[22]

This is precisely the poetry that cannot be read in the arena of cultural amblyopia or stunting. It is pervaded by invisible breaks and insertions that force it to violate the contract of making sense, even in the permissive lyrical way. Like the late Joycean prose that arises in Molly Bloom's monologue in the ultimate, "Penelope" episode of *Ulysses*, this discourse absents itself from the breaks and markers in flow that might clarify its intent. When coherent phrases begin to form, they are truncated by introjections that emerge from nowhere. "Turn / out of the last" begins, only begins to make sense at the top of this extract, when "out of accumulated" enters, pulling the rug out from under its sense making. This is a poetry of invisible seams and invisibly introduced bubbles.

And yet this is very much poetry, indeed. It opens up the matrices of meaning and sequential flow. It is radical in the sense that the poem exists both within and beyond the framework of "Amblyopia." Some of Bernstein's poems, notably "So really not visit a . . .", in *Controlling Interests*, consist entirely of this resistant, but volatile discourse. This particular poetic stuff, with its repudiation and intensification of poetic contracts,[23] may well hover at the radical extreme of language poetry's multifaceted, explicit, performative, and theoretical experiment.

The Trial of the Explicit

We come full circle as we close, asking ourselves if there is not some bill we pay as poetry moves toward the extreme of its own explicitness, or if perhaps the poetry of language offers us a theoretical tool that now helps us discern the glimmerings of explicitness within the ostensibly traditional and naive. The question is parallel to the one we ask when we ask if the overt experiments in line and color in modern painting do not ultimately speak to the representational issues taken up by, say, Memling or Rembrandt.

Once poetry has problematized itself theoretically, once it has performatively indicated and questioned its moves, can it ever be exactly the same as before? Perhaps not. Previously, poetic discourse had if nothing else irony to place its affirmations in relief and at a certain distance. It may be, though, that in a systematically experimental universe of letters, one joined, in different ways, by Joyce, Kafka, and Wittgenstein, as well as by more contemporary experimentalists, irony loses some of its pervasiveness and becomes one possibility amid a battery of distortions available to poetic and fictive discourse.

Must we experience this as a loss, this internal theorizing of poetry through the making explicit of its moves and attitudes? Here, both contemporary critical theory and the poetry itself have much to say. Rather than a loss or deprivation, this experiment constitutes an opening, vastly extensive, if a bit frightening. We are indeed fortunate that the experiment has been taken up in such a playful and inventive way.

THREE

Walter, the Critic

Culture is a sociological arena for entities that are by their nature, in their constitution, and at all times—textual. It remains a profoundly troubled and always contested question as to whether there are any manifestations of culture independent of textuality. Indeed, one paradox upon which this entire study is founded is the allure to the critic of an outside of language, often a quintessential, necessary condition for a particular intervention in writing. This outside may be posited and gauged historically, sociologically, ethnographically, geographically, technologically, even geologically, but upon close reading, it morphs into the very linguistic medium that was to be flown from, escaped, left behind. Based on the inquiries that I have managed to conduct so far, I would have to conclude that these "flights from language," which can be thought of as well as temporary erasures, obliterations, and forgettings, some of which are indispensable to the generation of new writing, end up invariably "grounded." But what a ground this is, this takeoff point and landing strip for escapades in script! It is infused with all the arbitrariness, accident, volatility, and materiality of the language that it is.

Culture is not only a locus, it is a metaphor. Like the self itself, it describes and circumscribes a space in which the effects of language and textuality rebound. There is no advantage to ignoring the metaphorics of culture in the same sense that there is little gain from categorically repudiating the appeal or the phenomena of selfhood and experience.

Any turn toward culture in the effort to bracket questions and effects of language is, congenitally, an oversight, blindness in a de Manian sense. The meditation on culture and its relation to language by the Frankfurt School is one of the most intense and sustained to be registered by twentieth-century Western discourse. It is part of an ages-old contrapuntal exchange through which, on the one hand, language makes itself intelligible by means of cultural institutionality, while on the other, ideology constructs genealogical myths of language whose effect is to domesticate its workings while grounding it in a particular community.[1]

Over the engagement, the *Auseinandersetzung*, that also embraces the Frankfurt School, cultural institutions and individual writers have often devoted vast expenditures of energy to representations of the transfer or the interface between ideology and metaphysics, on the one hand, and the material dimensions, dirty and lowdown though they may be, of textuality on the other. Instances of this unavoidable cultural and discursive myth are legion. They extend from the Platonic allegory of the cave, to Hegel's upending the undecidable and reciprocal play of forces in the "Force and the Understanding" and "Lordship and Bondage" passages of *The Phenomenology of Spirit*, to the *nummo*, the textually dynamic player-demigods of the Dogon cosmology as recounted in Marcel Griaule's *Conversations with Ogotemmêli*.

As Walter Benjamin set about assembling his own pointed intervention as a lifelong reader, cobbling together his own platform as a messianic, that is, society-redeeming and transforming critic, he found it incumbent upon himself to address the same interface, whether described as an entry, a void, or a hopeless disjunction, that is figured in the above-named works. The textual evidence indicates a deep commitment on his part to adapting and extending the speculative philosophy that had been featured so prominently in his education and to the Romantic theory and aesthetics that still exercised such a hold on his on his sensibility.

His ultimate destination, I would argue, was to be an astonishingly erudite and literate "full-service" critic, one capable of rising responsively to any occasion or set of emergent historico-cultural conditions significantly affecting the future of culturally inflected and motivated life. Within the framework of the present constellation of essays, this adaptability, this commitment to responsiveness and responsibility toward the unfolding transcript of the political conditions and cultural articulations emerging within a broad arena, whether known as an economy or as a civilization, is the ultimate mark of the critic. In this sense, Benjamin was not merely one other critic or cultural commentator. He labored long and hard to exemplify a labor, a sociocultural posture and bearing, that he had delved deeply and ranged widely in his readings in order to conceptualize. Out of an explicitly critical positionality, he managed to address both sociopolitical events and conditions and cultural artifacts of a bewildering diversity. He also devised critical responses, among them standard-issue academic essays, radio commentaries, and the genre breaker known as *The Arcades Project*, of such dissimilarity from one another that it is unbelievable that the same author produced them.

I am arguing, within the confines of this present intervention of my own, that Benjamin's commitment to a certain writerly occasion that was constant, but also constantly assuming new forms and posing new challenges, marks him above all, but in no simplistically exclusive way, as a critic, and in many senses as *the* critic. Benjamin's continued residence in this critical position (a commitment not unlike his ongoing residence in Europe, despite the mounting signs that it wasn't good for him) makes him, from a certain point of view, distinct from a philosopher (although his writing bristles with philosophical knowledge and awareness) and from what we would nowadays call a close reader (although his essays are exemplary in their foundation upon close readings that he conducted very much on his own).

Why, at a moment when, informed discourse, both in keeping with and in violation of what Derrida terms the law of genre, productively overflows and redefines definitions and distinctions such as "critic," "philosopher," and "close reader" do I persistently belabor them? I do so in the posture of a classroom lecturer, a position that is a feature of my own particular writing contract, as someone who would demonstrate, by a characterization of writerly roles also involving definitions and distinctions, the full palette of perspectival and compositional options available to his auditors. It is in this interest that I would again advance the philosopher's ultimate loyalty to a conceptual operating system in its historical and cultural evolution as what, roughly, somewhere in the performance, however polymorphous the "read-out" often becomes, distinguishes her from the critic. And I would propose the current, but by no means final or ultimate academic framework and unremittingly exegetical cast of close reading as what distinguishes close reading from the highly nomadic, iterable,[2] and adaptive bearing that the critic, under radically different conditions, regularly unpacks.

The transcript of Benjamin's evolving intervention, especially in the earliest of his works that embraced the full scope of his intellectual formation, gives every indication that he agonized over these postures and bearings, or their counterparts, as well. In the current chapter, I will survey the considerable debt to philosophy that Benjamin acknowledges in two major early pieces, "The Concept of Criticism in German Romanticism" (1920)[3] and "Goethe's *Elective Affinities*" (1924–25).[4] This debt is profound and revelatory within the framework of these two essays. It would reach crescendos in later works, including *The Origins of German Tragic Drama*[5] and "The Work of Art in the Age of Technological Reproducibility."[6] It would indeed be evident throughout the compass of Benjamin's writing. But it is not exclusively or even predominantly in the service of the refinement of a conceptual operating system that Benjamin undertook certain of his other major projects. Among these number his "memoires": *One-Way Street*,[7] *Moscow Diary*,[8] *Berlin Chronicle*, and *Berlin Childhood around 1900*.[9] And there is also the polymath compendium or print-medium Web site of materials deriving from and related to nineteenth-century Paris known as *The Arcades Project*, which was a major preoccupation during the last two decades of Benjamin's life.

1

One work in which Benjamin scrupulously pursues the emergence of the critic out of Romantic reactions to speculative systematicity is his 1920 essay "The Concept of Criticism in German Romanticism." As he surveys the possibilities for the critic as a pivotal catalyst within a literate culture, as the lineaments of this figure are to be discerned within the asystematic discourse of Friedrich Schlegel and Novalis, among others, he establishes, by dint of close and imaginative reading, at least the following seven logico-exigetical positions.

The first is, that subjectivity, for the early Romantics, was tantamount to a reflexivity that proceeded through complex dialectical steps of positing and correction with obvious implications for reading:

> On this state of affairs rests the peculiar character of the infinitude of reflection to which the Romantics laid claim: the dissolution of the proper form of reflection in the face of the absolute. Reflection expands without limit or check, and the thinking given form in reflection turns into formless thinking which directs itself upon the absolute. . . . These poles of reflection are simple throughout. . . . In order to distinguish these poles one would have to assume that absolute reflection comprises the maximum of reality whereas original reflection comprises the minimum of reality. This distinction among levels of clarity is . . . only an auxiliary construction.[10]

The distinction between absolute and original reflections, akin to that between truth and material contents that would be pivotal to the *Elective Affinities* essay, constitutes a confusion between "levels of clarity" that it is the critic's task to engage and unravel. Ironically, "reality" emerges only through the maximum "takes" of reflection. The critic maintains a sober gaze in the face of sublime reflexive displacement and expansion.

The second logico-exigetical position is that early Romanticism, for all its exploration of asystematic figures such as fragmentation and irony, which may be viewed as inevitable systematic byproducts, assumed systematic protocols and functions of its own. "Schlegel and Novalis did have, around 1800, a system. . . . What can be proven beyond any doubt is that their thought was determined by systematic tendencies and contexts, which in any even reached only partial maturity and clarity."[11] The infinity of Romantic reflection transpired within a context of systematic expansion and incompletion. Romanticism, for all its receptiveness to the ineffable, was not reducible to the forms of intellectual aimlessness that Hegel critiques in the "Freedom of Self-Consciousness" section of *The Phenomenology of Spirit*. The projects of Romanticism, and this may have implications for the vocation of criticism as Benjamin conceives it, were grounded in a very specific positivity:

> Schlegel's various attempts to define the absolute spring not only from a lack, not only from unclearness. What underlies them is far more a peculiar positive

tendency in his thinking. In this tendency is found the answer to the question posed above concerning the source of the obscurity in so many of Schlegel's fragments. . . . Certainly for Friedrich Schlegel in the *Athenaeum* period, the absolute was the system in the form of art. Rather than attempting to grasp the absolute systematically, however, he sought conversely to grasp the system absolutely. This was the essence of his mysticism.[12]

Schlegel's mysticism, according to Benjamin, is fraught with a tension between the indeterminacy engulfing all systematic projects and the critical terseness of formulation predicated by the aesthetics of fragmentation. With a vivid sense of this tension's implications for a responsive critical discourse, Benjamin pays it its full due: Schlegel "thus found himself—since his thinking did not unfold systematically, although it was indeed systematically oriented throughout—faced with the problem of combining the maximum range of thought with the most extreme truncation of discursive thinking."[13] In this instance, one byproduct of systematic overviews, from which, according to Benjamin, criticism cannot entirely detach itself, aphoristic formulation, arises to correct the imprecisions to which systematic aspirations inevitably give rise. Benjamin locates the critic very much in the interface between these unavoidable discursive gravitations, toward the fragmentary at the same time as the prolix.

The third logico-exigetical possibility for the critic that Benjamin discerns in "The Concept of Criticism in German Romanticism" is that, in Benjamin's words, "the doctrine of the medium of knowledge and perception is linked to the doctrine of observation, which is of immediate importance in the concept of criticism."[14] The model of observation in early Romanticism that Benjamin finds of direct consequence to criticism is one in which the object of contemplation, through the dynamics of reflection, thinks itself at the same time that the beholder observes it.

> It is not only persons who can expand their knowledge through intensified self-knowledge in reflection; so-called natural things can do so as well. . . . The thing, to the extent that it intensifies reflection within itself and includes other beings in its self-knowledge, radiates its original self-knowledge into these other beings. . . . Rather, the intensification of reflection in it suspends the boundary that separates its being-known by itself from its being-known by another; in the medium of reflection, moreover, the thing and the knowing being merge into one another. Thus, there is in fact no knowledge of an object by a subject.[15]

The notion of a reflexive modality of contemplation that Benjamin willingly draws from Romantic theory, one fitted out with its own artificial intelligence, is the cornerstone to a new epistemology of criticism, one in which the critic, under a Baudelairean sky, swoons into the aura of an artifact fitted out with autonomy, or, if you will, its own volition. Critic and artifact are conjoined in a vertiginous and endless tango of reciprocity, rather than confined to discrete sectors. Benjamin traces the interchangeability of observation (*Beobachtung*) and experiment (*Experiment*) in Romantic discourse. "Experiment consists in the evocation of self-consciousness and self-knowledge in the things observed. To observe a thing means only to rouse it to self-recognition."[16] The critic is as much an interloper in a conversation already in progress in the artwork as she who delivers judgment to a silent audience. The uncertain boundaries between critic and thing give rise to a structural irony: It is no longer possible to ascertain the position from which insight proceeds. "The medium of reflection and knowing coincide for the Romantics. The term 'observation' alludes to this identity of media; what is distinguished as perception and method of research in the experiment is united in magical observation, which is itself an experiment. . . . One can also call this magical observation in the Romantics' sense an ironic observation."[17]

Fourth, according to Benjamin, in the artwork, this Romantic inquest into systematicity, its discourse, and its limits is displaced to the realm of a specific materiality. All the more so does the critic merge with the thing, now an artifact, which effectively writes *her*. "Insofar as criticism is knowledge of the work of art, so is its self-knowledge; insofar as it judges the artwork, this occurs in the latter's self-judgment. In this last office, criticism goes beyond observation."[18] In trespassing beyond observation, criticism departs from its metaphysical, reflexive formation. It furthermore loses any sense of scientific objectivity. The artifact's autonomy enables the critic to step forward from a self-imposed scientific alienation and participate in the artifact's completion. Indeed, without the critic, the artwork is incomplete:

> This much is clear: for the Romantics, criticism is far less the judgment of a work than the method of its consummation. It is in this sense that the Romantics called for poetic criticism . . . declaring: "Poetry can be criticized only through poetry. An aesthetic judgment that is not itself a work of art . . . has no rights of citizenship in the realm of art." "This poetic criticism . . . will complement, rejuvenate,

newly fashion the work." For the work is incomplete. "Only the incomplete can be understood, can lead us further."[19]

In this fashion, the work of commentary becomes indistinguishable from the work of art. The critic merges strategically into the work of composition, abandoning secondary status.

Fifth, Romantic criticism thus declares itself in keeping with a new division of labor:

> The Romantics demand an immanent criticism. . . . This is . . . the foundation of a completely different kind of criticism—one which is not concerned with judging, and whose center of gravity lies not in the evaluation of the single work but in demonstrating its relation to all other works and, ultimately, to the idea of art.[20]

> These consequences can be expressed to three basic propositions. . . . The first principle . . . affirms that the judgment of a work must never be explicit, but rather must always be implicit in the fact of its Romantic critique (that is, its reflection). . . . That implicit judgment of artworks . . . is remarkable in a second way: it has no scale of values at its disposal. If a work can be criticized, then it is a work of art; otherwise it is not.[21]

Benjamin hitches criticism and creative improvisation inextricably to the same star. In return for an acknowledgment of the intuition, insight, and invention demanded by criticism in Benjamin's sense, criticism repudiates its claims to authority, whether in terms of objectivity, exteriority, reason, or systematicness. Benjamin thus establishes the ground rules for an activist criticism, one marked by the relativity in which the observer and contingency implode upon the reaction. Criticism's freedom to renounce the detachment that in an earlier regime invested it with authority is a key feature of its systematic irony, a trope whose explicit centrality to the Schlegels, Novalis, and Kierkegaard we briefly touched upon in Chapter 1. The critic that Benjamin situates at the crossroads between Romantic asystematicity and postmodern shock is a spinmaster of ironic nuance.

Sixth, however, in Benjamin's revised positionality of criticism, the critical object is as susceptible to transformation as the critic. If Benjamin teases out the mandate in Romantic theory for a synesthetic continuum *between* the genres, akin to the Borgesian figure of "The Garden of Forking Paths," at once a labyrinth, a lacquered writing cabinet, and a novel that can only be described as "a shapeless mass of contradictory drafts,"[22] he sets in relief the linguistic play that constitutes the commonality of the genres. Benjamin's engagement with certain formulations by the German Romantics whose suggestiveness has been highlighted above thus augments and consolidates our understanding of the critic's full range of responsibilities and liberties. The aesthetic of synesthesia that Benjamin appropriates from Romantic theory is neither mystical nor mystified: It prefigures the deconstructive notion of a textuality across the range of the artifacts of culture above and beyond conventions of genre and discursive modality. "All poems of antiquity link up to one another, until the whole is formed out of continually greater masses and members. . . . Ancient poetry is a single, indivisible, perfected poem. . . . All the classical poems of the ancients conjoin, inseparably; they form an organic whole, and are, rightly seen, a single poem, the only one in which the art of poetry is completely manifest."[23] In taking this formulation as his own, Benjamin not only continues to exploit the aesthetic implications of the Romantic ideal of organicism, he anticipates translinguistic constructs such as *écriture* of a far later provenance, underscoring the play of a medium literally underwriting the diverse manifestations of culture.

In the citations immediately above, poetics is to serve as the arena for this panlinguistic apprehension. But as the Romantics and Benjamin were aware, the medium of media may just as well be the novel. "Early Romanticism not only classified the novel as the highest form of reflection in poetry, but . . . found in it the extraordinary transcendent confirmation of its aesthetic theory. According to his conception, art is the continuum of forms, and the novel . . . is the comprehensive manifestation of this medium. . . . The idea of poetry is prose."[24] Unwilling to relinquish Romantic hopes for genre, Benjamin still invests poetry and the novel with the notion of a polymorphous linguistic substratum beneath all manifestations of culture. The closest to the Derridean notion of writing at which Benjamin eventuates here is prose, which he ironically elevates to the status of the very idea of poetry.

But the strategically contested no-person's land into which Benjamin wanders in this section of "The Concept of Criticism" is the turning point at which reflexivity—and the intensified mindfulness for which it allows—precipitates the residue, secretes the substance, metamorphosing it into textuality. At a certain moment, the pure play transpiring in the hall of mirrors, the endlessly fragmenting reflection of parabasis, becomes invested with the weight and substance, imperceptible though they may be, of materiality. In this instance, consciousness, the agent and medium of reflection, also known as Spirit, Mind, or *Geist*, a creature of the highest metaphysical provenance, becomes transformed into prose, a material element of human endeavor—or was that poetry?

The critic follows this alchemical transmogrification from mind to matter—from spiritual acuity, characteristic of sentimentalists and ministers, not just of the poet and the critic, over the brink. The leap from pure mindfulness or spirituality into the stuff of transcultural prose or poetry is over a life-claiming precipice. The critic, born into a pronounced state of mindfulness that can be characterized only as purely metaphysical, survives the leap and is left to negotiate the debris of history and its cultural forms with the shards of this literally fallen spirituality.

Seventh and finally, Benjamin, negotiating a highly volatile world, in the Heideggerian sense, whether of cultural or sociopolitical affairs, willfully pays homage to the tradition of sensibility constituting the critic's highest birthright. Even early on, he is aware that this intense mindfulness exists only to be degraded. It accumulates tension not of an entirely asexual nature only to spend it on a textual thing that cannot be fully appreciated in a culturally degraded world. On one flank, at least, criticism is thus an extreme of mindfulness, precipitating out of the Romantic problematic of reflexivity. Yet it is situated at the juncture where extreme perceptibility and sensibility and blatant materiality are one. The critic is the mind that can integrate, in the sense of late object-relations theory,[25] both sides of this divide.

The aesthetic of the artifact, extending from Romantic theory with extreme sensibility and materiality at once, Benjamin would later term "mechanical reproducibility." The Benjaminian cultural critic is she who, with full messianic pathos, with vivid memory of the idealism that motivated Romantic systematicity, embraces materiality and the literal impact of the material—shock—that enshroud the postmodern, endlessly reflexive thing in a degraded but textually articulate and explicit aura. In accounting for this dark turn in the intellectual endeavor, Benjamin marshals Hölderlin, who contributes to the aesthetic ethos "the principle of the sobriety of art." "Its connection with the methodological procedure of that philosophy, namely reflection—is obvious. . . . As a thoughtful and collected posture, reflection is the antithesis of ecstasy, the mania of Plato. Just as, for the early Romantics, light occasionally operates as a symbol of the medium of reflection, of infinite mindfulness, so Hölderlin."[26]

By virtue of its inherent aesthetic sobriety, mindfulness opposes ecstasy and the Platonic form of mania. Benjamin sets the stage here for an attentiveness to detail warranting Schlegel's "comparisons with manufacturing. But shouldn't the true author also be a manufacturer? . . . The Romantics were thinking of 'made' work, works filled with prosaic spirit."[27] It is under the gray, prosaic illumination characteristic of, say, Judge William's counterpoint to the aesthete's ebullient ironic vision in Kierkegaard's *Either/Or* that Benjamin constructs the unforeseen interface between infinite Romantic reflexivity and the throwaway, "the work of art in the age of mechanical reproduction."

Some of Benjamin's earliest direct addresses to the persona and function of the critic thus prefigure an exquisitely attentive reader who has, at her own peril, allowed an uncannily self-reflexive art object to overflow her own being, depositing there the detritus of an alien, but indissoluble materiality. To such a degree does the critic join the idealist surround of the artifact that she becomes a necessary condition for its completion. With one foot solidly planted in a materiality also predicated by the Romantics' speculations, the critic also contributes to the deflation of aesthetic mysticism and quasi-religious exaltation.

With this sensibility in hand, Benjamin assembles the auratic collection of artifacts that constitute his true signature. Baudelaire was enough the heir of German idealist aesthetics and metaphysics and enough the materialist in Benjamin's particular sense to circumscribe the composite critical project, to perfume it with a distinctive tone and flavor. The interface between extreme idealism and sober materiality is the location where Benjamin, astronomical *flâneur* of Paris as the capital of the broadest modernity, arranged the stars in the constellation of his taste and exhibited them in the sky of his prose.

3

Even the briefest survey of "The Concept of Criticism in German Romanticism" establishes the seriousness of Benjamin's conceptual aspirations for literary criticism. These arise in philosophy and intuit in criticism the potential for an aesthetically charged philosophical iteration or extension, one appealing, potentially, to a significant literate public. His long essay "Goethe's *Elective Affinities*" is a paradigmatic extended work of such criticism. It feels both comfortable and innovative as such and continues to furnish us with splendid suggestions as to what the most profound and meaningful literary realizations of philosophical thinking may be. In pursuing the vicissitudes of *Schein* (semblance, show, or apparition) in Goethe's novel of desire, *The Elective Affinities* (*Die Wahlverwandtschaften*), a pivotal construct of understanding shared, among others, by Kant, Fichte, and Hegel, Benjamin furnishes an exegesis of the novel in which the philosophical disputation of its age serves as the underlying operating system not only of its epistemology, but of the particular aesthetic devices and overall power that accord it a foregone sense of its inevitability.

> All genuine works of art have their siblings in the realm of philosophy. It is, after all, precisely these figures in which the ideal of philosophy's problem appears.— The totality of philosophy, its system, is of a higher magnitude of power than can be demanded by the quintessence of all its problems taken together. . . . Even if, however, the system is in no sense attainable through inquiry, there are nonetheless constructions which, without being questions, have the deepest affinity with the ideal of the problem. These are works of art. The work of art does not compete with philosophy itself—it merely enters into the most precise relation to philosophy through its affinity to the ideal of the problem. And to be sure, according to a lawfulness grounded in the essence of the ideal as such, the ideal can only represent itself in a multiplicity.[28]

Considering that *The Elective Affinities* is a novel in which characters pair off according to sympathies whose best correlatives derive from the rhetoric and metaphysical and procedural aspirations of chemistry and other physical sciences, affinities overpowering marriage and related social conventions, Benjamin's assertion of quasi-incestuous sibling pairings between philosophy and literature has to be a loaded statement. Philosophy, as Benjamin formulates it in this passage, one as pivotal to the overall direction of his work as to the elucidation of *The Elective Affinities*, is a pursuit mobilizing itself in the formulation of problems, which shimmer as transcendental indices to specific transactions.

Benjamin's image of philosophy as a matrix of problems anticipates Foucault's understanding of cultural history as a succession of *épistèmes* that at the same time set the linguistic and hermeneutic limits of an epoch and can thus be retrospectively deployed in conjunction with one another. Works of art, or, in the Goethe essay, of literature, demonstrate their quasi-incestuous parity with philosophy through their affinity to, their orientation toward, the problem—the problem of a particular moment whose articulation has been made possible, and made, by philosophy.

In its elective affinity for the problem, the memorable artifact of literature has joined in philosophy's work. This labor has been characterized earlier in the essay as a negotiation between material content (*Sachgehalt*) and truth content, as a trade-off between nature or language and representation, and as the crossfire between premonition and fate.[29] Literature joins philosophy as a sibling in the working through of the problem as an archaeological formation in Foucault's sense—but as a manifold, not as a unified, coherent theory, in the sense of a "unified field theory."

As Benjamin not only decodes Goethe's *The Elective Affinities* in this essay according to its shared orientation with philosophy toward the problem, but also performs the issues of exemplarity, appearance, and imagery that come up in the reading, criticism emerges as the deconcealment of and venue for this rich interface. The passage cited immediately above continues:

> The ideal of the problem, however, does not appear in a multiplicity of problems. Rather, it lies buried in a manifold of works, and its excavation is the business of critique. The latter allows the ideal of the problem to appear in the work of art in one of its manifestations. [*Sie läßt im Kunstwerk das Ideal des Problems in Erscheinung, in eine seiner Erscheinungen treten.*] For critique ultimately shows in the work of art the virtual possibility of formulating the work's truth content as the highest philosophical problem. That before which it stops short, however—as if in awe of the work, but equally from respect for the truth—is precisely this formulation itself. That possibility of formulation could indeed be realized only if the system could be the object of inquiry and therefore transform itself from an appearance of the ideal into the existence of the ideal—an existence that is never given.[30]

It is the business of criticism to unearth the problem common, in different ways, to philosophy and literature. But whereas in philosophical terms the problem is an epoch-setting phenomenon, from the perspective of the literary artwork, it is merely "one of its manifestations [*Erscheinungen*]." The above passage is replete with the imagery of appearances and manifestations that it will discover to be the truth content of *The Elective Affinities*.

The rapport between the philosophical operating system and the literary artwork, at this vital stage of Benjamin's development, is rich and intense, in keeping with a sibling rivalry, but is differentiated, as well. It can easily be described as being at a standoff. Philosophy has the honor of formulating the problem of which the literary artifact is one among many instances. Yet it is only in literature that the ideal embodied in the problem has any tangible existence. Philosophy "stops short" "of formulating the work's truth content." The "system" never quite manages to "transform itself from an appearance of the ideal into the existence of the ideal."[31] It is left for the literary artwork, in the case of *The Elective Affinities*, a text that literally hovers on the brink between semblance and nature, between the truth of the imaginary and the strictures of morality, to furnish a stage and a being for the ideal encompassed by the philosophical problem.

In the intricate *pas de deux* that Benjamin choreographs for philosophy and literature, the pivotal problematic of a distant epoch may not well serve the artwork that it is discovered to animate. As a showcase for this intimate and often secret connivance, Benjamin's gloss on *The Elective Affinities* is stunning for the degree to which it assumes accountability for certain material concerns of the novel's composition, including plot and characterization. The young female "lead" of the novel, Otillie, both completes the symmetry of its two counterposed couples and destroys this uneasy sexual and moral equilibrium—as her rapport with Eduard, the *major domus* and househusband of the *ménage*, explodes into passion. In keeping with the role that Benjamin has established for the philosophical operating system within the literary artwork, Otillie becomes a creature and figure for the semblance that is both a talisman for conceptual speculation at the moment and the novel's highest aesthetic epiphenomenon.

> With the semblance-like character [*Scheinhaftigkeit*] that determines Otillie's beauty, insubstantiality also threatens the salvation that the friends gain from their struggles. But if beauty is semblance-like, so, too is the reconciliation [*Versöhnung*] that it promises mythically in life and death. Its sacrifice, like its blossoming, would be in vain, its reconciliation a semblance of reconciliation. In fact, true reconciliation exists only with God. Whereas in true reconciliation the individual reconciles himself with God and only in this way conciliates other human beings, it is peculiar to semblance-like reconciliation [*scheinbarhaften Versöhnung*] that the individual wants others to make peace with one another and in this way become reconciled with God.[32]

This is a key passage in the philosophically motivated task of pursuing the emanations of *Schein* throughout the novel. Otillie is an embodiment of it. It is her beauty that prevents the novel from serving as a static schema, or, in toto, specifically as the ideal of a problem, the status of the transcendental under Goethe's particular cultural constellation. Yet her beauty, the aesthetic power she pinpoints, serves as one of many possible instances of "the existence of the ideal," which, according to Benjamin's overall blueprint for this project, the artwork encompasses and critical excavation unearths.

Yet by the particular inscriptive moment of the above extract, what was formerly an aesthetico-philosophical rhetoric that dominated the essay and gave it coherence has added a new vocabulary, ontotheological terms, of significance to the Abrahamic religions in general and to Judaism in particular. I think above all of "sacrifice," "conciliation," and "reconciliation."[33] The emergence of an ontotheological vocabulary through which Ottilie's significance as a literary figure of semblance can be measured is less, I think, a last-minute cat-out-of-the-bag production with the purpose of establishing the novel's ultimate religious meaning or interpretation. Through this development, rather, Benjamin gesticulates toward the widest horizon of the constructs implicated by criticism's syntheses and excavations. In terms of the above passage, the novel sacrifices Otillie, the figure of shimmering beauty and semblance, to maintain the possibility of other characters' and the novel's reconciliation (or resignation) to the ideal, whether it be the ideal of the truth or the ideal of the problem. Short of subscribing to any of these ideals (or any of the faiths or discourses that promise them), Benjamin assays the broadest investment that Western culture, in its manifestation as a secular art-religion under the aegis of modernity, maintains in the synthesis between philosophy and beauty (or poetics) in the artwork. Criticism, as Benjamin has defined it in this particular intervention, is at the service of this fusion or interface.

Hence it is that the possibility for hope itself hinges upon the vicissitudes of semblance that Benjamin traces out in "Goethe's *Elective Affinities.*" The dénouement of the essay, which after all, mobilizes only *one* of Benjamin's manifestations as a critic, is suffused by the broadest horizon of hope, under which the innovations of modernity, for better and for worse, transpire. In response to the hope that "shot across the sky above [the characters'] heads like a falling star" in *The Elective Affinities*, Benjamin writes: "With this comes to light the innermost basis for the 'narrator's stance.' . . . That most paradoxical, most fleeting hope finally emerges from the semblance of reconciliation, just as, at twilight, as the sun is extinguished, rises the evening star which outlasts the night. Its glimmer, of course, is imparted by Venus. And upon the slightest glimmer all hope rests; even the richest hope come from it."[34] The artwork, as well as the philosophical operating system whose workings criticism discerns in it, promises no reconciliation, whether with the truth, God, beauty, or pure faith. It delivers the "semblance of reconciliation," this essay's highest and richest synthesis. The semblance of reconciliation captures both the artwork's ongoing devotion to the philosophical problem and the hope that its shimmering images of beauty sustain.

The bittersweetness of this formulation, stopping short of resolution or finality, but not of their possibility, becomes a hallmark of the critic's dual posture, both as a nostalgist and as an avatar of shock, in Benjamin's consummate critical essays, including the "Theses on the Philosophy of History," "The Work of Art in the Age of Its Technological Reproducibility," and "On Some Motifs in Baudelaire." Nothing more monumental than the evening star, an unwavering pinpoint of light, stands a chance of outlasting the impenetrable night in which the experiments of modernity transpire, whose violence, percussion, and impersonality coincide with their flashes of brilliance. All this has been made possible by one particularly philosophically rigorous reading of a novel infused with its cultural moment, pivoting around the problem/figure of semblance.

And yet, as I have been suggesting, even this philosophically informed and beautifully orchestrated appeal to the philosophical operating system as the most rigorous accessible context for the public reception of the artifact is merely one of the guises under which Benjamin undertakes the task of the critic: media guru, bibliophile, children's announcer, travel writer, even food critic ("Food Fair," "Food," "Hashish in Marseille"). Each of these writerly stances diverged significantly from the academically irreproachable and conceptually labored frameworks that Benjamin devised for such projects, in addition to the *Elective Affinities* essay, as *The Origins of German Tragic Drama*. And Benjamin's scriptoral bearings differed radically from one another. Yet so unwavering was Benjamin in his devotion to the critical occasion that none of the postures he assumed was beneath him. Of course, the grounding of his varied interventions in a critical theory that he himself synthesized, in part based on his personal interactions with the estimable minds of his day, never failed him.

Although written in close proximity to "Goethe's *Elective Affinities*," his "Announcement of the Journal *Angelus Novus*" brings into play significantly different slants on criticism. Benjamin's précis of a journal that never came into existence alone would have been worth the price of any number of subscriptions. In composing this brief essay, Benjamin took upon himself the significant tasks of balancing the assertion of a journal's design and vision against "the function of great criticism . . . not . . . to instruct by means of historical descriptions or to educate through comparisons, but to cognize by immersing itself in the object [*durch Versenkung zu erkennen*]," an awareness gained by a literal sinking into the artifact.[35] How will *Angelus Novus* "proclaim the spirit of its age" without stifling the spontaneity of its individual contributions and collective vision through excessive explicitness and unnecessary erudition, without disrupting "the experience of a particular way of thinking"?[36] The launching of a vibrant journal, as Benjamin elaborates the problem, is much closer to the loose compromise we make with our unconscious in negotiating our everyday lives than to the possibly inhibiting expert testimony available to the psychotherapist and patient.

The inception of a journal that will bring a certain vision to the German readership, albeit one tempered by exhortations to wit and spontaneity deriving from a predecessor, the *Athenaeum*, that Benjamin specifically earmarks, is a quintessential occasion of idealistic anticipation. It is in fact in some of his less didactic presentations that the messianism with which he invests criticism receive their most tangible expressions. By the end of the *Angelus Novus* announcement, this messianic figuration becomes explicit: "According to a legend in the Talmud, the angels—who are born anew every instant in constant numbers—are created in order to perish and vanish into the void, once they have sung their hymn in the presence of God. It is to be hoped that the name of the journal will guarantee it contemporary relevance, which is the only true sort."[37] For all the quasi-religious fervor with which Benjamin endows the foundation of an institution that can uplift its audience through its philosophical grounding, its recourse to Romantic theory, and its commitments to sensibility, spontaneity, and the vitality of experience, he pays his full due to the evanescence of the artifacts that will be highlighted by the journal and to the fashions they inaugurate. The angels vanish after chanting their hymns into the void. It is this foregone annihilation that Benjamin installs into messianic time, the time of creation, of rigorous cultural work, that allows his critical postures and personae to be so diverse, to be written out in terms of highly specific, even momentary instigations and circumstances. The angels are the standard bearers for hopes, wishes, and the dream of transforming the world into a better place, but for all that, and even by virtue of that, they are quite fragile. Their exuberance has been invested in them with planned obsolescence. This pathos does not elude Benjamin's announcement of a journal whose fate is an apt expression of the issues and aporias it would, if granted life, set in play.

Known fatedness announces the birth of a veritable horde of Benjamin's critical angels: the writer of full-fledged memoires, including *One-Way Street*, *A Berlin Childhood around 1900*, and the reminiscences of his visits to Ibiza, who can drop the scholarly-philosophical pose entirely, but who still narrates his tale and composes its experiences in keeping with his full critical understandings, or the inventor of the print-medium historico-critical Web site, the utterly unprecedented genre, if that word in any way applies, known as *The Arcades Project*, in whose crystallization "passive" skills, including the assemblage of materials, montage, citation, and sequential ordering play a more prominent role than the thin, randomly distributed stratum of Benjamin's "active" critical commentary, as incisive as it often is. Benjamin offers a prolegomena for such a work in the numbered formulations of the "Program for Literary Criticism," where, under item 8 he writes, "Very good criticism can be made from both glosses and quotations. What must be avoided like the plague is rehearsing the summary of the contents. In contrast, a criticism consisting entirely of quotations should be developed."[38]

And the third angel of criticism whose meteoric flight I would like to pursue, distinct from the guiding light of the other two—his literary essays and diverse occasional pieces—is the inspiration for Benjamin's radio commentary. I think particularly of his 1931 children's broadcast on the 1755 Lisbon earthquake. Benjamin's solidarity with his youthful audience is so pronounced and his mindfulness of the parameters of the discursive occasion so intense that in this instance, and I am certain that it is not alone, Benjamin's voice will have to speak for itself:

> I feel like a chemist when I talk to you over the radio. My weights are the minutes, and I have to measure them out very accurately; so much of this and so

much of that, if the final mixture is going to come out right. "How come?" you will ask. "If you want to tell us about the Lisbon earthquake, begin by telling us how it started. And then you can go on to tell us what happened next." But if I followed this advice, I don't think the description would be much fun.[39]

The above do not begin to exhaust the host of critical angels, each substantially different from the next, which Benjamin released across the sky of modernity. The angels soared through the constellations of phenomena that were formed by modernity's frantic efforts to disrupt history and to appropriate it, to access that drive and control it, to discover new media and restrict access to them, to flood new markets with mass-produced commodities and hoard the profits, to engineer vast projects of human services, demography, transportation, administration, health, welfare, and defense, but also to turn them against human populations, if deemed expedient.

Each of Benjamin's angels of criticism existed among the isolation that in "On Some Motifs in Baudelaire"[40] ("*Über einige motive bei Baudelaire*") is a foregone conclusion. It is the fate of each angel to pursue a trajectory of exile, flaring up in poetry and illumination before subsiding into the obscurity defined by obtuseness and forgetting. Benjamin illuminated a host of angels vitally and plausibly engaged in the collective endeavor of cultural inscription. The meticulous pursuit of any of their trails across the sky of writing joins the messianic endeavors of cultural perceptibility, sensibility, reading, and elucidation.

3

As brilliantly thought through and put into play as Benjamin's project for a philosophically motivated criticism may have been—and here the essays we have been exploring thus far, "The Concept of Criticism in German Romanticism" and "Goethe's *Elective Affinities*," demand well-deserved prominence—the sequential reader of Benjamin's output cannot but be shocked, discombobulated, taken aback, even stoned, by the dawning of *One-Way Street* (*Einbahnstraße*, 1928) upon the atmosphere of his writing. This work sets the stage not only for other memoirs, such as *A Berlin Chronicle* and *A Berlin Childhood around 1900*, but for heterogeneous essays often composed of brief and hard-hitting sections, including "The Work of Art in the Age of Its Technological Reproducibility," "On the Concept of History" "Geschichtsphilosphische Thesen"),[41] and "On Some Motifs in Baudelaire," not to mention the utterly exceptional *Arcades Project.*

One-Way Street may be described as a loose and flexible collage of different discourses and figural modalities that circulate, in no predetermined or bounded way, around a number of obliquely related cultural phenomena, sociological trends, and autobiographical recollections that Benjamin drew into his endlessly reverberating text. Benjamin makes the decisive (but not irreversible) turn down a one-way—that is, open-ended—street in this composition when he suspends the primary task of making a case or argument before the arbitrating jury of culture in favor of performing the values that he advocates. With *One-Way Street*, allegorical inscription establishes itself as the horizon of his interventions and as a parameter of all critical commentary emerging from a world of modernist "structural fabulation," the postmodern simultaneity of all historical accretions, and psychophenomenological shock.

To be sure, Benjamin's philosophically motivated studies rehearse in a meaningful way the operating system that will underlie the extended allegories opening up after the turn down the one-way street. We can, for example, well understand why it was important for Benjamin explicitly to invoke the Romantic encomium for the critic to merge into the artwork, for the work to write *her* as much as the inverse. The shimmering *Schein* or semblance that Benjamin finds shuttling between Kant, Fichte, Hegel, and Goethe's consummate philosophical novel lends his allegorical essays their quintessential tonality and style. Yet when Benjamin crosses over from such works as "The Concept of Criticism" and the Goethe essay into the strikingly performative modality of *One-Way Street* and the texts with which it shares elective affinities, the unbounded reverberations from collisions common to the art world and "advanced" capitalist society definitively usurp the momentum of the occasion.

The thrust of the text is not so much a statement, however eloquent, or even the demonstration of a parity between the artifact and the prevailing conceptual operating system. *One-Way Street* gathers, within the framework of a single document, the open-ended feedback loop encompassing, in its indifferent continuity, radically heterogeneous cultural productions and sites. The appearance of *One-Way Street* in the sequence of Benjamin's substantial essays marks a radical turn in the direction of a commitment to relentlessly performative critical interventions. *One-Way Street* marks Benjamin's invention of an irreducibly critical performance art in the medium of discourse. This intervention holds itself relentlessly open to the contingencies in the aesthetico-conceptual field that Benjamin "covers." Although Benjamin is a splendid thinker and exemplar of philosophically astute interpretation, it became impossible after the moment of *One-Way Street* to reduce him to a purveyor of philosophical concepts or to restrict informed criticism in its wake to any form of summation, categorization, sequencing, or thematic readout that does not incorporate the dynamics of its own pretexts, counterforces, and rhetorical modalities.

I want, in this last substantial segment of the chapter, simply to unpack the passage between Benjamin's prior work and *One-Way Street* with you. The development, again, is not only decisive to Benjamin scholarship and the endeavor of culturally and aesthetically placing the important critic: It is momentous for our understanding and appreciation of criticism—its occasions, roles, and wide-open field for cultural intervention. It is a testament to the wildness of Benjamin's originality that the case on him will never be closed.

It may be of some small historical utility to recall that the crystallization of this work transpired midway during the composition, by Fernando Pessoa, on sandwich-paper, of the writerly scraps ultimately assembled into *The Book of Disquiet*. *One-Way Street* is surely Benjamin's first dream book, the liminal work in which he gives his dreams and personal experience (much of it romantic or relating his travels) full sway in an emerging textual constellation including, among its constitutive elements, not only texts themselves, but childhood, cities, maps, books, apartments, and money. There will be a significant "continuity of writing" along these thematic files, which also become nodal points in a map of writing, all the way through *The Arcades Project*. But more important than Benjamin's ongoing interests, which we may regard as primary scenes of composition, is the radical, nonlinear, and unpredictable leaping *between* these sites, which henceforth would serve as the only admissible basis for Benjamin's broader observations on art, literature, technology, and culture.

One-Way Street is also a memory book: It establishes recollection as one basis, among others, not only for a text-immanent modality of composition, but also for thinking. Had Proust not anticipated Benjamin on the scene of textually charged inscription, Walter would have needed to invent him.

Critical notation is henceforth to embody and perform the balletristic leaps linking a violently incongruous world, but also the anomalous counterforces at play in it and the discontinuities and disjunctions that preempt any easy conclusion. One dimension of the critic's vocation is to surrender herself to these forces, not knowing where she will come out on the other side. Were the results of these forays in any way objectifiable, the critic would be tantamount to an urban anthropologist of writing, not of "society." (The implications of a Benjaminian writing practice for the social sciences are as important as they are for literary and cultural studies.) The critical result or "finding" is thus hopelessly marked by the violence and shock prevailing within the textual register the critic perforce inhabits, calls "home," and in this commitment alienates herself from any "home base," national, urban, linguistic, or otherwise. To the degree that each scene or occasion of cultural elucidation elicits varying responses and writerly resources on the part of the critic, each critical transcript of a cultural encounter will be fundamentally different from all others in form, tone, style, thrust, even "genre." This is an implication of the Benjaminian practice of writing criticism forged in *One-Way Street* that wreaks havoc on the disciplinary expectations in which we couch the academic division of labor. It also does not bode well for a series of cultural institutions, among them universities, museums, theaters, and various publications, which, to the degree that they expect detachment and consistency from exegesis, undermine themselves.

Although far from Benjamin's longest work, *One-Way Street* contributes mightily to his shifting, ongoing endeavor of "founding a new genre" in prose. It is relentlessly fragmentary in composition. But what distinguishes *One-Way Street* is the pivotal role that section headings play within it and the intrinsic visual dimension they open up within the prosaic tissue. To judge from the titles that introduce every section or sequence of thematically related paragraphs in the text, *One-Way Street* is an urban phantasmagoria (a term accruing to Benjamin from his studies of nineteenth-century Paris), a sequence of prose pictures evoked by different sites and situations in the urban landscape. Each sequence of paragraphs is, then, the illustration or caption for a title that is its given. It functions as the verbal gloss on a title or caption initially deriving, in terms of an embedded compositional fiction and principle of hybrid form, from the visual register. The names or motives for the ensuing passages derive from "internal" and "external" locations ("Filling Station," "Construction Site," and "Manorially Furnished Ten-Room Apartment"). These sites may derive from an address ("Number 113"), what we would encounter in a shop window ("Chinese Curios," "Gloves"), or what we would read on a sign ("To the Public: Please Protect and Preserve These New Plantings"). Benjamin allows himself panoptical ubiquity in selecting urban pretexts for the offshoots of his prose. Yet once he assigns his legend, in this innovative, shock-dizzy, multiperspectival prose medium, to the different writing sites that make up *One-Way Street*, his prose diverges and wanders according to its intrinsic associative networks, as intricately crafted prose is wont to do. Cityscapes explicitly deriving from Berlin ("Mexican Embassy," "Stand-Up Beer Hall") morph into the "Travel Souvenirs" of far-flung and often exotic locations, places including Riga, Naples, and Marseille, with departure from Berlin hardly marked. Each of the ingenious titles that Benjamin crafts for *One-Way Street* thus functions intrinsically and extrinsically within the overall mapping performed by the text: It marks a site in the burgeoning, up-to-date, modernist city that the text embellishes, reenacts, and furnishes with a commentary, and it serves as a street sign or marker from which each word-site is free to digress and travel through the universes of language and semiotic dispersion.

It is primarily in the intense care and attentiveness that *One-Way Street* invests in book design, the conception of the book as a linguistic and communications medium, that it departs from Benjamin's earlier, more conventional productions of scholarly prose. It veers by implication into an exploration of media, their specific attributes as well as their status as figments of language. Benjamin maintains the standards of exegetical acuity that he established in "The Concept of Criticism" and "Goethe's *Elective Affinities*." But the emphasis, in the hybrid prose medium of *One-Way Street*, is far more on the exploration of the graphic, typographical, and citational resources of prose than on the culmination of a trend or argument. It may be thus said of *One-Way Street* that within its shifting boundaries "The Concept(s) of Criticism" receive an epoch-making and irreversible illustration.

Within the disorienting play of titles, captions, headings, and legends, one leading directly to the heart of an inquiry into the medium of critical prose, as into all media, Walter activates a continuum of seemingly unrelated issues—questions, exerting, if anything, a negative bearing on one another—but all indicative of the vectors and counterforces at play in cities and the media, and the phenomena accentuated by cities, among them labyrinths, maps, and sexuality. This constellation of nodes or sites of articulation, which includes dreams, love, childhood, books, maps, and apartments, becomes the ultimate map that *One-Way Street* furnishes with a legend. A major shockwave released by these phenomena is, quite simply, that there could be a space radical enough to house them in volatile communication. Let us call it the space of urban or cosmopolitan prose.

In no other work by Benjamin are the stuff of dreams and the melodrama of love so much of a piece with the other constituents with this impossible, but poetically compelling prose. In no other work, in other words, does he place material from his lived experience, his yearnings, dreams, and private language in general so much at the service of reminiscence, but, as in its Proustian inspiration, this memory work is anything but a personal expression. Not only does his on-once, off-forever romance with Asja Lacis, whom he had first encountered on Capri, furnish this text with its dedication: "This street is named / Asja Lacis Street / after she who / as an engineer / cut it through the author." The ill-fated subsequent visit that he pays her in Riga constitutes a digression in a travelogue branching off from the familiar streets of Berlin.[42]

This is anything but a psychoanalytical transcript. Indeed, *One-Way Street* establishes a new benchmark of openness to psychological material in Benjamin's writing. Dreams, dreams that Benjamin attributes to himself, form a significant swath of its fabric. But these dreams translate far more into the mapping of the cosmopolitan twentieth-century city than into the Freudian intrapsychic agencies and their vicissitudes. They configure the rebuses of narrative rather than of personality. Already the second section of the text, "Breakfast Room," characterizes the betrayal of the dream that coincides with its narration. "The gray penumbra of the dream persists there." "He who shuns contact with the day . . . is unwilling to eat and disdains his breakfast . . . thus avoids a rupture between the nocturnal and the daytime worlds."[43] The breakfast room is the foyer between dreaming and narration. It is first and foremost a scene of writing. Benjamin leads us there promptly, directly after tanking up in another sense at the "Filling Station." "Only from the far bank, from broad daylight, may dream be addressed from the superior vantage of memory. This far side of dream is

attainable only through a cleansing analogous to washing, yet totally different. By way of the stomach."[44]

This inaugural dream in the cityscape of *One-Way Street* is as enigmatic,
self-negating, exhausting, and inconclusive as any other, but it spends its
resources, discharges its energy, not in the illustration of psychic agencies
and their processes, but in illuminating a process of narration extending
beyond dreams to other narrative forms, as well. The breakfast room issues
out on the "further side of dream," where it "may be addressed from the
superior vantage of memory." But enlisting the dream's vivid memory and
its volatile flow in writing is tantamount to a fast, maintaining a hunger for
the dream, not a breakfast, in which the remains of the night are devoured
along with the morning's gastronomic offerings. The inscription of the
dream takes place in a breakfast room of detachment, as well as of material
comfort and plenitude, but it happens only in a restrained relationship to
satisfaction, whether of the psychic or corporeal variety.

It is not long before the guided tour of a house that takes up the inaugural substantial segment of *One-Way Street* deposits us in Goethe's study,
which becomes the scene of a dream narrative conventional in its form, but
pivotal in illuminating the complexities of Benjamin's writerly stance:

> In a dream I saw myself in Goethe's study. It bore no resemblance to the one in
> Weimar. Above all, it was very small and had only one window. The side of the
> writing desk abutted on the wall opposite the window. Sitting and writing at it
> was the poet, in extreme old age. I was standing to one side when he broke off
> to give me a small vase, an urn from antiquity, as a present. I turned it between
> my hands. An immense heat [*ungeheure Hitze*] filled the room. Goethe rose to
> his feet and accompanied me to an adjoining chamber, where a table was set for
> my relatives. It seemed prepared, however, for many more than their number.
> Doubtless there were places for my ancestors, too.[45]

We will, of course, never know if this narrative "clinically" corresponds
to a dream experienced by the historical Walter Benjamin or if it constitutes
a narrative improvisation. Or perhaps it constitutes the night composition
of the obsessive writer, the writing that gets done in our sleep. The Walter
of the dream narrative begins to "weep" with emotion at the sacrifices and
other considerations shown by the German Shakespeare to him, his family,
and his ancestors. Miraculously, Goethe breaks off his writing, bestows
upon Walter an urn deriving from the bedrock of Greek civilization, to

which, in *Faust*, the master poet dispatches his title character on an expedition to geological foundations and etymological roots,[46] and sets a table for Walter's family and forbears, largely Jews.

This dream opens itself to us and to the nascent webwork of *One-Way Street* on several facets. There is the pivotal figure of the urn, in many contexts a receptacle for the remains of ancestors, flesh burned out into ashes. Not unlike a dream or the text that transcribes one, the urn collects vestiges of the past, memories, literally, relations. Time itself is the ultimate material that gathers in an urn. Freud might well interest himself in why Walter rotates the urn between his hands, why the played-with object is more hollow than phallic, and in the "immense heat" the manipulation generates.

The Freudian theater, however, is a sideshow to the literary "commerce" that Walter, who begins the dream in a marginal position, establishes with the father of modern German letters, who could not be more accommodating. In terms of its sociological surround or setting, the dream stages a pronounced wish fulfillment to anyone who has undergone what John Murray Cuddihy termed "the ordeal of civility,"[47] the crisis of awkwardness and ill preparation for post-Enlightenment, Western European modernity on the part of Jews of recent provenance from the shtetl. In "setting a table before" Walter's entire tribe, Goethe in effect joins them as a Jew (or assimilates them into German society). This is the same Walter who under the name of Detlev Holz, which he assumed under conditions of considerable sociopolitical danger, would go on to introduce his collection of letters by *Deutsche Menschen*.[48] The utopic climax of the dream occurs when Walter sits cheek by jowl with Goethe and, through him, with the authorities and powers that be in the German academy and world of letters who would be immediately swayed by Goethe's recognition and acceptance of Walter. The dream thus bears the imprint of some of its author's natural and understandable ambitions. This is the same writer who would inscribe the anecdote "The Shirt," whose narrator achieves the "secondary gain" of this garment by living through a nightmare of pogroms in which everything else is lost.[49] The narrator is so destitute, in other words, that a dream in which he "escapes with his shirt" constitutes a tangible improvement of his conditions.

"I sat down beside Goethe. When the meal was over, he rose with difficulty, and by gesturing I sought leave to support him. Touching his elbow, I began to weep with emotion."[50] The relation of adjacency—of complete reciprocal parity and intimacy intimated by the gesture of lovingly touching an elbow—is enough to reduce Walter, at least in the dream "proper," to abject weeping. Yet even with this burst of restrained emotion, the transcript of the dream details a touch that doesn't happen, a contact that in fact doesn't take place, for Walter has to ask for permission. And elbows bend. The gesture of their touch is nothing if not ambiguous. The dream of contact and parity that Benjamin "experienced" or fabulated for *One-Way Street* thus leaves the messianic vision of establishing a productive and intimate foyer between German and Jewish letters wide open and largely unresolved.

The dream, however, is a marvelously suggestive and intricate text in its own right. It opens the compositional process by which *One-Way Street* constitutes a sustained, variegated celebration of dream works alongside cityscapes. Along the labyrinthine passageways of cities, telling objects, among them dreams, memories, apartments, books, storefronts, the postal system and its insignias on stamps—those arbitrary and strange enough to *stand out*—will collide violently and vividly enough with each other to configure an expansive imaginary world around us, one whose meaning cannot be fully read out. The ultimate calculus that will enable us to decode the urban dreamscape that Benjamin unleashes is that of the rebus, a notion that had also occurred to Freud, above all to the early Freud, who primarily served in the capacity of a linguist of consciousness.[51]

It is in another dream in *One-Way Street* that Walter demonstrates his own ability to truck in rebuses, a skill that would serve him well, both as a composer of critical allegories and as a close exegete. This other dream takes off from the word "Mexico," a curious signifier, a true textual "petit objet a," for apart from a glancing reference to the Mexican embassy in the German capital, Mexico has no explicit bearing on *One-Way Street*: "In a dream I saw barren terrain. It was the marketplace at Weimar. Evacuations were in progress. I, too, scraped about in the sand. Then the tip of a church steeple came to light. Delighted, I thought to myself: a Mexican shrine from the time of pre-animism, from the Anaquivitzli. I awoke laughing. (*Ana* = ἀνά; *vi* = *vie*; *witz* [joke] = Mexican church[!])."[52]

The Mexican shrine intrudes itself upon the present from the Anaquivitzli, a time so remote, not only pre-Columbian but preanimistic, that it constitutes a timeless time. The dreamscape here, as in the breakfast room, where the writing of the dream demands both appetite and restraint, is irre-

ducibly self-negating and paradoxical. The excavation down in Weimar
yields a church steeple pointing up. But the church is also a Mexican shrine
dating from pagan times. It is one of any number of hybrid objects and
bizarre amalgamations barreling down the one-way street, beginning with
the Asja Lacis of the epigraph, who is both a femme fatale and a civil engineer, and extending to the chief cathedral of Marseille, which, in Benjamin's
vignette, doubles as a "gigantic railway station."[53] It is in this overall metro-
politan context of inversion and what Freud calls condensation that the
word-thing known as "Anaquivitzli" dawns upon Walter, who's man
enough to dispatch its strangeness within the alien framework of the dream.
"Mexico" turns out to be a convenient exotic locale to which to append this
strange signifier. "Anaquivitzli" could just as well derive from Swiss German as from some exotic indigenous North American dialect. The "solu-
tion" to the rebus, suggests Walter, invokes the transfer and interpolation
of semes from radically different languages and contexts. The abrupt juxtapositions and condensations that could issue forth in "Anaquivitzli," which
pivot around the German word and syllable *Witz*, are just as dynamic to
jokes as to dreams.

The prominent place accorded dreams in establishing not only *One-Way
Street*'s cityscapes, but also its rhetoric and usage bespeaks a significant Benjaminian *ouverture* to mental life as a pivotal but by no means exclusive
component of experience. This mental dimension, which mobilizes itself
far more in writing and signification than through intrapsychic agencies,
also encompasses the effects of memory, desire, and shock.

> It is folly to brood pedantically over the production of objects—visual aids, toys,
> or books—that are supposed to be suitable for children. Since the Enlighten-
> ment, this has been one of the mustiest speculations of the pedagogues. Their
> infatuation with psychology keeps them from perceiving that the world is full of
> the most unrivaled objects for children's attention. And the most specific. . . .
> For children are particularly fond of haunting any site where things are visibly
> being worked on. They are irresistibly drawn by the detritus generated by build-
> ing, gardening, housework, tailoring, or carpentry. In waste products they recog-
> nize the face that the world of things turns directly and solely to them. In using
> these things, they do not so much imitate the works of adults as bring together,
> in the artifact produced in play, materials of widely differing kinds in a new,
> intensive relationship. Children thus produce their own small world of things
> within the greater one.[54]

Benjamin couches this major statement on the phenomenology of childhood and the culture of children in the form of a maxim that might well emanate from the Enlightenment philosophes and pedagogues he mentions. The moral would run: We don't need to produce an entire market of commodities directed at children, for attentiveness to the nature of their play circumvents and sidetracks this venture. But within the framework of this most sensible assertion, child's play emerges as a formidable radical, a process preempting the movements and postures of acute criticism without quite getting down to its conclusions. Child's play is combinatorial ("bring together . . . materials of widely differing kinds in a new, intuitive relationship"); it incorporates the material, and hence intractable and random dimension of cultural components; it zeroes in on the waste products of the fundamental, but for this reason evident and generative sectors of work and production.

The "intuitive relationships" that emerge from this artistry of the given or the at-hand bear significant resemblances to the enigmatic compositions with which the "dreams" of *One-Way Street* have begun to pique our wonder and challenge our reasoning. In far more profound a sense than empirical anteriority, childhood is a proving ground for dense, full-blown commentary. "Their own small world of things" that children "produce" is a simulacrum, a scale model of "the greater one,"[55] but with telling differences. Very much on the order of a memorable critical gloss, child's play reconstitutes the larger work from which it emanated, but unearths unsuspected materials and hitherto imperceptible relations there.

This is not an unproblematical mirroring between microcosm and macrocosm. Childhood is not, like Western eighteenth-century clothing, a smaller cut of adulthood with the same proportions. Child's play is already intuitive in its perceptions, innovative in its deployment of materials, and resolute in bringing its games to their tangible conclusions. In this sense, critical acuity in the "adult" world, in the spheres of institutional, legal, and financial arrangements, is not a training, taming, disciplining, or punishment of this childlike playfulness, but is, rather, tantamount to activating it on a long-term basis, to the skill of maintaining vibrant access to it. If childhood plays a role in the redemptive project of messianism or in the much worldlier task of educational reform, it is not as the terminus of the regression to a prior state of purity, but as the sustained freshness in perspective and the approach to cultural materials making vibrant criticism possible. As the above passage underscores, little in the way of tidiness or sedateness inheres in this condition, which is, rather, characterized by a rage and absorption in materials. It is in acknowledgment and tribute to the full-fledged critical training hard-wired into an untrammeled childhood that Benjamin dedicates such a substantial portion of his writings to this phase, both in the form of the recollections proliferating throughout his memoirs and in his explicit commentaries on the literature, graphic art, institutions, and material culture of childhood. He continues resolutely in the fulfillment of this task in the subsequent sections of *One-Way Street.*

In the comfortable setting of an upper-middle-class urban apartment, more on which below, Benjamin furnishes us with verbal "Enlargements" of what can only be childhood photographs. From what Benjamin and his commentators have already taught us, the subject matter and sequence of this miniature family album are almost predictable. Its vignettes are, in order, entitled "Child rearing," "Belated child," "Pilfering child," "Child on the carousel," "Untidy child," "and "Child hiding."[56]

We would hardly be reading Benjamin if the first snapshot in his collection did *not* capture a scene of reading. Benjamin addresses *his* reader directly, inscribing us in the intimate scene of nocturnal familial readings nonetheless instrumental in crystallizing the off-center, oddball inclinations constituting childhood's legacy to the critical sensibility:

> The peacefulness of the book that enticed you further and further! Its contents did not much matter. . . . The child seeks his way along the half-hidden paths. Reading, he covers his ears. . . . To him, the hero's adventures can still be read in the swirling letters like figures and messages in drifting snowflakes. His breath is part of the air of the events narrated. He mingles with the characters far more closely than grown-ups do.[57]

To the child, reading is an interaction and activity that mobilizes the ears, the skin ("he is unspeakably touched by the deeds"),[58] and even the breath, as well as the mind. The child literalizes the characters she encounters, taking a cue from allegorical practices prevailing in the Baroque German *Trauerspiel* that was the subject of the *Habilitation* that Benjamin preemptively withdrew in 1925.[59] The child traverses and thus pieces the text together in the tangential, indirect ways of "half-hidden paths." To the degree that childhood for Benjamin signifies above all the nascent perceptive and cognitive faculties consummated by authentic critical penetration, it is no accident that the remainder of the "Enlargements" in *One-Way Street* stress the child's resilience, decenteredness, intractability, and affinity for materials and materiality. It is against this backdrop that "Pilfering child," cinematographically, pursues the errant child's hand and its haptic sense that gathers forbidden treats in blind locations. The "Untidy child," whose dresser drawers "must become arsenal and zoo, crime museum and crypt,"[60] is a protocollector in the sense of the full seriousness and rigor that Benjamin ascribes to this adult preoccupation, and "Belated child," like Stephen's confrontation with Father Conmee in Joyce's *Portrait*, stages the child's alienation toward the predetermined strictures of school life.[61]

As suggested above, *One-Way Street* is very much a book of cities and the labyrinthian passages within and between them. Its narrator consults the "Pharus map" that will guide him through their involutions.[62] The personal touch is also, on occasion, capable of penetrating the complications: "A highly convoluted neighborhood, a network of streets that I had avoided for years, was disentangled at a stroke when one day a person dear to me moved there."[63] Yet the urban landscape of *One-Way Street* unfolds as much in the interior spaces of comfortable apartment buildings and the interstitial compartments of shop windows as it does in parks and public squares and on travels with no particular itinerary to yet-unknown destinations. The streets may teem with disreputable characters, such as "beggars in the South, forgetting that their persistence in front of our noses is as justified as a scholar's before a difficult text." Yet "The bourgeois interior of the 1860s to the 1890s—with its gigantic sideboards distended with carvings, the sunless corners where potted palms sit, the balcony embattled beyond its balustrade, and the long corridors with their singing gas flames—fittingly houses only the corpse. The domestic landscape of the Second Empire and after is as uncanny and treacherous to Benjamin as the street scenes are colorful. "This character of the bourgeois apartment, tremulously awaiting the murder like a lascivious old lady her gallant, has been penetrated by a number of authors."[64]

The thoroughfares between these complementary modalities of spatial disquiet are the shop windows in which Benjamin's favorite commodities—books, toys, and postage stamps—are arrayed. But the shop window serves merely as the paradigm of the window display that, in *One-Way Street*, Benjamin pursues in some of its less intuitive forms: the Parisian shooting gallery that opens out to Hell: "When its gates shut, a devil is seen tormenting a wretched soul. Next to him, another is seen dragging a priest toward a cauldron"; the Riga "stereoscope": "A low corner-house with a shop for corsets and millinery decorated with ladies' faces complete with finery, and severe bodices painted on a yellow-ochre ground. . . . The whole is like the façade of a fantasy brothel."[65] Or "A mechanical cabinet at the fair at Lucca": "Here stand Franz Joseph, Pope Pius IX, enthroned and flanked by two cardinals, Queen Elena of Italy, the sultaness, Wilhelm I on horseback, a small Napoleon III, and an ever smaller Victor Emmanuel as crown prince. Biblical figurines follow, then the Passion."[66] Urbanity, wherever it crystallizes, is the preeminent inspiration and site for the visual display encompassing the full richness of textuality. The cities of *One-Way Street*, exemplified by Benjamin's Berlin, but wandering far afield, are, above all, texts to be read in their complexity, illuminations to be glossed with a legend. Cities present themselves for elucidation in the form of rich visual displays. The Parisian shooting gallery and "mechanical cabinet" of Lucca incorporated by Benjamin into the trajectory of *One-Way Street* constitute allegorical windows upon the intimate, sudden rapport, akin to the fall of a target, the reversal of a mechanical doll, between seeing the urban visual array and acute elucidation.

Having evoked its three muses: dreams, childhood, and yes, love ("How much more easily the leave-taker is loved!"[67]), *One-Way Street* relentlessly sustains itself as a polymorphous, multidimensional, multiperspectival gloss on any artifact, experience, or set of sociopolitical conditions legitimately within the compass of twentieth-century, modernist, cosmopolitan urbanity, which the text exacts as much as it enumerates. Down *One-Way Street* Benjamin literally barrels with the erudition he has methodically attained, with the theoretical acuity he has crystallized not only out of philosophy, but from the social sciences (above all sociology), *Literaturwissenschaft*, and art history.

At stake in this all-out charge is nothing less than a full-fledged writerly empowerment, a license to synthesize, with reasonable expectations of cultural approbation, a critical notation installed with a full range of radical aesthetic features. Benjamin could not highlight the irreversibility of the shift in his writing's orientation and performance more noticeably than in his title, *One-Way Street*. We cannot know to what degree this irreversible turn is occasioned by the fiasco surrounding his *Habilitation* on the Baroque

German funeral pageant. But this much is certain: "full-service" cosmopolitan criticism has been implicated by Walter's streetwise tangent ever since.

The critical script thus inaugurated would aspire to a vast range of historical, aesthetic, technological, and social-scientific "coverage." It would encompass untold possibilities for the interconnection and recombination of the phenomena and experiences under its purview, and it would deploy a rich battery of compositional and rhetorical resources. The persona and writerly profile of the critic literally engendered, as in the sense of parenting, by Benjamin through the composition of *One-Way Street* would shrivel into irrelevance and insignificance by any hesitance on the writer's part to engage the full range of possibilities that Walter, with meticulous exactitude, has liberated for her. In the wake of *One-Way Street*, the critic is a vastly more exhibitionistic and dangerous character than before.

She pays for this above all writerly and perspectival notoriety by showing up on all the predictable "Wanted, Dead or Alive" posters: those issued by established and bounded academic disciplines seeking to regenerate traditions and maintain internal purity, by journalistic media dedicated to placating the general audience and excruciatingly attentive to the numbers, and, on occasion, by theoretical offshoots bent, at all costs, on assuring the integrality of conceptual operating systems. The cosmopolitan critic, as inaugurated and charged by Benjamin in *One-Way Street*, occupies a post rendered exhilarating and far-reaching in its polymorphousness, but is a relentlessly marginal, and hence expendable quantity.

The potentials for an aesthetically modeled, compositionally radical criticism first fully explored and put into play by Benjamin were seized upon and adapted by a full coterie of writers—among them, in very different ways, Adorno himself, Bataille, Barthes, Lacan, de Man, Derrida, Miller, and Agamben. The tasks and responsibilities, but also purview and license for the critic that Benjamin defined by the end of *One-Way Street* remain in effect today. But they are daunting in the full range of their resources and lines of articulation. Hence, in an era somewhat more politically stable and tolerant of expression than the one Benjamin confronted, the critic whose rights and range of interventions are demarcated and enacted in *One-Way Street* remains a liability.

And we have not yet completed our survey of the writerly and compositional resources, tools, postures, and guises that Benjamin integrated and coordinated into this epochal text. For the same composition that proceeds, by linear extension, from the streets of Berlin to Riga, Naples, and Marseille welcomes the sociopolitical analysis embodied in he paragraphs of the "Imperial Panorama: A Tour through the German Inflation."[68] By the engrained twist of the Moebius strip into which critical script metamorphoses itself in the wake of *One-Way Street*, social conditions are continuous with toys, postage stamps, and buildings on commentary's extended promenade. The strand of social commentary at play in Benjamin's "full-service" discursive writings from *One-Way Street* through *The Arcades Project* ranges from detached observation to a plaintive account rendered of lost human potential and opportunities for cultural upgrading. It is in addressing social phenomena that Benjamin allows his discourse the emotive range that elsewhere varies from nostalgic recollection to celebrating modern shock, the acceleration and variety of modern conditions.

Hence, along with "Imperial Panorama," Benjamin can observe that the accommodation of poverty preached by religious adages does not spare any particular individual disgrace and humiliation: "Filth and misery grow up around them like walls, the work of invisible hands. . . . Then he must be alert to every humiliation done to him, and so discipline himself that his suffering becomes no longer the downhill road of grief but the rising path of revolt."[69] Benjamin, a social critic as well as a cultural one, discerns amid postwar misery the stirrings of revolutionary fervor. Could this intuition encompass a certain degree of wishful thinking as well? From *One-Way Street* on, messianic hope is tempered by "depressive realism" in Benjamin's prose. The emotional landscape of his script becomes bipolar. "The freedom of conversation is being lost," observes Walter as his tour of the imperial adventure continues. "Irresistibly intruding on any convivial exchange is the theme of the conditions of life."[70]

Yet in the framework of dreamlike fabulation and vibrant textuality that Benjamin has established for *One-Way Street*, it does not take long for the elaboration of prevailing socioeconomic conditions to metamorphose itself into a kind of exegetical poetry.

> Warmth is ebbing from things. Objects of daily use gently but insistently repel us. Day by day, in overcoming the sum of secret resistances—not only the overt ones—that they put in our way, we have an immense labor to perform. We must compensate for their coldness with our warmth if they are not to freeze us to death, and handle their spiny forms with infinite dexterity if we are not to bleed to death. From our fellow men we should expect no succor. Bus conductors,

officials, workmen, salesmen—they all feel themselves to be the representatives of a refractory material world whose menace they take pains to demonstrate through their surliness. And in the denaturing of things—a denaturing with which, emulating human decay, they punish humanity—the country itself conspires. It gnaws at us like the things, and the German spring that never comes is only one of countless related phenomena of decomposing German nature.[71]

The philosophical commitment glaringly evident in "Goethe's *Elective Affinities*" enables Benjamin to take the long leap from social relations prevalent under the Weimar Republic, even ones affected by rampant economic inflation, to the correlative conditions of the Thing, the thing addressed in its materiality by disenchanted workmen, but also as an index of touch, hence intimacy, in everyday life. In this passage, by means of a prior philosophical meditation on the Thing, but by deploying the most elegant prose poetics, Benjamin effects an intervention of "object relations" at their highest conceptual level.[72] In a discourse that can only be identified as criticism, he traces the evolution, under the inflation, of the things of everyday life into uncanny outcroppings of a world unrelenting in its hostility that will never be warmed by the German spring. The social and human conditions set into play by the inflation are resolute in their indifference. Yet they belong as much to a collation of cultural and aesthetic signals at the critic's disposal—indeed, their unpredictable elucidation constitutes her primary vocation and task—as any more tangible cultural products, whether paintings, books, or theatrical performances. The social text that Benjamin explicitly registers on an ongoing basis from *One-Way Street* on thus opens the traditional parameters of "high" criticism onto an unexpected arena, but it remains within the register of an aesthetically inspired and text-intensive criticism.

Whether the referents of *One-Way Street* are material, sociological, geographic, economic, technological, or artistic-artisanal, and I am free to divulge this to you now, their ultimate destination, their workshop, as it were, is the very scene of writing that is the workshop of criticism, from whence critical discourse henceforth emanates. The compositional coup of *One-Way Street* is the seamless inclusion of several sections—themselves imaginatively composed—that not only *treat* writing as one topic or locution among others, but perform the inseparability of a current critical script from the cosmopolitan environment that gives rise to it.

It is in this sense that certain of the inventions to which Benjamin gave a critical cast in *One-Way Street*, and I think specifically of the section titles and such sequences of rampant association as "Enlargements" and "Travel Souvenirs," come closest to experiments that Joyce conducted in fictive space, above all in *Ulysses*. In view of the radical captioning that dominates the "Aeolus" episode of said novel, the fragmentary composition of "Aeolus," "The Wandering Rocks," and "Ithaca" and the allegorical naming that comes to a head in "Scylla and Charybdis," it becomes enchanting to speculate on the conversations that might have taken place between the two writers.[73] The pool of writerly innovations that the authors shared, deployed independently by each, also points to the intimate elective affinities between theoretically inspired fiction and philosophically astute criticism. Given the pronounced difference between the creative projects that Joyce and Benjamin assigned themselves, the commonality of their self-generated writerly tools and irregularities is nothing less than astonishing.

The critic's options *are* the concussions, violent juxtapositions, untoward relations, and technological surprises that the force field of the twentieth century generated. Critical script is very much of the cosmopolitan world, but in no simple way. The relation is distillation, catalyzed by the highest-powered conceptual matrices available and messianic commitment, not by mimesis or representation. In order to furnish the twentieth century, with its pronounced tendencies toward technological primacy, political hegemony, economic globalization, and administrative, military, and social systematization, with a viable, that is, responsive and exegetically acute legend, criticism, with all the subtlety and rigor it can summon, must pertain to the world that it qualifies. The trajectory of Benjamin's critical commentary from "The Concept of Criticism" to *The Arcades Project* is single-mindedly dedicated to this project: a tracing out of the displacements, substitutions, and transformations involved in the transition between an often exhilarating, harsh, impoverished, and inhumane twentieth-century European landscape in its cultural and sociopolitical dimensions and a discourse fitted out for both its characterization and generative critique. In *One-Way Street*, this endeavor attains for the first time its full expressive capabilities.

Hence it is that several striking sections of *One-Way Street*, grafted upon its overall economy by means of the privileged commodity and signifier of books, specifically address the exigencies, anomalies, and parameters of generating critical discourse at the moment. The wisdom that Benjamin volunteers to his writerly *compères* in some of these sections, such as "The Writer's Technique in Thirteen Theses," is nothing less than golden: "Let no thought pass incognito, and keep your notebook as strictly as the authorities keep their register of aliens."[74] Yet Benjamin is not above parodying a self-help approach to writing manifestly absurd in its counsel, as in "Teaching Aid": "Relationships that could be represented graphically must be expounded in words. Instead of being represented in a family tree, for example, all family relationships are to be enumerated and described." This will surely assist in the endeavor of writing "Fat Books."[75] Yet the aphoristic sections on writing itself, whether their dicta be productive or hilariously inadequate, draw attention to its compositional possibilities and technical features, including typesetting, and draw these into an urban labyrinth, a matrix of cosmopolitan expansion and an experience both configured and punctuated by trauma.

The accounts of the "Attested Auditor of Books" that Benjamin opens in a section of that title is, in fact, a miniature history of books over the broader modernity, whose inception coincided with Luther, printing, and global exploration.[76] The passage chronicles the end as well as the beginning of the Age of the Book:

> Script—having found, in the book, a refuge in which it can lead an autonomous existence—is pitilessly dragged out into the street of advertisements and subjected to the brutal heteronomies of economic chaos. This is the hard schooling of its new form. . . . The newspaper is read more in the vertical than in the horizontal plane, while film and advertisement force the printed word entirely into the dictatorial perpendicular. And before a contemporary finds his way to opening a book, his eyes have been exposed to such a blizzard of changing, colorful, conflicting letters that the chances of his penetrating the archaic stillness of the book are slight. Locust swarms of print, which already eclipse the sun of what city dwellers take for intellect, will grow thicker with each succeeding year.[77]

In this telling passage, Benjamin bemoans the eclipse of what his distant successor, Marshall McLuhan, will call the "cool" extreme of print media, consisting of books demanding concentration and a projective input of perceptual and cognitive data, by their "hotter" counterparts, advertising signage and print journalism, whose consumption, as described in the above passage, undermines conditions for close reading. In these phrases Benjamin invokes the climactic excess of a blizzard and a biblical plague of locusts to characterize the derangement of reading's premodern heritage, medieval in its nobility. In the final lines of *One-Way Street*, Benjamin again invokes journalism's effect upon reading in the sense of being upended into a vertical position. There, however, he transforms Rabbi Hillel's admonition against "learning Torah while standing on one foot" into the constructive ability instantaneously to derive telling sound bites from vast stores of information. This Benjamin performs in relation to the broad scope of *One-Way Street*. He attaches, in the end, this summative caption to the overall compositional effort: "They alone shall possess the earth who live from the powers of the cosmos."[78]

Thus, as suggested above, the manic celebration of modernist concussion never lingers far behind Benjamin's nostalgic pose. The contemporary scholar and student of culture is possessed of a preemptive weapon against the forces of overstimulation and distraction that undermine the heritage of reading. It is the card index, which opens the text to three-dimensional annotation. This image occurred, at the high point of structuralism, to Claude Lévi-Strauss, as well, to characterize his practice of isolating the structural elements of myths and narratives, those that also prevailed in a space beyond any particular version, a register that linked seemingly incompatible artifacts and that transformed the object of the researcher's quest—from themes and other substantive manifestations into structural relations.[79] The card index, both of the book and anticipating its future emanations, as characterized by Benjamin in the lines immediately succeeding the above elegy for the book, anticipates the cybernetic Web site and the hypertext. The hybrid text medium that Benjamin would secrete in *The Arcades Project* extends the principles that Benjamin enunciates in the succeeding lines on card indices and performs by means of the aphoristic cast and demonstrative typography of such sections as "Teaching Aid" and "Post No Bills."

> The card index marks the conquest of three-dimensional writing, and so presents an astonishing counterpart to the three-dimensionality of script in its original form as rune or knot notation. (And today the book is already, as the present mode of scholarly production demonstrates, an outdated mediation between two different filing systems. For everything that matters is to be found in the card box of the researcher who wrote it, and the scholar studying it assimilates it into his own card index.)[80]

Very much in keeping both with Benjamin's mapping of the city and its key components and appurtenances and with the formulations that Lévi-

Strauss would go on to crystallize in "The Structural Study of Myth," the card index is an expanding matrix of facets and dimensions open to multiaxial hermeneutic inscription. A 1937 photograph by Gisèle Freund shows Benjamin in perhaps his favorite haunt, the card catalogue of the Bibliothèque Nationale, rue Richelieu, at a time when he was no doubt adding to the convolutes that make up *The Arcades Project*, his prophetic work of and encompassing the history of the book. The card catalogue is both the source of the book and the print-medium version of what will succeed it. In the above passage, Benjamin demonstrates full awareness that the book medium to which he has devoted a lifetime has reached its limits.

The theoretically and methodologically explicit passage of *One-Way Street* entitled "Post No Bills" is itself subsectioned in an intriguing fashion. The smaller offshoots are entitled "The Writer's Technique in Thirteen Theses," "Thirteen Theses against Snobs," "The Critic's Technique in Thirteen Theses," and "Number 13." We obviously face a "number 13" problem or riddle here. Perhaps it is not an accident that Benjamin groups his aphoristic prose bombshells and summations of criticism's role, media parameters, texture, condensation, and effects under headings all measured by the numerical signifier 13.

Luther founded a religious tradition, one coincident with the history of the book, by nailing his ninety-five theses to the door of the church at Wittenberg. The repercussions of Luther's theological intervention included a culture exquisitely attuned to personal freedom and artistic expression, but also mandating a severe regime of self-regulation, a school discipline that Benjamin would excoriate in his earliest educational writings. Thirteen is a relatively low prime number marked culturally as a wild card or volatile, unpredictable shifter. Its magical leanings constitute a menace to any mainstream Western religious movement, even one of reformation. To supplant Luther's "original" ninety-five by a mere thirteen is to exercise postmodern skill in crunching numbers and dispatching vast stores of information.

The dispenser of aphorisms about writing, some exemplary and some very much the opposite, nonetheless couches them in forms and formats that will be decisive to any three-dimensional, multiregister, virtual future emanation of the book. As is not surprising from the author of "The Concept of Criticism," the formats of some of these sections had been rehearsed in the systematic philosophy of the Enlightenment and in the poetic critique of Romanticism: I think specifically of the Schlegels' and Novalis's aphorisms in the *Athenaeum*, and of the antinomies of pure reason that Kant's speculations reach, in many respects the *First Critique*'s most advanced productions.[81] The "Thirteen Theses against Snobs" under "Post No Bills" are arranged as double, self-negating formulations, to wit:

The artwork is only incidentally.	No document is, as such, a work of art. . . .
In the artwork, the formal law is central	Forms are merely dispersed in documents.[82]

Benjamin in this section, not unlike Kant in the wider movements of *The Critique of Pure Reason*, places us in the middle of two aphorisms arranged in a miniature antinomy. The multifaceted distinction between artworks and documents that Benjamin chooses to make in the crossfire between terse theses and their antitheses is a serious matter. But the form—and typographic format—in which he elects to do this work, a thematic that becomes explicit in "Thirteen Theses against Snobs," highlights the emergence of unorthodox scriptural notations out of the confluence of cities, dreams, childhood, buildings, and other components that make *One-Way Street* what it is.

Thirteen, as the Proustian epigraph to a section headed "Number 13," is to be sure a "loaded number." Thirteen may be an extension of "Number 113," the brief third section of *One-Way Street*. But I prefer to think of it as the numeration for Benjamin's faux Psalm 13, for each of its postulates begins with the formula "Books and harlots." In anticipation of a point that he makes even more forcefully in Convolute O of *The Arcades Project*, "Prostitution and Gambling," Benjamin, with the litany of a "responsive reading" in a religious service, draws parallels between the promiscuity, multiplication, openness, and economic calculus common to prostitution and publishing:

Books and harlots can be taken to bed. . . .
No one can tell from looking at books and harlots that minutes are
precious to them. But closer acquaintance shows what a hurry
they are in. . . .
Books and harlots have their quarrels in public.[83]

As venerable as the poetico-critical tradition of inserted aphorisms and antinomies may be, they constitute a radical scene of writing when they appear amid the phantasmagoria of an inscription that delivers itself over to the shock of the twentieth-century city, the untutored receptivity of childhood, and the calculated indifference of urban love. If "Goethe's *Elective Affinities*" launches the falling star that completes the trajectory between the messianism of the wish and the bluntness of postmodern materiality, *One-Way Street* for the first time crystallizes the constellation of figures and topoi from whose aura Benjamin's criticism would never depart. The stars composing the constellation may vary from one Benjaminian production to the next. By the time of "On Some Motifs in Baudelaire" and *The Arcades Project*, though, Benjamin's primary heavenly bodies are all present and accounted for. Some of them are already becoming familiar: cities, dreams, love, modern apartments, the media of mechanical reproduction, the image itself, and the process of imaging.

It was Benjamin's genius to synthesize a written medium in which these shimmering sites of thinking and articulation reverberated with and against one another in a fashion that produced an endless echo, aftershock, afterimage of the traumatic developments of the twentieth century. The inexhaustibility of reverberation and nuance set off by the aspirations of messianism, auratic mystique, and composition by fragment and constellation in no way disparages the aptness and precision of Benjamin's readings of the world. On the contrary: the critico-textual field opened up by Benjamin owes its sublime vastness and uncanny aptness precisely to the detail he was willing to pursue in a passage, to the concision with which he was able to phrase a far-reaching insight.

Benjamin's tortuous trajectory from Berlin's privileged West End to Portbou was at all times motivated by a stunning resoluteness of commitment to culture, literature, and writing. The readerly itinerary that we have pursued in this chapter proceeds from an early philosophical training and commitment to the *ouverture* of an unmistakably critical vocation. *One-Way Street* is the first text in which Benjamin unpacks the full kit of tools, devices, perspectives, postures, and compositional games developed in his "full-service" critical investigations.

Nevertheless, the trajectory of Benjamin's work and life was inflected by coincidence and happenstance at every turn. The intangibles of that life unchain an irresistible urge for biographical speculation. Would his writing have pursued this particular path and achieved this particular diversity had the *Habilitationsschrift* been accepted? Had he emigrated to Palestine in the mid-1920's? Had Germany not pursued the systematic disenfranchisement and persecution of several of its populations and subgroups? Had his academic ambitions been reasonably well realized, would Walter have written radio scripts for hearers of all ages?

We have intervened in his amazing writing process just at the point when the unmistakable philosophical bent and disposition of "The Concept of Criticism" and "Goethe's *Elective Affinities*" leap sideways and, without losing any of their momentum, morph, in *One-Way Street*, into something unexpected, something too polymorphous and writing intensive to be called philosophy proper. Subsequent history, the contributions of, among many others, Barthes, Foucault, Blanchot, de Man, and Miller, have taught us that this occasion-driven, situational, contextual, and heterogeneous discourse may be just as well be called criticism. Yet what is most exciting about the discourse, following in the path of the figure of the angelus novus taking flight in *One-Way Street*, is the open-ended spectrum of writerly bearings and positionalities emanating from its playful/rigorous experimentation.

It is in pursuit of this Moebius strip of script that Derrida can both philosophize—radiating outward from his earliest sustained encounter with Husserl to his groundbreaking rereadings of Plato, Kant, Hegel, Nietzsche, Freud, and Heidegger, among others—but also devise critical interventions in response to Joyce, Kafka, Ponge, Celan, and Blanchot that are as multifaceted and improvisational as the medium that Benjamin opens up in *One-Way Street*. Yet Derrida's most distinctive productions—distinctive in the sense of singular—may well be those, such as "Plato's Pharmacy," *Glas*, *The Post Card*, and "*Khōra*," in which a Benjaminian expansion of discourse to the threshold of shock remains at the service of the historically evolved conceptual operating system undergirding Western thought. The trajectory from "The Concept of Criticism in German Romanticism" to *One-Way Street* thus encompasses both facets of a complementarity that, by means of an intervention like deconstruction, allows philosophy to set the stage, furnish a format for critical elucidation, at the same time that criticism, relentlessly pursuing the occasions and immanent momentum of writing, honors philosophy through the performance of appropriating and disfiguring its etiquettes.

The one-way street whose maps and sidewalks Benjamin followed after his writing proved too protean, multifaceted, and resonant for the academy ultimately eventuates in the discursive complementarity that places the philosophical and the critical, as modalities of literature, in uneasy parity. There was no turning back. Walter pursued the track of cultural, messianic, and writerly commitments that declared themselves to him early in life long past their nominal fulfillment and the point of his personal comfort and safety. In different ways, a group of writers, pivotal to deconstruction and beloved by Benjamin and his *compères*—including Goethe, Hölderlin, the Schlegels, Kierkegaard, Nietzsche, Kafka, Brecht, and Proust—had already negotiated this turn. It was Benjamin who, in inscribing a gap and dissonance between philosophy and criticism in *One-Way Street* and in endowing criticism with its full cosmopolitan tenor, discovered the Northwest Passage between them.

It remains for us to exercise the readerly tact and writerly freedom that Benjamin liberated for us. For us to place at our disposal any less than the full palette of writerly tools, bearings, and postures that Benjamin brought to bear in and on criticism, whether in the name of the discipline, its subspecializations, the "market," or the numbers is to devalue his achievement and ignore his proliferating lessons. To review his legacy attentively is to persist in the uneasy interstice between joyous demolition and respectful celebration, between writerly play and philosophical oversight.

Man in a Café (oil on canvas, 1912) by Juan Gris. Philadelphia Museum of Art. The Louise and Walter Arensberg Collection, 1950.

Title page of "Hamafkid," *Tractate Bava Mezia*, chapter 3, of the Babylonian Talmud, the subject of the present chapter. The page derives from a facsimile edition of Munich Hebrew Codex 95, ed. Hermann L. Strack (Leiden: A. W. Sijthoff, 1912), courtesy of the Beinecke Rare Book and Manuscript Library, Yale University. Note that the configuration of the reproduced page, from a Talmud written in Paris ca.1340–70 A.D., has not yet reached the full typographical complexity achieved in post-Gutenberg editions. It is the more intricate and compartmentalized modern Talmudic page that serves as the pretext for the present discussion.

FOUR

Between the Registers: *The Arcades Project*, the Talmud, and *Glas*

If anything in the world of literature, of text, may be rightly characterized as a *thing*, it is surely Walter Benjamin's *Arcades Project*. Not a history; not a treatise; not even strictly a sourcebook, for it also delivers Benjamin's comments; not a work of criticism, in its utter disjointedness; not even, properly, a work. *The Arcades Project* may well be described as a thing that confronts us in its arbitrariness, its *Geworfenheit*, its thrownness,[1] its irreducible and irrefutable materiality. Its aggressive repudiation of any prior known or recognized genre qualifies it to be the literary counterpart of an exile. Its attenuated emergence from the past, historical commonplace, memory, and nothingness thus parallels, uncannily, its author's respective exiles—from his native city and homeland, Judaism, the intellectual communities of his elective affinity, his families, both by birth and marriage, his class, and ultimately, even from his most shockingly disclosed expectations concerning experience. *The Arcades Project* is an uncanny simulacrum, like the doll house in Edward Albee's *Tiny Alice* or like the backup file that my computer, autonomous of my volition, will create of this chapter as I compose it, a simulacrum of action taking place simultaneously to its call into being, in real time, in virtuality.

Over the same thirteen years during which Walter Benjamin's life advanced toward its seemingly inevitable annihilation, a life that proceeded by the systematic withdrawal of the socioeconomic and even material underpinnings that made it possible, *The Arcades Project* came to occupy a space and set of logical, generic, disciplinary representational conditions making it manifestly impossible. The phenomenon of Walter Benjamin and the composition of *The Arcades Project*, whatever it might be, and this is a major question, are inseparable. Although Benjamin's progressive loss, to whatever degree of his own connivance, of everything he ever valued, of everything with which he identified and in which he held faith, can only have been excruciating, his textual double, *The Arcades Project* emerges into being and persists solely on the ground of an impossible set of assertions. In their utter impossibility, an intransigence endowing cultural history and criticism and thinking itself with an unprecedented dynamic and flow, resides the only positivity that can be said to have emerged from Benjamin's tortured existential trajectory.

The Arcades Project is a Thing, I started to say, one of those bizarre and even humorous composites, like the hat that Charles Bovary is fated to wear into his new classroom at the outset of the novel named after his spouse who is so imprudent in her collusion with her drives, or like Kafka's Odradek:

> At first glance it looks like a flat star-shaped spool for thread, and indeed it does seem to have thread wound upon it; to be sure, they are only odd, broken-off bits of thread, knotted and tangled together, of the most varied sorts and colors. But it is not only a spool, for a small wooden crossbar sticks out of the middle of the star, and another small rod is joined to that at a right angle. By means of this latter rod on one side and one of the points of the star on the other, the whole thing can stand upright as if on two legs.[2]

The Arcades Project too is utterly anomalous. It arises to fill an impossible task, the reconfiguration of nineteenth-century Paris and the experience of living in it under the aura of the epistemological, cultural, and, yes, political formations that arose in its aftermath.

It may well be easier for us to acknowledge this dream of imaginative reconstitution when an author of fiction, perhaps of magical realism, assigns it to a character, as when Jorge Luis Borges has his consummate scholar of the peninsular Golden Age, Pierre Menard, compose several strategic passages of *Don Quixote*[3] without having read the novel, than it is for us to imagine the act of the textual reconstitution of Paris during the Second Empire that was achieved by an actual scholar, Walter Benjamin. In addressing *The Arcades Project*, it assembles an incompatible array of materials whose composite effect is to disqualify one another completely. Benjamin, in a strategy reminiscent of Marshall McLuhan's memorable analysis of the first page of the *New York Times*,[4] not only places historical firsthand accounts of the developments and events from the period of his interest, literary improvisations on the same motifs, popular documents, such as brochures and handbills, and historical, sociological, and critical retrospections of a much later provenance directly alongside each other. He makes sure to cite witnesses and analysts whose attitudes toward the unfolding developments could not be more antithetical.

As we will see, one of Benjamin's most cunning strategies in composing the *Arcades* is the subsequent disclosure of the political ramifications of works and assertions initially cited in a milieu of purported neutrality, "repressive tolerance," or "historical objectivity." Fourier and Grandville,[5] introduced in the early convolutes as endearing, spacey avatars of early nineteenth-century expansionism, eventually emerge, through Toussenel, whom they influenced, as early harbingers of the first, fin-de-siècle National Socialism. In keeping with the principle of textual openness, which is an ethical and existential as well as compositional article of faith behind the *Arcades*, Benjamin freely mixes, with the sparest commentary akin to the minimalist nods and grunts comprising the analyst's primary responses in psychodynamic psychotherapy, the formulations of his beloved radicals, whether Blanqui, Saint-Simon, Marx, Engels, or Adorno, with those of the proto-Fascists.

The textual openness that affords this ongoing, quasi-systematic incompatibility is both a compositional principle and a credo of unabashed belligerence. It is the measure of Benjamin's ethics that he answered systematic social segregation, humiliation, and genocide with what is at most a strategy of generic and compositional antagonism. Benjamin's call for an utterly unbounded text, an array of articulation so open and receptive that it becomes the sky across which the constellation configures its inevitable, but belated message, is largely what has made him, for a good thirty years already, so welcome to text-based thinkers, whether deconstructionists or rhetorical critics. "The dialectical image is an image that emerges suddenly, in a flash. What has been is to be held fast—as an image flashing up on the now of its recognizability. The rescue that is carried out by these means—and only by these—can operate solely for the sake of what in the next moment is irretrievably lost."[6]

This performance, as well as assertion, of largely laissez faire but strategically interrupted compositional receptivity, the only milieu receptive to the literal brilliance of the dialectical flash, cannot, on the other hand, be of enormous consequence to cultural critics for whom intellectual work is a read out of preconceptions, however complex or subtle they may be. Readers whose results tally with the principles of the disciplines that prompted them to undertake the reading, readers who discover in their research the results already inscribed in their premises, can only find in Benjamin an odd bird, both the inveterate exile who lived such an inconclusive life in several senses of the word and the textual amalgam, the *Arcades*, that functioned as his secret sharer and uncanny double for more than a quarter of his life.

1

It may well beg a number of significant theoretical questions to assert that there is some sort of "space" in *The Arcades Project* that can be discussed independently of its simply being a text. To what degree is there, as Maurice Blanchot, a text-oriented critic if there ever was one, would have it, a "space of literature?"[7] One could indeed argue, as deconstructionists and rhetorical critics implicitly do, that the truly significant notion of space is as a textual medium. Textually astute readers are constrained, I believe, at least to entertain the possibility that the text, however inflected by transtextual modalities of space, whether of the geographical, urban, colonial, cognitive, transcendental, phenomenological, or psychological varieties, is the only effective *expression* of these respective spaces as metaphors.

With all due respect to this fundamental theoretical consideration of space's status, I believe it fruitful, even inevitable, to explore the spatial coordinates of *The Arcades Project*. Indeed, the *Project*, in keeping with its inbuilt architecture, solicits us to do so. One way of appreciating this book is to think of it as the diffuse, panoramic background to two essays that Benjamin composed with an inconceivably greater density, the "exposés" or documentary synopses of 1935 and 1939, both known as "Paris, the Capital of the Nineteenth Century." These counterversions of the same essay justify Benjamin's assertion in Convolute N that literary montage, that is, the literary equivalent of the technique of violent, expressive, shocking film editing, is the underlying compositional principle of *The Arcades Project*:

> To cultivate fields where, until now, only madness has reigned. Forge ahead with the whetted axe of reason, looking neither right nor left so as not to succumb to the horror that beckons deep in the primeval forest. Every ground must at some point have been made arable by reason, must have been cleared of the undergrowth of delusion and myth. This is to be accomplished here for the terrain of the nineteenth century.

> Method of this project: literary montage. I needn't say anything. Merely show. I shall purloin no valuables, appropriate no ingenious formulations. But the rags, the refuse—these I will not inventory but allow, in the only way possible, to come into their own: by making use of them.[8]

Even though Benjamin, in keeping with Adorno's criticisms of the 1935 version of the essay, made significant modifications, both drafts introduce a certain narrative of nineteenth-century Paris by "cutting" between different scenes or loci of sociocultural activity. I would argue that the maintenance of this fiction of separate, but parallel spaces of sociopolitical, experiential, aesthetic, and personal or "private" development, the spaces orchestrated in literary as well as cinematographic montage, is as pivotal to the architecture of *The Arcades Project* as it is to the trajectory of "Paris, the Capital of the Nineteenth Century," in whichever version.

What is crucial about this highly condensed essay is that each of its sections is told from a different perspective and that the "camera angle" from which each segment is narrated implies a distinct and separate spatial compartment. "Fourier, or the Arcades," the initial segment of both exposés, takes place in the modern, commercial, inside/outside thoroughfares improvised "through whole blocks of buildings, whose owners have joined together for such enterprises."[9] A second section, extruded from the 1939 version, "Daguerre, or the Panoramas," occupies the photographic frame and the space enclosed by the parabolic panorama; section III, "Grandville, or the World Exhibitions," is set in the Champs du Mars and other sites of the spectacular trade shows initiated during the epoch of Benjamin's concern; section IV, "Louis Philippe, or the Interior," resides, literally, in the private urban living space that became standardized during this period. In the language of Walter Benjamin, the modern apartment became the cache where the bourgeois Ali Baba cum collector deposited his ill-gotten gains, oblivious to, but also exiled from the real urban ferment of the streets. Section V, "Baudelaire, or the Streets of Paris," takes place less in the streets of Paris than between the margins of the Baudelairean text. This segment opens up a panorama on Paris during the Second Empire from a "text's-eye view." The essay's ultimate section, "Haussmann, or the Barricades," reverts to the setting abandoned by the bourgeois, the avenues of class conflict and authentic cultural transmission.

The spatial, dare we say architectural? program of "Paris, the Capital of the Nineteenth Century" is rendered additionally complex by the division of all sections into dialectically counterweighted movements or subsections except for the one on Daguerre that appeared only in the 1935 version. The dialectical image not only captivates while it blinds through its visual explosion, it snares the reader by literally enclosing her in the absolutely inevitable and unavoidable space between images related not by logic, but by what Freud might call poetic condensation.

My favorite example of the Benjaminian dialectical image is the falling star of section IX in "On Some Motifs in Baudelaire."[10] When we first encounter this image, it is a vestige of the naïve wish that can still prevail in communities of tradition and belief, as opposed to ones dominated by industrial mechanization and large-scale capital. When Benjamin transmogrifies this falling star, "trailing clouds of aura," as it were, into the ivory ball of the roulette wheel, he is not only commenting upon the degradation of disarming (and, potentially, reactionary) belief into the hard and fast rules of the modern gaming table. He also shocks our reading experience by literally capturing us in the space between absolutely antithetical and therefore all the more inevitably intertwined images. The poetic condensation of images made intimate to one another through the impossibility of their affinity is what makes the dialectical image tick, or more precisely, makes it a ticking time bomb waiting to go off.

Benjamin engineers this dialectical bombshell, or at least its craters, into each of the spatially discrete sections of "Paris, the Capital of the Nineteenth Century." The first half of section IV, "Louis Philippe, or the Interior," places the bourgeois in his private residence and relates this entrenched privacy to the ethos of inwardness and the aesthetics of *Jugendstil*. The dialectical other shoe in this move, also within the frame of section IV, makes this private preserve the residence of the collector, "who bestows on [artifacts] only connoisseur value, rather than use value." The collector's things serve as stage props within his "dreams not only into a distant or bygone world but also into a better one."[11] In this fashion, Benjamin pursues the nineteenth-century man of the crowd into his gentrified interior space, where he functions both as an avaricious recluse and friend and protector of the arts and where the hard-sought objects of his *recherches* are mere accouterments to his lifestyle. The complexities of this interior preserve, itself merely one location in Benjamin's panoramic view of nineteenth-century Paris, already abound. The same can be said of the alternate spaces, whether the allegorical insides of Baudelaire's poetry or the conventions of spectacle launched like a hot-air balloon by the first international expositions, also spliced into the exposé.

What "Paris, the Capital of the Nineteenth Century" establishes for *The Arcades Project*, albeit on a miniature scale, is the construction of discrete, though semiporous compartments for different segments of the material. The expansive text of the entire *Arcades* switches off between the compartments demarcated in the exposé: the frame around the visual image, the public spectacle, the streets, Métro, parks, and even sewers of Paris, the domestic interior, the typographic innards of the text itself, linking Benjamin in this respect to the Joyce of *Finnegans Wake*,[12] all subsumed under the ur and ultra space of modernity itself, the Paris arcades. These spaces are the rooms in the apartment of Benjamin's massive array and collation. The implied hand-held camera in the text switches abruptly and seemingly at random from one of these rooms to the next.

If we grant that a notion or at least a metaphor of space holds true for *The Arcades Project*, the exposé grounds that space in complexity from the outset. Even while the loci of textual action shift back and forth as described above, the *Arcades* transpires in an hyperdetermined metaspace in which the spaces of Paris as a textual construct, the archive, and the medium of the book, with its typographic architecture, are seamlessly superimposed upon each other. The imagistic superimposition is reminiscent of the one that William Carlos Williams declares for *Paterson*, at once a man, a city, a waterfall, and a poem.

2

A register is distinct from a space. Legalistically, a register is a census or other listing made in the service of the king. The royal gaze thus has the aspect about it of a textual scanner. To register is to stray within the purview of the collective public gaze and be marked by it. Registration is being inscribed within the collation or list that is scanned by the optical organ or instrument of public scrutiny.

To the degree that a register is a spatialized text, an inscription situated in a particular document or public zone, a register is inherently spatial in nature. But as a text in its own right, a register is distinct from a discrete spatial compartment. The history of the book is deeply intertwined with the practice of its fragmentation into multiple registers, as if the repression instrumented by typographical codification produces resistance in the form of a proliferation of consecutive subtexts. The architecture of the book is made possible, in English, by a binding, the same term by which, in the biblical catachresis, in an episode from Genesis important to Kierkegaard and Benjamin, the restraint of Isaac is equated with Abraham's submission to God's sublime arbitrariness.[13] The codification of the Judaic law in the Talmud between the first and fourth centuries A.D. produces a reference work fragmented into a bewildering array of simultaneous, mutually supplemental, and mutually undermining registers.

This type of text could have only fascinated Benjamin, who as we know was captivated by interlinear translation, libraries, and the superimposed strata underlying the modern city. There is a degree to which the Paris of *The Arcades Project* is subdivided not only into discrete spaces, but into registers. There is a correspondence, in the sense of a beloved term that Benjamin appropriated from the poetics of Baudelaire,[14] a term incorporating gaping distances and differences as well as affinities, between the floors and levels of Parisian space and architecture and the registers of text design in the *Arcades*. Paris was increasingly the utopian, alternate world to which Benjamin relocated as the material and ideological struts were pulled out from under everything he held dear, but the textual architecture that Benjamin crystallizes in his imaginary reconstitution of the Second Empire is Talmudic in nature, belongs to the literature of multiregister texts, including, as well, illuminated manuscripts and illustrated canons. Benjamin's engagement with Judaism, like his rapport with women, was lifelong and painful. It underwent many ambivalences, rapprochements, diversions underground, and triumphant reemergences.

I am suggesting that *The Arcades Project* is situated at the poignant interstice between Paris, *Hauptstadt* of everything meaningful and still viable to Benjamin, and a registered oversight and composition that may well constitute the highest typographical expression of Benjamin's lifelong *Auseinandersetzung* with the Judaic sensibility. *The Arcades Project*, in other words, is Benjamin's Talmud, disguised as a text-medium Web site of nineteenth-century Paris. The *Arcades* not only offers insight into the diverse strands of reactionary and liberatory ideology and event that emerged from nineteenth-century Parisian commerce, art, politics, entertainment, architecture, and so on. It also illuminates the tectonic forces by which texts in general, exemplified by the Talmud and its analagons, organize themselves into registers of composition, reference, meaning, and misunderstanding, which then interact in modes of compression and dissemination pivotal to the dynamics of language and culture in general.

Benjamin plumbs the geological and architectural depths of Paris, then, not only in his hymn to the city, in his will, embedded in his nostalgist-modernist pose, to resurrect the *experience* of the Second Empire. He also is interested in the horizontal *zones* of the city as spatial markers of or preambles to textual registers, that is, as spatialized texts resounding, concatenating with others. It is in this context that we can appreciate that Benjamin incorporates into several convolutes material on such topics as Paris's ancient foundations and sewers, the basement of the Châtelet de Paris, where in a passage by Victor Hugo, "men condemned to the galleys were put . . . until the day of their departure for Toulon"; also where "almost all the argot songs were born"[15] and the horizontal bands that ironwork, in the form of balconies and balustrades, added to the facades of Hausmannian buildings on the *grands boulevards*. The confines of the present chapter allow me only one or two instances of the intense concern with horizontal zones and superimposed registers of activity and interpretation that indelibly mark *The Arcades Project*,:

> Paris is built over a system of caverns from which the din of the Métro and railroad mounts to the surface, and in which every omnibus or truck sets up a prolonged echo. And this great technological system of tunnels and thoroughfares interconnects with the ancient vaults, the limestone quarries, the grottoes and catacombs which, since the early Middle Ages, have time and again been

reentered and traversed. Even today, for the price of two francs, one can buy a ticket of admission to this most noble nocturnal Paris, so much less expensive and hazardous than the Paris of the upper world. The Middle Ages saw it differently.[16]

This extract, one of Benjamin's interjected comments, underscores the parallelism and difference between Paris and its subterranean double at the same time that it inscribes a historical reversal. Present-day spelunking in the caverns, asserts Benjamin, can deliver relief from the urban din above, while in the Middle Ages, the nether regions harbored the Devil. Of modern balconies, made possible by developments in iron production during the nineteenth century, Fritz Stahl, in his 1929 *Paris*, wrote:

> For the great architectural mass of the modern house, with its insistent lateral extension, this articulation could not possibly suffice. The architects' building sense required that the ever stronger horizontal tendency of the house . . . be given expression . . . and they discovered the means for this in the traditional iron grille. Across the entire length of the building front, on one or two stories, they set a balcony provided with an iron grating of this type, which, being black, stands out very distinctly and makes a vigorous impression. . . . In the case of adjoining houses, these balcony railings fuse with one another and consolidate the impression of a walled street.[17]

One of many importances that Benjamin ascribes to the widespread use of cast iron and glass in architecture is the ornamental scribing of horizontal bands on buildings.

Yet it is an uncited passage from Aragon's *Paysan de Paris*, a work realizing the aesthetic potential of the arcades in the manifestation of surreal juxtapositions, that discloses most powerfully the combined parallelism and disjunction characterizing the zones, scriptoral as well as architectural, according to which the *Project* is articulate. The strategy of *The Arcades Project* in no way preempts the possibility that the most telling passages of the works to which Benjamin, Paris, history, chance, and textuality itself lead us are *elsewhere*.

> Future mysteries will rise from the ruins of today's. Let us take a stroll along the Passage de l'Opéra, and have a closer look at it. It is a double tunnel, with a single gateway opening to the north on to the Rue Chauchat, and two gateways opening to the south on to the boulevard. Its two arcades, the western one, called Galerie du Thermomètre, are joined by two short cuts. . . . If we enter the

Galerie du Thermomètre through its opening between the café I have just mentioned and a bookshop, the Librarie Eugène Rey, having passed through the iron gates which at night-time bar the passage to all yearnings deemed contrary to public morals, we can see that whereas practically the whole length of the right-hand façade is taken up, at ground-floor level, by window displays of all kinds, a café, and so on, the upper storeys seem to be occupied by one single building. It is indeed a single edifice, stretching the entire frontage: a hotel whose rooms possess precisely the atmosphere and lighting appropriate to the laboratory of pleasures which the hotel offers as its sole justification for its existence.[18]

Only from a single vantage point, according to only one line of sight (or flight), made possible by the architectural sleight of hand of an obscure shortcut, does a hidden coherence of the second story of activity become evident or explicit. The architecture of the arcades encompasses as much of what is indirect and misleading as what is linear, in the service of unobstructed flow. It is an architecture of feints and false leads as much as it is one of easy traffic and free trade. Its vertical structure is familiar to any reader of Western metaphysical systems: At street level reigns particularity, the succession of discrete wares and enterprises, the cornucopia of goods and flavors, exacerbated by European Enlightenment and post-Enlightenment expansionism. In a most powerful sense, the linearity and double-sided structure endemic to all streets, ways, paths, and passages constitute an almost universal nexus of the experience of particularity. Directly above street level, in Aragon's vignette of Paris as an arcade, prevails an encompassing unity of purpose, as well as of architecture and visual display. In a Kantian universe, this superior purview and coordination would be ascribed to the transcendental. In the surreal Paris reconfigured by Aragon, and of such centrality to the imaginary of *The Arcades Project*, it belongs to sex by the hour, for the second story of the Galerie du Thermomètre is an hourly sex hotel, such as abound in our livelier cosmopolitan centers.

Aragon thus substitutes the universality of the drive for that of the transcendental. He establishes as well an architectural program in which the Paris of the Second Empire is configured by radically differing, even contradictory registers of activity, which are nonetheless complementary.[19] The serious atmosphere of business on the ground floor—for in the money economy initiated during the period of Benjamin's purview, *fric* is everything, and transactions are a serious matter—gives way on the second to the accumulation of pleasure and the frivolous expenditure of the pocket change held over from the fundamental profit motive. The radically divergent countereconomies of the Galerie du Thermomètre coexist side by side, vertically, that is. The sex industry and the world of legitimate business live off the same economy, yet they deploy energy and goods and invoke ideology in radically different fashions. The concurrent registers live off each other and illuminate one another; contradict each other and, in a vital sense, consummate one another.

This is not only a socioeconomic and architectural configuration pivotal to *The Arcades Project*, as well as to the Paris of its epoch, it is a program decisive for the architecture of books, at least those that would presume, in a systematic way, to account, compensate, or adjust, by means of running variants, annotations, and media of illumination, for their own major thrusts and assertions. Such works, whether the Talmud, *The Arcades Project*, or Persian and medieval European illuminated manuscripts, ornament a vast expenditure of the drive, sexual as well as writerly, for they both establish certain broad understandings, and bind culture to them, and witness and even orchestrate their unbinding and fragmentation. Hence, the crowning of the particular small businesses in Aragon's tour of the arcades by a sex hotel is not entirely by accident. The juxtaposition, the placement in parallel, of radically disjunctive scenes, theaters, and modes of apprehension, activity, and economy creates a need—might we say a market?—for an elaborate backup system of escapes, trapdoors, feints, and other indirections. Aragon's ongoing survey of the scene takes up this point, in a manner almost self-explanatory:

> Long corridors, like theatre wings, are strung with boxes, I mean rooms, all on the same side overlooking the passage. A dual system of stairways provides access to the passage at two separate points. Everything is contrived to facilitate hasty departure, to conceal from casual observers the trysts which will muffle some huge secret behind the faded sky-blue wallpaper of a banal décor. On the first floor, someone has had the idea of fixing up a door at the top of the farther staircase, so that if required this exit can be closed, although since the door is framed by nothing more than side posts all that need be done to get past it is to clamber over the banister at that point. This menace, swinging on its hinges, can provoke flights of dizzy speculation in the mind of anyone contemplating it. What can possibly be the significance of this door? . . . At odd intervals the corridors light up, but semidarkness is their favourite colour. A half-opened door releases a flash of négligée, a trill of song. Then happiness unravels, fingers un-

lace, and an overcoat makes its way down the anonymous day, towards the country of respectability.[20]

This latter extract is redolent of the human landscape that twentieth-century literature has invoked, whether in the crooked passageways of the court in Kafka's *The Trial* and "The Burrow" or the hexagonal galleries of Borges's "The Library of Babel," as settings of the crises and wonders of signification. The economy of concurrent registers, whether defined socioeconomically or textually, demands as much in the way of release valves and clauses as it asserts some overarching purview or metaphysical horizon.

Paris is at once a material and historical agglomeration that Benjamin reassembles and reconfigures out of its textual remains for purposes of strategic elucidation and already a book of a certain order that Benjamin literally presents to history as the remains of a certain cultural architecture and sensibility.

3

We cannot know for sure whether Benjamin's fascination and play with parallel registers of signification is motivated primarily by his exegetical, architectural, or historiographic interests. However, all these motifs conspire in the design and construction of *The Arcades Project*, Benjamin's most Talmudic work. I am arguing that *The Arcades Project*, in a particular sense, is a *translation* of the Talmud, in a distinctly Benjaminian modality, into a contemporary parlance. The Talmudic substratum of *The Arcades Project*, analogous to the caverns, grottoes, and limestone quarries to which Benjamin's sources (if not he himself) plumbs, may well teach us something of its architecture and illuminate an obscure facet of the translation process that the *Project* involved. In general, too, it is a rendition of and rationale for all memorable projects of mutiregister inscription.

The Talmudic story I want to discuss concerns the compression, fractal repetition and expansion, and thematic cascading and fragmentation characterizing a single Mishnaic proposition and its Gemaric elucidation and elaboration in an exemplary passage, taught early in any Talmudic education and surely known to Gershom Scholem, Martin Buber, and other of Benjamin's other compatriots and sources in Judaic studies. The passage in question heads the third chapter of Tractate Bava Mezia, literally, the "Middle Gate," and concerns the adjudication of disputes occasioned by failures or misunderstandings of delegated responsibility. The central column of the Talmudic page, the basis for all appended commentaries and glossaries, stages the alternation between the formulations of the Mishna, codified during the first generation of Biblical exegesis by Talmudists, dated by Adin Steinsaltz between A.D. 30 and 200,[21] and the expansive elaboration offered by the Gemara, assembled by the Rabbis over the next three centuries, extending to a vast range of subjects including ritual practices, legal determinations, and norms of propinquity.

We can say of the Talmud that, like other fractally organized works (and here I am guided by J. Hillis Miller's move toward a fractal reading of Proust in *Black Holes*),[22] a single structure and operating system of argumentative and rhetorical features suffices for the work as a whole, with all the expansiveness of its subject matter and the intricacy of the cross-referencing and cross-checking that it encompasses. In this sense, any section of Mishna and its Gemaric recapitulation harbors the seed structure characterizing the work as a whole. This is, for Miller, at the heart of fractility, as is the "self-dissimilarity"[23] established in each section of Talmudic argumentation and the question that occasions it as a highly distinctive local environment, irreducibly different from all others, even when, by process of cross-referencing, it is grafted onto thematically related segments.

The ongoing alternation between Mishnaic compression and Gemaric expansion, prolixity, cross-reference, and grafting, a fractal infrastructure, accounts for only the central column of the pointed Talmudic text, which achieved its enduring form in the decades following the Gutenberg Bible. Around this continuous central column are gathered the marginalia, indices, and canonical commentaries making each page of the Talmud a unique graphic composition and prayer to the abundance of typographical registers.[24] The structure of the Talmudic page itself is thus another instance of a fractility enabling even a canon that presumed vast authority in regulating communal and private behavior, even down to the level of personal habits and feminine hygiene, to fragment systematically in the face of being bound into a conceptual as well as physical compendium. Like the contract of marriage and the episode of Genesis regarding Abraham's travail in sacrificing Isaac to YHWH, known as the "binding" (*akeda*) of Isaac, it is the unique feature of the compendium, especially the multiregister work, to mark the explosion and fragmentation of the state of affairs that it presumably binds. The marriage contract purports to bind the sexual drive, which it can no way do, even though particular marriages may persist on some other pretext. The *akeda* episode of Genesis, as Kierkegaard is quick to note, inscribes a spiritual vertigo in no way resolvable by Abraham's willingness to sacrifice his best beloved and YHWH's magnanimous declination of the offer. And the codification of the law amid the comprehensive record of Rabbinic debate encompassed by the Talmud and the intricate typography of the Talmudic page signals as well a fragmentation of narrative and a cascading of response in irregular and skewed directions.

By the same token, the convolutes of *The Arcades Project* simultaneously encompass and codify a certain history and perform the demolition, in the progression toward fascism and anomie, of the utopianism promised by that history. Fourierism reaches a crossroads with Toussenel, at which it takes a sharp right. Little comes of Saint-Simon. The barricades fighter Blanqui can only attest to the boredom and blankness of petrified experience, repetition actualized. There is no better theater for the nullification of liberations dreamed in the Second Empire than the most comprehensive compendium of its textual remains.

To the degree that the individual convolutes constitute library stacks devoted to the themes that preoccupy them, Benjamin experienced the storage difficulties endemic to all libraries. Some of the later convolutes—I would suggest those after "V: Conspiracies, *Compagnonnage*"—have the feel of overflow repositories for material that Benjamin was unable to fit into the trimmer, better-contoured convolutes beforehand. The very expansiveness of *The Arcades Project*, like that of the Talmud, initiates a crisis of storage and memory.

The counterregisters that both ornament and supplement the central column on the Talmudic page include the running commentary of that French intellectual among the Rabbis, Schlomo ben Yitzhak (1040–1105), otherwise known as Rashi, and a compendium of his followers' readings known as the *Tosaphot*, literally "the supplements," set as a distinct typographical register. Editions of the Talmud published in Vilna added another ongoing gloss, an early one contributed by Rabbi Ḥananel ben Ḥushiel, who lived in North Africa between A.D. 990 and 1055.

Each of these registers of elucidation might hope or presume to stabilize an intent or meaning otherwise unclear, ephemeral, or self-undermining. Each register ultimately bears witness to the intransigence of the legal/moral picture that the law of the Mishna/Gemara would represent. The exact meaning takes flight the closer that each commentator comes to capturing it, a predicament shared by Humbert Humbert the lover and Vladimir Nabokov the lepidopterist. When we observe and contemplate the cumulative effect upon precise signification and adjudication registered by the assemblage or aggregate of commentaries inscribed upon each Talmudic page, the contrast between the contraction of significance, the precision of concurrent exegetical and social contracts, and the explosion of textual possibility becomes staggering, overwhelming. The Talmudic exegete worships God or whatever else we want to call him in the explosion of textual possibilities resulting from the perfectly understandable human impulse to pin down—to pin down a nuance as well as a butterfly.

God is the explosion of possibility, at once expansive and precise, celebrated as well in the intricacy and stylistic variation of illuminated Arabic script, the geometry of Islamic visual decoration, and in the algebraic figural multiplication adorning the major Hindu stupas, whether at Borabadur (Java, ca. A.D. 800), Angor Wat (Cambodia, ca. A.D. 1000), or Kajuharo (India, ca. A.D. 1000).[25] The bicolumnar architecture that Jacques Derrida devised for the typography of *Glas* is at once a simulacrum and commentary upon the precision and openness of the Talmudic play of exegetical registers.[26] By the same token, there is a residue of the Talmudic in the engagement with the book medium and the intricate lines of communication that it sets up in Avital Ronell's *Telephone Book*.[27]

The Talmudic passage evoking our interest concerns the responsibilities of delegated responsibility as it is adjudicated by artificial language in a Rabbinic court. The passage consitituted by a single Mishna and the Gemara arising to embroider upon it deliberates on ownership and the liability that accrues when property is left in the hands of a figure that Steinsaltz translates as the "bailee," but whose term derives from the Hebrew verbal root for watching or guarding, the *shomair*. A watchperson may be paid or unpaid. Obviously, a paying arrangement betokens both greater responsibility and legal liability. The Mishna, with astonishing compression, recapitulates the prevailing rule during the Amoritic period (again, A.D. 30–200). As the Gemara embroiders on a range of possible situations emerging from the Mishnaic strictures, states of affairs with varying degrees of logical complexity, likelihood, predictability, and premeditation, the wider issue that emerges through the variants of which property was left with whom and of which circumstances conspired to produce the damages is the issue of delegation.

In its breathtaking swings between Mishnaic condensation and Gemaric prolixity, the Talmud would presume to bring peace, in the form of broad articulate sensibility, what contemporary Buddhism might call mindfulness, to the very human torment often instigated by conflicts over property and the issues of responsibility and the degrees of its assignment and assessment. At moments, in a process whose name I will hazard as textual cascading, common to works such as the Talmud, *The Arcades Project*, and *Glas*, we cannot but smile as the Talmudic text conjures situations of escalating contingency and tenuousness before us, sometimes eventuating literally in what contemporary insurance companies would call "acts of God." This scenario surely has its academic correlatives, in which we have all played one role or another.

In their deliberately artificial condensation and closure, the Mishnaic propositions verge upon a legalistic speech act, a vow that will serve as a concrete basis for the rendition of justice, plain and simple. The first Mishna in the third chapter of Bava Metzia, which establishes a discursive and tonal landscape at the same time that it initiates a substantial strand of argumentation, runs as follows:

> Someone who deposits an animal or utensils with his fellow, and they were stolen or they were lost; [if the bailee] paid and did not want to take an oath . . . and be exempt . . . [if] the thief is found, he pays double payment. [If] he slaughtered or sold [it], he pays fourfold or fivefold payment. To whom does he pay? To the one with whom the deposit [was left]. [If the bailee] took an oath and did not want to pay, [and] the thief was found, he pays double payment. [If] he slaughtered or sold [it], he pays fourfold or fivefold payment. To whom does he pay? To the owner of the deposit.[28]

I cannot overstate how clipped and minimalistic the language of this formulation is, regularly eschewing basic pronouns and prepositions. The spareness of the formulation performs the clarity to which legalistic determination would purport. The explicit determination to which the formula reaches is of liability in cases where damage occurs to deposited goods.

Liability may accrue to either the negligent *shomair* or watchperson, who is possibly a thief, or to the owner who has instigated the legal controversy. It could emerge that on malicious grounds, the owner is the thief or adulterer of the goods, which can, of course, also be damaged or stolen by a third party, but this is to be determined by the court. The formulaic text would thus presume to execute two forms of preexistent punishment, double payment or its more onerous alternative, literally "fourfold or fivefold," liable to two potential agents, the negligent watchperson or thief, who are thus linked in reciprocal symmetry. The formula by the same token allocates the damages to two potential recipients, the watchperson or the owner.

Assessment of damages in the situation is to a considerable degree inflected by the watchperson's, and implicitly, by the thief's right to take an oath regarding innocence and degree of responsibility in a Rabbinic court of law. In the case of the performance of this speech act, the court is predisposed to grant credence to the party making it, but where, in the course of deliberation the oath proves false, the presumption of the speaker's guilt emerges, and higher penalties are assessed. Within the framework of the Talmud, the oath situation is a secondary language game grafted or templated upon the "primary" or empirical situation of damaged or stolen goods and the controversy they initiate. In keeping with a Judaic ideology of the sanctity of explicitness and self-regulated responsibility in human interactions, the court is predisposed to grant credulity to a formally correct oath, but the willful adulteration of this scrip or currency betokens malicious intent toward the community.

Yet taking an oath is a sociological as well as a rhetorical and formal act. There may be strategic, that is, interpersonal reasons for avoiding the oath independent of its role in establishing the facts of the case. For example, my taking the oath may unfairly implicate a potential suspect near and dear to me or someone in relation to whom I have a vested interest in the avoidance of public conflict. The Gemara in this chapter of Bava Metzia displays considerable sensibility to the ambiguity between the oath's role as a secondary truth value and its status in the sociological struggle for the moral, that is, communal high ground. This is of considerable interest to all of us who, having enjoyed and benefited from the revolution in criticism and scholarship toward language-oriented models, wish to trace the intricate intertwining between textual dynamics and the laws—and I deploy this term with deliberation—of social life.

The first Mishna of the chapter, set in a scenario of damaged goods, thus leaves us with an aggrieved owner and a paid or unpaid watchperson who has either exempted himself from legal damages with an oath or has not. The intrusion of a third party, the thief, aggravates the always already tenuous situation of trust. The Mishnaic text establishes different levels of punishment to the negligent watchperson, and it opens the question as to whether the thief's punishment, in the form of legal damages, accrues to the owner, that is, the depositor, or to the watchperson from whom the property was diverted. It serves as a template upon which subsequent Mishnas and their Gemaric embroideries will play variations, for the Talmud, like *The Arcades Project* and other multiregister works, is a matrix of permutational play and elaboration. It establishes a context in which the willful public misrepresentation of the facts, which are not necessarily the same as some abstract or transcendental truth, is as egregious a misdeed as the empirical act of theft or fraud. The strategic importance of this Mishna is magnified by the fact that it establishes an entire culture of delegation at the same time that it establishes a framework and mechanisms for the determination of certain forms of property liability.

The body of Gemaric elaborations upon this stripped-down miniature legal code understandably gravitates from the most tangible to the most unlikely hypothetical instances. The specifications of the Gemara do not belong to case law, but rather to speculative law. The instances that the Gemara belabors are speculations, and their progression is from rootedness in material probability to "acts of God," the most tenuous of outcomes.

The Gemaric elaboration of the first Mishna in the chapter runs a full gamut from logical and sociological analysis to figural performance, at times flamboyant. Its first questions are the predictable ones, easily addressed on a substantive level: Why, for one, does the Mishna specify a deposit of either animals or utensils, thus encompassing organic and inorganic categories of property? In the case of a lost animal, should penalties take into account potential accretions of value, including shearings and offspring? On this point, Rabbis Rami ben Ḥama and Meir part ways, the latter contesting the former's assertion: "Surely a person cannot transfer ownership of something that has not yet come into the world."[29] The inquiry into the futurity of ownership segues quite well into an analysis of the oath situation proper, in which a commitment regarding the future as well as the past is made. What are the sociological as well as ethical implications of paying damages without taking an oath as opposed to taking the oath without wanting to pay? The distinction between a compensated watchperson (*shomair sahar*) and a gratis watchperson (*shomair ḥinam*) is factored into the possibilities engendered by the oath. Compensation for losses, according to the Gemara, is indeed eventually accorded to watchpeople who could have exempted themselves from damages by means of the oath, but who allowed the facts of the situation, including their innocence, to emerge through the proceedings. This analysis establishes at least two motives for a party's taking the oath in a dispute: not wanting to pay and preempting the appearance of guilt. Paying damages without swearing, on the other hand, suggests hesitation regarding the truth value embodied in the oath or future legal amplifications or charges yet to emerge.

A distinctive Talmudic feature evident in this passage is that the level of performativity, itself constituting the interruption of conceptual elaboration by means of assonance, refrain, and incantation and other material features of language, augments as the argumentation reaches toward finer, sometimes even tenuous distinctions. The Gemaric text is at times constrained to perform the proliferation of semiological and sociological complexity that the situation of loss and speech action occasions. In this context, Kafka's "Parable of the Doorkeeper," consummating a legalistic novel in which a preliminary interrogation has already transpired in an audience that can only be a Talmudic academy, opens up a scene of exegesis whose scope of proliferation can also be only Talmudic.

The debate as to whether our Mishna stresses the anticipatory or the assertive function of the oath of nonliability, whether the oath is primarily a strategic (performative) or assertive (constative) speech act, rises into a concantenation of commitments to pay. "The Tannaim of the School of Rabbi Ḥiyya and the school of Rabbi Oshaya" conclude that the constative and performative thrusts of the oath "were taught next to each other": "It is obvious [that if] he said: 'I will not pay,' and then he said: 'I will pay,' surely he said 'I will pay.' But [if] he said 'I will pay' [34B] and then he said 'I will not pay,' what [is the law]? Do we say he has retracted, or perhaps he stands by his word, and he is putting him off?"[30] The litany of "I will pay" and "I will not pay" here stages the concrete performance of the oath at the same time that it inquires into the logical intedeterminacies that the oath occasions.

The oath itself arises in a concantenating refrain, the reverberation of a knell or *glas*.[31] In the bicolumnar typography of his work of this latter title, Derrida stretches the mutually reinforcing thrust of the ongoing registers encompassed by the Talmudic page. Derrida glosses the problematical and even hypocritical Hegelian pronouncements of family ethics and law with an opposed column of text devoted to the scandalous Rabbi Genet. Yet the sustained dissonance and supplementarity of discourses wreathing themselves around the problematic of idealization itself surely extends the Talmudic play of registers.

The outbreak of music and lyrical poetry within the staid deliberations upon the law signals, metaphysically and ideologically, that there is something higher than the resolution of the case at hand, and even higher than the opinions of those fellow academics, the Rabbis. This something can be named only in two ways: YHWH himself or the mechanism of the language that can associate such assonance and rhythm.

The Gemara, proceeding to the liability of the *shomair's* sons in the event that he dies while in possession of the deposit—alas, in my own citations, I can no longer evade the gender-specificity of the Judaic law—rises to an even more impressive concantenation of "ifs" than in our preceding example:

> Do we say he has retracted? . . . [If] he said "I will pay," and he died, and his sons said "We will not pay," what [is the law]? Do we say they have retracted, or perhaps they stand by their father's word? . . . [If] the sons paid, what [is the law]? . . . [If] he paid the sons, what [is the law]? . . . [If] the sons paid the sons, what [is the law]? [If] he paid half, what [is the law]? [If] he borrowed two cows and paid [for] one of them, what [is the law]? [If] he borrowed from partners and paid one of them, what [is the law]?[32]

In a very concrete manner, as tangible as the interpersonal relations that the Talmud aspires to orchestrate, the text performs the lacunae and stutters that enter the case upon the *shomair's* death.

Throughout the disputation, the registers of Rashi, the Tosaphot or supplements, the Torah Or, and Ein Mishpat Ner Mitzvah monitor the action taking place in the central column, in the main frame, as it were. Impartial observers to a contention that may well go awry, the alternate registers constitute the symptom of a crisis of textual and moral codification at the same time that they would supply a guardrail, a restraining order. On the very first point of our Mishnah, for example, Tosafot asserts that the case is limited to the theft of the deposited property; the penalties that the Talmud takes under consideration do not really pertain to the situation of loss.[33] This is a pivotal specification, and subsequent argumentation is indeed slanted toward a theft situation and the malicious intent that it implies. Rashi and Ra'avad enter a particularly pointed dispute as to the accrual of liabilities to the watchperson's sons. "*Ra'avad* argues," according to Steinsaltz, "that the Gemara must be referring to a case where the depositor dies after the animal was stolen,"[34] whereas Rashi insists that the theft predated the death. The architecture of the Talmudic page places the additional registers of traditions, commentary, and cross-references *around* the central column of Mishnaic/Gemaric elaboration and give-and-take. The secondary registers are as close to a physical scaffolding as text allows. Yet it is precisely the explosion of potential formulation and meaning that the support apparatus documents and ornaments. The Talmud and its *semblables* in the universe of multiregister works both register and celebrate the unlimited self-engendering of script.

Of course, the columns of *Glas*, as opposed to those in canonical works such as the Talmud, were constructed as much to crumble as to stay firm. The skyline of *Glas* is the product of cantilevered philosophical narratives. The deconstructive performance of *Glas* unearths tectonic vectors complementary to the prevalent myths by which its subjects, Hegel and Genet, are remembered. In the left-hand column, Hegel's adultery and concurrent second family give the lie to the sanctimonious ideology of culture enunciated in *The Philosophy of Right* and other texts. On the right hand of the pages, Genet's neighborhood of crime, perversion, and the abject conditions of prison is revealed to harbor a far more compelling version of idealism than the Hegelian metaphysics would allow. The counterforces enabling *Glas* to "band erect," to stand on its own, thus consist of debunked sanctimony and hypocrisy, and, on the other hand, purported deviance restored to its humanity. Deconstructive design sits astride both wings of this diptych or hinge. Indeed, the deconstructive position inheres far more in the complex infrastructure of this dual debunking/affirmation, the hinge of critical scrutiny, than in the play of cultural epigones and demons, whether Kant *avec* Sade,[35] Hegel *avec* Genet, James *avec* Proust, or Hemingway *avec* Kerouac.

In their design and architecture, then, the counterpoised columns of *Glas* are calculated to crumble, to veer away from the logical imperative of holding their own, or holding their end up, of a dialectical tension or standoff, like the extremes of a bridge. Both columns of *Glas* bulge and bubble with arbitrary grafts and accidental typography. In this fashion, the extremes of moral and cultural possibility reveal that they are far more complex than meets the eye; that they verge toward each other; that they are in fact inscribed within each other; that their field is in fact a single range or continuum of assertion, ideation, diversion, and perversion.

Hence, it is of little surprise, but of enormous wit and inventiveness, when the Genet column fragments at the point of its most articulate "banding erect," opposite, it turns out, extracts of Hegel's idyllic prenuptial correspondence with Marie, his wife. This moment of typographical anomie and ironic matching occurs, in fact, several pages after the Genet column has abandoned its "normative" typography[36] and has entered an "italicism" underscoring a far-ranging exploration of the subsemantic and "material," as de Man would say, potentials in the word and syllable *glas*.

The *glas* of language, we might want to generalize at some risk, as it emerges from the pages of Derrida's Talmudic study, consists in the assonant and arational dimension of signifiers undercutting their roles in logic and meaning and their place in ideology. The "glassle," if not glottal, or sybillant, for that matter, resonance or substratum that persists along with language's higher metaphysical aspirations and undermines them is a material operator of the disruption and subterfuge that the Genet column of *Glas* performs in relation to the sanctimonious mainstream of the Western tradition. In the instance of our current concern, the Genet column falls apart at a moment when the ongoing narrative, signified by the major typeface common to both columns, discusses sucking, and suckers (*ventouses*) in relation to adoration. This typographical display of a split or breakdown in drift or clear intention has been preceded by a long excursis in italics that has allowed the Genet column to explore several matters reverberating significantly upon the ongoing material substrate that sustains ideology and meaning while severely disfiguring them. It also allows it to incorporate extratextual materials from wide-ranging "sources."[37] The Genet column at this point hazards the subsyllabic implications and disruptions of the consonant combination "GL."[38] It has quoted and explored the meaningful/nonsensical music of Edgar Allen Poe's "The Bells," an instance (and author) of literary "glassality" as extreme and significant as any.[39] Indeed, the typographical crisis that attends the emergence of suckers in the Genet column climaxes the work's most sustained exploration of the subsemantic, subsyllabic dimension of language upon which ideological claims of purpose and meaning founder. These marginal "outside elements" are at once covered over by Hegel (and by whomever would presume to speak for the predominant drift of Western civilization) and utterly generative (if not central) to the marginal, minor, and deterritorialized barrios of this system, whether occasioned by crime, homosexuality, ideological dissidence, nihilism, or whatever. This is merely one instance of the intellectual work that went into the typographical inconstancy of the ongoing columns that structure the text of *Glas*.

The openness of both columns to citation, to the incorporation of material not proper to the Hegel narration-exegesis or to the Genet narration-exegesis, already installs a radical potential for both discursive registers to proceed indirectly, even to about-face, to fragment, to diverge, even, on occasion, to cross. The textual grafts in both columns of the material are characterized by a modernist tendency to diversity, variation, and collage. When the talk turns to organs on the Genet side of the text, as it often does, Derrida grafts a citation regarding the musical organ from 1619 by Michael Praetorius, in its Gothic typeface from the period, adding, as does Pound in the *Cantos* and Williams in *Paterson*, to the work's typographical repertoire.[40] If Derrida limited his play on the dialogic column architecture of *Glas* to citation, he would already have considerable resources for undermining and varying this megastructure.

Yet Derrida is too systematic, and, I would add, too *visual* a critic to stop his critique of the entire tradition by which metaphysics, whether it arises in a Western or non-Western provenance, by configuring a restrictive inside and outside to itself, a column A and an opposed column B, to limit the transformative potential of the *Glas* columns to citation. This is the point at which both the columns fragment, in some instances split down the middle, take on marginal notation, and bubble in the sense of including foreign material in unexpected doses and typographical shapes, including the arbitrary typesetting of poetry. Derrida also takes the liberty to play with the continuity and discontinuity of material set in the standard typeface for the work. Especially in the Genet column, but occasionally in its Hegelian counterpart, there can be long gaps of absence in the typesetting. In one of them, Derrida inscribes his signature; in another, the capitalized word "PARANTHESE," parenthetically enclosed.[41] Derrida can completely enclose cited material, on either the right or left-hand side, by the standard columnar typeface, creating exactly the effect through which certain typographical elements are cornered by others in the Talmud.[42] It should be noted, though, that some of the cited material, especially the poetry, resides at the center, as opposed to the sides of the columns. Some of the off-sides citations are so brief that they become, in effect, marginalia to columns already highlighting the marginality of text, thus continuing the tradition of self-ironic marginalia common to Sterne's *Tristram Shandy*, Coleridge's "The Rime of the Ancient Mariner," and chapter 2.2 of *Finnegans Wake*.[43]

With astonishing consistency, these typographical improvisations embellish work taking place on a conceptual level in the vicinity of their outbreak. From the outset of *Glas*, the figure of the eagle, homonymic in French with the pronunciation of Hegel, is a property of the left-hand, that is Hegelian, column of the pages. But at a certain moment, when Derrida glosses Genet on the inspirational power that the Cluny unicorn tapestries exercised over him, the figure of the eagle migrates to the Genet column, one example of the crossover I hinted at above.[44] It is precisely where the eagle occupies center stage of the Genet column that Derrida splits the typography down the middle, exploring mythological and Christian sources of this figure in the right subcolumn and maintaining the Genet eagle narrative on the left.[45] By the same token, the column dedicated to Hegel neatly divides between an account of Hegel's Platonism and a digression into the mythological sources behind that interest.[46] The overall effect, though, is an undermining of the divide that mainstream judgment and metaphysics would set between Hegel and Genet in the first place, an undermining that proceeds, as in Sterne, Joyce, Proust, Stein, Pound, and Borges, through expansion and proliferation.

The bubbles, splits, and divergences that happen in the typography of *Glas* are epiphenomena of the same tendencies potential within texts in general. The disputation of a Talmudic Gemara may culminate in a cascade of tenuous possibilities, or with the invocation of the Angel of Death (or of women, every bit as much a disruption according to the Judaic laws of genre), but the design of the Talmudic page does not bless expansion and proliferation in the law. This is a moment at which deconstruction parts ways from a tradition of minute argumentation and meticulous exegesis that obliquely inspired it. This divergence is as ambivalent and pained as it is irreconcilable.

4

In all likelihood, I am culpable, perhaps to the "extreme decree," of straying far from Benjamin's home, his final one, an imaginary home, situated somewhere in the Paris of the Second Empire. What could, after all, the obsessive disputations of the Amoritic and Tannaitic periods have in any significant way to do with such phenomena as the development of the arcades, the initiation of international trade expositions, the massive deployment of cast iron and plate glass in construction and design, the spread of prostitution and gambling as economies marginal to a voracious, fast-paced brand of capitalism, the invention of photography and industrial techniques of mass production, the emergence of the modern mass media, and the disturbances of 1848 and the Paris Commune? No two phenomena could be more distant than the Talmudic academies of Palestine and Babylonia—in places such as Sura and Pumpedita—and Paris during the nineteenth century. The later convolutes of *The Arcades Project* register a blurring of the distinct camera angles organizing the exposés of 1935 and 1939. They witness the cascading of such excessive historical and documentary material into venues where they no longer pack a concentrated punch. And what could these two highly unlikely points on a connecting line have to do with the program and carefully designed typography of *Glas*?

Surely what could link the Talmud, *Glas*, and *The Arcades Project* is a radically democratic textuality, an open space or medium questioning the authority and determination underlying even stringent religious practice. These works not only open their medium: They allegorize the spatial play of language by activating compartments of signification and speech action. The registration of language, its buttressing-undermining of itself in architectural units, is both its legal defense against the accusation of its systematic indeterminacy and the most incriminating evidence supporting this charge. Works of this nature, configured in registers as they are, marshal themselves in ecstasy, at the Wakean "proteiform graph itself . . . a polyhedron of scripture," the "ruled barriers along which the traced words run, march, halt, walk, stumble at doubtful points," the "sounds in utter that, in signs so adds to, in universal, in polygutteral, in each auxiliary idiom, sordomutics, florilingua, shaltafocal, flayflutter, a con's cubane, a pro's tutute, strassarab, ereperse and anythongue athall," so as to "begin again to make soundsense and sensesound kin again."[47]

Textual registers may be thought of as places or locations of signifying, representational, and ideology assertive-critical activity, as microenvironments within overarching, we might say canonical enterprises of cultural formation and disfiguration. Each one establishes a certain microclimate joining an overall atmosphere of cultural, ontological, epistemological, and metaphysical understanding. There are political, material, technological, and other pretexts and subtexts affecting the massive multiregister or canonical work that any sociocultural formation establishes and consults during its tenure, the epoch of its validity. In different ways, the Talmud, *The Arcades Project*, and *Glas* all speak to the excruciating difficulty, the tenuousness, and even the force underlying these purported society-wide or culture-wide understandings. Their demarcation of registers is the insignia as well as the symptom of the violence and fragility with which the ground, the architectural floor of common knowledge, is fraught, in all places and at all times.

Yet if it be granted that Benjamin, the man and the writing, immersed himself as few others of his era in the being, design, and vicissitudes of books, his peers in this regard being the likes of Kafka, Proust, and Joyce, the considerable affinities between the Talmud and *The Arcades Project*, the massive, final, and unfinished preoccupation of his life, are in no way farfetched. Indeed, during the last days of his residence in Paris, Benjamin confided the manuscript of his yet and constitutionally unfinished treatise to Georges Bataille. Had Bataille not successfully fulfilled the responsibilities of the *shomair ḥinam*, the unpaid watchperson, we would not have the pleasure of puzzling over *The Arcades Project* today. Both works, the Talmud and *The Arcades Project*, configure themselves in multiple, simultaneous, ongoing registers of elucidation and activity. Both works arise out of and perform the cultural material that makes them possible. Both works prefigure contemporary cybernetics by configuring their various topics into print-medium Web sites and by developing a typography of windows. Both works set into play an open-ended textual cascading over the categories and boundaries that they themselves establish.

Through Scholem, Buber, and others, the Talmud indeed constituted part of the cultural landscape to which Benjamin belonged from early on in his formation. The Talmud resided in Benjamin's close vicinity in the same way that political formations, some of a venerable and outmoded pedigree, including "nomadic despotism" and feudalism lurk, according to Deleuze and Guattari in *A Thousand Plateaus*,[48] just beneath the surface of modern, constitutional, presumably "safe" and liberal societies.

We think of Benjamin in conjunction with Kafka, Proust, and Joyce, among many others, because he was engaged in a wide-ranging exploration of textuality in its narratological, interlinguistic, material, temporal, and spatial dimensions. Multiregister works, whether the Talmud, *The Arcades Project*, or *Glas*, clearly capitalize on certain spatial and typographical features of texts in order to highlight the dialogic, polysemic, exegetical, and glossematic features of writing. The spatial experimentation of the Talmud, *The Arcades Project*, *Glas*, *Tristram Shandy*, *Finnegans Wake*, and related works belongs, in this respect, to what Maurice Blanchot has termed "the space of literature." It is both in this space and on this space, hopefully with a slightly aggravated sensibility to its intricacies, that the present chapter closes.

FIVE

Deterritorializing the Text: Flow-Theory and Deconstruction

Gilles Deleuze and Félix Guattari, in a chapter of *A Thousand Plateaus* entitled "10,000 B.C.: The Geology of Morals," indicate an architecture of stratification and doubling germane to the enterprise of establishing a flow
theory embracing both textual and extratextual phenomena:

> God is a Lobster, or a double pincer, a double bind. Not only do strata come at
> least in pairs, but in a different way each stratum is double (it itself has several
> layers). Each stratum exhibits phenomena constitutive of *double articulation*. Ar-
> ticulate twice, B—A, BA. . . . Double articulation is so extremely variable that we
> cannot begin with a general model, only a relatively simple case. The first articu-
> lation chooses or deducts, from unstable particle-flows, metastable molecular or
> quasi-molecular units (*substances*) upon which it imposes a statistical order of con-
> nections and successions (*forms*). The second articulation establishes functional,
> compact, stable structures (*forms*), and constructs the molar compounds in which
> these structures are simultaneously actualized (*substances*).[1]

The inexact symmetry of lobsters, ticks, prawns, and other creatures from
the natural world becomes the infrastructure for a kind of doubling, or what

Borges, in "Death and the Compass," calls "maniacal repetition," which is a feature in the architecture of culture.[2] *A Thousand Plateaus* is, in one of its facets, a deranged, antilinear history book. Each chapter is named by a temporal marker, a year or period in apposition to a major breakthrough in what Foucault would characterize as archaeology, the genealogy of culture in an invariably discontinuous sequence of epistemo-linguistic formations. The year zero, pivotal to Christian iconography, is linked to a phenomenon that Deleuze and Guattari name "faciality,"[3] the maniacal reinscription of facial traits across the gamut of major civilizations and a staggering range of artifacts. The structural unit of faciality is "probe-heads," another biologically derived feature interchangeable with and introducible into artifacts of what we might call a higher symbolic order.

Within the same discontinuous historical sequence, 1227, the year in which Genghis Khan died, is accorded special status in the formation of nomadology, or the war machine. Nomadic despotism, as Deleuze and Guattari have culled it from source materials by Hegel, Marx, Nietzsche, Durkheim, and others, is an irrational, violent, and pathogenic substructure upon which all organized societies, including modern "liberal" ones, are grounded. The despotic machine, more like the Freudian preconscious and the Lacanian pre-Oedipal than the Freudian unconscious, is a massive, collective will to anomie, incest, and death capable of crystallizing and deranging bourgeois society at any moment. Deleuze and Guattari, only partially successful in their attempt to avoid dialectical and/or genealogical schemata, make a point of distinguishing this chaotic, destructive happening from a massive sociological regression, which it would otherwise closely resemble, naming it an "involvement."[4]

The most precipitous deployments of the mobilization of the despotic machine in the waning years of the last century were Hitler, the Kmer Rouge, and the genocide in Rwanda, while an American blitzkrieg that can be directed anywhere is an irradicable feature on the current geopolitical map. The rise and meaning of Hitler are memorialized in a chapter of *A Thousand Plateaus* entitled "1933: Micropolitics and Segmentarity." Hitler's takeover of the German chancellery and Reichstag becomes an exemplary occasion for showcasing the fluctuations between what Deleuze and Guattari term "molar" and "molecular" movements.

In the distinction between classes and masses, postmodern flow theory opts for the latter. Masses release themselves from the "molar segmentarity" defining the conventional division of labor in advanced societies.[5] Like the despotic machine that generates them, the masses are a trump card, a loose cannon, whose unpredictable wills and movements are able, at any moment, to upset the hierarchically defined socioeconomic order defining distinct classes and assigning them different roles and functions. Deleuze and Guattari favor the "molecular notion" of masses "that do not have the same kind of movement, distribution, or objectives" as classes and "do not wage the same kind of struggle. . . . *The notion of mass is a molecular notion* operating according to a type of segmentation irreducible to the molar segmentarity of class. Yet classes are indeed fashioned from masses; they crystallize them. And masses are constantly flowing or leaking from classes."[6] The unpredictable turns of the masses are a social factor that a postmodern flow theory indeed wishes to chart and keep within its sights. For Deleuze and Guattari, 1933 was a moment at which the play of molarity and molecularity was particularly fruitful in terms of social overcoding, on the molar side, and molecular mutation. It was a banner year in the history of segmentarity, the Kafkaesque communication gap between the operative segments of a modern liberal society.

As was Karl Marx in his own day, contemporary cultural critics are torn between the allure and self-generating conceptual infrastructure of "high theory" and the social injustices and cultural misprisions of actuality. Marx had clearly read his Rousseau, Kant, and Hegel well. While an exemplary expositor of the simultaneous and linear processes that were emerging in the big industry of his day, Marx dealt with this conflict of interest with a bit of segmentation of his own. In *Capital*, his social critique and sharp vituperation at the miseries and injustices perpetrated by capitalism—the inhuman working conditions, minimal wages, interminable workday, and exploitation of child-labor—alternate with his more dispassionate analyses of the rise of surplus value and the intricate circuits in which materials, money, and commodities circulate with increasing velocity.[7] Cultural critics today, however, having benefited from the stunning writerly performances of Nietzsche, Heidegger, Benjamin, and Derrida, design their discourse so as to span the same conceptual-actual interstice, but without the Marxian linear segmentation. They demand the same script to critique *épistèmes* and deconstruct conceptual architectures and to address the injustices and miseries of race, class, and gender discrimination.

If any two critics position their discourse so that it might fill this rather tall intellectual order, it is Deleuze and Guattari. They do so by resisting the impulse to segment textuality off from other registers of human behavior and activity. Their experiment comes at the cost of registering some ambivalence toward rigorous textuality, a point at which we will arrive below. Their postmodern flow theory monitors the possibilities for action and exchange across a theater of operation extending from ticks and the animal in general to political formations, music, social-science theory, the hypothetical human subject, and a coterie of privileged texts, including, among others, Spinoza's philosophical disputations, Kleist's dramas, and Kafka's fiction.[8] There is no doubt a price to pay when criticism flies in the face of the Husserlian critiques of the psychological and the historical or de Manian and Derridean questioning of the thematic and deterministic at the expense of the rhetorical, and this give and take, the tax levied on a critical model positing a flow both textual and transtextual, will be assessed below.

My survey of a possible exchange between deconstruction and Deleuze and Guattari's postmodern flow theory begins with a blatant and easily overlooked point. The extract at the head of this essay, like one that will be appended shortly below, dedicates itself to the elaboration of a conceptual scaffolding barely accessible, let alone present, if one were to allow oneself the term, to mind. *A Thousand Plateaus* is a rhizomatic constellation of infrastructures known as machines, assemblages, and planes that never coheres and always stops short of actuality. This virtual discourse is a *précis*, a "before," to an intellectual machine work or system whose *Zusammenhang* never emerges in any definite sense, yet Deleuze and Guattari characterize its details and workings with utter seriousness, with a near-positivistic sense of its actuality, a sense that they term a "pragmatics." In the temporality of their discourse, Deleuze and Guattari sandwich us between a future presented as fact and a past overflowing with indeterminacy. Like the psychotics such as Freud's Schreber who furnished the founding case histories of schizoanalysis as well as psychoanalysis, Deleuze and Guattari insist that we take their projections of a highly privatized and singular conceptual system, which is always a potential one, a theory of the as-if, with the utter seriousness with which they do.

There is an odd cohesion to the clinical observations of psychosis, however diverse the multiple vantage points. Whereas Freud focuses upon the grand scale achieved by the system of Schreber's delusions, its interconnection by rays and its service as a medium for communication with God, Lacan emphasizes the verbal hallucination without which no event can be truly termed psychotic:

> A claim against people who are supposedly against you is not enough for us to have a psychosis. . . . People have always known how to define the paranoic as a touchy, intolerant, and distrustful gentleman, who is in a state of verbalized conflict with his surroundings. But for us to have a psychosis, there must be disturbances of language—this is at least the rule of thumb I suggest you adopt provisionally.[9]

A distortion or collapse of reality is tantamount to a disturbance of language, which for Lacan is the medium of flow within the subject and in her interaction with the world. The verbal hallucination, which for Lacan is the primary specification for psychotic conditions, entails a dissolved border between an existing and a created reality. Lacan continues:

> What indicates a hallucination is this unusual sense the subject has at the border between the sense of reality and the sense of unreality, a sense of proximate birth, of novelty—and not just of any novelty but of novelty over its use breaking through into the external world. This is not the same order as what appears with respect to meaning or meaningfulness. It is a created reality, one that manifests itself well and truly within reality as something new. Hallucination . . . here constitutes the support for what the subject is experiencing.[10]

The Lacanian psychotic prefigures Deleuze and Guattari's schizo, yet where Lacan remained firm to the linguistic nature of psychotic and nonpsychotic psychological manifestations, Deleuze and Guattari would pour them out into the extratextual and transtextual spheres.

There is a characteristic grandeur to Deleuze and Guattari's theoretical claims with which readers of the Schreber's pronouncements will be familiar. Conceptually and allegorically, these critics reconstitute a nomadic despotism, a being to animality and even to death underlying the organized nation-state. The role of the critic that they implicitly mandate, whether her discipline be literature, painting, music, anthropology, history, or psychoanalysis, is to sense and monitor the flow of signifiers, money, products, and even bodily secretions normally just beneath the stratum of public scrutiny and achieving explicitness at moments of social catastrophe.

> The *territorial machine* is therefore the first form of socius, the machine of primitive inscription, the "megamachine" that covers a social field. It is not to be

confused with technical machines. . . . The social machine is literally a machine, irrespective of any metaphor, inasmuch as it exhibits an immobile motor and undertakes a variety of interventions: flows are set apart, elements are detached from a chain, and portions of the tasks to be performed are distributed. Coding the flows implies all these operations. This is the social machine's supreme task, inasmuch as the apportioning of production corresponds to extractions from the chain, resulting in a residual share for each member, in a global system of desire and destiny that organizes the productions of production, the productions of recording, and the productions of consumption. Flows of women and children, flows of herds and of seed, sperm flows, flows of shit, menstrual flows: nothing must escape coding.[11]

Such reads the omnivorousness of flow, or the omnivorousness of the discourse starting from the assumption that flow is the ultimate form of articulation, that flow precedes the social institutions and even discourses structured to register and mark it, that critical reading and social awareness monitor and evaluate the vicissitudes of different modalities of flow. The primary philosophical intervention marking *Anti-Oedipus* and *A Thousand Plateaus* thus may well be the restoration of two often-overlooked thinkers to their potential place in a postmodern reading of civilization and culture: Heraclitus and Spinoza. The primacy of an a priori and autonomous flow to civilization and to the language that records and measures it could well constitute a belated tribute to Heraclitan flux, while the blueprints for despotic and other social machines and the architecture of knowledge pivot around a plane of indifference, the "plane of consistency" adapted from Spinozan monadology.

The implied critic or intellectual is not necessarily a free-flow advocate, however. Whereas Freudian psychological health involved a salutary restoration of the drive's free flow, Marx saw more evil than good in the mass and speed with which money, goods, and profits circulated during the first age of industrialized capitalism. Yet the critic implicit in the pages of Deleuze and Guattari's "Capitalism and Schizophrenia" diptych is more a machine watcher and flow monitor than a close reader. Even with their marked fidelity to the exposition of Spinoza, Kleist, Marx, Freud, and Kafka, Deleuze and Guattari tend to pick and choose, from the artifacts they observe, substantiation for the particular elements of their own discursive machine or assemblage under scrutiny. They are not bound, as is the close reader, by the convention of exploring the multiple and discordant strands that constitute an artifact's imposition and meaning.

Deleuze and Guattari remain inveterate and astoundingly loyal readers of texts, even if they do not define themselves officially as close ones. In the spirit of Paul de Man and J. Hillis Miller, they demonstrate fidelity to an assemblage of texts that has congealed in the course of their investigations.[12] Deleuze and Guattari fashion the psychotic air castle known as the despotic machine out of their readings in the authors mentioned a paragraph above and in others. At the peak of their psychotic elaboration, in the "Geology of Morals" chapter of *A Thousand Plateaus*, where they draft the blueprint for a barely articulable, rhizomatic, labyrinthine, but arbitrarily structured system of knowledge, they are still reading something—specifically, the triple-structured mass of memories and associations through which the analysand proceeds at the very end of *Studies on Hysteria*. Deleuze and Guattari's characterization of the strata structurally pivotal to the social machine and its system of knowledge is strikingly reminiscent of the psychic material in the earlier Freudian description: "We may therefore use the term the central layer, or central ring, for the following aggregate comprising the unity of composition of a stratum: exterior molecular materials, interior substantial elements, and the limit or membrane conveying the formal relations. There is a single *abstract machine* that is enveloped by the stratum and constitutes its unity. This is the Ecumenon, as opposed to the Planomenon of the plane of consistency."[13]

Through a complex of vertically, concentrically, and haphazardly arranged psychic material, the original neurotics of the psychoanalytical field proceeded backward in their quest for the inadmissible thought whose unearthing would obviate the need for a symptom or complex of symptoms. The socioconceptual architecture that Deleuze and Guattari fashion out of the at-hand materials, however, is more forbidding and less negotiable than the psychic landscape traversed by the originary neurotics. The rehashing of this architecture early in *A Thousand Plateaus* is, in typical Deleuzian/Guattarian fashion, an *extension* of the Freudian initiatives that becomes an obfuscation, a fugue, and a derangement. Structure, in this postmodern de-contraction of the potentials both highlighted and held in check in Freud, becomes even more pronounced and arbitrary than it was in 1893, 1900, and 1905 in the genesis of a science of consciousness:

Forms relate to codes and processes of coding and decoding in the parastrata; substances, being formed matters, relate to territorialities and reterritorialization on the epistrata. . . . Nomadic waves or flows of deterritorialization go from the central layer to the periphery, then from the new center to the new periphery, falling back to the old center and launching forth to the new. The organization of the epistrata moves in the direction of increasing deterritorialization. Physical particles and chemical substances cross thresholds of deterritorialization on their own stratum and between strata; these thresholds correspond to more or less stable intermediate states, to more or less transitory valences and existences. . . . Not only are physical particles characterized by speeds of deterritorialization— Joycean tachyons, particles-holes, and quarks recalling the fundamental idea of the "soup"—but a single chemical substance (sulfur or carbon, for example) has a number of more and less deterritorialized states. The more interior milieus an organism has on its own stratum, assuring its autonomy and bringing it into a set of aleatory relations with the exterior, the more deterritorialized it is. That is why degrees of development must be understood relatively, and as a function of differential speeds, relations, and rates. Deterritorialization must be thought of as a perfectly positive power that has degrees and thresholds (epistrata), is always relative, and has reterritorialization as its flipside or complement. An organism that is deterritorialized in relation to the exterior necessarily reterritorializes in its internal milieus.[14]

This passage fuses semiosis to the scenario of movement, acceleration, and the transfer of valences taking place only somewhat independently of it. The architecture of planes, strata, parastrata, and epistrata is an infra-structure arising in part to frame, in part to instrument this a priori, categor-ical, and category-blurring movement. The nomadic waves chronicled in the extract transpire both on historical-empirical and infrastructural levels. These waves launch from an established order onto or into a fertile territory and then fall back.

The anthropological stratum of Deleuze and Guattari's discourse is open to the notion of the universe as a play of preexistent vital and destructive forces celebrated both in Eastern thought and in the cultures of tribal peo-ples such as the Dogon, chronicled meticulously by Marcel Griaule and known well to the authors.[15] Deterritorialization, Deleuze and Guattari's rough equivalent to what deconstructive theory means by marginality, is arranged in the above passage with reterritorialization in an oscillation be-tween immanent and extraneous locations. The organism squeezed to the margin, and in Deleuze and Guattari this can be in a biological, sociological, or semiological sense, is already experiencing a reterritorialization, a reorientation to normative coordinates, whether Cartesian or ideological, even while being marginalized. The stage has been set for the despotic machine by an architecture incorporating waves of invasion and retreat, complementary yin-yang shifts between interior and exterior locations, between dominance and subordination.

The despotic machine underlying the civility of the liberal public sphere also demands, according to the above passage, an architecture that can include changes in speed and movement. In a nutshell, the attention to acceleration and corporeal movement may constitute Deleuze and Guattari's most radical revision of a critical movement or history that, beginning with Heidegger and Benjamin and the extensions of their work into the semiotically inspired French structuralism of Barthes and Foucault and into the textualism of de Man and Derrida, has tended to suspend time and to situate reading, thought, and linguistic activity in a spatial field, one tending toward insulation—if not from historical contingency, then from specific historical events. Deleuze and Guattari are nowhere more brilliant than in militating for theoretical discourse to make provisions for changes in speed and corporeal location. "Still less" is the Spinozan plane of consistency, the basic architectural unit in the infrastructures of flow theory, "a regression leading back to a principle":

> It is on the contrary an *involution*, in which form is constantly being dissolved, freeing times and speeds. It is a fixed plane, a fixed sound plane, or visual plane, or writing plane, etc. Here, fixed does not mean immobile: it is the absolute state of movement as well as of rest, from which all relative speeds and slownesses spring, and nothing but them. Certain modern musicians oppose the transcendent plan(e) of organization, which is said to have dominated all of Western classical music, to the immanent sound plane, which is always given along with that to which it gives rise, brings the imperceptible to perception, and carries only differential speeds and slownesses in a kind of molecular lapping: *the work of art must mark seconds, tenths and hundredths of seconds.*[16]

A conceptual model that can incorporate music is, in shorthand, one that has been calibrated to acceleration, and, as we will see, implicitly calibrated to corporeality.

The discourse of Deleuze and Guattari demands the anomaly of a moving architecture. By definition, architecture would seem to predicate structures of ongoing if not permanent program and value, structures that don't move. To the extent that Deleuze and Guattari's theory is receptive to flow as well as to semiosis, to the extent that it bridges the gap between textual spatialization and the hydraulic model common to Hegel, Marx, and Freud, among others, it requires the utter antinomy of a shifting architecture, a structuration whose strata, projections, and other annexes respond—with motion of their own—to fluctuations in the persistent flow of signs, money, goods, traffic, bodily fluids, and so on that is the ontological ground of Deleuze and Guattari's discourse. By opening the door to questions of acceleration and speed, this theory makes itself susceptible to the recriminations that phenomenology and deconstruction have addressed to conceptual operations of causality, determination, and temporal sequencing and prioritization. Yet the grounding of this theory in what would be best described as a transcendental flow introduces the transient and febrile into the solid, dissolves into the seascapes and aquatic media made familiar to us by Proust and Calvino, hospitable to lobsters and other instances of asymmetrical, binary, arational structuration.[17]

Even where not physically evident or present, a body is a necessary condition inhering to a conceptual system that is both text-oriented and flow-oriented. A body is not a corpus or a corpse, but a marker or placeholder in an assemblage that would presume to encompass the temporality of flow.[18] Flow and its temporal implications necessitate the construct of a body, even where there is no body in the house—where the house is not haunted by bodies. Deleuze and Guattari's body is one without organs, and not only because this disarticulation goes along with deterritorialization in the putatively external world. As a shifter, the marker of a flow transpiring prior to and independently of it, the body needs neither organs nor the division of labor that organic systems bring about. The body is a construct and creature of flow changes: invasions, retreats, accelerations, slowdowns, shutdowns.

> The BwO [Body without Organs] causes intensities to pass; it produces and distributes them in a *spatium* that is itself intensive, lacking extension. It is not space, nor is it in space; it is matter that occupies space to a given degree—to the degree corresponding to the intensities produced. It is nonstratified, unformed, intense matter, the matrix of intensity, intensity = 0; but there is nothing negative about that zero, there are no negative or opposite intensities. . . . That is why we treat the BwO as the full egg before the extension of the organism and the organization of the organs, before the formation of the strata; as the intense egg defined by axes and vectors, gradients and thresholds, by dynamic tendencies involving

energy transformation and kinematic movements involving group displacement, by migrations: all independent of *accessory forms*.[19]

We read here one of the more abstract characterizations of the body without organs, the body commissioned, as it were, by a theory setting out with a counterpoint of multiple flows and establishing the protocols of reading and exegesis only later. This body is less a compartment for an individuated subject than a field in which drives, intensities, and impulses are registered, corresponding to the full egg prior to mythographic differentiation.

Who constitute, for Deleuze and Guattari, the last residents of the BwO in a culture in which the body has become just another instrument, tool, factory in a stratified division of labor? The schizo inhabits a BwO of necessity. It is the junkies and sadomasochists who volunteer for BwO service. They are the last-ditch squatters in the BwO, holdouts for the disarticulate conjunction between the flows of mind and body.

> After all, is not Spinoza's *Ethics* the great book of the BwO? The attributes are types or genuses of BwO's substances, powers, zero intensities as matrices of production. The modes are everything that comes to pass: waves and vibrations, migrations. . . . The masochist body as an attribute or genus of substance, with its production of intensities and pain modes based on its degree o of being sewn up. The drugged body as a different attribute, with its production of specific intensities based on absolute Cold = o. . . . A junky does not want to be warm. He wants to be cool-cooler-COLD. But he wants The Cold like he wants His Junk—not outside where it does him no good but INSIDE so he can sit around with a spine like a frozen hydraulic jack. . . . There is a continuum of all the attributes or genuses of intensity under a single substance. . . . A continuum of all substances in intensity and of all intensities in substance. The uninterrupted continuum of the BwO. . . . Drug users, masochists, schizophrenics, lovers—all BwO's pay homage to Spinoza. The BwO is the *field of immanence* of desire, the *plane of consistency* specific to desire (with desire defined as a process of production without reference to any exterior agency).[20]

Crucial to Deleuze and Guattari's theory is its gravitation to fields and continua at the expense of points and binary oppositions. The body commissioned by a postmodern flow theory is postoperative, postorganization. No longer the inner sanctum of individuation, it is the field for movements operating prior to and independently of it. It is home to a psychotic experience.

Deleuze and Guattari's postmodern flow theory is a complex concept game in need of a body. For worse rather than better, Wittgensteinian analysis also required a body, in the latter case because the philosopher insisted on an epistemo-corporeal source for the sensations and feelings that could be expressed only with so much trouble, inexactitude, and pain. For all that the fabric of textuality in deconstructive discourse, say in "The Double Session," embroiders space—the space of the hymen, the veil, the tympany, the heliotrope, and so on—space is linguistico-phenomenological, rather than corporeal.[21] Organic corporeality flies in the face of philosophically rigorous essays at delimiting the metaphysical because the organized body is home to the spirit. Even artifacts exploring the intricacies of body writing, say Peter Greenaway's cinematic updating of Sei Shonagon's *Pillow Book*, arrive at a divide at which the semiological nuance of tattoos and the play of desire on the part of surrogates endowed with motives and interests take separate paths.

The disarticulation of corporeality into a body without organs is a psychotic symptom, ultimately traceable to the nineteenth-century breeding ground of psychiatry, another psychotic manifestation of a discourse that preempts its impossible referent, articulating it with utmost seriousness. Both individual experience and civil society are always on the verge of dissolution into mechanical automaticity. The body and the judicial and war machines always breaking out in Deleuze and Guattari's discourse might seem at first to be mere illustrations of the limitations of subjective metaphysics and the logocentrism that, in deconstruction, distrusts all mechanical processes. But in text-based and rhetoric-oriented theory, it suffices to ascribe all features of mechanics and automaticity to the linguistic medium. Deleuze and Guattari insist on a psychosocial gravitation of the liberal and the rational into the machinal. The despotic machine and the fluctuating waves of deterritorialization take place, constantly, in the actual world as well as on the page. Nothing less than the liberal public sphere and the constitution of subjectivity within it are constantly on the verge of a breakdown into psychotic automation and interconnectedness.

Text or Not Text?

The preeminent strength of Deleuze and Guattari's postmodern flow theory must surely be, as we have assayed it so far, its spanning at high levels multiple registers of meaning and experience and its achievement of stunning and unexpected connections between seemingly disparate phenomena. This is particularly helpful for critics who feel constrained to address artifacts not limited to a textual articulation, ones more time intensive, such as music or video, or ones inscribed on media less space-bound than the page. Artifacts in this latter category might include Christo's fencing in of the California desert or the Tet Offensive during the Vietnam War. As I hope has been established, Deleuze and Guattari do not make it easy to shift from the traditional foci of philosophical and critical attention to artifacts and events seemingly actual and "more in the world." A solid background in Spinoza, Kant, Hegel, Kierkegaard, Marx, Durkheim, Nietzsche, Freud, Lacan, Dumézil, Greimas, Barthes, Foucault, and Derrida is a salutary preparation for understanding the transformations enabling Deleuze and Guattari to place ticks, Kafka's animal parables, and everything in between in apposition.

The strength and distinction of this approach may well constitute its Achilles' heel. Indeed, one major cost of Deleuze and Guattari's innovative contribution to social and critical theories may well be some waffling on the pivotal question as to whether flow *is* textually constituted or whether it bridges the textual to the nontextual or transtextual. The minds of these two thinkers are capacious enough to advance both possibilities. It falls upon us, agents in the endeavor of reading and re-presenting culture, to determine how transigent Deleuze and Guattari are on this pivotal point and at what cost. Let me raise at this juncture the compromising hypothesis that Deleuze and Guattari could be thinkers and critics of enormous value to the readerly and writerly communities even if they fail miserably in the consistency of their approach to text.

It is of great consequence to Deleuze and Guattari's theory and our own ability to draw upon it whether language constitutes an urflow, a model for the other registers of signs, objects, and values that circulate through knowledge and culture, or whether language is merely one currency moved and disseminated by a preexistent and therefore transcendent flow. The evidence, as suggested above, seems to point in both directions. On the one hand, a certain coterie of modern writers in English places fiction in a privileged position to register the flow and the experience of the body without organs that is often the unique province of schizos. In *A Thousand Pla-*

teaus, on the other hand, we will learn that the plastic arts and especially music are even more intrinsically flow-oriented than writing.

> Strange Anglo-American literature: from Thomas Hardy, from D. H. Lawrence to Malcolm Lowry, from Henry Miller to Allen Ginsberg and Jack Kerouac, men who know how to leave, to scramble the codes, to cause flows to circulate, to traverse the desert of the body without organs. They overcome a limit, they shatter a wall, the capitalist barrier. And of course they fail to complete the process, they never cease failing to do so. . . . But through the impasses and the triangles a schizophrenic flow moves, irresistibly; sperm, river, drainage, inflamed genital mucous, or a stream of words that do not let themselves be coded, a libido that is too fluid, too viscous: a violence against syntax, a concerted destruction of the signifier, non-sense erected as a flow, polyvocity that returns to haunt all relations.[22]

This passage fluctuates from schizo madness to neurotic repression, from grammatical language to word salad. It hails from the anti-Oedipal wing of the "Capitalism and Schizophrenia" diptych, which in general traces the psychosocial implications of the tension between despotic and capitalist machines in our ("advanced" Western) culture, while, in general, again, *A Thousand Plateaus* explores the speculative and systematic architecture erected over this schism. The passage is an effective blueprint of Deleuze and Guattari's impasse: Here, literature is the medium by which the flow and its antagonism to organized society and psychological rationalism make themselves known. Yet language, and specifically ungrammatical schizophrenic discourse, is merely one in a number of other flowemes, including inflamed genital mucous and drainage. Could Deleuze and Guattari invoke the polyvocal, disseminative privilege of a flow deriving its dynamics from language, but then insist that there are nonlinguistic registers of flow? This compromise may well turn out to be the case.

Deleuze and Guattari frontally address the status of language both in and apart from a spectrum of other registers of order in a chapter entitled "587 B.C.–A.D. 70: On Several Regimes of Signs." The historical moment corresponding to the emergence of several telling registers of meaning and order in organized society corresponds to the period between the destruction of the First and Second Temples in Jerusalem. The various exiles and subjugations of Jews, in other words, are paradigmatic in establishing a complex interplay between the territorial, despotic, authoritarian, and abstract machines at work explicitly and at the edges of complex, bureaucratic, organized societies. It is in this chapter that Deleuze and Guattari take up the intellectual work of coordinating "regimes of signs," whose potential authoritarian rigidity they indicate by designating them "regimes," but which they situate squarely in a semiological realm, with a certain configuration known as the "abstract machine," which is, as we will see, both linguistic and nonlinguistic, organized by principles that may well be semiological, but producing a tangible effect in the sociopolitical realm. If there is any intellectual work in the "Capitalism and Schizophrenia" diptych that puts the consistency of Deleuze and Guattari's approach to language to the test, it is this configuration of the abstract machine in the wings of organized society that somehow feeds on regimes of signs, but transcends them, is *aufgehoben* beyond them, in serving as an effective sociological matrix, if not an actual force.

The abstract machine forms only one segment of the socioepistemological machinery that Deleuze and Guattari assemble to demonstrate the complex interplay between language and tangible sociological happenings in the discursive construction of history. Their understanding of sociopolitical formations is as a palimpsest of outmoded organizations that still persist at the margins of our so-called advanced technological society. The sociohistorical traces of feudalism have been registered in what Deleuze and Guattari term the "territorial machine," the power expectations stemming from land ownership.[23] They designate the vestiges of the nomadic invasions that overran and co-opted mainstream cultures—from the Hyksos to the Mongols—the "despotic machine." Garden-variety capitalist societies fall under the sway of the "authoritarian machine," which is neither so picturesque nor in certain senses so direct and speculative as the nomadic and despotic machines. Undergirded by these separate territorial, nomadic, and authoritarian machines, contemporary liberal societies are chaotic registers of outmoded and current politico-epistemological formations, and it was the deterritorialization of the ancient Hebrews that inaugurated a complex interplay of sociological vestiges and semiological registers still current today. It is in the sense of this approach to society that Deleuze and Guattari advance a pragmatics that is at once "*generative* since it shows how the various abstract regimes form concrete mixed semiotics, with what variants, how they combine" and "*transformational* . . . which shows how these regimes of signs are translated into each other, especially when there is a creation of a new regime."[24]

The question as to whether language structures all thought or is an ideological and political tool is pivotal to their way of doing pragmatics.

> For language is a political affair before it is an affair for linguistics; even the evaluation of degrees of grammaticality is a political matter.
>
> What is a semiotic, in other words, a regime of signs or a formalization of expression? They are simultaneously more and less than language. . . . As Foucault clearly shows, regimes of signs are only *functions of existence* of language that sometimes span a number of languages and are sometimes distributed within a single language. . . .
>
> But at this point, everything turns around, and the reason why a regime of signs is less than language also become the reasons why it is more than language. . . . Now contents are not "signifieds" dependent upon a signifier in any way, nor are they "objects" in any kind of relation of causality with the subject. They have their own formalization and have no relation of symbolic correspondence or linear causality with the form of expression: the two forms are in reciprocal presupposition. . . . This is what we call the *abstract machine*, which constitutes and conjugates all of the assemblage's cutting edges of deterritorialization. We must say that the abstract machine is necessarily "much more" than language. . . . A true abstract machine has no way of making a distinction within itself between a plane of expression and a plane of content because it draws a single plane of consistency, which in turn formalizes contents and expressions according to strata and reterritorializations. The abstract machine in itself is destratified, deterritorialized; it has no form of its own . . . and makes no distinction . . . between content and expression, even though outside itself it presides over that distinction and distributes it in strata, domains, and territories. An abstract machine in itself is not physical or corporeal, any more than it is semiotic; it is *diagrammatic* (it knows nothing of the distinction between the artificial and the natural either). It operates by *matter*, not by substance; by *function*, not by form.[25]

The abstract machine is like the answer to a riddle we struggle to "get" from a rather drawn-out and anomalous narrative of clues. It has the feel to it of Odradek, from Kafka's "The Cares of a Family Man": We listen to the uncanny syntheses between organic and inorganic materiality, between human and inhuman speech, and we wonder what the thing might be. The abstract machine is more and less than language. On the outside, it establishes linguistic structures and distinctions; on the inside, it is, like the body without organs, destratified, disarticulated. It is this moreness and lessness than language that must, as readers familiar with the expectations of text-based conceptual models, intrigue us.

While the overall thrust of the argument here is to assert that language is political before it is formally linguistic, any explicit characterization of language in Deleuze and Guattari's discourse reinforces the intransigent formal mechanics of language at the expense of its neat function as a political or capitalist tool. (This is in spite of the assertion that the abstract machine, "within" its precincts, eschews form-content distinctions.) Although Deleuze and Guattari gain us unprecedented theoretical access to the corporeal, the sociopolitical, and to artifacts, such as music, that are primarily articulate in time, they never outgrow the ambiguity of the division of labor they assign to language. Indeed, this schizo double bind is absolutely formative of their discourse. Criticism can pass with equanimity from microscopic, formal linguistic analysis to a macroanalysis of institutions, culture, and their interrelation, only at one expense—entering a condition of schizophrenia. All in all, this is not too high a stake to place on the gambling table of a critical game that so responsibly opens up the status and analysis of culture.

The abstract machine that is one of the major indicators and monitors of the manic flow just beneath the surface of liberal organized society is a social force in the guise of a language generator, a linguistic agent embued with social power. Never assuming the tangibility of a computer or political machine, the abstract machine eschews such purely logical distinctions as that between form and substance, operating at a level we may term presystematic, in the sense of pre-Oedipal. To be *diagrammatic, material* (though not physical), and *functional* is to operate as a language, but Deleuze and Guattari insist on a sociopolitical sphere of activity for the abstract machine, "a moment at which nothing but functions and matters remain." It does not play on the stage of history, for it is also prehistorical, but it "produces continuums of intensity, effects conjunctions of deterritorialization, and extracts expressions and contents."[26] In brief, it establishes the Foucauldian *épistème* according to which knowledge, for an age, is defined.

The abstract machine marshals and coordinates what we might call different stages of semiosis, again, in a sociolinguistic version of a Freudian-Lacanian model in which thoughts, memories, and signifiers pass from preconsciousness into the conscious and beyond: The abstract machine sets into play presignifying, signifying, countersignifying, and postsignifying semiotics, each corresponding to a degree of order and a manner of coding that a particular sociopolitical configuration or moment will allow. Allowing for a multiplicity of semiotic regimes, the abstract machine is the site for the "analogical transformations" by which the power relations of society are translated into differing discourses—rap songs, say, and the op-ed page of the *New York Times*.[27] From the perspective of the work done in departments of languages and literatures, the transformations and translations taking place under the aegis of the abstract machine are crucial. They have been well marked by our most polyvocal and synesthetic modern/postmodern authors, from Pound, Joyce, and Stein to Borges, Pynchon, and Acker.

It may remain an open question as to whether signs allow themselves to be hyperorganized into regimes, whether in the form or guise of machines, signs achieve sociopolitical actuality and effectiveness. It is to the threshold of this antinomy that Deleuze and Guattari lead us in their scenario of a palimpsest of outmoded and actual sociolinguistic machines fueled by "regimes of signs." Theoretically suspect as this impasse may be, it empowers philosophically responsible readings of cultural artifacts by linguistically acute readers at the same time that it remains an "open book." So powerful is Deleuze and Guattari's advocacy for a sociopolitics grounded in language but also for a language at the service of sociopolitics that this impasse must ultimately be left in their own terms:

> All methods for the transcendentalization of language, all methods for endowing language with universals . . . have fallen into the worst kind of abstraction. Regimes of signs are not based on language, and language alone does not constitute an abstract machine, whether structural or generative. The opposite is the case. It is language that is based on regimes of signs, and regimes of signs on abstract machines. . . . There is no universal propositional logic, nor is there grammaticality in itself, any more than there is signifier for itself.[28]

By Way of Inconclusive Conclusion

Deconstruction does not qualify, in the passage immediately above, as one of the discourses revolving around a transcendental signifier. With enormous philosophical rigor, it pursues a flow of quite mutable signifiers, marking their seeming convergences and divergences with a range of ideologies and the closure that such systems would implement. Deconstruction would surely not take issue with postmodern flow theory on its hypostatization of a language machine underpinning the formations of society and sociopolitical institutions. So where does the parting of the ways between this theory and deconstruction take place?

One place to start is the spatial agenda that Heidegger sets for language-intensive theory when he situates *Sein* in a clearing, implicates it in the play between a historical World, with affinities to the Saussurean *parole*, and a synchronic Earth whose activity and timeframe correspond rather to the Saussurean *langue*. Even by filling in *Sein*'s temporal dimension by dramatizing its invigoration through death, *Sein*, and by implication the discourse that modulates itself through the ongoing disclosure of and adjustment to its intractable linguistic features, remain the curious wards of a spatially configured world. The acuity of phenomenological and Frankfurt School models does not allow for the rehistoricization of flow theory in any simple or wholesale way, but a flow-oriented conceptual model is inherently keyed to matters of time. Surely Deleuze and Guattari are more concerned with matters of sociological formation than they are with history per se. It may well be that their vocation of accounting for social institutions and artifacts favors the temporal dimension opened up in discourse through the dynamics of flow.

As has been suggested above, it is the *jouissance* of flow theory to encompass and bring into mutual communication and illumination multiple registers of oversight: linguistic, psychosexual, political, visual, musical, whereas deconstruction tends to translate phenomena into signifiers or semiological signs and allegorical events. Flow theory revels in establishing *connections* between seemingly inimical phenomena and through these links or rhizomes in constructing a *system* striking in its psychosis as well as in its extent and power. The psychotic assemblage at which this discourse eventuates will be appreciated, decoded, or not. The route to these assemblages is somewhat of a one-way street.

Deconstruction, on the other hand, revels in disclosing, demonstrating, and allegorizing certain philosophico-critical *facilities*. These fit in quite well with a Western aspiration for intellectual transcendence in place at least since the foundations of modern aesthetics. While certain themes, such as flow itself, rhizomes, and corporeality are iterable from Deleuze and Guattari and will therefore generate mountains of "applications," the assemblages and machines that are their ultimate creations display a high degree of singularity and are hence dead-end constructions or fabulations. The achievement of deconstruction is therefore, oddly one more easily matched and measured against other approaches vaunted in the academic marketplace.

Yet in its pick-and-choose practice, flow theory will tend to see only its mania of the moment, whether for schizo culture, or claws, or chemically induced hallucinations, or picturesque sex, in what it addresses. The deconstructive ethics of reading, on the other hand, mandates a rather exhaustive exploration: of dissonances between concepts and constellations of signifiers, between signifiers and the ideological systems based on them, and of transformational relationships *between* signifiers. Flow theory is more idiosyncratic and specific in its choice of sites for critique and exemplification, while deconstruction is more general in its applicability. Virtually all signifying artifacts are ultimately qualifiable by deconstructive economies and countereconomies of signification, totalization, logocentrism, writing, trace, *différance*, dissemination, re-mark, and so on.[29]

Both theoretical models may be said to be infrastructural. In certain cases, there are even striking parallels between flow-predicated and deconstructive infrastructures, say between deterritorialization and marginality, between flow itself and dissemination, between segmentarity[30] and *différance*, between sociolinguistic and writerly machines. Yet postmodern flow theory deploys and works through the kinds of dialectical operations and paradoxes for which Hegel is famous, while the thrust of deconstructive readings is a modulation or resistance to dialectical structuration and thinking.

At the same time, the psychohistory in flow theory that moves toward a genealogy of the schizo state is so systematic and deep-seated that it dissolves the singularity of individual clinical cases, absolving individual schizos of responsibility for their actions in an always already schizoid world. In keeping with, above all, Guattari's ethos of liberation psychiatry, the schizo is more laudable, more open to a flux suppressed in banal normality, than culpable. Deleuze and Guattari are obviously not alone in this theoretical scenario. Lacan details the situation in which the subject belatedly enters the chain of signifiers that she must to some extent misrecognize or defile. The language that deconstruction addresses is certainly not idiosyncratic privatized discourse. For all deconstruction's questioning of the metaphysics of the individuated human subject and its spirituality, this discourse maintains a more urgent sense of personal ethics, in this case, applied at the hermeneutic level to an implicit (reading) subject, than postmodern flow theory, with its vision of a forbidding landscape under capitalism constituted by an assortment of different inhuman epistemological machines.

Binary structures are one of the raw materials that Deleuze and Guattari locate in the background of virtually all epistemo-sociological formations and whose workings they incorporate into their discourse. A particularly pivotal one of these oppositions on which their discourse builds is between the linguistic and the nonlinguistic. Their theory purports to offer access to nontextual or extratextual registers, but remains ambiguous regarding its own status. As we have seen, in places, their discourse repudiates pure textuality, yet elsewhere characterizes flow as a pure semiosis or writing. This ambiguity extends to their effort to distinguish such manifestations of unresolved flow as becoming death, becoming animal, and becoming music from simple regression, terming it instead an "involvement." It is at times impossible to escape the regressive tenor of the schizoid drives always capable of overcoming and redirecting society.

Deconstruction, for all the febrile play it traces between signifiers, tends to distribute them, as we have seen, in a spatial field, although its oversight surely encompasses sequences in signification. Postmodern flow theory accounts for speed, as well as territory or space. It therefore inherently presupposes a body and explores the conceptual and anthropological implications of certain corporeal paradigms. As we've noted, its openness to questions of temporality, velocity, and corporeality may make it the preeminent theoretical discourse for approaching music and possibly film in our day.

It is at the notion of the body that this provisional dialogue between text-based and flow-oriented theories leaves us. Both critical models have already generated and will continue to generate considerable bodies of textual and cultural analysis. There are unavoidable divergences between these bodies. Deconstruction lends a particular force and focus to the aspect of Kafka's writing intuiting the textual dynamics and constitution of culture, knowledge, and social institutions. The parable "Vor dem Gesetz" ("Before the Law"), which appears independently and terminates the "cloudy spot" near the end of *The Trial*, achieves its most powerful illumination as an allegory of textual production, displacement, and indeterminacy within the purview of deconstructive theory. Such a reading captures the famous parable's processes of interpretative proliferation and exclusion, as well as its resistance to monolithic meaning. It underscores the parable's function as a recapitulation, in miniature, of the novel's key motifs and theoretical issues. The inevitability of deconstruction to the parable's productive elucidation is indicative of its unique attunement to modernism's *jouissance* in the apriority of language to knowledge and culture.

But we need something else to deal with the uncanny whistling emanating from Josephine and the subterranean rodents who are her cohorts in "Josefine die Sängerin" ("Josephine the Singer or the Mouse Folk"). We could call the whistling textual, but its articulations are random and minimal, possibly falling below ordinary specifications of discourse. Whereas this parable, from a deconstructive viewpoint, details a textual oddity, presents us with a singular object, a threshold or borderline text, it occupies a solid position in several of the scenarios that coincide to construct flow theory. The "mouse folk" reside in a position of deterritorialization, a status akin to the deconstructive margin, but with sociopolitical resonance, as well. Their animality bespeaks a cultural gravitation to faciality and animal icons that Deleuze and Guattari situate at every stage of political formation registering on the palimpsest of history. Josephine is a pack leader in a devolution or "becoming animal" that remains an ongoing potential in the most sophisticated cultural configurations. Musicality, as embodied in her uncanny piping or singing (Kafka leaves its exact nature indeterminate), is a communicative register residing on the underside of discourse in advanced, rational, segmented, specialized culture.

The reading of the "Josefine" text that Deleuze and Guattari make possible responds to the Kafka who was uncannily sensitive to the implosion and destruction that lurked just beneath the surface of the early twentieth century's most efficiently or repressively organized societies. Flow theory is no more foolhardy than deconstruction in rushing to "fill in" the piping's significance and message. But it does build out a nonreductive context for the consideration of important sociopolitical conditions of economic, racial, ethnic, and gender domination that an increasing number of critics incorporate into its readings. Flow theory cannot outdo the rigorous, meticulous, ethical reading that deconstruction can furnish "Vor dem Gesetz," but it does open a space for the linguistically sensitive turn to social issues and institutions in criticism. It allows language to stop at viscosity before attaining the stratification of a structural architecture and an institutionally oriented discourse. It is a viscous architecture, one founded on soft structure, that this chapter, at its head, situated in Deleuze and Guattari.

Deconstruction and flow theory relate to one another in the supplementarity that it was Derrida's seminal inventiveness to articulate. They are different. They do things at least slightly differently. They do certain things better than each other. They both occupy a highly honored place on the palette of contemporary conceptual models. Having them both at our disposal is of considerable comfort and use in continuing the labor of cultural articulation in a millennial environment, when the public's investment in all modalities of literacy, in so-called "advanced" societies, is shakier than it has been for some time. This very attenuation is itself a superb subject (or is it object?) for analysis, whether by text or by flow.

SIX

Derrida as Critic: A Joycean Odyssey

At the outset of his essay "Ulysses Gramophone: Hear Say Yes in Joyce" (1987), which breaks new ground—it may well contain Derrida's most exuberant literary criticism—Derrida points out the anomalies to which straying into the vernacular gave rise in Descartes. Yet the commentary on Joyce there is advanced enough to stage the wider enquiry, one is tempted to write "allegory," into the ongoing implications, effects, suggestions, and heritage of deconstruction that characterizes much of the work since the late 1980s, especially deconstruction's extensions into religion, politics, and psychoanalysis:

> When at the end of the *Discours de la méthode*, Descartes explains why he had decided to write in the language of his country, the Latin translation of the *Discours* simply omits this paragraph. What is the sense of writing in Latin a sentence the gist of which is: the following reasons illustrate why I am now writing in French? It is true that the Latin translation was the only one violently to erase this affirmation of the French language.[1]

Why indeed, if the *Discours* is appearing in *Latin*, still the lingua franca of its day, should it specify that it is not in French? This is an absolutely logical question to raise at the outset of an exploration of Joyce, who will emerge on the photographic plate of the Derridean sensibility as a polylingual babeler and as a founding figure in a literary institution whose complexities are the equal of its ubiquity.

Descartes' Latin Translation

Descartes, according to Derrida's specification, was still quite susceptible to the linguistico-cultural politics that prevailed between the dominant tongue—the language of government, science, and social administration—and the vernacular. The latter tongue, whose domain coincided with local geography, had already usurped a considerable share of authority and credence formerly restricted to the Latin tradition and domain. Claims of priority, authority, and influence were at stake in the obvious elision of the claim, in a document in one language, that it is not in another.

It is not entirely by accident that the circumstances surrounding Descartes' Latin translation arise early in an essay that surveys Joyce's relation to deconstruction. Derrida's *Auseainandersetzung* with the Joyce establishment is a tour de force of professed ignorance on his part, disarming disclaimer, and ironic polemic, one that can easily extend to his status as an academic and an institution in his own right:

> All of you are experts, you belong to one of the most remarkable of institutions. It bears the name of a man who did everything, and admitted it, to make this institution indispensable, to keep it busy for centuries, as though on some new Tower of Babel to "make a name" again. . . .
> And you call to strangers to come and tell you, as I am doing in replying to your invitation: you exist, you intimidate me, I recognize your paternal and grandpaternal authority, recognize me and give me a diploma in Joyce studies.[2]

Professing the status of a "stranger" to the Joyce "family,"[3] Derrida counterpoises deconstruction's radical positionality and tropological reprogramming to the authority claimed by organizations, meetings, degrees, and chairs. Yet the image of Joyce that emerges from this process of photocritical development has already been scribed with interests and scenarios iterated from other scenes of deconstruction, whether prior or subsequent to "Ulysses Gramophone."

> *Finnegans Wake* is the sublime babelization of a *penman* and *postman*, the motif of postal difference, of remote control and telecommunication. . . .
>
>   Joyce experts are the representatives as well as the effects of the most powerful project for programming over the centuries the totality of research in the onto-logico-encyclopaedic field, all the while commemorating his own, proper signature. A Joyce scholar . . . has at his command the computer of all memory, he plays with the entire archive of culture, at least of what is called Western culture, and, in it, of that which returns to itself according to the Ulyssean circle of the encyclopaedia.[4]

Joyce's work, especially the late fiction, literally begs to be read in terms of the issues of translation, postal communications, and archiving that had or would come to the fore in such texts as *The Post Card*, "Des Tours de Babel," "The Eyes of Language," and *Archive Fever*.[5] By incorporating the paradox of Descartes' Latin translation into his intervention on Joyce, Derrida explicitly raises issues concerning "deconstruction's" relations to a range of affiliated literary, critical, exegetical, and cultural projects that it might have engendered, inspired, focused, or clarified, but that also might have functioned autonomously from its articulation, dissemination, and powerful persuasion, concurrently with its interventions or even, possibly, prior to them.

"Deconstruction," given the variegated division of labor it has taken on and the labyrinthine intricacy with which its complex tropes and radically refitted terminologies have been derived and set into motion, rapidly ceases to be a blanket term that one can apply with any degree of credibility. It names a broad compendium of attitudes, interventions, and positionalities still expanding, when last I looked, with an astonishingly wide-reaching public recognition factor for a set of readings, interpretations, and aesthetic projects (architecture, painting, and music are only a few of the art forms to have been powerfully affected in this sense) extending from or affiliated with Derrida's writings and public appearances. My personal encounters with deconstruction as a cultural construct, as it appears in journalism and the popular media, suggest that its subversive or destabilizing effect on what it addresses has come to the fore. Its linguistic bent and the rhetorical organization of its interventions or "acts" have also filtered into its wider public reception to a remarkable degree. Deconstruction is as much an atelier, the rubric for a more or less collective project with shared takeoff-off points and bearings on the part of its participants as it is the body of writings by Jacques Derrida and the rich array of his devices.[6] The Derridean project is so compelling in part due to the explicitness, rigor, and ethicality with which it mandates its challenge to the most pervasive because culturally transparent and systematically installed conceptual infrastructure underlying Western cultures. Yet even with this persistent questioning, disclosure, and reprogramming of conceptual givens as part of its express undertaking, as a community, "deconstruction" mobilizes the more or less shared attitudes characteristic of aesthetic or critical contracts. In a deconstruction-inspired study of my own, *The Aesthetic Contract*, I pondered the motives and conditions for such often-implicit agreements, which go a long way in characterizing the sequence of styles, experiments, and schools in the histories of art, literature, and speculation.[7]

The paradigm of Descartes' Latin translation in turn raises the questions of the affiliations and working agreements between Jacques Derrida's writings and other projects said to be deconstructive, whether direct products of the atelier, by longtime colleagues or students, inspired or in certain cases planned in conjunction with Jacques, or productions pulled into the deconstructive orbit through its momentum and gravitational force. These may consist of allied projects, such as the rhetorical readings whose specifications were so rigorously but also affectively formulated by Paul de Man. The cast of de Man's project and the drift of its intervention had been set long before the pivotal Derridean year of 1967. Yet by 1979, it was clearly in de Man's interest to inscribe a deconstructive scene or theater in each of the essays making up his *Allegories of Reading*, which became his major transitional work, transforming his productions from individuated critical essays, each with a specific philosophical and scholarly strategy, into reflections both joining and commenting upon the expansive body of contemporary critical theory.

Writing on Nietzsche, de Man characterized deconstruction as a demonstration[8] that transpires "with any use of language": "The deconstruction states the fallacy of reference in a necessarily referential mode. There is no escape from this, for the text also establishes that deconstruction is not something we can decide to do or not do at will. It is co-extensive with any use of language, and this use is compulsive."[9] In the context of detailed de

Manian readings in which artifacts and texts consistently retract the schemata configured for their intelligibility and in so doing deface and disfigure the deeper systemic motives for these figures, there is every reason for de Man to exemplify deconstruction as a rhetorical function located, as it were, within the articulation, transpiring consecutively with it. Within the deployment of what I have termed "critical contracts,"[10] a subinstance of aesthetic ones, in this performance, de Man lends his own formidable project's support to the gathering tide of deconstruction and appeals to its immanent public reception and effect. In return, de Man assures a certain minimum threshold for the recognition and effect of his own highly distinctive project, which like any other erudite intervention in the world of letters, circumscribed to a readership defined by shared hurdles of reading and schooling, runs the constant threat of consignment to obscurity.

The appropriation of deconstruction cited immediately above, while surely in keeping with de Man's precise and intricate stagings of figures at once quietly pervasive and congenitally flawed, both is and is not appropriate to its subject. To the degree to which deconstructive interpretations are uncannily adept in culling and then dissecting the often-occulted terms upon which entire systems (of logic, belief, government, and so on) hinge, de Man is right on target. Yet "deconstruction" was in a radical condition of evolution and reconfiguration in 1979, as it is today. Its definition as an infratextual battery of tropes and readings does not necessarily account for the full range of effects it has worked through the dispersion of its theater to a broad range of institutional and sociopolitical situations.

Derrida worked long and hard, with an intensity that de Man was able to recognize in its full Hegelian and Jamesian senses, to crystallize the most memorable deconstructive tropes, among them the *pharmakon*,[11] the gift,[12] the veil,[13] the heliotrope,[14] the knell,[15] the frame,[16] and the event,[17] out of unrelentingly intense readings. Yet he also exercised the liberty to displace these figures that both exemplify and deface meaning to other textual settings, that is, to additional sites of scriptural programming, where he recast and recombined them and directed them to a variety of tasks, some within and some beyond the constraints of close reading. As the library of deconstruction expanded and proliferated, it even became possible for Derrida to achieve a certain shorthand through the mobilization of existing figures or infrastructures, themselves resulting from precise exegeses, in what I would call superthematic readings of further artifacts, events, and states of affairs.

What are the stakes in the stock market of attributions linking method-ological paradigm to methodological paradigm, linking exegetical project to exegetical project? The lines of affiliation are at best tenuous, the reflux of influences vertiginous. Case in point: In 1974 or so, largely enabled by mind-boggling and utterly transformative participation in Derrida's spring 1971 seminar for American visitors to Paris under the auspices of Cornell University, whose subject was the proto-Surrealist nineteenth-century writer Lautréamont, I composed an early full-fledged "deconstructive" reading of Kafka's *Der Prozeß*, with an emphasis on the role of the parable "Before the Law" as a textual allegory or scene of writing. The approach was fresh enough at the time to enable the piece to appear in the January 1977 issue of *PMLA*.[18] Five years later, Derrida delivered his "Before the Law" to the Royal Philosophical Society in London and, later that summer, at Cérisy-la-Salle.[19]

The deconstructive purview on Kafka shifted away from one of many possible novices in the atelier to that of the inventor of deconstruction him-self. Derrida took the occasion to explore the multifaceted guises of "the Law" in Kafka's novel, including its status as a philosophical construct and moral imperative in systematic philosophy as epitomized, above all, by Kant. The fictive distortions and displacements to which Kafka subjects "the Law" become an instance of where and how literature as a perform-ance and an institution takes off from philosophy. "Before the Law" is not only a notable contribution to the "body" of "Kafka criticism." It is a semi-nal node in Derrida's negotiations with jurisprudence as a social institution as well as an academic discipline. As we will see, addressing such ongoing Western institutions as the law, politics, psychoanalysis, the Abrahamic reli-gions, and literature itself is a vital task in deconstruction's excursis and dissemination of its own relevance.

Indeed, deconstruction's extension to social institutions, its mobilization as a rigorous modality of social critique, constitutes a major intervention preempting Derrida's relegation to the status of a technical philosopher of language, a more strictly academic sphere of operation akin to being a struc-tural linguist. Derrida's insistence that deconstructive positions are more relevant to some of Western society's most deeply entrenched impasses than the procedures evolved by traditional social science constitutes a major step beyond the first wave of deconstructive elaborations, which are of the pro-cedures and instruments of representation, communications, and transmission: the postal system, the telephone, and eventually cybernetics.[20] Left on their own, even the pivotal exegeses constituting Derrida's studies of Husserl, Heidegger, Kant, Hegel, Nietzsche, and Freud would deposit him in the status of a linguistically driven philosopher with strong technological side interests.

Derrida's later engagements with religion, psychoanalysis, and the academy occupy the position first taken, in the canon of psychoanalysis, by *Jokes and Their Relation to the Unconscious* and later by such additions as *Totem and Taboo* and *Moses and Monotheism*. The unconscious was surely as tough a commodity for Freud to sell to the public as the complex circumlocutions by which ideology founders on the sign systems and other media that announce and enact it. Religion and politics are social institutions almost as pervasive as the Freudian laughter that "proves" the existence and activity of the unconscious, or some parallel archive, by erupting before reason, understanding, or the conscious can "process" the joke's messages.[21] Without the bridge to social relevance, however intricate its engineering, furnished by Derrida's explorations into religion, politics, and psychoanalysis (the latter largely concurrent with his lifetime commentary), he would be held hostage to the debunkings of logocentrism that he devised and performed with unprecedented focus and breadth.

As an atelier of thinking, deconstruction consistently functioned as an environment in which a student or a colleague could take a "first crack" at a major work and subsequently learn of the results crystallized by the inventor. Indeed, over the years, much of deconstruction's agenda, tones, and directions have been set by its students. This is surely one of the distinctive features of the Derridean environment. A major motivating factor in deconstruction's outreach to psychoanalysis, religion, law, and politics has been its students' call for tangible engagements with the persistent impasses exasperating the contemporary world.

When I performed my early, full-fledged deconstructive exegesis of *Der Prozeß* in 1974, I was not prepared to ponder the law as a concept conditioned by the broader history of Western philosophy or to project the history of literature as an infraphilosophical body of artifacts. Thirty years later, I am not much better prepared to argue on that level than I was in those days. I subscribed and submitted at that time to a division of labor whose tasks and bearings I associated with literary criticism. My first and foremost obligation, I assumed, was to the puzzlement presented by Kafka's novel. Although my treatment would need eventually to draw some conclusions with regard to the work's significance and place within the overall trajectory of European culture, the large question mark to which *Der Prozeß* was coequal broke down into a host of dimensions: compositional, formal, rhetorical, grammatical, syntactic, semantic. My critical role carried with it a responsibility for addressing every dimension of the novel's mystery that was discernible to me, to produce a reading, moreover, that established some coherence between the respective responses to its multifaceted challenges. I was not terribly preoccupied by any consistency between the response that *Der Prozeß* would elicit from me—between the particular materials and reactions that it would mobilize—and my scriptoral response to the next big puzzle, the next major artifact, in my intellectual trajectory.

With Derrida's delivery and subsequent publication of "Before the Law," I was upstaged, in the world of Kafka criticism, by the writer through whose marvelous teaching I was first primed to recognize Kafka as a compelling literary interest. This vertigo of hints, resonance, elective affinities, and appropriations extends to the cultural properties to which deconstruction first gravitates. Did certain of the compositions of Artaud,[22] Ponge,[23] Blanchot,[24] Kafka, Celan,[25] and Joyce inspire readings by Derrida because of some "intrinsic" inventiveness, or because they were already "scored" or inscribed with deconstructive figures and scenarios? Is the Borgesian library of texts by the quite singular Jacques Derrida a compendium of cues that he took from modernism's progenitors, among many literatures he has assimilated and to which he had recourse? Or did the likes of Kafka, Ponge, and Celan have to meet prescribed deconstructive criteria before they qualified to elicit Derrida's critical scrutiny? It was gratuitous, unnecessary for Descartes' Latin translation to declare that a variant of it had earlier appeared in French. Once the still extending veil and texture of deconstructive figures coalesces, what is the status of the cultural materials out of which they were woven? Are they "masterworks" whose deconstructive readouts simply join existing responses under the auras of different critical paradigms? Or are these cultural "properties," these occasions for critical inscription, easily substitutable prompts to masterful writing, whose future cultural currency largely consists in their deconstructive treatment?

Joyce under the Aura of Deconstruction

In the remarkably inventive and playful essay "Ulysses Gramophone,"[26] the Joyce literature gains one of its most performative contributions and Der-

rida takes the opportunity to address an already long-simmering controversy between his script and literary scholarship, particularly as practiced in
the United States. The essay hardly sounds like a work of systematic philosophy, and for reasons that it is quick to make explicit, violates many of the
standard expectations surrounding literary criticism. Following in the wake
of "The Double Session," it breaks new ground in articulating what the
literary might entail from a philosophically rigorous point of view. Indeed,
in the narrative that it encompasses and stages, partly autobiographical (or
otobiographical),[27] one roughly contemporaneous to the playful experimentation of *The Post Card* (1980), "Ulysses Gramophone" constitutes a literary
work in its own right. This text, in the bold swath it cuts through the field
of general writing, thus surveys a megadifference that has begun to prevail
between deconstruction's hybrid discourse and the preexisting conventions
of literary knowledge—its reception, annotation or archiving, and dissemination. It serves in this regard as a useful context for differences in the
critical division of labor that it is the current study's ambition to elaborate.

It is clear that Derrida's overall response to the task before him, namely,
to address the 1982 meeting of the International Joyce Society, was to compose a text, in an obliquely Joycean vein, that would supplement the existing
literature without subjugating itself to its already operative laws. More specifically, he substitutes a text, another text, for a structured, or predetermined "contribution." Derrida's reaction to a summons—with full Kafkan
overtones—to appear before the regulative body of an "intellectual field"
so structured as to be exemplary of all disciplines and studies so constituted,
that is, founded on the possession, empirical "treatment," and control of a
certain "property," in this case "literary," is to supplement Joyce's writing
with a text reverberating off it, but one alien to the regulative protocols that
have arisen since the Joycean composition, even if these standards were to
some extent dictated by Joyce himself. Derrida responds in a general sense
to the commission he has accepted by synthesizing an occasional text, one
receptive to Joycean inventions and tonalities, but one also extending and
predicating the expansive network of deconstructive scenes and figures.

One does not frontally enlarge or redirect "fields of knowledge," argues
Derrida by means of this stratagem. "All" one can do is to secrete texts
along resonant lines of composition. Joyce may provide the "occasion" for
Derrida's current composition, the text of "Ulysses Gramophone," but it is
only in a limited sense that even the great "Irish modernist master" "dic-

tates" or determines this critical commentary. One may sense a resistance on Derrida's part to the institutional dimension of this scholarly occasion, the Joycean congress, just as on other occasions he points out resistances to his own megaproject. Yet one can "read through" this contrary attitude an empowerment, indeed responsibility, on the part of other writers with exegetical tasks, to generate their own texts, however idiosyncratic or problematical, rather than acquiesce to a mechanical and to some degree mindless "filling out of the field."

What are the elements of the singular, thorny text that Derrida composes in the wake of *The Post Card* and for the Ninth International James Joyce Symposium?

First, in a Joycean vein and in keeping with his critique of "The Law of Genre," Derrida incorporates a narrative into his own "critical essay," and it is one colored by the coincidences and chance meetings of the sort highlighted in *Ulysses*. In the Joycean text, of course, coincidences abound around the meaning of "throwaway." Personae, whether Bloom, Stephen, Molly, Simon, Nosey Flynn, or the H.E.L.Y.S. sandwichmen, circulate randomly throughout the city, scraps of meaning as much as "characters." In "Ulysses Gramophone," "Jacques Derrida," "driving along with my mother . . . in a Paris Street," catches sight of the same Jean-Michel Rabaté with whom he has been arranging his International Joyce Conference appearance. "This coincidence must have been 'telephoned' in some way" is the critical summation, introducing the technologies of communication, reproduction, and transmission pivotal to deconstruction's linguistic purview as to Derrida's decoding of Joyce.[28] In Tokyo, a place in *Ulysses* and a spot in Derrida's global odyssey at the time, Jacques discovers a title in a hotel bookshop, *16 Ways to Avoid Saying No*, with uncanny resonance for the issue of affirmation, both the signifiers "yes" and "oui," and as a rhetorico-philosophical figure and event constituting Derrida's most purely conceptual interest in Joyce. Yet in its orthography, "Tokyo" is inextricably linked to "Ohio," another place in *Ulysses*, but also the seat of the James Joyce Foundation at the time and the source of the Dannon yogurt brand whose slogan is "Bet You Can't Say No to Yes."[29] (The fact that "Tokyo" and "Ohio" both contain doubled "o"s, combined with the linkage of this dominant vowel to the French affirmative, "oui," points to a subverbal and even subsyllabic instance of a coincidence that Derrida finds pivotal to language and the rigorous exegesis of the ideological constructions manufactured out of it. He productively explores this microscopic linguistic slippage and dissemination, above all in "The Double Session" and *Glas*.

Derrida lards "Ulysses Gramophone" with the narrative not only of his contemporary Homeric travels, but also of his appearance at the International Joyce Conference and what it means to him. The storytelling of *The Post Card*, in which Jacques engages in an epistolary exchange that is and is not "romantic," shuttles between Oxbridge, the United States, and other locations. This jet-setting criticism is the framework for piecing together the traditions and anomalies of transmission radiating from a medieval print of Plato dictating to Socrates and extending to Heidegger and Freud.

This critical storytelling, or this narrative absorbed within a critical task, takes on a somewhat different cast and tonality when its cultural occasion becomes "Joyce." The ultimate story of *The Post Card* may well concern the emergence of a reading and the crystallization of the traits of a megatradition amid a sequence of intellectual and academic transactions. The narrative element of "Ulysses Gramophone" forces us to reconsider the nature of scholarly contributions at a moment when, through "The Law of Genre," their traits and parameters have entered an unprecedented, but always implicit fluidity.

Second, Joyce's refusal to confine his later fiction to any single linguistic culture or nationality prompts a Derridean meditation on translation, so central to Western civilization that its canonical allegory, the "Tower of Babel" episode, appears quite early in Genesis. "The affirmation of a language through itself is untranslatable. . . . According to a distinction I have hazarded concerning history and the name of Babel, what remains *untranslatable* is at bottom the only thing to *translate*, the only thing *translatable*. What can be translated of that which is translatable can only be untranslatable."[30] These are anomalies that had been most fully explored by Walter Benjamin in "The Task of the Translator,"[31] whose implications for Hebrew as both a sacred and a secular language Derrida would explore in "Des Tours de Babel."

Derrida sets out from problems surrounding the translatability of the affirmative "yes" or "oui," which is perhaps his philosophically most far-reaching point—the affirmative, whether of language's intelligibility or communicability, embedded in the basic performatives of language itself, including the signature. In *Ulysses*, this arbitrary affirmation may well receive its most telling literary staging. The problems of translation to which it precipitously gives rise push the analysis toward the polyglot babelian amalgam of *Finnegans Wake*.

Third, Derrida's most sustained literary intervention with respect to *Ulysses* is a pointed questioning of the long-standing characterization of "Penelope" as "Molly's monologue." The primary feature of this segment that resonates most tellingly for Derrida is its role as a medium for Molly's affirmation, often taken synecdochically as the summation of all affirmation in the novel. Derrida, much in keeping with his evolving project, opens up a differential field for the "yeses" and "ouis" throughout the novel and even within the microclimate of "Penelope." If "Penelope" is itself dialogical, and even polyphonic, then some of the truisms of the Joyce literature, especially attributing unities, whether to "Penelope" or to *Finnegans Wake*, strongly stand in need of reconsideration.

Fourth, the title of Derrida's intervention links it directly to his long-standing fascination with communications media, the telephony and telegraphy that elaborate the Husserlian scenario of representational autoaffectivity so central to Derrida's early studies of that philosopher,[32] and with the cybernetics highlighted in his later work. It is no accident that a significant portion of "Ulysses Gramophone" gravitates toward the "Aeolus" episode of Ulysses, set in the editorial offices of *The Evening Telegraph* and consisting of fragmentary interjections cast as newsflashes, each with a catchy journalistic title or caption. This chapter occupies an analogous position in Joyce's fiction to that occupied by "The Work of Art in the Age of Its Technological Reproductability" in Benjamin's. "Ulysses Gramophone" consolidates Derrida's intervention into the field of critical media studies, which had begun in earnest in *The Post Card* in its exploration of the postal system.

Fifth, in appropriating Joyce as a fellow impresario of Western ideology's convolutions and aporias with respect to language and the media of representation, Derrida is most attentive to Ulysses' embedded religious allegory, particularly with respect to Bloom's "outsider" status as a Jew. One could well argue that the religious drama of "Ulysses Gramophone" is pivotal, for in shifting the field toward the literary and away from the more conceptual illuminations of Levinas,[33] Hegel (in *Glas*), Heidegger,[34] and even Jabès,[35] Derrida opens deconstruction to the more empathic and forgiving approach to religion that one senses in his later, theology-oriented pieces. I will attempt to consolidate this point in the closing chapter, "The Fourth Abrahamic Religion?"

In his reading of *Ulysses*, Derrida gravitates to the messianic strain of Bloom's Judaism that Joyce underscores. This includes not only the fabulation of "ben Boom Elijah" at the end of "Cyclops," but the references to fundamentalist American evangelism centering on the figure of Alexander J. C. Dowie. Derrida attributes the narrative voice of the cry to Jerusalem to "Open your gates and sing" to "the Gramophone, the character and the voice"—like the affirmation, an *im*personal figment/function of language to which Joyce's ". . ." gives free rein.[36]

In keeping with the strand of semi-autobiographical narrative that he has installed in the essay, Derrida diverts the mock-heroic prophetic messianic hyperbole that Joyce applies to Bloom to Elie, the French form of "Elijah," which happens to be his own familial, nonpublic name. The strong presence of Elijah in *Ulysses* links the infrastructural figure of affirmation in language to the mission shared by the three Abrahamic religions:

> I pronounce *Elie* in the French way, but in the English name for Elijah, Molly's *Ja* can be heard echoing. . . . And the voice of the one who says "yes." Elijah saying to those who are in the *vibration* (a key word in my view) that they can call him any time, straightaway . . . without using any technique or postal system, but going by the sun . . . we could say photophone or heliophone.[37]

The figure Elijah indexes the graft or suture between a certain affirmative thrust or draw in the impersonal network of language and a technology of immediate communication with the transcendental built into the mythology shared by the Abrahamic religions. It turns out as well that:

> I too am called Elijah: this name is not inscribed, no, on my official documents. But it was given me on my seventh day. Moreover, Elijah is the name of the prophet present at *all* circumcisions. He is the patron, if we can put it like this, of circumcisions. The chair on which the newborn baby is held is called "Elijah's chair." . . . A Midrash tells how Elijah had complained about Israel's forgetting circumcision. God is then supposed to have given him the order to be present at all circumcisions, perhaps as punishment. This scene of signature could have been marked with blood connecting all the announced passages concerning the prophet to the event of circumcision, the moment of entry into the community, of alliance and legitimation. At least twice in *Ulysses* there are references to the "collector of prepuces."[38]

This is a pivotal passage in "Ulysses Gramophone," supplying a very personal interest, his familial name, that Derrida takes in *Ulysses*' "programming over the centuries . . . over the entire archive of culture—at least of what is called Western culture."³⁹ This passage offers an exegetical, ultimately linguistic scenario for the entrance of an individual into a "family" or community, a community of interpretation, by means of the rite of circumcision that would come to the fore, and foreskin, in "Circonfession."⁴⁰ *Ulysses* also "takes cognizance" of this rite of socialization and identification with a community. The Prophet's diegetic address to the community that he hopes to reform, to prepare for messianic redemption, is highly redolent of Derrida's *Auseinandersetzung* with the Joyceans. This stance, which is antagonistic, but in a loving and pedagogical way, is in turn emblematic of the philosopher's posture: the role assumed by one who has labored hard over many years to delineate, translate, and reprogram a vast, encompassing civilizational operating system as he addresses the priesthood of the local religion, corrupt and self-interested through ingrained habits of stewardship and preservation, if not through stupidity. In this encounter, someone is going to lose a foreskin. And while Derrida graciously telegraphs ahead the bases on which his may disappear—"All of you are experts, you belong to one of the most remarkable of institutions"—he is not without his own preemptive strikes pointing to the priests' congenital limitations.⁴¹

The encounter between Jacques and the Joyceans is highly suggestive, if not paradigmatic, for all the essays that make up the chapters in the present volume, because it furnishes a scene or setting for the inherently flawed dramatic script juxtaposing for immediate disqualification and rejection the prevalent discursive models available to cultural commentary—poetry, philosophy, close reading, and "criticism proper"—that I hope to set into play for the benefit of the critical community, among other purposes, but doing so only after a thought process I consider intrinsically worthwhile. Even within the always tentative categories that I posit, "Ulysses Gramophone" is, above all, a respectful, rigorous, and brilliant contribution to the *critical* literature.

That Jacques on occasion—and occasion is pivotal to my own idiosyncratic *mise en scène* for criticism—could function admirably, even exemplarily, as a critic is a testament to his own polymorphous discourse, akin to Joyce's polylingual one, and a decisive rejoinder to "The Law of Genre." But the performance of "Ulysses Gramophone" is preceded and, in some nonconventional sense, predicated by years of decoding and intervention at the infrastructural level of the philosophical operating system undergirding

Western thought and to some degree characterizing non-Western systems. Lest we mistake some of the controversies prevailing in the community or family whose dynamics are indicated with such lucidity in the above passage and throughout "Ulysses Gramophone"—say between "critical theory" and "cultural studies" as "essential"—we need to devote careful attention to how the contemporary discursive division of labor, as exemplified by the standoff between the inventor of deconstruction and the "conventional Joyceans" affects our productions and our "findings."

In keeping with the issues and criteria articulated with such lucidity in "The Law of Genre," but "signaled ahead" by the interdiscursive experiments on the part of, among others, Baudelaire, Mallarmé, Kafka, Joyce, Benjamin, and Pound, contemporary discourse synthesizers are free to wander in the specific sense between the discursive parameters of poetic enunciation, philosophy, and close reading as the situation or occasion arises, demands, and allows. To explore this liberty in some detail, however provisional, may disseminate a degree of empowerment not evident throughout the entire critical "family." The responsibility sure to supplement this "difficult freedom" will be increased attentiveness to the range of discursive, rather than essential or politically motivated differences within the overall factory of disciplinary letters. There surely are politically significant differences between segments and members of the academic community. But these, as the likes of Derrida, Miller, and de Man have been teaching for two generations now, are more likely the outgrowth of discursive modalities, whether described as tropological, rhetorical, or performative, than the inverse: the dictates of predetermined, essentialistically antagonistic political stances.

Last of all, having ushered in his far-reaching project with serious qualifications to exterior/interior compartmentalizations constituting the very ground plan of reductive thought, Derrida, in his Epistle to the Joyceans, nevertheless marks, straddles, and effaces such boundaries. He resorts to bearings and positions founded upon the very parameters that they delimit.

Derrida addresses the Joyce establishment as a stranger, an outsider, yet his contribution to its collective literature and archive makes him very much "one of them." By placing his intervention at the outer benches of the Joycean Talmudic academy, Derrida initiates and joins in an empathic reception of and meditation upon the tangible Other, the stranger, the immigrant, which reaches a humane crescendo in "Hostipitality."[42]

Joyce remains a stranger to me, as if I did not know him. Incompetence, as they are aware, is the profound truth of my relationship to this work, which I know after all only [in]directly. . . .

On the other hand, it must be realized at the same time, and *you realize this*, that the signature and the *yes* that occupy you, are capable—it is their distinction—of destroying the very root of this legitimacy, of its domestic interiority, capable of deconstructing the university institution. . . .

Hence the mixture of assurance and distress that one can sense in "Joyce scholars." From one point of view, they are as crafty as Ulysses, knowing, as did Joyce, that they know more, that they always have one more trick up their sleeve. Whether it is a question of totalizing summary or subatomistic micrology . . . no-one does it better. . . . But from another point of view, this hypermnesic interiorization can never be closed upon itself. . . . So you have the feeling, given that nothing can take you by surprise from inside, that something might eventually happen to you from an unforeseeable outside.[43]

Joyce is as much a "stranger" to Jacques as he applies the same term to himself, an expert witness of sorts, summoned to testify before the "experts, belonging to the most remarkable of institutions." Yet in the second extract immediately above, Jacques switches from a direct apostrophic address to his "insider" Others, who "realize . . . that the signature and the *yes* . . . occupy you" to the alienated characterization of his auditors in the third person—crafty, but capable of a solipsistic self-enclosure, obsessive and archivistic, rendering them obtuse to "surprise," to unforeseen "happening" in their exegesis and thinking.[44] Derrida literally switches off the interlocutors he engages, from first-person intimacy to third-person remoteness. Unbeknownst to them, he ascribes to them an authentic interest in the affirmative of language and the event of the signature. He inscribes them within these deconstructive rhetorico-linguistic scenes. Yet he constantly performs and demarcates a tangible distance from these conventional critics, even at the expense of professing an "intimidation" before them.[45]

On a subliminal level, then, Derrida invests in a writerly "outside"—a surprise that might issue from "an unforeseeable outside"—whose conceptual basis he has put under exquisite questioning since the outset of his written traces. This outside may well go the way of the necessary rhetorical delusions inevitably "deconstructed," in Paul de Man's apt rhetorical exegeses, by further rhetorical constructs generated within the specific texts in which the *fatae morganae* appear. The surprise capable of bursting on the scene from this outside may well be related to Joyce's general divorce from academic institutionality, to whatever degree he may have "primed" a few studies by associates and contemporaries, including Stuart Gilbert[46] and Frank Budgen.[47] A construct something like this general "outsideness" may well inflect certain of the less explicitly philosophico-academic interventions by Walter Benjamin.

I would like to conclude this hardly systematic review of Derrida's critical intervention in "Ulysses Gramophone" by suggesting some of its fault lines that allow for the diegetic *Auseinandersetzung* between Jacques/Elijah and the International Joyce Society membership and that I posit as indicative of some of the options along the continuum or family tree of contemporary cultural elucidation. As in the case of any critical rendering of artifacts and the figures who offer them up, we need to check the plausibility of the rousingly affirmed, but also significantly updated profile of Joyce that emerges from his essay.

The image of Joyce that Derrida contributes both to the collective body of Joyce studies and to his own proliferating intervention is one that both extends the knowledge and wisdom that have accrued now for eight decades and affirms, after the fact, deconstruction's scenography and tropology. Derrida attributes to Joyce "the declared project of keeping generations of university scholars at work for centuries of babelian edification," a project that

> must itself have been drawn up using a technological model and the division of university labor that could not be that of former centuries. The scheme of bending vast communities of readers and writers to this law, of detaining them by means of an interminable transferential train of translation and tradition, can equally well be attributed to Plato and Shakespeare, to Dante and Vico, without mentioning Hegel and other finite divinities. But none of these could calculate, as well as Joyce did, his feat, by modifying it in accordance with certain types of world research institutions.[48]

Taking off from the status of major Western universities in the 1920s, the Joycean imaginary was surely capable of extrapolating the contemporary research university and its position as a node in a vast and expanding global information network. Joyce was an inveterate newspaper reader and collector of clippings that he found, in some register, striking. The extremely erudite and capable archivists at one of the universities where I teach, the University at Buffalo, a city whose Abbott family happened, beginning in the 1920s, to assemble one of the preeminent collection of Joyce materials in the world, assure us that the phrasings and word sequences of *Finnegans Wake* draw heavily on Joyce's singular practice of reading and storing newspapers. My university *owns* Joyce's newspaper clippings.

But the degree of Joyce's commitment to the reception and global preservation, analysis, and dissemination of his works and reputation and his attentiveness to institutions, the substrate for such work and its facilitation, may be a bit overstated. The biography and the journalistic sources suggest that while priming the pump for the emergence of a Joycean institution—as Freud did for his clinical practices and the publications they occasioned—James Joyce lived at a relative remove from institutions and the support, disciplinary constraints, and sociological imperatives that they offer. The "immediate" Joyce family suffered material deprivations and social disorientation for years as the result of the author's insistence on aesthetic and writerly "autonomy," whatever that might be. His highest academic appointment, with no benefits, was as an instructor of English at the Berlitz institute in Trieste. Joyce did not achieve anything resembling financial stability until the late 1910s, when he secured the patronage of Harriet Weaver, Sylvia Beach, Eugene Jolas, and others.[49] Derrida was surely more a creature of "world research institutions" than Joyce was, or Benjamin, for that matter.

It has been obvious since 1922, when *Ulysses* first appeared, and likely beforehand, given Joyce's talent for drumming up interest in his works "in progress," that Joyce was intensely aware of the media and the means of the reproduction, transmission, dissemination, and distribution of script and writing. Not only the newspaper office scene ("Aeolus"), but also the recurrent references to the Dublin tram and water systems (in "Ithaca," for example)[50] make this point. But Derrida's descriptive language, in the above passage, of Joyce "bending vast communities of readers and writers to this law, of detaining them," resorts to uncharacteristic force and violence. It may not be Joyce who is caught up in this system of institutional affiliation, support, housing, preservation, discipline, and sanction to the systematic degree that Derrida asserts. It may not be Joyce who has calculated, as one who prepares an investment portfolio, the returns he may accrue from the network of typography-gramophony-telephony-radio-television-cybernetics-World Wide Web: a study that Derrida has managed to take at least one turn beyond the overview synthesized by the "Irish modernist master."

Surely, although in no simplistic way, matters including the nature, degree, and stability of financial support and institutional affiliations do affect the production of writing. These factors become inscribed in the tangible synthesis of a written medium, as registered in generic choices, rhetorical ploys, stylistics, and related features. In both *The Post Card* and "Ulysses Gramophone," Derrida's narratives implant an anecdotal level within demonstrations by a globe-trotting, highly visible and sought-out professional philosopher. These anecdotes do not bear the same architectural stress as, say, the "free-standing" narrative structure of *Ulysses*, for which, however schematically ingenious, Joyce was compelled to make far-reaching decisions concerning time, place, sequence, characterization, and the "appropriation" of fictive experiment to episode and "event." Through a dynamic that I have elsewhere attempted to formulate, the "creative artist" is forever pushing the envelope of innovation, the effacement of existing paradigms, and the anomalous, but within a broader contractual understanding of the "state of the art" at the moment.[51] In both *Ulysses* and *Finnegans Wake*, Joyce assumes this particular mantle of "the artist," with magnificent results. Given the risks he took in producing both works—he committed considerable chunks of time to projects whose prospective recognition and acceptance were at best iffy—his ultimate rewards were considerable. The risk taking, of course, puts Joyce more in the position of the Hegelian "master" than that of the "bondsman," but had rewards been his sole motivation, Joyce could have "accessed" far more dependable enterprises into which to sink his time and efforts.

Surely, as Derrida speculates in "Ulysses Gramophone" and throughout his *Acts of Literature* interview with Derek Attridge, literature is an institution.[52] I, for one, among so many others, belong to it. For different reasons, other writers, including Joyce himself, Kafka, Pound, and Benjamin, were not nearly as successful as Derrida—and, for that matter, the rank-and-file full professor—in forging these ties of ongoing support and disciplinary and professional recognition. The world of letters is surely all the richer for the detachment maintained by and imposed upon these and the other inventive modernists. It bespeaks a temporary and fated "outsideness" that provokes the most resonant access to the equally chimeric "inside," incubator for the initially idiosyncratic "private" cries, musings, and "introjections" serving as the springboard for aesthetic utterance.

The division of labor implicit in Derrida's address to the Joyceans as a "stranger" or some sort of Other is that one has already been effaced and disqualified, to a significant degree, *before the fact*. After all, Derrida had read *Ulysses* closely several times and counted its "yeses" in at least two different languages. In his work on Joyce—and this is true of all of his interventions—he does not shy away from the pedestrian labor of accounting and indexing performed by the Bartlebys of literature, and indeed by all of us who engage in the dirty work of tracing the vicissitudes of specific signifiers through intricate and multilayered texts. Derrida's philosophical speculation, indeed, has been marked from the outset by the elbow grease he has been willing to expend on hard-core scholarship, etymological excavation, and simple tabulation. His dedication to the general task of inscription has not preempted him, as a philosopher of writing, from undertaking the actuarial and archival labor demanded by his interventions. Derrida recognized an important facet of his own work among the Joyceans in the audience of the Ninth International Joyce Conference. These were not drones mired in mindless functions of storage, filing, and annotation. Among them numbered full-fledged critics, such as the notorious Jean-Michel Rabaté, who have brought the formats, categories, and meditations of philosophy to bear on Joyce. Beyond the framework of "Ulysses Gramophone," these scholars would morph into the denizens of *Archive Fever*, the workers who implement contemporary culture's rage for information, records, documentation, and proof.[53]

In the interview with Derek Attridge that heads *Acts of Literature*, Derrida specifically addresses the interface between philosophy and literature:

> There are hierarchies, there are relations of force: as much in literary criticism, moreover, as in philosophy. They aren't the same ones. The fact that literary criticism is dealing with texts declared "literary," and of which we were saying just now that they suspend the metaphysical thesis, must have effects on criticism. It is difficult to speak *in general* of literary criticism. . . . As an institution . . . I think it must have tended, precisely because it wanted to be theoretical, to be more philosophical than literary criticism itself. . . . It is perhaps more metaphysical than the literary texts it speaks about. . . . In general literary criticism is very philosophical in its form, even if the professionals in the matter haven't been trained as philosophers, or if they declare their suspicion of philosophy. Literary

criticism is perhaps structurally philosophical. What I am saying here is not necessarily a compliment.[54]

In this passage, criticism emerges as the philosophical supplement to literature, whose speculative pretext is often effaced or elided, but which stops shy of fully assimilating philosophy's protocols and lessons. It is, in the terminology of science fiction, a philosophical cyborg: In many respects, it looks and sounds the same, but doesn't quite share the same wiring. With respect to literary criticism, as to the collective enterprise of Joyce studies, Derrida is drawn to the institutional, as opposed to the discursive manifestations of the entity, to its sociological installation. Activating a form/substance distinction, Derrida allows criticism the *form* of philosophical reasoning, but minus the *pith* of some of its lessons and minus the *momentum* and *refinement* of its training.

This sense of the difference between philosophy and its critical Other has been derived from years of shuttling between the two camps. It is surely authoritative. As significant as Derrida's cumulative sense of the different products engendered by both institutions is the parallel course on which he sets the two discourses. Were he to extend this highly suggestive "take" emerging under conditions of a "live" interview, he might want to specify further criticism's inherent deficits in relation to philosophy and also to posit the inverse, to enumerate the functions and postures with which philosophy tends to dispense and that literary criticism takes upon itself as its implicit mission. Among these *Aufgaben* are surely the motive to relate ideational investments to formal improvisations and the assimilative effort to work a broad range of data sources stemming from the artifact into a broadly coherent, if not logically cohesive explanatory narrative.

Derrida's greatest and most enduring legacy, a notion he develops comically in *The Post Card*, may well consist of the empowerment he has liberated, through meticulous reading and the inventive (structured) deployment of linguistic resources, for all writers as individuals engaged in an interchange and negotiation with culture. The figures that he deploys and resources that he accesses, through his always rigorous, specific, and in this sense, respectful readings, are available to the entire spectrum of cultural workers, whether self-professed theorists or editors. It is in this sense entirely misrecognized and even tragic that the distance and division of labor implied in Derrida's address to the Joyceans should haunt our academic departments, professional associations, and even senses of our own personal worth and self-esteem. This haunting may well constitute the pivotal figure in Derrida's writings on religion (and other subjects), to which we will turn below.

Participation in the community of what I have elsewhere[55] termed "literacy workers"—teachers, journalists, publishers, artists, museum curators and other "arts managers," as well as disciplinary academics—thus requires an active engagement with the ghosts of this tradition, a predetermined cultural division of labor. Derrida would call it a "responsible" engagement. It helps for us to carry along a traffic map of what we can and cannot expect from the diverse strands and registers of our discourse, and I will continue in my effort to draft that map in this and the remaining chapters. But the drift of Derrida's "Law of Genre" is surely a collective scene of writing within which, assuming rigor and respect—respect, for example, for the "local difference" between texts and between other specific cultural microclimates—it is possible to cross and dissolve gender lines in the ex-orbiting process of inscription and cultural annotation.

By Way of Intervention

In light of contemporary critical theory's multivarious contributions over the past forty years, we now require a definition of higher education much akin to the negotiation between two tongues, between an individual's "patrimonial languages," as replete with biases and cultural baggage of all sorts as we would expect it to be, and the discourses of the respective disciplines, we would hope "set" to the highest degree of theoretical rigor possible. We need to distance ourselves from such traditional models of formation as a subject's socialization into a wider community or inculcation into a profession, the latter with an inherently salutary specialized science and practice.

It is incumbent upon us, in the flow and aftershocks of the theoretical reformatting of intellectual and cultural work, to rethink the assignments extracted from students throughout the history of "education" as the proofs of successful transmission or progress. A student's response to a course of study should be less the microcosm of or a contribution to an existing field of study of which the instructor is a professed master than an intervention within the being in the world that has been opened up, set into play, by the artifacts or "material" under scrutiny. There is literally a world of difference between an assignment, the standard term paper (a phrase also linked to prison terms) and an intervention, a pointed response by an enfranchised language operator and cultural programmer in training (and who among us is not still such a trainee?) whose qualification resides in an informed encounter with issues of representation, figuration, textuality, difference, dissemination, and mediation. In this sense, a plausible intervention that may be asked of students is a response, in the Derridean sense of responsibility, in any discourse, medium, or material at hand, to the provocations, possibilities, and hypotheses posed by the artifact. To empower the interventions of students and associates, it is particularly crucial to recognize the viability and fertility of the media and sign systems in which they may elect to couch their responses, regardless of our fluency in them.

It has occurred to all of us that a stage or film adaptation of an artifact involves the same process of exegesis, "sifting and sorting" between readings and interpretative models, and at some level "willed misreading" as an addition to the scholarly literature. The viability of an intervention consists not in the "objectivity" or the "expertise" of its findings, but in the differential literacy of its performance. It behooves us to make ourselves comfortable, but not complacent in a world in which students' and associates' interventions assume the forms of photographs, dramatic scripts, musical compositions, and Web sites responding to artifacts whose impacts and reverberations we may share with them, and not only of "learned," "academically disciplined" prose. As I've noted before, after all, if *The Arcades Project*, the results of Walter Benjamin's epic foray into nineteenth-century Paris and the artifacts, narratives, and accounts that it inspired belong to any currently conventional art form or genre, it would be to that of the cybernetic Web site, even if, at the moment of its composition, it was typeset within the parameters of the print medium.

Even within our plodding academic accounts of artifacts and our encounters with them, to the extent that these writings constitute our interventions, we are empowered, before the fact, to incorporate a range of discourses and registers, whether the "miracle of poetic prose" prophesied by Baudelaire and taken up as a rallying cry by Benjamin; the de Manian close reading, so rigorous that its overall format can be extrapolated for heuristic purposes by Andzrej Warminski;[56] or the specifically occasional critical embroidery whose vibrant responsiveness comes at the cost of acknowledged congenital "blindness," error, and "limited shelf life," if not "planned obsolescence."

Long before the inscription of "The Law of Genre," Derrida availed his inscriptions of the possibilities of morphing into at least the above-mentioned three prose forms that might be held distinct from the philosophical elucidation at which he is so adept. He reserved some of his early writings, notably "The Double Session" and "Plato's Pharmacy," as occasions for the synthesis of his own "poetic prose," as wild and contingent as any we might encounter in French Symbolism or Surrealism. Particularly his core readings of Rousseau,[57] Plato, Kant,[58] Hegel,[59] Freud, Heidegger, Husserl, and Levinas are so meticulous, attending both to the nuances of keywords in pivotal passages and to the historical status and accretion of significance by these terms, that they claim the status of close reading (although they tend to improvise context-specific figures in their conceptual-textual allegory, rather than to refer back to the traditional Western compendium or textbook of rhetoric). I would hope to have implied that in embellishing the occasion of his intervention on Joyce, in iterating and imposing upon the Joycean text a by no means exhaustive set of his ongoing interests (among them, translation, the technologies of communication and reproduction, messianism, and the "local difference" of tropes), and in eventuating in a specific, because idiosyncratic reading, Derrida has gracefully assumed the mantle of a "full-service" critic.

The medium of Derrida's own "poetic prose" is a receptive environment for all the major scripts or registers in memorable discourse, just as his philosophy solicits, even demands, the often suppressed or dismissed positionalities that mainstream concepts and terminologies will not accommodate. The chapters that make up the present volume are dedicated to the continuum of discursive modalities tolerated together, but within a modulated and precise medium of writing by the likes of Baudelaire, Joyce, Benjamin, and Derrida. Only by acknowledging the full range of nuances already embedded in the modalities of the discourse in which we have already attained literacy do we approach a "full palette" for our cultural interventions. We arrive at the "outside" evident in Joyce's fictive inventions and the critical elucidations that Benjamin projects onto the persona of a "wandering outsider" only through an "insider's" familiarity with the discursive nuances (i.e. differences) over which we dispose. We struggle to infuse our own interventions with the freshness of this "outside," even knowing that the subtleties of our own language and its embedded thought work won't allow us to go there, that it was all a delusion in the first place.

SEVEN

The Fourth Abrahamic Religion?

The itinerary I plan to follow in this chapter is problematical, to say the least, verging on incredulity for any serious student of culture, its underlying conceptual software, and its interventive options. Jacques Derrida's grouping of Judaism, Christianity, and Islam as the three "Abrahamic religions" has been a suggestive and illuminating tack in its own right, attributing a certain degree of common infrastructural programming and shared responsibility to the three religio-political cultures whose mutual hostility, undermining, bigotry, repression, exclusion—and sharing—has been of nothing less than epic, possibly mythical proportions. In this line of commentary, I propose to posit the attitudes and positionalities known as deconstruction as a fourth and hypercritical station in this collective Western advent and adventure of three thousand to almost six thousand years (depending on your calendar). The considerable religious dimension of deconstruction, long understood, but now gaining particular focus in the work of Hent de Vries[1] and others, may be approached by thinking of deconstruction as a site of religious discourse (not a working denomination, faith, sect, or cult) in its own right, the latest in a long history of close exegetical encounters, discursive raids, and friendly and less than friendly takeovers proceeding from Judaism, Christianity, and Islam, counterbalanced from the outset by (Greek) philosophy's status as an ontotheological commentary in the secular sphere serving as a supplement and alternative to that dimension of religious life mobilizing itself in speech acts and rituals. (For purposes of the present discussion, the latter may be thought of as dramatically and ceremonially realized performatives or speech acts.)

At first glance, and in keeping with the specifications set down by deconstruction's savants and even its inventor, deconstruction, which prescribes no rites, which owns or manages no sites or places of worship, and which ordains no priests or clerics, could not possibly be situated further away from a practicing faith or religion. Deconstruction, through "The Law of Genre," indeed has quasi-systematically made incursions into other discursive heritages. However, the institution with which deconstruction has been most consistently associated—philosophy, whether we regard it as setting into motion with the pre-Socratics or with Plato—is a discursive reaction, critique, or commentary of a sort far more consistent with an academic movement or critical contract than with a religion. It is, of course, of greatest relevance to my present writing project under what conditions we would identify deconstruction with philosophy, say as over and against religion, education, or some other installation of sociological infrastructure, and under what conditions we would spread or disseminate it along the discursive continuum extending to poetics, "close reading," and criticism "proper."

I want to formulate and entertain the hypothesis that deconstruction mirrors, mimics, or performs a religion, specifically an "Abrahamic" one, a religion in the tradition of creation, divine presence, revelation, prophesy, redemption, annunciation, and the engendering and entry into history rehearsed, more or less sequentially, by Judaism, Christianity, and Islam. Why, other than in the name of absurdity, would I advance such a hypothesis? For a number of related reasons:

First, to the degree to which deconstruction "empties out" the ground principles of Western ontotheology, constructs including presence, spirituality, and purity—empties them out by disclosing them in the complexes of sense, articulation, and reference in which they gather their authority and effectiveness—it attributes to Western religions a site or a register in which they acknowledge and negotiate the vacuity and facility of their own vocabularies and the performatives founded upon them. This is in fact a sign and act of great respect on Derrida's part toward the amalgamated religious heritage. It attributes to each of the primary elements in the history of Western religion—a tradition constituted as much by mutual reading, strategic misreading, appropriation, and grafting as by a succession of theological revelations, narratives, liturgies, and so on—a *philosophical project* to excavate, elaborate, translate, reconsider, correct, and reinstitute *itself*. In relation to Judaism, Christianity, and Islam, deconstruction retrospectively installs itself in those sectors of the religion, whether in canonical texts, commentaries, or "acts" of religion, where the work of critical self-reading at the level of founding (almost in the sense of *revealed*) keywords and definitive sociopsychological infrastructures takes place.

To the degree that this intensity of foundational reading at the "deep structural level" of initiatory (hence "divine") language in its etymological roots and affiliated networks is endemic to deconstruction, deconstruction claims, as it extrapolates the communal system of the Abrahamic religions, the status of the site or temple at which the systemic blindnesses and biases, but also the aspirations of the respective religions, are brought to language, rendered to an explicitness that comes as close as possible to a positive deconstructive religious value. The precedents of deconstructive elucidation demand that the composite "Western religion" and the constitutive religions be read in their own terms, in the phrasings and conceptual apparatuses that they bring to bear on their own existential, cultural, aesthetic, and behavioral systems. As the encompassing arena in which the limits of religion join the other features accounting for the distinction of specific Western theological traditions as existence systems, deconstruction is as much a religious *partner* of the three Abrahamic religions, and not a "negative" one, as it is a "philosophical site" for detached commentary upon them.

In order to posit a case as to how deconstructive discourse furnishes the format for a supplemental, theoretically rigorous rejoinder to the Abrahamic faiths assuming certain of their bearings and lines of inquiry, one no less than marvelous in disclosing the dynamics of all life systems comprehensive enough to be credibly designated "religions" and opening up an interface between the Western religions grouped as "Abrahamic" and other religious traditions, I will need to shift the field of the theoretical religious investigations thus far undertaken, including by Derrida himself. The two minor displacements in my own intervention pertain to placing religion's sociohistorical and effective prominence in human culture alongside the tropological and infrastructural readings that have been the thrust of commentaries offered by Derrida himself, de Vries, Rodolphe Gasché,[2] and others and to positing a generic similarity between all religious cultures powerful enough to allow existing deconstructive approaches to pertain to them, to other cultures such as Taoism, Buddhism, Hinduism, and to certain indigenous religions not yet welcomed into this conversation. Derrida's profound and ingenious approaches to such constructs as *khōra*, the name, messianism, and hospitality have, in keeping with deconstruction's heritage, based the inference of particular rituals or behaviors on the teasing out of ideology implanted at the infrastructural level. The implied attitude here, a distinctive feature of the deconstructive signature, is that specifics of institutionality and practice derive from language, that the base tropes of language already have the behaviors implanted in them, whether these are the making of sacrifices, the Eucharist, praying, or, in Judaism, donning the tallith. This formulation furnishes an intriguing occasion for thought and debate: To what extent is a religious manifestation, for example a ceremony, a prohibition, or a ritual, always already inscribed in pivotal tropes themselves, and to what degree does it constitute an accretion of social practice over time, a practice possibly motivated by other than ideological factors?

In raising such questions, we may eventuate at a juncture where the traditional social sciences, especially anthropology and sociology, can profitably work together with deconstruction. The question may now be less what constitutes the deep, underlying figures in a religion and the beliefs they occasion, for deconstruction has already elaborated several splendid pivotal examples in this direction, but rather *what* is believed and *how* it is enacted in particular communities. Indeed, now that deconstruction has sketched out new paradigms for discerning the precipitation of ideologies, morals, and even cultural icons out of canonical or enabling language, the specification of the effectiveness of this distillation in the world may well have emerged as a pressing overarching mission for the descriptive social sciences. While avoiding a relapse into the historical and sociological *determination* of religious meanings and values, the status quo that deconstruction inherited, it is in the interest of contemporary, theoretically nuanced interventions to allow for the specifications that the social sciences can indeed furnish. From this point of view, their empiricist tendencies constitute an asset, rather than a detriment. Deconstruction's scenarios of the precipitation of ideology, metaphysics, and belief out of pivotal keywords and figures should furnish the focal point of social-scientific assessments of organized religion. So "primed," the social sciences will be freer to explore multiple motivations for religiosity and to examine which, if any, "Abrahamic" figures and tenets demonstrate extensions or parallels "beyond the fold" in such cultures as Hinduism, Buddhism, and indigenous religions.

Deconstruction emerges as a place or site (*khōra*) where, in the name of something more precise, explicit, and open, the span of Western theology can offer up its biases, misprisions, misreadings. In this linguistic responsibility, Judaism, Christianity, and Islam offer a (by no means ultimate) corrective to the slants, biases, and violence to which they have given rise. Singular though its exegetical interventions invariably are, deconstruction establishes a community to the degree to which it renounces exclusion, violence, and, in the sphere of pronouncement and articulation, obtuseness and oversimplification.

It remains in an Abrahamic sphere to the degree that Judaism, Christianity, and Islam have furnished its interventions with their imagery, metaphysics, and tropology. Thus, in the context of Derrida's searing analyses of, for example, sacrifice,[3] redemption, and pardon,[4] deconstruction is the discursive venue offering the existing Western faiths whatever possibility they have of redeeming themselves, a redemption both corrective and broadening: widening the arena of theological thoughtfulness and deepening the apprehension of keywords and core concepts.

At least initially, I wish to set out on this quite literal *essai* in wonder at the broad *Grundprinzipe* that deconstructive thinking has added to the possibilities of studying religion as an institution of near-global parameters. I want to sketch out the purview that my own formation as a student of deconstruction, as one of the most negligent of its students, has afforded me in introducing my own young students to the comparative religions dimension of World Civilizations. Even before availing myself of the opportunity to read Derrida's luminous writings on religion, especially the later pieces demonstrating if not his embrace of it, at least a "philosophical relaxation," in the name of religion's human preponderance and deep sociological foundation, of the neutral distance toward it that Derrida maintained early in his career, I knew at least the following.

Far and away the preeminent site for what we know as the "history of religion" is the margins around canonical texts, not the battlefield or the "hearts of men." To the degree to which religions struggle against each other for "market share," the "world's major religions," occupying prominent places within the archive of recalled culture, each manifest an inbuilt capitalism or expansionism. The primary tactic by which competing religions, that is, ones regionally adjacent or coterminous, "pitch" for larger market share involves projecting their worldviews and doctrines within the *margins* of antagonistic faiths' core texts. These border-zone transactions, which highlight deconstructive scenarios of marginality, assume the form of appropriating terms and tropes from other religions; inserting or introjecting language within those antagonistic margins, and grafting the articulations of the religious culture aspiring toward success and succession upon preexisting religious canon, in the sense of a hostile takeover.

Indeed, the "Abrahamic religions" form a natural grouping within deconstruction's extrapolation of the underlying operating system of Western metaphysics, and its reprogramming of those parameters is in no small measure due to the volatility and richness of the textual frontier separating and joining the Old Testament, the New Testament, and the Koran. Monumental studies in the archive of world culture have already been devoted to the projections, extrapolations, retrospective property disputes, and takeovers that have been rife, at least since the rise of Christianity, along these borders. Indeed, the textual Yugoslovia of "Western culture" anticipated the political one by many centuries.

Among the primary instances of these marginal epiphenomena of mutual reading and interpretation is, for example, the retrospective confirmation and adaptation by a verse in Matthew 2. "So the words spoken through Jeremiah the prophet were fulfilled: 'A voice was heard in Rama, wailing and loud laments; it was Rachel weeping for her children, and refusing all consolation, because they were no more'" (17–18). Another is found in the "prospective" formulations in Jeremiah 31:

> Hark, lamentation is heard in Ramah, and bitter weeping,
> Rachel weeping for her sons. She refuses to be comforted: they are no more.
> These are the words of the Lord:
> Cease your loud weeping, shed no more tears;
> for there shall be a return for your toil,
> they shall return from the land of the enemy.

You shall leave descendents after you;
your sons shall return to their own land. (15–17)

Indeed, the most compelling instance of a Christian messianic prophesy in the Old Testament, in Isaiah 8,

For a boy has been born for us, a son given to us
to bear the symbol of dominion on his shoulder;
and he shall be called
in purpose wonderful, in battle God-like,
Father of all time, Prince of peace.
Great shall his dominion be,
and boundless the peace
bestowed on David's throne and on his kingdom, to establish it and sustain it
with justice and righteousness
from now and for evermore (6–7)

is framed by an instance of marginal textual appropriation quite similar to the one above, in this case from Matthew 4:

When he heard that John had been arrested, Jesus withdrew to Galilee; and leaving Nazareth he went and settled at Capernaum on the Sea of Galilee, in the district of Zebulun and Naphtali. This was to fulfill the passage in the prophet Isaiah which tells of "the land of Zebulun, the land of Naphtali, the Way of the Sea, the land beyond Jordan, heathen Galiliee," and says:

The people that lived in darkness saw a great light;
light dawned on the dwellers in the land of death's dark shadow. (12–16)

These latter verses are an exact, but advantageous quotation of Isaiah 9:1–2, which set the stage for the prophet's joyous proclamation of the birth of the Son.

Transcripts of Islam's intense intertextual conversation and *Auseinandersetzung* with both prior religions "of the book" are furnished throughout the Koran, notably in the sura known as "The Table Spread":

Allah made a covenant of old with the Children of Israel and We raised among them twelve chieftains, and Allah said: Lo! I am with you. If ye establish worship and pay the poor-due, and believe in My messengers and support them and lend unto Allah a kindly loan, surely I shall remit your sins, and surely I will bring you into gardens underneath which rivers flow. . . .

And because of their breaking their covenant, We have cursed them and make hard their hearts. They change words from their context and forget a part of that whereof they were admonished. Thou wilt not cease to discover treachery from all save a few of them. But bear with them and pardon them. Lo! Allah loveth the kindly.

With those who say: Lo, we are Christians, We made a covenant, but they forgot a part whereof they were admonished. Therefore We have stirred up enmity and hatred among them till the Day of Resurrection, when Allah will inform them of their handiwork.

O People of the Scripture! Now hath Our messenger come unto you, expounding much of that which ye used to hide in the Scripture, and forgiving much. Now hath come unto you light from Allah and a plain Scripture.

Whereby Allah guideth him who seeketh His good pleasure unto paths of peace. He bringeth them out of darkness unto light by His decree, and guideth them unto a straight path.[5]

The tendentious attitude toward Judaism and Christianity in this pivotal passage is ameliorated by the intimacy of the engagement with the religions that the passage also betrays. These lines, before rendering their judgment on Christianity, recapitulate Christianity's departure from Judaism, and they critique Judaism from a Christian perspective. The leaders of the twelve tribes of Israel have become both "chieftains" and "apostles." With the phrase "They change words from their context," these verses tap into Christianity's initial competitive claim that Judaism was a creed so submerged in its own details and technicalities as to obscure the transcendent humanity embodied by Christ. Yet Christianity, having "forgot a part whereof they were admonished," has also strayed from the purity and lucidity of Abrahamic values that Islam now reinstates, redirects. The trajectory from darkness to light that God, by whatever name, will now restore derives from the very core of Abrahamic theological imagery and tropology. It goes back to the scene of creation in Genesis. Derrida has marked and scored this imagery well since the outset of his own conceptual odyssey, in religious and philosophical contexts.

This quintessential endeavor, in the world of competing or comparative religions, the enterprise of claiming precedence, essentiality, and authority, is first and foremost a *textual* transaction of reading and exegesis. Marginality, the volatility at the *outskirts* of culture's canonical texts, is the medium within which these hostile actions and acknowledgments transpire. The highly ambivalent and complex amalgam of mutual hospitality/hostility to which religions are driven, in the name of both "domestic accord" and "foreign affairs," has been condensed into one vibrant trope by Derrida and tellingly emboidered in "Hostipitality."[6]

Second, I want to propose the hypothesis that deconstruction mirrors, mimics, or performs a specifically "Abrahamic" religion because the world's religions, particularly those sharing adjacency or territorial coincidence, operate and configure themselves in a differential space, as Saussure declared signs to be differential, whose *différances* deconstruction has elaborated to a delicate degree of nuance. It is in this sense that the dietary prohibitions of the "Abrahamic religions" are supplemental to one another, share in the deconstructive "logic of the supplement," both in the interplay between prohibited foods and generalized fasting and on the menu of forbidden nourishment. Judaism limits fasting to five days spread throughout the calendar and assembles a substantial index of proscribed foods and food combinations. Christianity and Islam go heavier on fasting (Lent and Ramadan), but are more permissive in the menu of comestibles. Judaism and Islam, of course, proscribe pork, while Christianity tolerates it. This "Western" etiquette of eating practices is one-upped by substantial sectors of Hinduism and Buddhism, which advocate vegetarianism and proscribe the slaughter and consumption of cattle.

Enduring religions thus promulgate themselves within a differentiated field[7] and marketplace whose competing enterprises relate through mutual difference. Religions, as highly political organizations, promote their differences with the competition so as to ensure domestic unanimity. But of course, the dynamics of differentiation and supplementarity prevail as much within the "major religions" as between them. One might argue that certain of the metaphysical aspirations, say toward purity and presence, common to the "Abrahamic religions" make them particularly susceptible to intramural instances of doctrinal fragmentation, usurpation, appropriation, retrospective grafting, and mutual supplementation. To a large degree, the sequence of these positionings, backbitings, and hostile takeovers, whether successful or not, is coextensive with what we call "the history of religions." Each religion, through a mixture of intramural refinement and "foreign affairs," establishes a distinctive rhetorico-hermeneutic climate in which certain figures of speech and exigetical moves attain prominence. It is these rhetorical traditions and engrained hermeneutic practices that come to the fore in many instances of religious sectarianism and splitting. Obvious examples include the Iconoclastic Controversy so formative to the Eastern Orthodox Church, the issues of metaphor and metonymy raised by the opposed interpretations of the Eucharist at the moment of Protestantism's crystallization,[8] and the relative degrees of literalism and figurality mobilized by the Shi'ite and Sunni traditions of Islam.

"Differences" between religions, and between sets of religions, are first and foremost a matter of rhetorical climates and traditions (i.e., practices continuing and entrenched over time), distributed over the continuum or palette of likely possibility. Talmudic disputation, for example, favors the *Kal va-ḥomer*, the a fortiori inference of Aristotelian logic,[9] at the expense of certain of the other appropriated logical figures. If we are indeed to achieve the "tolerance" and diversity publicly espoused already for centuries by the "modern democracies," especially in light of the simmering tensions belied and ignited by episodes such as 9/11/2001, it becomes a matter of urgent exigency to "map" the rhetorical landscapes of the persistent religions, those with historical constituencies and traditional "catchment areas." A disproportionate share of the intractable impasses in current events can be plausibly ascribed to a global constriction and entrenchment across the differentiated field of the historical world religions. From this point of view, it becomes possible to imagine the play of "world religion" over history as a mass rhythm of systolic and diastolic constrictions and releases, tolerances and persecutions.

Indeed, the heart of Derrida's varied, discontinuous, but substantial theological project—and it makes utter sense that it arises in the traditional site or place (*khōra*) of philosophy—consists in a scrupulous demonstration of how the keywords of Western ontotheology *differ from themselves*. Even before Derrida's "turn to religion" became long-standing and explicit, the project was embedded in his early deconstruction of presence as the milieu of a range of constructs at the service of Western ideology, spirituality, and the favored communications medium known as "voice." Hent de Vries formulates the early, pivotal situation of presence in relation to the overall project as follows:

> In fact, one did not need to wait for the publication of the most recent writings on religion in order to realize that Derrida's deconstruction of the notion of presence—or of nature (for example, in the second part of *Of Grammatology*)—

was hardly inspired either by the philosophy of absence, or for that matter, by its shadow, empiricism. . . . Nor can Derrida's resistance to the notion of immediacy, whether of nature or some other presence, be adequately characterized by comparing it with a "contemporary culturalism."[10]

Particularly in Derrida's early *Auseinandersetzungen* with Heidegger, themselves embroidering on issues of language and experience that he raised in his Husserlian investigations, presence—as a stress-bearing pivot of spirituality and immanence—emerges as a highly ambiguous construct, infused with values as ambivalent as Western culture's approach to the uncontrollable technomechanical features of language itself.

In *Speech and Phenomena*, Derrida quite clearly formulates the strategic position that presence maintains in relation the overall capacity for idealization in Western thought:

> The unique and permanent motif of all the mistakes and distortions which Husserl exposes in "degenerated" metaphysics, across a multiplicity of domains, themes, and arguments, is always a blindness to the authentic mode of *ideality*, to that which is, to what may be indefinitely *repeated* in the *identity* of its *presence*, because of the very fact that it *does not exist*, is *not real* or is *irreal*—not in the sense of being a fiction, but in another sense which may have several names. . . . This nonworldliness is not another worldliness, this ideality is not an existent that has fallen from the sky; its origin will always be the possible repetition of a productive act. In order that the possibility of this repetition may be open, *ideally* to infinity, one ideal form must assure this unity of the *indefinite* and the *ideal*: this is the present, or rather the presence of the *living present*. The ultimate form of ideality, the ideality of ideality, that in which in the last instance one may anticipate or recall all repetition, is the *living present*, the self-presence of transcendental life. Presence has always been, and will, forever, be the form in which we can say apodictically, the infinite diversity of contents is produced.[11]

Even with the volatile proliferation of Derrida's interests, the deconstruction of presence over time remains interminable. Over time, it reemerges with urgency with respect to theological core concepts and conventions. Derrida was still reading the theological implications out of Heidegger's philosophy in "Faith and Knowledge" (1994), a decisive position in the sphere of his disputation and a vital link to the more accommodating—while still unstintingly rigorous—theological bearing of recent years.

In its most abstract form, then, the aporia within which we are struggling would perhaps be the following: is revealability (*Offenbarkeit*) more originary than revelation (*Offenbarung*), and hence independent of all religion? Independent in the structures of its experience and in the analytics relating to them? Is this not the place in which "reflecting faith" at least originates, if not this faith itself? Or rather, inversely, would the event of revelation have consisted in revealing revealability itself, and the origin of light, the originary light, the very invisibility of visibility? This is perhaps what the believer or the theologian might say here, in particular the Christian of originary Christendom, of that *Urchristentum* in the Lutheran tradition to which Heidegger acknowledges owing so much.[12]

Derrida's disclosure of an aporia, which we might think of as an almost sexual mutual friction or rubbing within a Heideggerian notion of revelation prevalent, at least, in a stark Protestant theology, is a gesture that has been repeated in several instances over the history of deconstructive interventions. In this case, Protestant revelation (*Offenbarung*), by virtue of many factors, including homonymy, rubs shoulders with and takes off from a revealability (*Offenbarkeit*) that may fly unfettered not only from Protestantism in particular, but from organized religion in general. The Western urconstruct of revelation, with important workings upon Judaic and Catholic theology, thus harbors something alien in itself, diverges from itself. It is in this sense, in the passage directly above, that the vision that immanent revelation would presumably facilitate is inextricable from a certain lurking blindness or invisibility, as Derrida directs us to see in this scenario. *Offenbarkeit*, a general condition of apprehension endemic to thinking and knowing, may well be encrypted in *Offenbarung*, an opening (or escape hatch) to which conventional theology blinds itself.

Revelation, which in several senses describes the condition of spiritual intuition, is thus other than and other from what the traditions and institutions of religion have described it to be. In his reading of the above-cited passage, Derrida demonstrates that the "reflecting faith" is not as relentlessly reflexive as faith would have it. Western religions have manifested a pervasive tendency to cover over their own dissonant or incompatible elements.

Yet for all the shortcomings of this order that Derrida encounters in his readings of theological texts—Derrida's critique here is consistent with unveilings of closure and obtuseness that he has performed with respect to atheological as well as religious constructs—the above passage keeps the lines of communication open to "the believer or the theologian." Derrida affords a certain plausibility to positions that have already proven susceptible to critiques of blindness, metaphysical, generic, or disciplinary, whose heuristic *address*[13] has coincided with his project, countersigning deconstruction's willingness to engage them thoughtfully. While perhaps as much an amelioration of tone and bearing as a decisive sea change, this attribution of plausibility to positions whose intrinsic difficulty has been clearly marked nevertheless signals an overture toward and an embrace of groundbreaking philosophy's radical Other—entrenched customs, compromised idealism, or in Avital Ronell's term, stupidity.[14] This is not, on Derrida's part, a messianic capitulation to the persistent dullness motivated by prior investments or commitments undertaken under conditions of limited conceptual lucidity because "they know not what they do," but rather a commitment to the work of tropologically motivated sociocultural correction that will never consummate itself in a definitive sense.

Derrida thus takes the liberty to differ from himself. In the later essays, the change in the tonality of the address to ontotheological constructs over and against the critiques delivered in *Of Grammatology*, *Writing and Difference*, and *Glas* is palpable, if not systematic—at the same time that it sets in relief the differences of philosophical keywords and core concepts from themselves. And if Derrida can isolate rich, but unsettling double messages in each of religion's core concepts, including God, the name, and the abyss, one after the next, it follows that the more issue-oriented dimensions literally bristle with the anomalies that surface, under the aura of sustained thoughtfulness, from the current religious pieties. It is in this context that Derrida, in "Interpretations at War," can find greater difficulty and even conceptual violence in Hermann Cohen's assumption of "'the innermost kinship (*die innerste Verwandtshaft*)' or affinity of the German spirit with Judaism" at the time of the First World War than in the political positions of Karl Schmitt and Martin Heidegger during the Second.[15] In a letter to Franz Rosenzweig that Derrida glosses in "The Eyes of Language,"[16] Gershom Scholem postulates the systematic linguistic anomalies and sociopolitical pressures attending Hebrew's transformation from a sacred tongue into a secular—and official—language. With these elaborated examples, Derrida demonstrates that theology's difference from itself migrates into the sociopolitical and cultural receptions of religion.

The at times violent, self-disciplining torsion that religious thought applies to itself is nowhere more apparent than in the transition from the law of theology, which serves as an instance of divine principle and unwavering justice, to the law of sociopolitical institutions, where, in the writings of Benjamin that Derrida illuminates in "Force of Law,"[17] "the compulsory use of violence . . . consists in the use of violence as a means toward legal ends."[18] Law turns out to be a capital occasion for Derrida's religious thought: Along with his work on Joyce, Derrida's comments on the appeal to "the Law" in Kafka's *The Trial* mark a turning point toward a more systematic approach to literature as both an exception to philosophy and a privileged window upon (or gopher hole into) its workings than is evident in earlier commentaries.[19] Derrida makes sure, when he turns to the implicit violence in the extrapolation of legal institutions and processes from legalistic discourse in relation to Benjamin's attentiveness to these matters, to inscribe, in response to and anticipation of the obvious platitudes, a rather comprehensive set of the paradoxes and anomalies emerging from the Holocaust, the consummate violence in the "living memory" of sanctioned violence in the West. Benjamin's early musings on workers' rights to resort to violence under untenable bargaining conditions and on what legitimate responses are available to the state furnish Derrida with an opportunity to invoke a rich network of constructs coalescing around the law. Given deconstruction's distinctive signature, it is no accident that this "theologico-legal complex" should crystallize among three aporetic situations to which Benjamin's "Critique of Violence" leads Derrida, "The Epokhē of the Rule," "The Haunting of the Undecidable," and "The Urgency that Obstructs the Horizon of Knowledge":[20]

> At no moment, it seems, can a decision be said to be presently and fully just; either it has not yet been made according to a rule, and nothing allows one to call it just, or it has already followed a rule—whether given, received, confirmed, preserved, or reinvented—which, in its turn nothing guarantees absolutely. . . . This is why the test and ordeal of the undecidable, of which I have just said it must be gone through by any decision worthy of this name, is never past or passed [*passé ou dépassé*], it is not a surmounted or sublated [*relevé*] (*aufgehoben*) moment in the decision. The undecidable remains caught, lodged, as a ghost at least, but an essential ghost, in every decision, in every event of decision. Its ghostliness [*sa fantomaticité*] demonstrates from within all assurance of presence, all certainty or all alleged criteriology assuring us of the justice of a decision, in truth of the very event of a decision.[21]

Building toward vertiginous formulations in which the deity of the Abrahamic religions himself shuttles between transcendent fullness and luminousness and an utterly obscure void, Derrida stages the particular justice characterizing a Western religion's tangible, socially accessible guarantee. And indeed, justice, which can never be certain, residing in the temporal crossfire between the actuality and potentiality of its rules, is as spectral not only as God but as an entire sequence of ideals whose trajectories Derrida has traced, ideals including social justice (as embodied by Marx), authority, and sacrifice. Justice, like religion, is haunted by an elusive ghost. Its undecidability links it inextricably to deconstruction, the "experience of impossibility"[22] and the "science" of indeterminacy. To the degree that justice, unbeknownst, harbors its own undecidability, its study is "always already" deconstructive. In the above passage, deconstruction figures as a character in a legal drama in which, through conceptual determinations and temporal indirections, justice has already gone awry. Deconstruction, by the same token, is embedded in a close reading of the Abrahamic deity, a character in the adventure disclosing that if any substantial presence dwells in the Holy of Holies, it is akin to the Wizard of Oz. Deconstruction assumes the mantle of religion in part through its knowing partnership in an undecidability at the very fulcrum of Western theological core concepts.

Within the context of its inherent impossibility, justice becomes tantamount to a messianic promise. It takes on the casts of mysticism and madness:

> This "idea of justice" seems indestructible in its affirmative character, in its demand of gift without exchange, without circulation, without recognition or gratitude, without economic circularity, without calculation and without rules, without reason and without theoretical rationality, in the sense of regulating mastery. And so, one can recognize in it, even accuse in it a madness, and perhaps another kind of mysticism [*une autre sorte de mystique*]. And deconstruction is mad about and from such justice, mad about and from this desire for justice. Such justice, which is not law, is the very movement of deconstruction at work in law and in the history of law, in political history and history itself, even before it presents itself as the discourse that the academy or the culture of our time labels deconstructionism.[23]

The injustice that theology promises is resolute, almost to the point of madness. In the above passage, it interferes with religious mysticism, which Derrida, a few pages earlier, has characterized as "a silence walled up in the violent act; walled up, walled in because this silence is not exterior to language."[24] Mysticism is a moment of silence that religion takes out from the deluded and maddening activity of its own self-founding and imposition.

Montaigne, whom Derrida carries forward, noted the "mystical foundations of the law's authority."[25] Religion's mad faith in the justice served by legal authority runs counter to what institutions, including religious ones, know and always have known about language. The *persistence* of faith in justice, the inability to dispense with or ignore this belief in the availability of justice, in its delivery by divine if not human law, along with the delusion of *purity* in thought, conception, sense, or motive, would be at the heart of a deconstructive psychopathology, were one so uncircumspect as to posit one. The mystical moment of silence through which religion as well as religion-based institutions take a breather is a response to the violence done to language in the necessity and name of the law: The silence is *of* language, not other to it. Deconstruction, as the inscription of the faith in justice persisting after the blind and violent imposition of the law, takes on or assumes, with no messianic aspiration, the madness that such oversight engenders. A displacement if not transference of madness takes place here. As a persistent register of the torque applied to language in the production of the delusion that justice inheres in the law, deconstruction is an expression of madness, or madness's symptom or victim. At the expense of its own lucidity, its own summation and translation, deconstruction furnishes a running transcript of the excesses to which culture gives rise in the forced gagging of language. The transcript is not an easy one to read, ethically or semantically.

The betrayal of the ideals or ideation of the Abrahamic religions by the strong-arm tactics that they apply to language, forcing declarations and confessions, if not entirely squelching expression, becomes a persistent motif in Derrida's address to the existing Abrahamic religions. This is nowhere more evident than in the hostility that Derrida discerns as a "secret sharer" in these religions' profession of altruism and hospitality as the apotheosis of human social values. Rarely does Derrida achieve in the title of an essay alone, "Hostipitality," the fluctuation between hostility and welcome, detainment and support, betrayal and blessing, and accusation and pardon, upon which the entire piece of writing pivots.

If every concept shelters or lets itself be haunted by another concept, by an other than itself that is no longer even its other, then no concept remains in place any longer. This is about the concept of concept, and this is why I suggested earlier that hospitality, the experience, the apprehension, the exercise of impossible hospitality, of hospitality as the possibility of impossibility (to receive another guest whom I am incapable of welcoming, to become capable of that which I am incapable of)—this is the exemplary experience of deconstruction itself, when it is or does what it has to do or be, that is, the experience of the impossible. Hospitality—this is a name or an example of deconstruction.[26]

This passage extends from the enunciation and elaboration of the paradoxes surrounding a very particular core value common to all three Abrahamic religions, hospitality, to a very broad characterization of deconstruction's role within this religious tradition. It is possible, and upon this distinct possibility I base the argument of this entire chapter, that deconstruction *joins* the discursive platform shared by the Abrahamic religions precisely as the "experience of their impossibility," the site or interface (Derrida's *khōra*) at which the patient explication of their maddening contradictions, paradoxes, and other anomalies, such as surround the imperative to hospitality, defines their prevalent features and thrust. If hospitality is indeed "a name or an example of deconstruction," then any firewalls invoked conceptually in order to compartmentalize deconstruction's language immanence from the putatively more tangible or concrete domain of sociology or social relations have been, from the moment of this formulation, irreparably compromised.

Deconstruction displays no small redemptive aspiration of its own when it assumes, *takes on*, transferentially enters this madness for the purpose of bringing it to the fore and before the jury of contemporary cultural debate. In the case of hospitality, then, it is no accident that the Messiah can be interpreted as "hôte, about the messianic as hospitality, the messianic that introduces deconstructive disruption or madness in the concept of hospitality, the madness *of* hospitality, even the madness *of the concept* of hospitality."[27] This willingness, whether of an idealistic person or a decisive positionality, to serve as host is of course fraught with double messages, as the fascination with the position of the *hostage* common to Emmanuel Levinas and Louis Massignon in their radical projects of engaging otherness makes clear.

Massignon, the notable French Orientalist who, long before it was fashionable to do so, espoused Islam's position on the continuum of the overall experiment and adventure of the Abrahamic religions, is the presiding spirit over Derrida's meditations on hospitality. "A central theme that inspires Massignon's entire exegesis" is "that the three monotheistic religions, as Abrahamic religions, are issued from a patriarch that came to this earth as a 'stranger, or hôte, a *ger*,' and a kind of saint of hospitality." Levinas by the same token, "always says that the other, the other man, man as the other is *my* neighbor, my universal brother, in humanity." Yet, as Derrida elaborates, there is a moment in the hospitality that Levinas and Massignon share "where the welcoming [*l'accueil*] is second, no longer subject to the visit, to the visitation, and where one becomes, prior to being the *hôte*, the hostage of the other."[28] This volatile switching and reversal in a fundamental Western value and particularly in a fundamental value of Judeo-Christianity and Islam marks "the self-contradiction, the self-destruction of the concept of hospitality. And with this concept of subjectivity or of ipseity as hostage, we have the inseparable concept of *substitution*—of the unique as *hostage* responsible for all, and therefore substitutable, precisely there where [*là même où*] he is absolutely irreplaceable."[29] Under the purview of deconstruction, the duplicity in a multireligious core value not only initiates an ethical debate, but foregrounds a movement—substitution-of broad and general philosophical interest, particularly as a philosopheme coinciding with a feature of language and representation. By way of the duplicity joining hospitality to the hostage, Western religion's messianic impulse to harbor and protect and in the same gesture to reinforce mores of altruism becomes indicative, in a deconstructive homily, of a generalized substitution, sometimes between strikingly dissonant values, that prevails in language and throughout its manifold deployments.

Derrida does not hold back in tracing out the broadest psychocultural arena for this theotropological duplicity:

Being-present as absent to the hôte? Must one be there (living, or surviving, or not)? *Unheimliche*: absence as presence. Must one be present or not, and how, to the hôte? The hôte always passing through (road and itinerary, iterability: come; come back [*viens: re-viens*]). But must one hold back [*re-tenir*] the passing hôte? When does holding back and retaining [*retenir*] him become detaining [*détenir*] the other as hostage? (to hold, to hold the other, to entertain and support [*entretenir*] the hôte (entertain and sustain: art of conversation, without labor nor program, no constraint nor commerce: leisure, gratuitousness, grace, art salon, music salon, etc.).

Moments of hospitality follow each other but do not resemble each other.

The question: does hospitality presuppose improvisation? Yes and no.[30]

This passage begins bearing the full weight of Western spirituality, nostalgia, respect for the dead, and ghostliness as coalescing in the uncanniness around which religion constructs its shrine and to which psychoanalysis pays its dues and fee. This is a religio-ontotheological complex that Derrida could conjure forth with increasing ease as his critique of theology extended itself in different projects. Yet the passage, always on hospitality and its possibilities, ends in an abrupt and unpredictable, we might almost say untenable stutter step around the French verb *tenir*, a dance leading nowhere with an inconsequentiality surely of concern to the Abrahamic religions. Hospitality itself suffers from the uncanny divide fusing intimacy with ghostliness, extending from the familiar scenario of monolithic idealism and awe to a concantenation, a *glas*, of Latinate elements (*venir* joins *tenir*) whose outcome is by no means so certain. Like so many of the bases upon which the Abrahamic religions rest, hospitality is far more than it might seem, is not a simple matter, differs from itself. The somewhat familiar drama or passion of the hôte eventuates in an etymological cloud chamber in which the staples of Western religion bounce off one another.

This volatility, the ongoing possibility in religion for dissonant worldviews and values to precipitate out at any moment, becomes as endemic to the Abrahamic creeds as to "Western metaphysics," in Derrida's view. It is in this context that in Judaism/Christianity/Islam, the forgiveness at the very core of the possibility for redemption is increasingly related to betrayal. Responding to a long passage from *Totality and Infinity* in which Levinas sets the impossible encounter between the subject and the Other against a backdrop of time's progression toward death, Derrida writes:

> This inscription, so necessary, of forgiveness in betrayal and betrayal in forgiveness, is what enables saying to the other or of hearing oneself tell the other and hearing the other tell oneself [*s'entendre dire par l'autre*, hearing oneself told by the other] and hearing, understanding what is thus said: you see, you start again, you don't want to forgive me, even on the day of Atonement, but me too, me neither, a "me" neither, we are in accord, we will forgive each other nothing, it is impossible, let us not forgive each other, agreed [*d'accord*]? And then comes the

complicitous burst of laughter, laughter becoming mad, demented laughter [*le rire dément*].

Le rire dément, demented laughter, laughter denies. Yes, laughter denies. It is mad, this demented laughter, and it denies lying [*et il dément mentir*]. This laughter is, like every laughter, a kind of denegation of lying which lies still while denying lying or while avowing lying—or, if you prefer, which says the truth of lying, which says the truth in lying, thus recognizing that a logic of the symptom will always be stronger than an ethic of truthfulness [*véracité*].[31]

The religious core concept is never more violent than in the burst of Nietzschean laughter that erupts in place of forgiveness. Indeed, to the degree that hospitality demands a sublime effort of restraint and denial, what Freud might well call sublimation,[32] it harbors or hosts within it a sequence of values that could not appear more antithetical to itself: hostility, hostage taking, sustained, almost unquenchable resentment (imaged, perhaps, in Exodus's burning bush), lying, and denial. The pretension to transcendental forgiveness, to an overcoming of the resentment predicated by denial and restraint, is drowned out in peals of complicitous laughter giving the lie, with the speed and spontaneity of the Freudian joke, to the entire system of promise and reward based on repression, self-denial, and sacrifice. The laughter erupting in place of "true," that is, ideologically sanctioned forgiveness, the captivity imposed upon the guest at the moment of the host's presumed largesse and self-sacrifice: these manifestations signal a "planned obsolescence" installed into the religio-ideological complex in which hospitality plays a prominent role. In keeping with his long-standing philosophical address to Freud, Derrida is on target in treating such epiphenomena as symptoms. The wink attending this demented laughter is a communal acknowledgment, from the outset, before the framing of the social contract, that the self-proclaimed mission of the Abrahamic religions is, constitutionally, too facile, Pollyannaish, quixotic for its own good and for its realization.

Deconstruction is the home, locus, site, and *khōra* where this complicity and unmasking take place (more on this below). As such, deconstruction opens an abyss or shrine where another Western "variety of religious experience" takes place. Deconstruction's sustained engagement with Judaism/Christianity/Islam is too intense and complex for this encounter to be reducible to philosophy or to criticism, that is, to be a neutral or purely secular commentary issuing from the singularity-free or sanitized sphere.

Deconstruction's insistence on the elaboration of *différance* is in the service of a singularity preempting philosophy's claims of a disciplinary neutrality that would make it substantially other from a religion, a creed, a local culture. In the duplicity, ambivalence, and alienation that deconstruction sustains, deconstruction, as it addresses religion, ironically absorbs certain of the cultic features against which it rose in indignation.

It transpires in a time-space of ongoing dialogue and conversation so vast, not quite infinite, that its analyses can never do justice to its preoccupations, ontotheological or other. Derrida often struggles against while also acknowledging the limits of his own attention and conversation in reaching, encompassing, all the nuances of the issues and topoi that he raises.[33] This repeated gesture of apology can issue only from a site or *khōra* in which the "infinite conversation," the total commentary, is imaginable, if not actually forthcoming. There is a murky region—not quite a Holy of Holies—in which deconstruction becomes susceptible, to the religious preoccupations that it has taken on, manifesting the vulnerability at the heart of authentic critical engagement. This does not make it a religion, but it does not antiseptically quarantine it from one, either. Does this make Derrida's work on religion over the past two decades an instance of "philosophical relaxation," the accommodation of and a gesture toward what had been, previously, philosophically unacceptable, below standard, inadmissible? We will ponder this riddle, however elusive its decisive response.

Deconstruction's Theological Abyss

No edifice of human striving has been grander in its pronouncements, as pervasive in its social outreach and institutionalization, and erected on more questionable linguistico-rhetorical and conceptual grounds than religion. This may go a long way toward explaining religion's fatal attraction to deconstruction, a seemingly fated overflow and mixing of their very different accounts. Organized religion becomes haunted to an increasing degree by spectrality, once Derrida has developed this notion in *Specters of Marx*, there in relation to a complex of technoscientific and administrative concerns. As Derrida's theological writings proceeded, religion was seen increasingly to stage the mysteries that its theology leaves unresolved in the name of its professed transcendence. Yet to whatever extent deconstruction succeeds in demonstrating the degree to which the Abrahamic religions, in their ideological self-promotion, have overdrawn on the accounts of their credibility, the discourse of Western theology has issued forth in a vast store of pronouncements of compelling interest to its parallel universe in philosophy, whose operating system, even when in the service of the church or other theological institutions, appeals to a secular audience and a secular theater of operations.

Confining their interventions to the miniature scale of dense and formally demanding lyrical poems, the English metaphysical poets of the seventeenth century applied their ingenuity to mapping in figurative and rhetorical terms the complexities in the interaction between the deity and people whose expression is modulated by conditions of individuation and increasing self-reliance. Against the backdrop of the negative theology that had been evolving since Jewish/Christian/Islamic Neoplatonism, poets including Donne,[34] Herbert,[35] and Crashaw[36] infused the human address to the deity with all the rhetorical and "personal" ambiguity pervading human relationships in general, especially erotic ones. Indeed, Derrida's "Sauf le nom,"[37] an extended gloss of a prayer cycle, Angelus Silesius's (Johannes Scheffler's) *Cherubic Wanderer*, could just as well emerge from an anthology of religious poems by the above-named English poets.

Just as George Herbert, in *The Temple*, formally fits out his poems to simulate the sites, activities, and stages of an intense religious exchange with the deity, Derrida, as his religious writings evolved over the years, touched upon the major stress points and elements in the architecture of an Abrahamic megareligion. While remaining faithful, invariably, to his long-standing project of situating the terms and figures of his elaborations in the linguistic heritage of Western culture, he addresses at least the following issues of pressing theological concern: the divinity himself and the spectral conditions in which she must be couched, an inquiry leading into the name itself; the rhetorico-conceptual constraints upon the hymns and prayers addressing the deity; the dynamics of translation, by which revelation is disseminated to alien cultures while the divine assumes explicit terms in any single language; the lieu or site (*khōra*) where the divine mysteries or anomalies merge into the intractability of language; and the economy of a priori obligation, forgiveness, and pardon that may well come closest to "the theology of everyday life." The cumulative effect of these various interventions, extending as they do from the ontotheological investigations of

Husserl and Heidegger and from a long-standing encounter with Levinasian ethics, is to map, acutely and critically, without subscribing to it, the parameters of a philosophically plausible working religion. In this sense, deconstruction generates the language, the conceptual program, not only for a shadow or negative religion, but for one in an ongoing project of self-elucidation and self-correction. As suggested above, the theological flank of the deconstructive project simulates, in a virtual sense, the dimensions and functions of the Abrahamic religions as they have evolved to this date.

Paradoxically, but very much in keeping with prior investigations, Derrida situates in Greek philosophy, Western culture's secular institution of transcendental metaphysical meditation, a means of access to the aporias activated by Abrahamic theology that is more germane, more "direct," than is found in the canonical texts of the three Abrahamic faiths themselves. The notion of *khōra* that Derrida elaborates from Plato's *Timaeus* uncannily parallels such Abrahamic "mysteries" as a deity who is at once everywhere and nowhere and who issues forth from a Holy of Holies, a deity better understood from the attributions of negative theology than by any tangible traits or actions. He likewise elaborates a language of prayer both addressing the deity and about him, as well. Plato, in the *Timaeus*, with an unsettling mixture of anticipation and appropriation, shadows the inner workings of Western theology, as he does in the *Phaedrus* with regard to the unsalutory effects of the body on the soul and the manifold possibilities for a spiritual afterlife. Isolating the philosopheme *khōra* in the bedrock of Greek philosophy and appealing to its quasi status as a "neutral observer" of the sectarian exigencies of the Abrahamic religions afford Derrida the possibility of "translating" the interest-motivated discourses of the established faiths into the ongoing operative language of Western philosophy—and of working in the other direction, as well. In the sense that Derrida never relinquishes his allegiance to and investment (if not faith) in this ongoing Western conceptual operating system, the threshold furnished by *khōra* is necessary to a full ontotheological intervention on deconstruction's part. Both exegetically and ideologically, then, the figure of *khōra* serves as a departure, deviation, or exile by means of which deconstruction, as a supplement to Western ontotheology (among multiple traditions) is free to inscribe its disinterested illumination.

Khōra, in other words, concentrates the sublimity, mystery, secret, and self-effacing paradox by means of which all three actual Abrahamic faiths claim ideological justification and camouflage their conceptual vulnerability, but in the academic setting of philosophy, that is to say, in the foyer of more or less free inquiry that philosophy established on the outskirts of the sacred district, whether adjacent, metonymically linked, to the temple, church, or mosque. *Khōra* simulates and articulates what spiritual presence, immanence, and transcendence would be if they could undergo this displacement to the zone of thoughtfulness that functions almost autonomously of the institutions of religion. As the margin of its existence, its capacity for being is so frail and tenuous, it comes as no surprise that *khōra* is veiled in mystery. At every turn it embodies and presents us with a riddle.

> *Khōra* reaches us, and as the name. And when a name comes, it immediately says more than the name: the other of the name and quite simply the other, whose irruption the name announces. This announcement does not yet promise, no more than it threatens. It neither promises nor threatens anyone. It still remains alien to the person, only naming immanence, even only an imminence that is alien to the myth, the time, and the history of every possible promise and threat. . . .
>
> Hence it might perhaps derive from that "logic other than the logic of the *logos*." The *khōra*, which is neither "sensible" nor "intelligible," belongs to a "third genus" (*triton genos*, 48a, 52a). One cannot even say of it that it is *neither* this *nor* that or that it is *both* this *and* that. It is not enough to recall that *khōra* names neither this nor that, or, that *khōra* says this and that. The difficulty declared by Timaeus is shown in a different way: at times the *khōra* appears to be neither this nor that, at times both this and that, but this alternation between the logic of participation and that of exclusion—we shall return to this at length—stems perhaps only from a provisional appearance and from the constraints of rhetoric, even from some incapacity for naming.[38]

Sheathing *khōra* in the mystery that it presents to him, Derrida first articulates this ultratheological site and figure deriving from beyond the pale of theology as a multifaceted (dis)embodiment of the provisional. Alternating "between the logic of participation and that of exclusion," it hovers at the possibility of placement. It presents a name before we can even know what to expect from naming, let alone what its name delineates. It defies logic on every level, whether Platonic and Aristotelian systems dividing the universe between "sensible" and "intelligible" and establishing definitive genders, rhetorical as well as biological, once and for all; or in the more pedestrian, formal/grammatical formulae of inclusion (either/or) or exclusion (neither/

nor). Occupying space, being there, seizing the word before there can be any rationale for its assertion, *khōra* is as questionable rhetorically, gyrating unpredictably as a figure, as it is systematically, logically, ontologically, geometrically, and generically.

Khōra, not unlike another product of Derrida's engagement with Plato, the *pharmakon* of "Plato's Pharmacy,"[39] is an exasperating metatrope whose resistance to meaning, placement, and conceptual functionality, whose sloughing off of these necessary and expected roles, at the same time excavates, brings to light of day, some of the real violence and uncertainty conditioning Western thought, culture, and theology precisely where they are founded. To acknowledge the excruciating difficulty of naming, defining, translating, and paraphrasing *khōra*, in spite of its pivotal role within the economy of Plato's *Timaeus*, is tantamount to acknowledging the tenuous rhetorical and conceptual basis on which Western core institutions, including Judaism/Christianity/Islam, are founded, the fragile platform upon which their sectarian pronouncements stand. In figures such as the *pharmakon* and *khōra*, forbidding murkiness, exasperating complexity and proliferation of meanings, themselves sometimes contradictory, and undeniable centrality to constellations of speculation, belief, and ideological assertion converge.

Khōra's elusiveness is at the core of its meaning and import. Yet however compelling and irresistible the challenge it issues to tie it down, to fill it in, its relations with entire complexes by which Western thought renders itself intelligible and tolerable are at best problematical, if at all they can be said to exist.

> "*Khōra*" seems never to let itself be reached or touched, much less broached, and above all not exhausted by these *types* of tropological or interpretive translation. One cannot even say that it furnishes them with the support of a stable substratum or substance. *Khōra* is not a subject. It is not the subject. Nor the support [*subjectile*]. The hermeneutic *types* cannot inform, they cannot give form to *khōra* except to the extent that, inaccessible, impassive, "amorphous" (*amorphon*, 51a) and still virgin, with a virginity that is radically rebellious against anthropomorphism, it *seems to receive* these types and *give place* to them. But if Timaeus names it as receptacle (*dekhomenon*) or place (*khōra*), these names do not designate an *eidos*, since *khōra* is neither of the order of the *eidos* nor of the order of the mimemes, that is, of images of the *eidos* which come to imprint themselves in it. . . . *Khōra* is not, is above all not, is anything but a support or a subject which would

give place, by receiving or by conceiving, or indeed by letting itself be conceived. How could one deny it this essential significance as a receptacle, given that this very name is given to it by Plato? It is difficult indeed, but perhaps we have not yet thought through what is meant by to receive, the receiving of the receptacle, what is said by *dekhomai, dekhomenon*. Perhaps it is from *khōra* that we are beginning to learn it, to receive from it what its name calls up. To receive it, if not to comprehend it, to conceive it.[40]

Khōra, a venerable foundation of Western metaphysics, is not only inimical to the pivotal architectural supports upon which this edifice literally stands (subjectivity, substance, logical types). It eludes the very framework, structure, or architecture by which traditions are founded, concepts are comprehended, principles find support, and attitudes and ideas are received and collected, stored in receptacles. In *khōra* Derrida isolates a founding principle that is constitutionally inimical to the architectural as well as conceptual framework, the canonical or core structure, according to which traditions, beliefs, and institutions are received, transmitted, supported, and sustained. Not only does *khōra* pull the rug out from under the format of support on which traditions and religions depend,[41] it maintains a respectful distance from the rhetorical tropes, above all, metaphor and metonymy, by which such functions as support, transmission, and reception are instrumented.

To be sure, Derrida would not dedicate such pitched attentiveness to *khōra* were it merely an abyss of nonmeaning or insignificance. From his Platonic readings and explorations of the existing scholarship, he knows that the term is "properly a mother, a nurse, a receptacle, a bearer of imprints or gold." Yet even in this respect, "its scope goes beyond or falls short of the polarity of metaphorical sense versus proper sense," and it "exceeds the polarity, no doubt analogous, of the *mythos* and the *logos*."[42] For all the indeterminacy in which it is shrouded, for the multifaceted support functions that it abdicates, *khōra* does indicate the sites, the formats, in which the deceptively violent work of establishing Western values and institutions takes place.

By distancing itself from the site proper of Western theology, the temple, church, or mosque, *khōra* becomes an ambiguous model for all oracles, sacred precincts, Holies of Holy. *Khōra* is the theological installation of the Western scene and framework of the abyss, a construct whose decisiveness for thought and representation Derrida has carefully extrapolated in a variety of contexts. Derrida places great emphasis on the spatial dimension and specification of *khōra*, yet what kind of site, exactly, does *khōra* constitute? *Khōra* is both the extension and embodiment of a chasm that opens up right in the midst of the *Timaeus*'s "encyclopaedic" dimensions, its aspiration to serve as "a general ontology, treating of all the types of being," including "a theology, a cosmology, a physiology, a psychology, a zoology":

> And yet, half-way through the cycle, won't the discourse on *khōra* have opened, between the sensible and the intelligible, belonging neither to one nor to the other, hence neither to the cosmos as sensible god nor to the intelligible god, an apparently empty space—even though it is no doubt not *emptiness*? Didn't it name a gaping opening, an abyss or a chasm? Isn't it starting out from this chasm, "in" it, that the cleavage between the sensible and the intelligible, indeed, between body and soul, can have place and take place? Let us not be too hasty about bringing this chasm named *khōra* close to that chaos which also opens the yawning gulf of the abyss. Let us avoid hurling it into the anthropomorphic gulf of the abyss.[43]

Khōra, in context, opens up as a void in the midst of a philosophical work with claims on being the comprehensive philosophical work of its generation and in the Platonic canon. Even in the relatively secular domain of philosophical discourse, an abyss opens up, one that, in spite of Derrida's admonitions against demonizing it and humanizing it, links *khōra* to such Western metaphysical manifestations as oracles, ghosts, apparitions, messengers, and underworlds staged by classical and Renaissance drama; also to Hell, magic, and alchemy. Secular discourse thus binds *khōra* to the entire complex of supernatural constructs and apparatuses both epitomizng faculties of speculation and imagination and undermining their purity and lucidity. Indeed, the ultimate wizardry that, as a certain kind of place or site, *khōra* mobilizes is the composition of the text that would presume to account for thinking and its inscription:

> If there is indeed a chasm in the middle of the book, a sort of abyss "in" which there is an attempt to think or say this abyssal chasm which would be *khōra* . . . is it insignificant that a *mise en abyme* regulates a certain order of composition of the discourse? . . . Is it insignificant that this *mise en abyme* affects the forms of a discourse on places [*places*], notably political places, a politics of place entirely commended by the consideration of sites [*lieux*] (jobs in the society, region, territory, country), as sites assigned to types or forms of discourse?[44]

In its indelible traits, *khōra* proves elusive, both as a location or setting and as a known quantity. Yet *khōra* is not fated to the isolation of exile, to remaining utterly off on its own and incommunicado. To the degree that the roles and functions emerging from its abyssal architecture (receptacle, imprint bearer, etc.) embody principles of composition, they extend into the hub of communications and involve those language programmers known as writers, speakers, and orators. Among the spaces in Western thought, religion, and culture that *khōra* configures is a theater, and the action on this allegorical stage definitely has the political cast registered in the citation immediately above. Space is inherently social. There is no exclusively formal space. *Khōra*, as a substrate that is not fundamental, a framework that renounces support, is from the outset programmed with roles and functions that will be set into play, activated, by the consummate actor to stride across its stage, the philosopher. The philosopher is she who programs and reprograms the conditions of thinking and writing that, in lieu of principles, categories, types, and genres, configure the abyss of *khōra*. Socrates is not *khōra*, but his sociopolitical roles and his actions as a discourse programmer have to some degree been conditioned by *khōra's* anomalous setting.

> Socrates *effaces himself*, effaces in himself all the types, all the genera, both of the men of image and simulacrum whom he pretends for a moment to resemble and that of the men of action and men of their word, philosophers and politicians to whom he addresses himself, philosophers and politicians to whom he addresses himself while effacing himself before them. But in thus effacing himself, he situates himself or institutes himself as a *receptive addressee*, let us say, as a *receptacle of all* that will henceforth be inscribed. He declares himself to be *ready and all set* for that, disposed to receive everything he's offered. . . . Once more, the question returns: what does *receive* mean? What does *dekhomai* mean? . . .
>
> Socrates is not *khōra*, but he would look a lot like it/her if it/she were someone or something. In any case, he puts himself in its/her place, which is not just a place among others, but perhaps *place itself*.[45]

The philosopher is less a player in the arena of action than a figure of self-effacement, receptivity, readiness to be marked, scored, influenced, changed. Her ongoing state of preparedness for a thoughtful event always on the verge of being defined and structured implies a very specific temporal bearing and attitude toward time. The philosopher who thinks and reprograms on the stage of *khōra* maintains, like the prophet, the priest, and

Christ, a privileged relation to the abyss designated as the foyer, the shifter in Western culture, leading toward divinity and transcendence. But whereas the prophet, the priest, and even Christ presume to speak in the name of the deity, to express and in so doing to establish and stabilize certain eternal truths regarding the deity and the configuration of society, religion, and culture that the deity determines and predicates, Socrates acts only by abdicating, by abandoning the terra firma of existing ideology and by opening up the space for incredulity, speculation, and thinking whose features are those of *khōra*. In this respect, Derrida's Socrates is a distant, but discernible descendant of Kierkegaard's.

Khōra extends. It "stretches out," not with the infinite expanse and pliability of the void at the beginning of Genesis, but into the arenas of cultural activity and organization. Its features merge not only into the figure of the philosopher, but also into the self-effacing reprogramming that the philosopher performs. *Khōra* bespeaks the paradoxical temporal bearing maintained by the philosopher, progressing from certitude to something less, but something more mobile. It expands into the discursive media that the philosopher deploys. Discursive mastery, in the philosopher's hands, is a vehicle toward the astonishment and wonder at the far side of knowledge. In its revolutionary, open-ended theater, *khōra* characterizes not only the medium of writing, but also the dynamics of narrative.

> Now what is *represented* by virgin wax, a wax that is always virgin, absolutely preceding any possible impression, always older, because atemporal, than anything that seems to affect it in order to take form *in it*, in it which *receives*, nevertheless, and in it which, for the same reason, is always younger, infant even, achronic and anachronistic, so indeterminate that it does not even justify the name and the form of wax? . . . Each tale is thus the *receptacle* of another. There is nothing but receptacles of narrative receptacles, or narrative receptacles of receptacles. Let us not forget that receptacle, place of harboring/lodging (*hypo-dokhè*), is the most insistent determination (let us not say "essential," for reasons which must already be obvious) of *khōra*.
>
> But if *khōra* is a receptacle, if it/she gives place to all the stories, ontologic or mythic, that can be recounted on the subject of what she receives and even what she resembles but which in fact takes place in her, *khōra* herself, so to speak, does not become the object of any *tale*, whether true or fabled. A secret without secret remains forever impenetrable on the subject of it/her [*a son sujet*].[46]

The first part of this extract addresses the medium of inscription. Under the aura of *khōra*, communications are impressed on tablets of wax whose virginity bears within it an attitude toward time. *Khōra's* legends always transpire before the fact. They constitute a "soft writing" that is atemporal, inimical to its array on a structured framework or stand of temporal priority, progression, and causality. The medium of writing retains an infancy and febrility resistant to these calculations. Impressed into service to trace progressions in language, the soft milieu of writing extending from *khōra* can establish only a repository strewn with abandoned segments of narrative: imprints of tales communicating only onto more tales. This is the landscape that Derrida surveys in the second part of the extract. *Khōra* thus "gives place" not only to all stories, but to the format, the template out of which all stories, indeed narration itself, emerge. *Khōra* has no status outside of precipitating, crystallizing this format. There is no tale or history, whether of nobility, transcendence, or perdition, in which *khōra* plays a part, yet *khōra* opens the terrain of all narratives.

The ground of *khōra* thus underlies the narrative that is the pretext, rationale, and thrust of religion. But it is *khōra's* role as a site and station for textual production—textuality as the outgrowth of philosophy's etiquettes and projects, and not to the degree that it has been claimed by one Abrahamic subculture or another—that marks its soft and passive decisiveness for Derrida. By reading *khōra* as an unobtrusive pretext to writing deriving from the philosophical sphere, Derrida can delineate his own interpretation of this complex, pervasive trope from the Heideggerian appropriation, which allocates it to "the question of the meaning of being."[47] Derrida's image of a landscape composed of "nothing but receptacles of narrative receptacles, or narratives of receptacles of receptacles," which are both the fullest extension of *khōra* and the pretext of the structured fictions indispensable to Western science and law as well as religion and literature, approaches the vividness of Plato's most memorable poetic crystallizations, whether the charioteer of the *Phaedrus*, the cave of the *Republic*, or the aviary of the *Theaetetus*. The landscape of receptacles deriving from the *Timaeus* indeed joins the Platonic *pharmakon* as a telling figure emerging in the place of a cosmological origin, a historical foundation, a prescriptive logic, or a definitive ethics. This is a figure indecisive in its passivity, confusing in its polymorphousness, but it does not abandon its station as an enabler and catalyst of further articulation and thinking. Such a figure is *all* that Derrida has to offer by way of ontotheological ground.

Khōra, then, stands in for the origin and firm substrate that philosophical systems dictate for themselves, assumes the qualities of the inscription emerging in place of these mythical foundations, as their only viable and indeed only available alternative, and anticipates the role of the philosopher and conceptual reprogrammer, whether Socrates, Kierkegaard, or Heidegger. *Khōra* also encompasses the capability to stage or perform itself. It is possessed of "hard" allegorical wiring. The proliferation of narrative receptacles or elements that Derrida figures, in other words, can claim a theatrical expression. *Khōra* opens a space of abyssal mimetic repetition, *différance*, and disfiguration. This setting is as close to a comprehensive "scene of writing" for the diverse branches of Western idealistic striving as can be allowed. At the outset of the magisterial Western tradition, *khōra* claims the role that Kant assigns the *hypotyposes* at the climax of *The Critique of Judgment*: It is a metatextual, metarhetorical performer.[48]

To know that the substrate of all inscription is so configured, is installed with allegorical circumspect and ironic qualification, severely brackets the claims of originality, authenticity, authority, and rectitude that can be made, whether by discourse in its disciplinary genres or by religion.

> The discourse on *khōra* thus plays for philosophy a role analogous to the role which *khōra* "herself" plays for that which philosophy speaks of, namely, the cosmos formed or given form according to the paradigm. Nevertheless, it is from this cosmos that the proper—but necessarily inadequate—figures will be taken for describing *khōra*: receptacle, imprint-bearer, mother, or nurse. These figures are not even true figures. Philosophy cannot speak directly, whether in the mode of vigilance or of truth (true or probable), about what these figures approach. The dream is between the two, neither the one nor the other. Philosophy cannot speak philosophically of that which looks like its "mother," its "nurse," its "receptacle," or its "imprint-bearer." As such, it speaks only of the father and the son, as if the father engendered it all on his own.[49]

Khōra not only assures a place for figuration in philosophical discourse, it qualifies any formulation that Western philosophy—or religion—might be so bold as to issue as irreducibly figurative, rhetorical, and writerly. In this regard, establishing a long tradition in philosophy, *khōra* occupies a feminine position or posture. Philosophy can henceforth speak only in parables. The same can be said of religion. The Christian Gospels are particularly responsive in relation to this point. Western discourse, already abyssal, figurative, passive, and openly receptive, cannot presume to speak directly, to pronounce under the presumption of direct access to the truth, rectitude, or the divinity. All the less is it justifiable to *act* on the basis of discourse, of inscription itself framed by or set against the backdrop of *khōra*. Given *khōra's* passiveness and receptivity, any concerted action, the acting out of principles, dicta, or pronouncements presumably "contained" by discourse, whether religious or discursive, is irreducibly violent. It matters not whether such action is hospitable or openly aggressive, whether it is undertaken by recognized governmental, administrative, or religious organizations or agencies, or whether it is impromptu. *Khōra* not only stages the theater of Western thought and inscription, it harbors the traces of an ethics whose fullest articulation may well await the fourth Abrahamic religion. This is an ethics of the nonviolence that precipitates from the intricacies, nuances, colorations, and tonalities of language. We may often fall beneath the state of preparedness for what deconstruction, through *khōra*, reminds us: If we insist on imagining Western art, science, religion, and government as a grand edifice, it is founded, irreducibly and incontrovertibly, on nonviolence.

A Moment of Philosophical Relaxation?

Given Derrida's longstanding elucidation of telling religious constructs and values, particularly where they merge with and affect the evolving conceptual operating system that is Western philosophy's paradigmatic preoccupation, a palpable shift in his attitude, say toward the Torah scrolls near the conclusion of the Genet column of *Glas*[50] and the tallith in "A Silkworm of One's Own,"[51] warrants notice and commentary on the part of his readers. If one can argue that a relaxation takes place in Derrida's attitude toward religion in general, in full view of religion's historical intolerance and violence and its ideological and ethical closure, it is a rapprochement, not a lending of credence. And such a diminution, if not dissolution of tension, comes to us by way of the oto/autobiographical register of his writing[52] that, setting out in full force in *The Post Card*, is almost as old as *Glas*.

Any comfort that gradually invades Derrida's address toward a canon of texts and a set of institutions whose history is as checkered as religion's— indeed, the treacheries of religion *are* the discursive/disciplinary limits of history—does so through an increased intimacy in his rapport with Judaism, his "home" religion. But his *Auseinandersetzung* with Judaism, as with anything, is first and foremost mediated through philosophy in its ongoing experiments in conceptualization through articulation. He had known since the outset of his project that the inscription of his or any author's singularity bears the privacy and uniqueness of his signature. It can well be argued in general that Derrida's growing intimacy with religion in general is a facet of his own singularity that is Jewish-Algerian, that has submitted to a Jewish upbringing in a Muslim society, itself subjected to a French nationality whose religious bent is a Catholicism fitted out to secular modernization. Indeed, any study of "comparative religions" is a panorama of colliding singularities. These singularities demand expression, being rendered explicit, and a literate, articulate working through before an individual can eventuate in a Levinasian embrace of alterity, in what post-Enlightenment Western ideology imprecisely couches in a rhetoric of preordained and universally understood and accepted equality and tolerance.[53]

Through the engagement with and inscription of his proper singularity, Derrida opens a dialogue with religion in general by way of his own quite particular Judeo-Muslim early formation. "I would like to sing the very solitary softness of my tallith, softness softer than softness, entirely singular, both sensory and non-sensory, calm acquiescent, a stranger to anything maudlin, to effusion or to pathos, in a word to all 'Passion.' "[54] It is not only Derrida's tallith that has opened and softened to him, offering him a very private refuge. Yet for all the warmth in which Derrida's sheath or veil envelops him, he will not allow himself or his readers "Passion," the adulteration of his radical positionality through sectarian allegiances or appropriations.

Derrida remains the radical reprogrammer of philosophical operating systems, yet his position toward religion, initially very hard and ironic, in keeping with the rigor of a reprogramming from the perspective of "language's eye-view" and toward the philosophy of writing, softens. The sea change in cultural bearing that Derrida orchestrates—not only toward language, but also in relation to the protocols of the arts and sciences—is the most comprehensive in memory. How do we account for the seeming about-face on the part of a thinker whose intervention has been unusually consistent with itself since its inception? Is such a mood change entirely unprecedented in the work of a thinker whose purview is as systematic as his writing is volatile and arbitrary?

The peace that Derrida, in "A Silkworm of One's Own," finds in his tallith is not entirely unlike Kant's willingness, in his *Critique of Judgment*,[55] having annotated beauty's sexual allure, to welcome aesthetics as a full-fledged domain of systematic philosophy. It bears striking similarities as well to Wittgenstein's acknowledgment, in *On Uncertainty*,[56] of the pathos of thinking and knowing, this after a career—in the names of logic and rigorous formulation—of severely bracketing the roles of subjectivity and psychology in learned discourse. Kant's scripting of a seductive scenario in which philosophy first dismisses and resists beauty primes the pump for the theatrically begrudging acceptance of aesthetics as a legitimate theater of intuition and field of knowledge. A touching irony and disingenuousness attend this long-delayed détente, one transpiring after years of spirited, highly creative resistance.

It is thus less accurate and less useful to speak of a softening or amelioration in Derrida's stance toward religion than to underscore the particular openings toward not only its attitudes, but also its practices that emerge in the later studies. These not only include, in the context of a dialogue with Hélène Cixous, a highly generative critic and theorist whose Algerian-Jewish background he shares, a meditation on his tallith or prayer shawl. It is surely in this context that Hermann Cohen ("a university professor . . . the first Jewish professor of that rank in Germany") shored up his hope that Germany would serve as "the true homeland of every Jew in the world, 'the motherland of their soul,'" with patriotic support of that nation's position in World War I and a strategic discretion with regard to anti-Semitic discrimination in university student organizations.[57] Derrida recognized in himself a fellow academic of unusual distinction and Jewish extraction whose political opinions matter.

In contradistinction to Cohen, Derrida applies the full force and refinement of his philosophical distillations to his comments on religious politics. Hence, he "takes a stand" for Algeria in an essay of that title,[58] and he declares, at the outset of "Interpretations at War," which he delivered in Jerusalem, his "solidarity with all those, in this land who advocate an end to violence, condemn the crimes of terrorism and of military and police repression, and advocate the withdrawal of Israeli troops from the occupied territories."[59] In "The Eyes of Language," by the same token, he brings the full lucidity and rigor of his readings of Rosenzweig, Benjamin, and Scholem to bear on the transformation of Hebrew from a "spiritual language" to a secular one encoded with the political territoriality and force of a national entity replete with cultural institutions.

Derrida's increased willingness in his later writings to address such often exasperating questions does not in any way transpire as a Sabbath from or suspension of his evolving positionalities. Yet he can also recognize certain aspects of his own situation and experience, as he did in the case of Cohen, in the biblical Abraham's wanderings and emigration, his status as a *ger*, or stranger. "For Abraham calls himself again, he recalls that he is destined by God to be a hôte (*ger*), an immigrant, a foreign body abroad, a strange body to the stranger [*un corps étranger à l'étranger*]."[60] Surely no philosopher and academic has been as "nomadic"[61] as Derrida, both in his early emigration from Algiers to the École Normale Supérieure in Paris and in the Homeric global trajectory of his subsequent seminars and lecture appearances. This initial and ongoing status of a stranger to several languages, nationalities, and academic discourses and disciplines at once has been momentous for the radical positionality from which Derrida joins any conversation, although at a dislocating remove. Again, any "softness," first toward Judaism and then toward its Abrahamic sibling religions that these considerations indicate, emerges above all from Derrida's embrace, in writing, of his own multifaceted singularity. Religion thus furnishes him with one particularly compelling lieu, *mihrab*, *bima*, or stage in his writing in which singularity addresses ideology.

Surely no turn of phrase is more emblematic of Derrida's very specific détente with religious thought than the "diminutions" casually appearing at the outset of "A Silkworm of One's Own."

> Stop writing here, but instead from afar defy a weaving, yes, from afar, or rather see its diminution. Childhood memory: raising their eyes from their woolen threads, but without stopping or even slowing the movement of their agile fingers, the women of my family used to say, sometimes I think, that they had to *diminish*. Not undo, I guess, but diminish, i.e., though I had no idea what the word meant then but I was all the more intrigued by it, even in love with it, that they needed to diminish the stitches or reduce the knit of what they were working on. And for this *diminution*, needles and hands had to work with two loops at once, or at least play with more than one.[62]

The parallel case to Kant's seduction, toward the end of his career, by the beautiful and its rhetorico-aesthetic ramifications, to Wittgenstein's quasi-mystical uncertainties at the tain or underside of precise formulation may be, in Derrida's case, nothing more momentous or earth-shattering than a "diminution," an adjustment surely distinct from a deviation or change of heart. (In its evolution, Derrida's vast project has been far more a dance of side steps, stutter steps, and digressions of elucidation than a dialectical drama of grand assertions and retractions.) The diminution whose source is a weaving practice among the women of Derrida's family, a weaving that produces, among other garments, the enveloping Jewish prayer shawl or tallith, entails a change in tonality and modality, rather than in substance. "Talking music, you can, decrescendo, diminuendo, attenuate little by little the intensity of the sound, but also 'diminish' the intervals. Whilst in the language of rhetoric, a little like litotes, like extenuation or reticence, a 'diminution' consists in saying less, sure, but with a view toward *letting* more be understood."[63] The diminution in weaving that the women in Derrida's family make part of their practice, also when producing religious garments, thus, like any other figure worthy of Derrida's underlining, operates above all in a rhetorical domain, as an understatement, saying less in order to intimate more.

The figure of the tallith thus spans the shoulders of one religious tradition, Judaism, and rhetoric. Its woven mode of production places it in a long tradition of veils, fabrics, and membranes in Derrida's writing: the hymen, tissue, sails, swan's wings, foam, and fold from "The Double Session,"[64] where such figures not only thematically proliferate but become the signature of the Mallarméan poetics. This work anticipates the not inconsiderable elaboration of veils in "A Silkworm of One's Own."[65] In this dimension, the tallith serves as one local figure of textuality. It has been embroidered with the subprogram of the deconstructive project that has bracketed conceptual claims of efficacy by means of a relentless attentiveness to the textual features of discourse. The tallith situates deconstruction's theological commentary squarely (but also roundly) within the precinct or *khōra* of textuality.

The "diminution" situated at the outset of a far-ranging dialogue with Hélène Cixous signals an adjustment, within the deconstructive discourse of theology, an adjustment such as occurs in the sizing of a garment. And

Derrida's exposition of what his tallith has meant to him signals the overall drift of his more relaxed approach to questions of theology and religiosity:

> So I no longer wear it, I simply place my lips on it, almost every evening, except when I'm traveling to the ends of the earth, because like an animal it waits for me, well hidden in its hiding place, at home, it never travels. I touch it without knowing what I am doing or asking in so doing, especially not knowing into whose hands I am entrusting myself, to whom I'm rendering thanks. But to know at least two things—which I invoke here for those who are foreign (get this paradox: even more ignorant, more foreign than I) to the culture of this tallith, this culture of shawl and not veil: blessing and death.[66]

This passage arises in an uncanny intimacy with an object alien and foreign, very much of a piece with the narrator's kitten/lamb in Kafka's "Eine Kreuzung" ("A Crossbreed/A Sport"):

> Sometimes I cannot help laughing when it sniffs around me and winds itself between my legs and simply will not be parted from me. Not content with being lamb and cat, it almost insists on being a dog as well. . . . It has the restlessness of both beasts. . . . For that reason its skin feels too tight for it. Sometimes it jumps up on the armchair beside me, plants its front legs on my shoulder, and puts its muzzle to my ear. It is as if it were saying something to me.[67]

Derrida's tallith is an inheritance from his family, as is the bizarre creature who is the talisman of the Kafkan character's difference, his literarity, the creature who gazes at the narrator in utter familiarity while the narrator ponders ending its misery in sacrificial fashion, with a butcher's knife. This is a specific literary counterpart to a moment in the *Gespräch mit Cixous* making a sharp turn toward the poetic. The passage ends with a new *différance* added to the domain of deconstructive textuality: shawls, with their enveloping warmth, precipitate out of veils, and perhaps other weavings. Derrida's tallith never travels. It is a creature of his home. Yet precisely because the tallith and its culture remain "foreign" to him (here Derrida professes an ignorance of Judaic culture not borne out in such writings as "Des Tours de Babel," "Interpretations at War," "The Eyes of Language," and "A Silkworm of One's Own"), he relates to it physiotropically, with his *tongue*, both as a particularly visceral corporeal organ and as a keyword for language. Derrida's tallith is a complex mantle of alienation and Otherness. It is foreign to him, while in intimate rapport to him and his ("original" and extended) families. It marks him as the *ger* or foreigner he has been for so many decades in relation to academic disciplines, universities, colleagues, even governments. The endurance of the paradoxical vacillation between intimacy and uncanniness that the tallith prompts initiates the Derrida persona of the dialogue into the tallith's culture of blessing and death.

Whether blessing enters Derrida's purview on ontotheology, religion, and ideological constellations in general, it is indissolubly linked to a certain death: whether the death of cultures in desuetude, the death of systems, the death of old crystallizations, or of lives and the minds that endow them with distinction. The "diminution" that played a generative role in the tallith's spinning out thus orchestrates the slightest adjustment in Derrida's bearing toward religion and the conceptual/ideational formations that it encompasses, but one nevertheless pivotal.

The gestures of warmth and intimacy—of blessing—in this "diminution" are palpable. Even with regard to the vexed questions of Jewish nationality and the role played in it by the Hebrew language, it is possible to discern an openness to theological questioning in no way mitigating Derrida's pronounced and ongoing opposition to nationalisms, violence, and a priori exclusions.

In "The Eyes of Language," Derrida meditates on a letter from Gershom Scholem to Franz Rosenzweig on the anomalies resulting from Hebrew's transformation from a "spiritual" to a "secular" language. The essay begins quite literally in an abyss, one known, if not familiar to Derrida's readers of the past two decades: a multiuse, linguistically constituted venue and dynamic for often-spiritualized cultural phenomena traditionally relegated to such constructs as "spirit," "the underworld," "the imagination," and "the ghostly." By diverting his own project into this abyss, Derrida effects a contrapuntal shift in emphasis, enabling spectral linguistic epiphenomena including repetition, recursivity, iterability, concantenations, and assonance to come to the fore, effects largely muffled in traditional theological discourse constructed around spirituality and its manifestations, including pure evil, the unconscious, and the uncanny. Indeed, if deconstructive spectrality enters into a counterpoint with traditional spiritualized scenarios for otherworldliness, such productions as Kierkegaardian repetition, Nietzschean "eternal recurrence," and the Freudian "return of the repressed" are particularly momentous, being translatable into both notations, conventional and deconstructive, of this double-entry accounting.

Derrida's insinuation, as in the instance of *khōra*, of a spectral dimension within the matrix of language itself furnishes deconstruction with an overture to addressing some of the most patent values in Abrahamic theology: altruism, sacrifice, and redemption. The pivotal works in which Derrida effects this transposition include *The Gift of Death* and *Specters of Marx*. The complex encompassing ghosts, specters, revenants, and the abyss also is the single most prevalent strand of imagery among the essays collected in the English-language anthology *Acts of Religion*.

In terms of "The Eyes of Language," the essay that Derrida dedicates to the establishment of Hebrew as a state language, this development is a "catastrophe," a term that Derrida takes over from Scholem, one involving "the terrifying return of a ghost."[68] There is no theoretical discourse by which the return of Hebrew as a secular language can be debated, say by Rosenzweig and Scholem, Derrida demonstrates, that does not activate a rhetoric of ghosts and the abysses they haunt.

> Can one not say, consequently, that Scholem speaks, in a certain manner . . . a sacred language? Yet he does so in German (Hebrew figures in the German language) and in order to speak the evil that has happened, that will happen [*pour dire le mal qui vient d'arriver, qui va arriver*] to the sacred language, but will happen to it [*advenir*] to it as much through a certain return of the sacred language that will *come back* as through its departure, through the experience in which we separate ourselves from this language as we depart from it? This country is a volcano, then, and language inhabits it. Language dwells, as one says, *on top* of a volcano.[69]

Language, then, is not the substrate or subtext of the nation, whether conceived of as sacred or secular. It is a decisive factor, up front, "from the top down." Scholem duly recognizes, in the face of Rosenzweig's defensive posture to the effect that "Zionism is a secular form of Messianism," that the institution(s) of language will be explosive to any state.[70] As the nation is inflected linguistically, not the reverse, linguistic matters will detonate from the outset, explicitly, rather than subliminally.

The restorers of Hebrew, in Scholem's scenario, its translators from sacredness to secularity ("spellbound [but they are also sorcerers, sorcerers' apprentices]")[71] are thus, to borrow a figure from Wallace Stevens, "connoisseurs of chaos." Hoping to conceal the abyss, they unleash its unsettling potentials all the more. Derrida opens a sobering yin-yang for all who would aspire through religious renewal to redeem the insufficiencies and intangibles of political public life: the more the goal seems attainable, the more imminent the sociopolitical volcano's explosion.

> But these sacred names, precisely those that the blind men bequeath to our youth without seeing and without knowing [*sans voir et sans savoir*], they are the abyss. They conceal the abyss—in them the abyss is concealed. . . . The abyss is in the name, one could say, if such a typology were representable, if the bottomlessness of the *Abgrund* could still let itself be included, inscribed, comprehended. At bottom, the bottom of the bottomlessness [*au fond de ce sans-fond*], what the blind sorcerers of secularization do not see, is not so much the abyss itself, over which they walk like madmen, but rather that the abyss does not, any more than language, let itself be dominated, tamed, instrumentalized, secularized. The abyss no more than language, for both take place, *their* place, without specifiable topology, in the name" *Sprache ist Namen*, language is Name."[72]

The recourse to Hebrew is abyssal, as Scholem senses and Derrida elaborates—indeed deconstruction's relentless making explicit marks one of its pervasive and always understated intersections with Judaism—and it is in the nature of this linguistic substrate, pretext, scene—of writing, reverberation, mumbling, moaning—to brook no control, no domination. Jews can just as easily join the community of madmen who would presume to fill and direct this abyss, to inaugurate a regime of linguistic purity[73] as, say, Germans, Serbo-Croatians, and the mullahs. It is to a violence perpetrated in the sphere of linguistic primordiality that Derrida wishes to direct our attention when we contemplate the Middle East and other zones of intractable sociopolitical conflict. Here is where the violence erupts. Only by retracing the reverberations of this set of shortcuts, abridgments, and foreclosures will there be any possibility of détente and healing in the sociopolitical domain. It is in contemplating possible solutions to persistent impasses such as those surrounding Hebrew that Derrida approaches the discourse of a theological speculator in his own right. The openness toward ontotheological thinking that does not allow him to dispense with religious figures in wholesale fashion motivates his quest for varieties of religious experience within the framework of language itself. The play in Scholem's thought between sacred and nonsacred "produces an experience of the edge, the edge of the abyss, between two places [*entre deux lieux*]. The immanent sacrifice, at once past and impossible, makes appear, or rather announces, the sacred language as such, the very sacredness that is *of language* [*qui est de la langue*]."[74] Even in light of Hebrew's intense borderline difficulties, the "experience of the edge," Derrida explores a sacredness that might be endemic to language itself, according to which language's sacrifice might be comprehensible. Such sacrifice "has two significations or two virtues. It can destroy the sacred but, in so doing, it can . . . make the sacred as such manifest, save it thus in the sacrifice, pay homage with, or give the gift of, a destruction [*faire homage ou don d'une destruction*], indeed of a murder or of a death, to the sacred."[75] To think the sacredness of language is both to open up a radical lieu for the redefinition of the sacrifices that have already been made, some horrific, and to reconsider the metaphysics of sacrifice itself.

> One must therefore tie what we have just said of sacrifice to the responsibility proper to our generation, the one undergoing the trial of this nonlanguage that secular Hebrew is—a generation of transition (*das Geschlecht des Übergangs*), a generation of passage and of access. The transition is not interpreted solely according to the present sense of the biological or natural chain of generations. . . . The gravest responsibility must be exercised at the moment of the greatest danger: without rule and guarantee on the edge of the abyss, above the abyss. On the edge of the abyss or above the abyss—it comes down to the same thing [*cela revient au même*].[76]

Madness, henceforth, is not in the province of behavioral, psychiatric, or clinical nosologies; it articulates itself as a rapport with sacredness, which is, in turn, a feature of language, not of spiritual, sociopolitical, or cultural entities. As part of an ongoing strand of Derrida's thought meriting elaboration on its own terms, madness (or psychopathology) is tantamount to object-relation theory's "immoderate demands" imposed upon language: Language should deliver expressive, experiential, or emotional "purity." As a medium, it should retain "perfect" memory and in so doing control time. These aberrations in the form of language desires or wishes are doomed to failure and are hence evocative of negative emotions, and possibly of "symptoms," that may be experienced on personal ("private") or collective levels. They form the basis of a deconstructive mode of psychology and psychotherapy, a regime of response and intervention, of (lines of) questioning, and of potential healing as coherent and conceivable as the other schools currently in operation, whether Freudian, Lacanian, object relations, humanist, or existential. The extrapolation of the bearings and addresses in a deconstructively nuanced modality of psychotherapeutic treatment is as unavoidable and compelling as the projection, attempted in these pages, of Abrahamic religion in the wake of deconstruction.

In his work on the broadest philosophical implications of the return of Hebrew as a state language and on the debate accompanying this historical development, Derrida does not simply dissociate himself and deconstruction from the "madness" of which modern Hebrew is a symptom. In keeping with the nuance and gradation that deconstruction demands, in psychotherapeutic fashion, he makes an "alliance" with this madness. He engages himself with the madness of linguistic purism and absolute retentiveness in order to piece together a sense of generational responsibility of the abyss, literally on the brink. In this particular swath of discourse, he writes not as one accomplishing a definitive act of repudiating conditions repugnant to him, but rather as an advocate of collective responsibility for them in the very particular sense that accrues to this term. Indeed, responsibility, both as response and departure, will be a tenet central to any counter-religion or fourth Abrahamic faith that can be culled from the literature of deconstruction. Whether as part of a mature relaxation of earlier positionings that Derrida might share with other major contributors to philosophical tradition or through the process of diminution that he himself stages, deconstruction opens itself to and accepts liability, assumes responsibility, for ontotheologically derived articulations and conditions of the most controversial and problematical nature for its sustained project and projection.

Religion under the Aura of Deconstruction

In closing this review of Derrida's religious writings from the 1980s on, we are challenged to ponder not that it exists, will exist, or even *should* exist, but what a deconstructively inflected sphere of religious activity might encompass. I do not foresee any particular group, cult, sect, or tangible community emerging from this exercise. To be sure, Derrida allowed himself to serve as the occasion for the formation of a numerous, boisterous, smart, erudite, and irreverent community of international scope, but it would be difficult to characterize this pack of deconstructionists as religious in its mission (although it might not be excessive to ascribe an implicit theological interest to this singular dialogue).

Yet the challenge of imagining a deconstructively configured religious lieu or *khōra* is *there*. It has emerged or happened in the wake of a congenitally flawed history of exclusive and tendentious religious practice that has accompanied a parallel history of religious imaginativeness, inspiration, caring, learning, and speculation as old as human communities. Religious practice and institutions impinge upon us. They are in the world.

The Abrahamic religions, precisely because they are coded with figures redolent of mysticism, mystification, and ages-old superstition, pose a striking challenge to rigorous philosophy, close reading, and memorable criticism. If we assume that traditional organized religions will continue to play some role in contemporary culture—as part of a hybrid secular religion whose elements, among others, include professionalism, technology, consumerism, sports, and entertainment—it is hardly dismissive of deconstruction to assume that it might offer something vital and indispensable to the projects of religious reprogramming, correction, adaptation, and renewal. On the contrary. If the ambitious and audacious secular counterdiscourse of philosophy has offered any ongoing gift to the societies and institutions that might have been foolish enough to sustain it, and we need only to reread "Plato's Pharmacy" to recall what a complex figure this is, it has been precisely the gift of a *counter*, a resource for radical and potentially corrective reprogramming at the figural level.

Even the slightest sensitivity to the theologically nuanced language that has crept into my last sentences will bear witness to the need for such a persistent counter. This potential for productive revision retains the gift of an ongoing articulation of what Derrida terms "the experience of the impossible," the always obscure, aporetic, and difficult counters to the force and momentum of prevailing systems, whether they be sociopolitical, economic, juridical, or, in terms of the present discussion, religious. There is no "promised land" of a positive deconstructive religion into whose futurity we can peer, like Moses at the culmination of his politico-prophetic mission. But we can begin to ask ourselves how the three Abrahamic religions will differ from themselves in the wake of deconstruction's sustained elucidation of them and how deconstruction may serve as a *khōra* or lieu of this indispensable updating.

As always, the first recourse that we have to deconstruction's potential prescriptions to the existing Abrahamic religions is to Derrida's specific formulations. It has not been beneath him, on occasion, to characterize the overall attitudinal resetting that would be necessary to a more conceptually viable and constructive theological culture in the West. It is in these loosely prescriptive statements that we isolate the first lineaments marking deconstruction as a religious site of correction rather than addition, of dismantling rather than reformation. It will then be possible, based on the persistence and depth of the ethico-ontotheological reprogramming that Derrida has already performed at the tropological level, to generate certain of the aphorisms pertaining to this updated religious sphere.

RESPONSIBILITY AND RELIGION

> The temptation of knowing, the temptation of knowledge, is to believe not only that one knows what one knows (which wouldn't be too serious), but also that one knows what knowledge is, free, structurally of belief or of **faith**—of the fiduciary or of trustworthiness. The temptation to believe in knowledge, here for example in the precious authority of Benveniste, can hardly be separated from a certain fear and trembling. Before what? Before a scholarship that is recognized, no doubt, and legitimate and respectable, but also before the confidence with which, authorizing himself without trembling through this authority, Benveniste (for example) proceeds with the cutting edge of assured distinction. For example, between the *proper* meaning and its other, the *literal* sense and its other, as though precisely *that itself* which is here in question (for example, the response, responsibility or religion, etc.) did not arise, in a quasi-automatic, machine-like or mechanical manner, out of the hesitation, indecision and margins between the two ostensibly assured terms. *Scruple*, hesitation, indecision, reticence (hence modesty <*pudeur*>, respect, *restraint* before that which should remain sacred, holy or safe: unscathed, immune)—this too is what is meant by *religio*.[77]

It is not the delusions of knowledge themselves that are so disastrous to our collective deliberations and actions, qualifies Derrida, but the faith, a quasi-financial investment we make in them. It is not merely possible, but likely, when it comes to questions of faith, to overinvest, in Benveniste's terms, in the "proper" and "literal" interpretations. As a counter to the pervasive *assurance*[78] extending even into Benveniste's distinctions, Derrida invokes a series of terms whose effect is to calibrate responsibility as an overall aesthetic of finitude: as a scruple, hesitation, indecision, reticence, modesty, respect, and restraint capable of mitigating our interested convictions. The terms do not predicate action or behavior so much as they predicate the fashion in which we read the data, apprehend and evaluate the actions and volitions of others, share in cultural resources, and mobilize ourselves in institutional settings, whether these be political, social, or religious in nature. The most promising possible *redemption* from the Western religions' pronounced tendencies to reductiveness and literality is the assumption of a multifaceted sense of limitation not entirely inimical to the religions themselves. The various cultures of religion form the lineaments of an exegetical, if not theological sensibility—the modalities, postures, even tactile grips or *prises* of reading—as Derrida elaborates them in the sequence of his conversations with philosophy, whether with "the sources," his predecessors and contemporaries on the European intellectual scene, or his colleagues, students, and adversaries.

Scruple, hesitation, modesty, restraint: This is, if religion be possible, a religious vocabulary of caution, care, nonviolence, applied far more to language and acts of culture than to actions and studies of their "impact." Derrida gives the attentiveness to nuance and to minute, but telling detail that, to him, encompasses both philosophical responsibility and, in any possible religion, an "immediate" application as he extrapolates a double tradition, a split orientation, in the articulation of *religio* itself:

And yet, one tells oneself, **one must still respond**. Within the Latin sphere, the origin of *religio* was the theme of challenges that in truth were interminable. Between two readings or lessons, therefore, two provenances: on the one hand, supported by texts of Cicero, *relegere*, what would seem to be the avowed formal and semantic filiation: bringing together in order to return and begin again; whence religio, scrupulous attention, respect, patience, even modesty, shame, or piety—and on the other hand (Lactantius and Tertullian) *religare*, etymology "invented by Christians" as Benveniste says, and linking religion to the *link*, precisely, to obligation, ligament, to debt, etc., between men or between man and God. At issue would still be, in an entirely different place, on an entirely different theme, a division between the source and meaning (and we are still not yet done with this dualization) . . . because the two competing etymologies can be traced to the same, and in a certain manner to the possibility of repetition, which produces the same as much as it confirms it. In both cases (*re-ligere* or *re-ligare*), what is at issue is indeed a persistent bond that bonds itself first and foremost to itself. What is at issue is indeed a reunion <*rassemblement*>, a reassembling, a re-collecting. A resistance or a reaction to dis-junction. To absolute alterity.[79]

Yet responsibility is not exhausted by its restraining functions. It is defined as well as a certain urgency, if not imperative of reaction, always, of course, on the critico-linguistic plane. The interface that an *exegetical bearing* opens upon actual religious communities is the deconstructive sense that a modulated response to the prevailing ideological parameters of culture is incumbent upon readers whose senses of difference and articulation are calibrated to a certain degree of sensitivity. This response, scribed all the way down to the level of textual particularities is incumbent, specifically, on those engaged in responsible, that is, specific, finite, meditation and ongoing revision of their own orientations and tendencies. If the traditional Western religions and deconstruction communicate at all, it is in the foyer linking shared commitments to a meticulous reading of theology and to the revision of misunderstandings promulgated by prior exegetical lapses, whether blind spots or motivated misrecognitions. Deconstruction and communities of exegesis speak to one another at the point that they acknowledge their shared predilection to a certain *activism*, if we understand this notion as a willingness to follow through on a radically finite and meticulous exegesis, to undertake whatever adaptations and revisions to their own nomenclatures and procedures are implicated by this ongoing close re-reading.

The passage quoted immediately above scores the dual religious parentage by *legere* and *ligare*. It places both of these possible derivations in the modality of repetition made possible by the prefix "re." Deconstructive responsibility stems from a dual etymological derivation: harvesting and gathering, on the one hand,[80] and linkage, binding, and obligation on the other. Within this etymological arena, religion is both the site of communality and community and the site of self-assumed books of public obligation. The singular imprint with which we are left as Derrida reworks responsibility, a term customarily exhausted by the truisms attending the *sensus communis* and the moral imperative,[81] is that of the urgency, the activity, and the implications of our freedom for the responsibility whose provenance and dynamic is exegetical. The degree of active responsiveness and personal accountability that Derrida grafts onto a notion of responsibility that is also tempered by restraint is striking indeed.

The configuration of religion through responsibility is unavoidable, Derrida argues in "The Force of Law":

> This responsibility before memory is a responsibility before the very concept of responsibility that regulates the justice and appropriateness [*justesse*] of our behavior, of our theoretical, practical, ethico-political decisions. This concept of responsibility is inseparable from a whole network of connected concepts (propriety and property, intentionality, will, freedom, conscience, consciousness, self consciousness, subject, self, person, community, decision, and so forth). All deconstruction of this network of concepts in their given or determinate state may seem like a move toward irresponsibility at the very moment that, on the contrary, deconstruction calls for an increase in responsibility. But in the moment that the credit or credibility [*crédit*] of an axiom is suspended by deconstruction, in this structurally necessary moment, one can always believe that there is no more room for justice, neither for justice itself nor for the theoretical interest that is directed toward problems of justice. It is a moment of suspense, this period of *epokhē*, without which there is, in fact, no possible deconstruction. . . . This anguishing moment of suspense . . . cannot be motivated, it cannot find its movement and its impulse . . . except in the demand for an increase or a supplement of justice, and so in the experience of an inadequation or an incalculable disproportion. For in the end, where would deconstruction find its force, its movement or its motivation if not in this always unsatisfied appeal, beyond the given determinations of what names, in determined contexts, justice, the possibility of justice?[82]

So pressing are the exigencies of a responsibility whose modalities derive from interpretation that they encompass and radically redefine the practices of justice itself. The fact that the parameters of responsibility might be most clearly discernible in national questions of language policy, for example—as in the instance of Israel—in no way dilutes their tangible and potentially disastrous consequence. Issues of justice are raised by all instrumental, deliberative, actionable, executive, and executed processes, which can be carried out with *justesse* only if they bear residues of *khōra*, only if they have transpired under the aura of thinking.

The crisis of responsibility unfolds on the edges of an abyss, both site to the crisis of the invalidation of a system and the scene of writing, as Derrida has developed the figure since his early writings on Freud.[83] A phenomenon as intangible as representation haunts the perimeters of every immanent historical disaster scene. Derrida's only prescription for the staving off of disaster is the sharing of responsibility by the actors and the antagonists, this in a countersignatory act by which a critical apprehension of situational consequences—as enunciated under the aesthetics of modesty and restraint—is passed all around. The countersigning of responsibility, which accounts not only for the relation between parties in a contract or treaty, but also between an author and her readers, is the only precondition under which the vexing impasses of the sociopolitical domain—Israel's constitution and its interactions with its neighbors are a telling example—may be approached.

> One must therefore tie what we have just said of sacrifice to the responsibility proper to our generation, the one undergoing the trial of this nonlanguage that secular Hebrew is—a generation of transition (*das Geschlecht des Übergangs*), a generation of passage and of access. . . . The gravest responsibility must be exercised at the moment of the greatest danger: without rule and guarantee on the edge of an abyss, above the abyss. On the edge of the abyss or above the abyss—it comes down to the same thing [*cela revient au même*]. There again, we should follow the thread of an analogy—only an analogy, of course, between a certain movement of this Scholem of 1926 and that of a certain Heidegger in the years that are going to follow. . . . The "we" who signs this confession belongs, then, to this *Geschlecht des Übergangs*. He engages himself both in this passage and in this responsibility. . . . The responsibility is ineluctable, and as paradoxical as this may appear, it finds the sign of its freedom in this fatality, in the bond of this obligation, which is not the formal or formalizable obligation of a practical universality in the Kantian sense. This is the responsibility of a generation. It does not replace itself, does not delegate itself. It is unique: in a place, at a moment of history, in a language, before [*devant*] a language; but also and of course first of all, and by way of all this, before God, the voice of whom will have marked the covenant in the experience of *this* language. The signature of this "we" countersigns the covenant; it says "our generation" by countersigning, by so responding to a commitment already taken, to a promise, and it sees its autobiography assigned, the commitment already taken, to a promise, and it sees its autobiography assigned, the autobiographicity [*l'autobiographicité*] of the "we," out of the call that resonates in this sacred language.[84]

RESPONSIBILITY WITHOUT PURITY

If a genre is what it is, or if it is what it is destined to be . . . then "genres are not to be mixed"; one should not mix genres, one owes it to oneself not to get mixed up in mixing genres. Or, more rigorously, genres should not intermix. And if it should happen that they do intermix, by accident or through transgression, by mistake or through a lapse, then this should confirm, since, after all, we are speaking of "mixing," the essential purity of their identity. This purity belongs to the essential axiom: it is the law of the law of genre, whether or not the law is, as it is considered justifiable to say, "natural." This normative position and this evaluation are inscribed and prescribed even at the threshold of the "thing itself" . . . if something of the genre "genre" can be so named. And so it follows that you might have taken the . . . sentence in the first person, "I will not mix genres," as a vow of obedience, as a docile response to the injunction emanating from the law of genre. In place of a constative description, you would then hear a promise, an oath. . . . I promise you that I will not mix genres, and, through this act of pledging faithfulness to my commitment, I will be faithful to the law of genre, since of itself it invites and commits me in advance not to mix genres.[85]

The passage immediately above is most striking in its projection—from a literary artifact, a text—of the very *voice* of purity, the prescriptions against mixing, mixture, inclusion, and contamination directly extending from the categorical imperative in Western thought. On the occasion of Blanchot, Derrida somehow wrenches an entire tradition and cultural-ideological matrix into a posture in which it admits, concedes, blurts out, confesses the bigotry and categorical profiling that, at an infrastructural level, power and advance it. The purity mandated and implemented by these faiths is multidimensional. It is conceptual, operational, and demographic. It not only establishes denominational, sociological, and communal boundaries, it sets distinctive styles and tonalities for the very rhythm of life. It is applied to space, time, marriage, food, clothing, and other tangible domestic arrangements. Do the features of a historically evolved communal lifestyle dissolve when the platform of purity supporting this continuity is stripped away? This is another question facing the leaders and participants in the surviving Abrahamic religions as they deliberate on their status under conditions of critical apprehension.

BEARING BEFORE LAW

Deconstruction is too polymorphous in its approaches to constitute a sustained position. It values performance, articulation, nuance, specificity, minute particulars, and *différance* too highly to be conflated with nihilism, radical skepticism, or negative theology. It is too responsive, in ways suggested above, to the particularities of the contexts in which cultural articulation arises to import or iterate a finite or known toolbox of operations, procedures, or methods to its variegated scenes of writing. In what, then, does a sustained sequence of cultural interactions conducted under the aura of deconstruction eventuate? At most, a bearing, an indeterminate address[86] to the directions, prohibitions, justifications, encomia, fantasies, and exhortations into which culture issues for its own good, to assure its continuity and intramural repressive tolerance. A bearing—of respect, responsibility, nonviolence, suspicion, skepticism, sustained and detailed attentiveness, resolve to articulate states of affairs in something approaching their "full" complexity—for a set of interventions that have been invoked as widely and momentously as deconstruction, such a bearing is a rather modest end product, far more so, say, than a system, a movement such as Futurism or Surrealism, an epochal project such as psychoanalysis or structuralism, or a method, such as the New Criticism. A *bearing* is nothing more substantial than an address, a posture, a broad strategem always being modified in the name of particularity in anticipation of unannounced happenings. It is a very singular kind of opening or openness: one "primed," perhaps, by memories of the varieties of repression and violence that have been entertained and sanctioned by Western discourse, but open, through a resolute commitment to close reading and local difference, to the artifact at hand, in its painful and demanding particularity.

I must concede here, openly and without reservation, that what I here term a "bearing" has never sufficed as the sufficient condition for a religious community in the past. In relation to the world's traditional religions, a bearing is at most a submerged and elusive pretext, often left unstated, like questions of communal lifestyle. A bearing, within the context of the traditional faiths, intangibly contributes to a religion's overall flavor or reflex attitude, say Christianity's affinity for childlike wonder or Hinduism's approach to the sublime through multiplication. But the traditional religions, as they go about engineering a life system housing, among other elements, a lifestyle, a collective ethos, and institutions of morality and justice, vastly exceed the suggestibility of a bearing as they conjure up a universe, distinguish right from wrong, and determine a host of behaviors ranging from rituals to the conventions of domesticity and sexuality.

An exegetical bearing of the sort that deconstruction both designs and sets into play offers far less than this in the way of tangible prescription and direction. Deconstruction's minimalism, in other words, the restraint by which it falls short of definition, prescription, and institutionalization, its contentment with itself as an inflection, rather than a hard-core model or agency of intellectual procedure, scores an indissoluble barrier between itself and anything resembling a practicing, practical religion. Yet it is precisely the bearing that deconstruction crystallizes over the course of its multiple encounters with canonical artifacts of many different orders—core texts of civilization, philosophical overviews, ideological milestones, literary reprogrammings of conceptual-ideological configurations, and scholarly contributions symptomatic of wider systemic impasses—that constitutes the primary resource that it offers to the same religions. The diligent, respectful, dispassionate, relentlessly articulate and incredulous but meticulous bearing that deconstruction coalesces is precisely an attitude facilitating the self-questioning that the current traditional religions, now more than ever, desperately need, above all at the interface between ideology and behavior and with regard to the reprise of traditional internal debates and differences and the reopening of traditional frontiers between them and Other creeds and faiths.

It serves us well, then, to pause over how an end product as constitutionally inconsequential as a bearing, yet whose precisions have deeply affected the contemporary discourses of law, architecture, political theory, and the "hard" sciences, as well as philosophy, could emerge as a vital, ongoing element in deconstruction's intervention. We are circling around the persistent and no doubt contested issue of the profound, far-reaching, tangible, and "practical" effects—existential, historical, sociopsychological—of the negotiations conducted on the fields of inscription, encoding, decoding, and reading. So much impinges on something so frail as an attitude of reading! Only in this apprehension of the power of small things, of what Rodolphe Gasché terms "minimal things,"[87] does deconstruction appeal to the attitudes of mindfulness and nonviolence in cultures so far afield from Western metaphysics as Tibetan Buddhism. Religion may well serve as the preeminent cultural site for the registration of the multiple and far-reaching implications of nothing more imposing than a critical bearing. To the degree that deconstruction has facilitated the full-throttle, explicit opening of criticism's play and options, deconstruction's glosses on religion highlight the cultural impacts, verging into shock, of exegetical options, critical stances.

THE COMMUNITY OF DECONSTRUCTION

The question of community is a vexing one to deconstructive discourse. The activities of interpretation, disputation, and publication all depend on supportive social infrastructures. But the critique of the conventional pre-texts of social belonging, unity, and organization delivered by deconstruct-ive inquiry is so finely tuned and vibrant that Derrida, for one, resigned from the discourse of community rather than retrofitting or updating it. Responding, in *Specters of Marx*, to Francis Fukuyama's celebration of the apotheosis of core Western values at the end of history, he writes: "This end of History is essentially a Christian eschatology. It is consonant with the current discourse of the Pope on the European community: destined to become a Christian State or super-State, this community would still belong therefore to some Holy Alliance. It is thus not unconnected with the alli-ance spoken of explicitly in [Marx's] *Manifesto* which also named the Pope at that point."[88]

Community, at least the overarching sociopolitical organization marshal-ling serious ideological artillery simply in constituting itself, is hopelessly tainted from the perspective of responsible deconstructive critique. The metaphysics of friendship is a venue in which Derrida cannot entirely avoid the lineaments of a protocommunity, but any collective matrix of inter-action so emerging is, in keeping with Jean-Luc Nancy's recuperation of communal constructs, "inoperative." In *The Politics of Friendship*, Derrida elaborates the communal possibilities emerging from a careful extrapolation of two pivotal underlying mores of friendship—avowal and silence—in Nietzsche's *Human All Too Human*:

> This day of joy, as we recall, will be one of a shared rejoicing (*Mitfreude*), not fellow suffering (*Mitleid*). For there would then be two communities without community, two friendships of solitude, two ways of saying to oneself—keeping silent, keeping it hushed—that solitude is irremediable and friendship impossi-ble; two ways for desire to share and parcel out the impossible: one would be the compassionate and negative way, the other affirmative, which would attune and join two disjointed rejoicings [*jouissances*], conjugated at the heart of the dissocia-tion itself: heterogeneous allies, co-affirmed, perhaps affirmed in total darkness. An ecstatic rejoicing but one without plenitude, a communion of infinite wrenching.
>
> In the meantime . . . you had better keep silence to preserve what remains of friendship. And as the friends know this truth of truth (the custody of what can-not be kept), they had better keep silent together.[89]

Nietzsche's canny extrapolation of the social mores surrounding what is, interpersonally, dearest to us, invested with the greatest hope, produces a tangle of mixed messages—not double-talk—in Derrida's projection. Friendship is as much a matter of silence and discretion, hence disavowal, as avowal. The threat to friendship, triggered by the violation of the implicit vow of silence, issues from the within the relationship, not from "outside."

The uneasy alliances of friendship, prompting Derrida's endowing them with a political dimension, never go away. This does not bode well for the notion of communities writ large, collectivities marshalling an even thicker and wider network of associations than the conspiracy of friends. And prospects for viable community are in no way improved when the collectivity or association is motivated by the exalted idealism of religion, by the intervention or even the will of God. Indeed, one could argue, the ideals of religion add only additional weight and impediment to alliances already strained in their convenience and duplicity. The politics of friendship, as Derrida elaborates its principles and underlying dynamics, must content itself with qualifying "a community without community," or several varieties of this protocommunity before the fact.

The "community without community" may go as far, however, in characterizing the nodes and cells of readers who share their reactions to cultural artifacts and who responsibly read each other's composed reactions to them, as it does in delimiting both the exaltation of friendship and the communities seeming to accrue from it. In full cognizance of the liabilities attending the associations of avowal and enforced silence, both Nancy and Agamben go on to project the highly qualified and limited prospects for community that remain.[90] Derrida does not join them in this venture. On this point, there is a parting of the ways in the discourse of deconstruction. Yet Derrida's comments on friendship and community, which are of direct consequence for the makeshift collectivities (or "packs")[91] of reading and exegesis, are nonetheless germane to the possibility of the quasi-religious occasions and events transpiring in the wake of deconstruction.

The community of deconstruction, such as it exists, manifests itself in disinterested reading groups, informal discussions, and exchanges of letters and e-mails. (Indeed, all three Abrahamic religions may have inspired similar communities and modalities of interpretation, whose work was always, however, inflected and constrained by certain doctrinal bottom lines.) The shibboleth of deconstruction marks an inchoate community to be sure, but one in keeping with the textual artifacts and dynamics motivating it, summoning it into being. An aura of the underground, of understatement, if not actual conspiracy, hovers over this noncommunity as an inoperative affinity group. Borges's "Tlön, Uqbar, Orbis Tertius" projects the image of a "secret society" of intellectual magi who maintain, from generation to generation, an alternate universe in an a priori state of deconstruction. In this text-based universe, fictions are the only possible truths, mathematics is limited to sliding values, and archaeological relics emerge from dreams, not from the earth. The community of deconstruction operates under the onus of a similar cabal, one that might balk at the assistance of Borges's Ezra Buckley, "a freethinker, a fatalist, an apologist for slavery,"[92] of questionable moral character, perhaps, but an outsider of deconstructive bearing. The liens that bind this possible and indeed, under finite conditions, existent community, may well be rhizomatic in nature, in Deleuze and Guattari's sense.

> Unlike trees or their roots, the rhizome connects any point to any other point, and its traits are not necessarily linked to traits of the same nature; it brings into play very different regimes of signs, and even nonsign states. The rhizome is reducible neither to the One nor the multiple. . . . It is composed not of units but of dimensions, or rather dimensions in motion. It has neither beginning nor end, but always a middle (*milieu*) from which it grows and which it overspills. It constitutes linear multiplicities with *n* dimensions having neither subject nor object, which can be laid out on a plane of consistency. . . . Unlike a structure, which is defined by a set of points and positions, with binary relations between the points and biunivocal relationships between the positions, the rhizome is made only of lines: lines of segmentarity and stratification as its dimensions, and the line of flight or deterritorialization as the maximum dimension after which the multiplicity undergoes metamorphosis, changes in nature. These lines, or lineaments, should not be confused with lineages of the arborescent type.[93]

Even with the almost palpable differences in grasp and drift between the deconstructive and Deleuzian/Guattarian projects marked by this passage, it is intriguing to imagine the community of reading and writing arising under the aura of deconstruction as a rhizome. Indeed, it is Deleuze and Guattari's insistence on projecting positivistic figures for philosophical thinking (in the sense of their being decontextualized and put forth as positive, existent options), figures such as assemblages and lines of flight, even at the expense of lapsing into a psychotic or not countersigned language, that gives their "Capitalism and Schizophrenia" diptych such appeal to intellectuals whose work is invested with the wish for certain tangible socio-political payoffs.

I would argue that deconstructionists perform their work within a rhizome even while they might well take issue with the positivism of its articulation, with its incorporation of "nonsign states," with the formation of certain registers of signs into "regimes," and above all, with the power relations willy-nilly introduced into the semiological sphere. Deconstruction transpires, if at all, within the impersonality and to some degree ahistoricality of the pack, an imaginative term that Deleuze and Guattari develop along with the rhizome, in this case as part of their effort to comprehend animality within the assemblage of ongoing human sociolinguistic activity. It behooves us all to contemplate what we gain as units of a pack as opposed to stalwarts of institutions or ideologically constituted communities:

> You can never get rid of the ants because they form an animal rhizome that can rebound time and again after most of it has been destroyed. Every rhizome contains the lines of segmentarity according to which it is stratified, territorialized, organized, signified, attributed, etc., as well as lines of deterritorialization down which it constantly flees. There is a rupture in the rhizome whenever segmentary lines explode into a line of flight, but the line of flight is part of the rhizome. These lines always tie back to one another. That is why one can never posit a dualism or a dichotomy, even in the rudimentary form of the good and the bad.[94]

The reprogrammings and reconfigurations effected by deconstruction can gain force and focus only when understood to arise in a context whose historical and institutional underpinnings are at best problematic, in a milieu circling back upon itself, with only a middle, whose boundaries and ends have been foreclosed. This acutely characterizes the *khōra* or abyssal setting generative of texts themselves conducive to thinking.

ADDRESS IRRESPECTIVE OF GENDER

"Do," "do not," says "genre," the word *genre*, the figure, the voice, or the law of genre. And this can be said of all genres of genre, be it a question of a generic or a general determination of what one calls "nature" or *phusis* (for example, a biological genre, or the human genre, a genre of all that is in general), or it is a question of a typology, designated as non-natural and depending on laws and orders which were once held to be opposed to *phusis* according to those values associated with *technē*, *thesis*, *nomos* (for example, an artistic, poetic, or literary genre). But the whole enigma of genre perhaps springs more closely from within this limit between the two genres of genre, which, neither separable nor inseparable, form an odd couple of one without the other in which each evenly serves the other a citation to appear in the figure of the other, simultaneously and indiscernibly saying "I" and "we," me the genre, we genres, without it being possible to think that the "I" is a species of the genre "we."[95]

To contemplate a successor to the Abrahamic faiths in which the law of gender has been thought through with deconstructive rigor is to undertake an overhaul that is the most far-reaching and hence dangerous imaginable, and yet the one on which any future credibility and viability of these traditions most depends. Western religion without gender, in the sense that Derrida accords it? Can the leopard change its spots? If the pivotal architectural scaffolding underlying Western religion (and Western science) is the law of genre, won't the edifice simply collapse with any questioning or modification of this support?

Indeed, Derrida's chief concern is that God serves as the pretext, rationale, model, and allegory for the many exclusions, categorical discriminations, orders, and prescriptions emanating outward from the possibility and implementation of genre. If the continuing Western faiths are to conduct a review of the play and compass of genre within their respective ideologies and practices, then this meditation will not be limited to the excision of references to God the Father or to the inclusion of additional possible generic features or coordinates within God. Such a theoretically rigorous and critically motivated self-encounter will entail, rather, the most elaborate and elaborated review possible of causal, categorical, and discriminatory attitudes, practices, and tonalities within the less tangible way of life engendered by the faith, as well as in its formal services.

It is difficult to imagine that such a revisionary critical reprise of the continuing faiths will be undertaken by a large share of their practicing members. This is in light of the fact that conceptual or philosophical rigor is rarely the motivation behind affiliation with or membership in religious organizations. Indeed the emotional payoff of such belonging is often the senses of tradition, historical continuity, community, and spiritual inspiration or transcendence that are the motivating problems, if not the nemeses of the deconstructive investigations. Yet such a critical and philosophical reworking of the faiths will be indispensable to those aspiring to draw on their considerable linguistic, literary, and existential resources and artifacts in an authentically thoughtful ambiance. In the wake of such a reconsideration, undertaken by core users of the faiths and their practices, it will be surely possible to mix and match wisdom that has accrued over the course of all three enduring Abrahamic religions, for there will no longer be a site or a rationale for their mutual exclusivity and segregation.

PERFORMANCE NOT RITE: CEREMONY AND PRAYER UNDER THE AURA OF
DECONSTRUCTION

Indeed, I can think of no more edifying a challenge before the existing Abrahamic faiths than reforming, reformulating, and reformatting themselves in response to a series of challenges that Derrida has placed before the idealizing, totalizing, and categorical tendencies of Western thought. What would the vestiges of these traditions entail if we could correct them for such powerful and unavoidable features as their valorization of spirit at the expense of body and matter; their imposition, by dint of the metaphysics of presence, of a direct, personal responsibility defined in terms of ethnic loyalty; their thinking categorically, under the law of genre; their gravitation toward several modalities of purity; their appeal to texts, but only ones that have been canonically invested with a certain trustworthiness, and to the exegesis of these canonical artifacts, as long as it results in the reaffirmation of core ideological values and images? It is with the profoundest irony that deconstruction—the most sustained and intense setting in relief and questioning of ideological and theological formations and imperatives to date—is the body of commentary most suggestive of the tangents and redirections still open to these traditions.

In deconstructive terms, the religious intervention turns out to be a responsible act of reading and inscription whose effect will be to limit the claims and effectiveness of a particular organized religion, to whatever degree the acts of interpretation have arisen in its name. It is no accident that a recitation of scripture, and often, a theologically orientated affirmation of what is taken to be the "message," meaning, and thrust of the selected reading, is at the heart of Sabbath and holiday services in all three Abrahamic religions. Toward the end of *Glas*, Derrida takes humorous pleasure at the memories of concrete fetishism literally surrounding the Torah as a literal body of sacred script during the Jewish services of his childhood.[96] Derrida can readily acknowledge the reverence toward texts and the deliberations upon their meanings powerfully affecting Abrahamic theology. What elicits a sustained and interventionist critique on the part of deconstruction are the self-interested strings attached to the three separate Abrahamic affirmations of sacred writing and exegesis, the ideological liens imposed on the storytelling and recitation even before they have taken place.

A deconstructively inflected religion—whatever other ties and rituals it may program—holds an ongoing funeral or memorial service for itself as a functioning community or worldview.[97] Yet this apprehension of the religion's former effectiveness does not preclude the ongoing synthesis of prayers, ceremonies, and rituals in the distinctive idiom, inflection, and rhythm that the religious ecology has historically established. Precisely because religions are artifacts of culture composed of programs and texts, it is possible for them to persist in the wake of their own cultural dominance and communal jurisdiction. Indeed, in view of deconstruction's ongoing purview, the conditions of a religion's persistence are close to the status of any archived and consulted artifact. Even if no believers in a given religion survive—and we need at least to consider the possibility that there are no absolute believers in any religion—the religion persists as long as there are readers who think and act in its vein.

As unabashedly skeptical as deconstruction has been toward the ideological platform shared by the Abrahamic religions, it by no means declares a moratorium on the performative repertoire that this theological matrix has evolved, even toward the end of orchestrating and implementing major points of faith. Deconstruction neither promotes nor condemns the performativity of language, one of its built-in dimensions. The issue is not to declare the bankruptcy of language's capabilities to perform, enact, or figure not only its own functions, but also significant human relations and conditions, but to revise the common understanding of what is at stake in these performatives as it is embodied in the speech-act theory of John Austin and the meditations on it by subsequent philosophers of language. As J. Hillis Miller penetratingly elucidates, in the "Jacques Derrida" section of *Speech Acts in Literature*, the essays dedicated to speech-act theory—"Signature Event Context" and "Limited Inc abc . . ."—are not merely formal arguments of considerable technical virtuosity that Derrida raises with his notable colleagues. He "includes a new concept and practice of performative utterances as a fundamental part of all his work, especially his later teaching and writing."[98]

> Derrida's new conceptions of politics and ethics depend on a reversal of speech-act theory whereby the performative utterance creates the conventions it needs in order to be efficacious, rather than depending on their prior existence for its felicity. It thereby transforms the context it enters rather than presupposing it and being based on it. Such a speech act is a historical event in the sense that it deflects, in however small a degree, the course of history. Only a performative theory of the historical event can account for historical change. Only such an explanation of speech acts will go beyond the sterile opposition between, on the one hand, a static structural concept of history that sees a given historical "episteme" or discursive regime replaced suddenly and inexplicably by another one and, on the other hand, some oversimple idea of historical materialism.[99]

Nothing less than our basic understanding of history, including the past and future of the core religions, is at stake in the distinction between a stable, ongoing framework in which speech acts transpire, including declarations of war and treaties, and a more dynamic notion in which linguistic articulation creates the arena—and understandings—in which such situations eventuate. The renegotiation of the terms of events, historical as well as linguistic, as well as of the contexts in which they take place, that Derrida works out on the occasion of his reading Austin and Searle is decisive for our understanding of all social institutions, whether religious, political, cultural, archival, or educational in nature. An institution, even one so venerable as a religion, is no longer a transhistorical venue for vows, blessings, lamentations, and other attestations and commitments attaining, by virtue of this iterability, a transcendental status. An institution is, rather, a marketplace in ongoing flux whose transactions gain meaning from the contextual conditions with which they have been, before the fact, infiltrated.

> For an ungrounded or self-grounding performative to work, it must convey the illusion, fable, or fiction of having a solid preexisting ground or law to erect itself on, while claiming for itself autonomous performative force. The document itself is open to both interpretations. Textual support for either way of reading can be cited, although the two readings are incompatible. This is quite different from the relativism of Austin's "It depends on how you take it." In Derrida's understanding, both ways of reading are commanded by the text, though it is impossible, logically, to have both ways at once.[100]

Every text, artifact, or document with performative repercussions vacillates between grounding its legitimacy and enacting its avowed purpose. Deconstructively inflected practices would take every measure to render explicit the pretexts to the religious occasion, to incorporate into the scripted event the self-service that prompts and drives it. Indeed, this rendering explicit of occasions and motives contributes to the thinking whose promotion is at the core of any deconstructive intervention. Provided that the prayers and rituals of religion can be thoughtful, deconstruction is no more inherently opposed to them than to the arguments, dispositions, and judgments of law or to the declarations, laws, treaties, and other acts of government. It remains possible, and even intriguing, to imagine prayers and religious ceremonies retaining their inherent performative thrust while dispensing with the many valuations binding them to the Abrahamic and Western metaphysical patrimonies. In this respect, certain of the stances and formulations registered in non-Western religious canons (e.g., the Rg Veda, Uphanishads, and Buddhist Sutras), even while deconstructable to the degree that they also deploy mechanisms of idealization, sublimation, universalization, exemplification, and so on, nevertheless intimate certain directions that ceremonies and prayers composed under the aura of deconstruction might take.

The community of a ceremony or service is occasional. It does not affirm the perpetuity, tradition, or purpose of an ongoing human group, whether defined ethnically, culturally, or in any other nonfunctional, that is, essentialist, way. The ceremony or service embellishes a happening—in the rigorous sense of surprise—with texts, music, and other linguistic artifacts selected by virtue of resonance they may share with the occasion and nuances of meaning they may disseminate to it.[101] Where, in keeping with Abrahamic tradition, the service or ceremony opens an allegorical or exegetical abyss within itself through the consideration of an exemplary text judged illuminatory to the occasion, the process of interpretation is open-ended. There are no predetermined ethical or theological payoffs or homilies. The elucidating text may do as much to cast doubt upon the ceremony at hand as to affirm it.

The service, provided its participants have agreed to its aims and format, may implement certain actions, that is, may encompass a performative dimension, whether the implementation of a unit for reproductive or legal purposes, the mourning of death and the orchestration of a burial, the public celebration or bemoaning of any number of surprises and events affecting the assembled group of individuals. The language of the service is poetry. Indeed one definition of prayers as plausible as any other is the following: poetry impressed into the service of theology. Under the aura of deconstruction, the only future for prayer in the ceremonies and services of noncommunities crystallizing to mark certain nodal events in the ongoing text of experience is the reclaiming of the poetic subtext of prayers, as this poetics has been articulated by twentieth-century phenomenology, notably by Heidegger. The service of prayer, in the wake of the traditional Abrahamic theologies, is the assumption of the burdens and releases of thinking, either as individuals or in an assembly crystallizing around an occasion, one declared in advance and agreed to by its participants. The mutual support that individuals gain in such a service of prayers and the ceremonies that may enhance and embellish them as an accompaniment or supplement is the affirmation of the task of thinking that cannot be abdicated, not the confirmation of an ideology or the collective destiny of a people. In this, we—the category of all beings fitted out with language and the sensibility, perception, and cognition programmed by language—have an enormous amount to offer one another in affirmation, acknowledgment, articulation, and responsibility.

The kind of prayer or poetry service I am referring to is far more thrown together than an established and iterable canon of archivally correct texts. Like one of Heidegger's compelling essays, the prayers in a deconstructively nuanced religious practice are nothing more than composites of thrown-together words, words assembled to embellish an occasion in cognizance of the particularity and evanescence of that moment. Let's take Heidegger's "What Are Poets For?"[102] as an instance of a text grounded in nothing more substantial than a constellation of words: chief among them "composing" or "composition," (*dithten*), "trace" or "track" (*Spur*), "ground" (*Grund*), "abyss" (*Abrund*), "nature" (*Urgrund*), "venture" (*wagen-Wagnis*), "balance or scale" (*wage*), "drawing" or "draft" (*Bezug*), "the open" (*das Offene*), "concealment" (*Verborgenheit*), "unshieldedness" (*schutzlossein*), and "conversion" (*Umkehrung*). And yet the formulations that this occasional piece is capable of generating, touching upon some of the German poets most resonant to Heidegger (above all Hölderlin and Rilke), offer substantial intimations of the qualities and tendencies of the hymns in a contemporary religion chief among whose aspirations is thoughtfulness. Indeed, as a composite performance, the essay may be read as a hymn to the possibilities in thinking and cultural improvisation realizable through processes of poetic composition and conceptual reprogramming at the infrastructural level.

"What Are Poets For?" is an excursion through the clearings that open up when the confluence of philosophically laden and poetically resonant terms, for example, "poetic," "venture," "draft," and "deconcealment," is thickest. In the textually foliated woods of Heideggerian philosophy, a clearing arises only in the density of a thicket. Heidegger's most memorable passages stop us dead in our reading tracks, effecting the imperative mission on which Benjamin sets the dialectical image. The way stations of Heidegger's prose, at which we arrest our readerly progress because the density of composition and thinking compel us to, are prose poems set into the etymological network of the text, poetic terminals constructed in keeping with the linguistic features that the Heideggerian excursion unearths, passages in turn presaying if not predicating a poetics of openness, linguistic respect, and celebration of the human (and occasionally inhuman) potentials and activities in thinking, poetizing, inventing, building, and dwelling. The volatile prose nodes or stations at which Heidegger's etymologically driven formulations abut themselves program and generate a poetry strikingly redolent both of the poetry that has inspired the philosopher and of the poetry capable of marking and ornamenting the occasions designated by a deconstructively thoughtful religion.

Any such present or future hymns are above all, for Heidegger, artifacts of language. As such, they issue forth from "the precinct (*templum*), that is, the house of Being."[103] Only the sober encounter with poetry can gain entry to this house. With his "whole being and vocation / a poetic question,"[104] Hölderlin is a poet who has sustained this encounter.

> But there would be, and there is, the sole necessity, by thinking our way soberly into what his poetry says, to come to learn what is unspoken. That is the course of the history of Being. If we reach and enter that course, it will lead thinking into a dialogue with poetry, a dialogue that is of the history of Being. Scholars of literary history invariably consider that dialogue to be an unscientific violation of what such scholarship takes to be the facts. Philosophers consider the dialogue to be a helpless aberration into fantasy. But destiny pursues its course untroubled by all that.[105]

Regardless of the disruption that the dialogue between thinking and poetry poses to the standard intellectual academic division of labor involving philosophy and literary history, only from this engagement can emerge the texts capable of delimiting the parameters of the human situation in an open-ended way. In the terms that Heidegger improvises for this essay, these texts are situated on the trajectory leading into the open of the venture.

Heidegger does not neglect, in this essay, to indicate the commerce and exploitation apparent when venturesomeness crassly subordinates itself to will.[106] The poetic programming of Being nevertheless arises in an affirmative mood of venture or draw: The occasion for compositional improvisation draws the reader/thinker/writer into the open of possibility and invention. "Drawing this way, the venture ever and always brings the ventured (*Gewagte*) toward itself in this drawing. To bring something from somewhere, to secure it, to make it come—is the original meaning of the word *Bezug*, currently understood as meaning reference or relation."[107] The fine-detail work that Heidegger performs with respect to the profound philosophical and cultural implications of inscriptive activity such as drawing, in this essay as script or scribing, to pull or draw (*ziehen*), or as relationship (*Beziehung*) or in "The Origin of the Work of Art" in conjunction with the rift or outline,[108] is characteristic of the first major phase of his project. Heidegger places the trajectory of a language-based and reconfigured ontology and metaphysics directly in the *draft* of an impulsion toward openness. To open metaphysics, and by implication theology, to the linguistic infrastructure and underpinnings that first made their pronouncements possible is to highlight the poetic condensations and indeterminacies in sacred texts.

The distinctive atmosphere of this Heideggerian open, amid the clearings that open up amid the woods of language and thinking, is particularly hospitable toward questions concerning the wider implications and precinct of human activity. This line of inquiry is less a humanism or quest for spiritual meaning than a recasting of invention and productivity in terms of the linguistic processes and possibilities that facilitate them. It enables the discursive thread of "What Are Poets For?" to veer toward the threat of death, itself attenuated by the demands of willing, as a limiting factor in the realization of human creative potential.

> What has long since been threatening man with death, indeed with the death of his own nature, is the unconditional character of mere willing in the sense of purposeful self-assertion in everything. What threatens man in his very nature is the willed view that man, by the peaceful release, transformation, storage, and channeling of the energies of physical nature, could render the human condition, man's being, tolerable for everybody and happy in all respects. But the peace of

this peacefulness is merely the undisturbed continuing relentlessness of the fury of self-assertion which is resolutely self-reliant. What threatens man in his very nature is the view that this imposition of production can be ventured without any danger, as long as other interest besides—such as, perhaps, the interests of faith—retain their currency.[109]

What must interest us here is the "natural" drift of an essay on the pivotal role of poetizing within culture, a centrality so pronounced that it revises our understandings of metaphysics and ontology into a domain of commentary on "man's place in the universe" usually reserved for Abrahamic theology. The revised text of Heidegger's 1936 essay treats the atomic bomb as the extreme instance of the willing that will truncate and debilitate the realization of Being in poetry and other thoughtful activity. The figurative explosion of such a bomb in the midst of Heidegger's poetic meditation discloses the inherent ontotheological underpinnings of the discourse on the pivotal and irreducible role of language in thinking and indeed in all structured endeavors. The excavation of this crater enables us as well to see the connection between Derrida's early inquiries into the prevailing Western drift toward logocentrism and into Husserlian and Heideggerian phenomenology and his far-reaching explorations of the Abrahamic religions.

From the outset of his polymorphous project, Derrida maintained an acute sensibility to Western ontotheology's inventive capability to reinstate itself and its orientations, even in the most thoroughgoing and radical theaters of creativity and thought work. Hence, his own Heideggerian investigations are attentive to the rebounds of spiritual presence and other manifestations of immanence and teleology in Heidegger's groundbreaking formulations. Heidegger's meditations on poetry still serve us well as an intimation of what the prayers and other scripted occasions in a deconstructively nuanced religion might entail: an affirmation of the linguistic facilities and processes making human cultural and interaction thoughtful; a declaration of the commitment to make thinking, deliberation, and the nonviolent conventions of interpretative and cultural reprogramming the basis for any action—national, administrative, or personal—with its inbuilt ideological and reductionist tendencies, which might foreclose creative and empathic possibility; and, a celebration of the diversity and otherness in occasions, worksites, and settings that bring people together and foster their responsiveness and responsibility.

It is, then, not entirely by accident that this inquiry into the fourth possible Abrahamic religion ends in the poetry that is both the inspiration and crystallization of so many of the conditions making human affairs *possible*. The condensation of wide arcs of meaning into a few words, the Mallarméan dance of signifiers on a page, the translation of the piebald input of the sensory organs and nerves into a shorthand of hitherto undiscovered phrases: This is not merely a distraction, the way to pass a few hours innocuously or the intriguing scramble of what is otherwise only too well known. We submit our poems, along with the dialectical images that crystallize for us in our open-ended exegeses of culture, as prayers in the endeavor of illuminating the world with language. In all likelihood, results of this frantic collective enterprise will be imperceptible. At stake in it, though, is the trembling and reconfiguration of an ontotheological system only too familiar to us in its purism, brutality, and systematic foreclosure.

To Heidegger, this recentering of dense and terse poetic composition in the forefront of constructive human enterprise is emergent on the horizon. What we have learned from Derrida's meticulous and responsible exegeses of Heidegger makes many of us wary of the destiny that he sees as following from this movement. The photographic emergence of the dialectical image on the light-sensitive plate of poetic composition remains the surprise joining the schools and subgenres of discursive work together and lending their formulations any authenticity they can claim.

> The poet thinks his way into the locality defined by that lightening of Being which has reached its characteristic shape as the realm of Western metaphysics in its self-completion. Hölderlin's thinking poetry has had a share in giving its shape to this realm of poetic thinking. His composing dwells in this locality as intimately as no other poetic composition of its time. The locality to which Hölderlin came is a manifestness of Being, a manifestness which itself belongs to the destiny of Being and which, out of that destiny, is intended for the poet.[110]

Coda

We are reminded, in negotiating the close of a study that has pursued the division of labor between scripts conspiring in memorable discourse, of the vow made at the end of a Borges story by a criminal to the astute, but unimaginative reader who brought him once before to justice. "'The next time I kill you,' said Scharlach, 'I promise you the labyrinth made of the single straight line which is invisible and everlasting.' "[111]The Borgesian setting of "Death and the Compass" has expanded into an exegetical labyrinth of time as well as space in which the detective story will repeat its possible outcomes at the same time that it charts the labyrinth of crimes that Scharlach has plotted over the space of a city that can be identified only as Paris superimposed on Buenos Aires. Scharlach has woven a triangular net of murders, acts overdetermined by coordinates of location, directional coordinates, colors, costumes, and times of occurrence, with the avowed purpose of trapping a reader, Lönnrot, a detective and ratiocinator good enough to assemble and plot the clues to their logical conclusion, but not so intuitive that he takes in the bearing, drift, address, grain, static, and rustle of the system.

The full extent of Scharlach's victory over Lönnrot is registered by the morphing of a "staggered series of bloody acts"[112] arranged in a triangle into a labyrinth whose parsimony allows it to compress itself into a single line while it encompasses the daring, imaginative leaps and unpredictability of a text or a rhizomatic configuration. Red Scharlach belongs to the long tradition of literary transgressors, but in his imaginary gift, he is a philosopher, one who "cracks," violates, and subverts the limits of the systems whose residual effect is the thwarting and oppression of the people who live in their shadows and under their sway. Following in the wake of Borges's imaginary criminal/philosopher, Derrida discerns and articulates the systematic platform encompassing three Abrahamic religions traditionally understood as branching out in categorically different directions. Like Lönnrot, he discovers the "labyrinth made of the single straight line" into which the core Western religions verge, in spite of their claims to inherent and absolute uniqueness and divinely sanctioned right. If philosophy and theory can claim any magic, it resides in the deconcealment of a coherence underlying and connecting the seemingly most divergent tracks of ideology, tradition, and communal identity.

Once again, Derrida's multitiered project intimates the labyrinth whose stunning coherence and insight does not belie the richness and complexity of the elements making it up. Ecstatically diverging from the law of genre, we can now well picture to ourselves the creative abyss or *khōra* within whose compass the telling "partners in discourse" catalyze, feed, interpenetrate, counteract, and cannibalize one another, all within a dynamic of inventive supplementarity and mutual affirmation.

Fragmentary Script as the Enabling Legislation
for Modern Criticism

After the lengthy exercise that we have just completed, I can hardly claim that a philosophico-rhetorical survey of the confluences and stress lines between poetics, philosophical discourse, religion, close exegesis, and criticism has never been undertaken before. Prior to terminating our inquiry, however, perhaps one more footnote is due, an extended one at that, one acknowledging our ongoing debt to early Romanticism as the scene of cultural production in which "full-service" criticism first became viable and attained its modern parameters.

Indeed, one of the preeminent features endowing the term "Romanticism" with a personality, enabling it to intimate substantially more than a broad-based literary and cultural production arising between two dates, is a certain intimacy and dialogue between the prevailing conceptual operating systems of the moment and the contracts for artistic production and intellectual work transpiring under its aegis, in its name. Particularly in light of the brevity of its duration, from 1790 to 1840 or so in Europe, perhaps extending to 1860 in the United States, the image as well as the experiments of Romanticism have recurred with a particular power. Romanticism, in meditations as diverse and far-flung as Kierkegaardian repetition[1] and the Nietzschean eternal recurrence,[2] even went so far as to theorize its own uncanny staying power. This title for a period doubles, then, as the icon for a moment at which the continuity and follow-through between a series of aesthetic experiments and the operating systems that inform them and undergird them is particularly striking. This creative interplay between conceptual programming and aesthetic reconfiguration and dislocation is so intense that it haunts subsequent scenes and theaters of production. Marx's scenarios of class conflict and the dialectical progression of history are already marked by a conceptual working through *and* aesthetic vocabulary common, in significant senses, to Kant, Hegel, Schlegel, Kierkegaard, Blake, Wordsworth, and Coleridge. In countless ways, Freud, too, returned to this ur engine of conceptual-figurative coordination: whether in providing the groundwork for such phenomena as obsessive compulsion or uncanniness or in elaborating the dynamics prevailing between the intrapsychic agencies and between the strata of consciousness.[3]

In other words, a powerful auratic allure emanates from a moment of cultural production in which there is a free and easy—not to mention profoundly problematical—exchange between the terms most critical to the conceptual rationale and the programming of the current cultural/ideological agenda and the most vibrant figures facilitating aesthetic inventiveness. Romanticism, through a coordinated and interlocked set of overarching projects, which it sustained with unflagging persistence, effected a thoroughgoing critical retrofitting and recalibration in which discourse and aesthetic invention shared as coconspirators. Among the different ecologies of cultural work needing to be encompassed under this umbrella project are the following: charting the parameters of the transcendental, its uncanny suspension in relation to the empirical; the momentum toward systematicity in speculation and social organization, as well as the disruptions of this trend posed by fragmentation; a sustained dissonance in logical operations and narrative perspectives resulting in irony; an absorption in the image as an indisputably visual element of cognition and experience programmed with all the abruptness, discontinuity, and potential radicality attending the fragment; and finally, a polymorphous double vision attending this ongoing disparity.

I am arguing here that the aura in which Romanticism is framed inheres more in the aesthetico-conceptual interface or follow though between its operative terms and figures than in the allure or uniqueness of its most memorable cultural producers or artifacts. It can reasonably be assumed that there is always some leakage or overflow between the pivotal terms in the conceptual operating program of the cultural moment and that moment's imaginary (or spectral) working through of its issues in literature, drama, or the visual arts. Yet not every scene of cultural articulation retroactively identified as a historical epoch or moment bespeaks the focus in rhetoric and vocabulary indicative of Romanticism. The fluidity of the interface between conceptualization or theory and aesthetic play casts a certain utopianism on Romantic experiments before the fact: the hope and at least remote expectation that ground can be gained, that progress can be made within a matrix of problems spanning sociopolitical reality and culture.

It is not by accident that a near-continuous succession of generations of intellectual crystallization and striving kept reverting to Romantic theory and poetics as to the scene of some unavoidable crime. The allure of a coordinated field theory—if not a "unified" one—a theory interconnected by the plays of fragmentation, systematicity, imagining, doubling, and irony—remained compelling within the frameworks of these subsequent ateliers of cultural and intellectual programming. But underlying this unusual if not one-time coherence of cultural inquiry is a script, in the sense of a medium of notation, constituting the conditions of possibility for this outstanding, periodic thrusting into focus of disparate intellectual projects.

A pervasive and undeniable *joy* hovers over Schlegel's *Critical Fragments* and *Athenaeum Fragments*, as over the Kierkegaardian texts, notably *Repetition* and "The Diary of a Seducer,"[4] which Schlegel's discontinuous musings undoubtedly inspired. This is the joy at the precipitation of a writing medium that, as a "universal poetry," can link the disparate art forms and genres and can claim revolutionary repercussions on conceptual work at the infrastructural level. In moments of intellectual utopianism, the degree of hope and investment in the processes of articulation and inscription themselves cannot be overestimated. The concerted work that Friedrich Schlegel, in conjunction with his brother, August Wilhelm, Novalis, and Schleiermacher performed with respect to fragmentation, wit, genre, irony, and the image throughout the 1790s is not merely the fortuitous encounter of an aesthetic vocabulary worth pursuing. It is, rather, a profound collective intuition of the working dimensions of writing as they had been set into play under a particular set of historico-cultural conditions. Such elements as the fragment, wit, and irony not only characterize aesthetico-cultural projects whose pursuit is viable and edifying as of that moment, they both earmark and perform the tenor, neighborhood, and ecology of intellectual programming at a particular time and in a specific cultural venue.

The genius of selecting and working through, in a variety of fragmentary contexts, these particular features and potentials of cultural inscription—and the *Athenaeum* writers were dedicated not merely to the elaboration of genius's conditions—is that they pertain equally as well to a broad range of aesthetic experiments and to the theoretical discourse in which the aspirations for a self-engendering and self-regulating speculative narrative of human potentials, achievements, and responsibilities are set out. We might even go so far as to postulate the efforts, above all by Fichte and Hegel, to configure self-regulating and modulating systems of cultural inquiry and commentary as the inaugural—set in print medium, to be sure—experiments in artificial intelligence. Grounded in the Kantian equations for the precise cosmological bearings between the empirical and the transcendental, these partially self-motivated machines of thought set a powerful stage for literary fabulations including Frankenstein's monster and Olympia, the clockwork love object of E. T. A. Hoffmann's "Der Sandmann."[5] As suggested above, it is the dual effectiveness and applicability of an aggregation of figures and terms, striking in its specificity—to aesthetic invention and philosophical specification—that endow this scene and moment of collaborative cultural programming at the infrastructural level with an attractiveness and an allure not yet effaced from cultural memory.

Fragmentation, in the overall framework of an Enlightenment insistence on the human source, motivation, and contribution of the principles and modalities of government and social organization and of the intuitions and discoveries of science, art, and technology, is not merely a style of inscription or an experiment in truncated writing. It is the very dimensionality of cultural inscription itself. The human, and by dint of the human, the intuitive, incisive, spontaneous, and creative can be brought to the lyceum of public conversation only through a medium that is itself abrupt, truncated, and above all, spontaneous. Fragmentation, as Schlegel and the *Frühromantik* elaborated, calibrated, and refined it, disrupts and hopelessly deranges language marshaled in the propagation of and service to the a priori tran-

scendental. Fragmentation performs this incapacitation to an entire economics of language—representation—as well as to the long-standing
cultural modus operandi of conceptual and historical determinism before
the fact, before, that is, the full transcript of fragmentary features and interventions has been assembled. Like the Freudian notion of wit or the joke,
whose raucous effect well in advance of the elaboration of its rationale establishes a definitive setting for the unconscious, whether it constitutes a
mathematical "proof" for this entity or not,[6] fragmentation is a modality of
inscription and cultural notation whose necessity and inevitability are already embedded in its performance. For Friedrich Schlegel and his interlocutors to encounter and grasp the vitality of fragmentation not only as a
mannerism of writing, but as a mode of intellectual sensibility and intervention was already in large measure to intuit the signature of an entire cultural
theater and its effect on subsequent generations of speculation and experimentation.

It is not entirely by accident that Romantic fragmentation transpired
with the explosiveness and arationality of the Freudian joke, and this was as
true of the major British Romantic poets as of their counterparts in Germany. Wit and irony, although they branch out to different spheres of operation, share a certain condensation: They encompass a particular
temperament or atmosphere of engagement *and* they correspond to certain
technical conditions of rhetoric and discursive performance. To declare that
wit is a precondition or feature of intellectual and aesthetic interventions is
to insist that activity on the intellectual plane of public culture now assumes
a certain brevity, compression, and playfulness not by and large in the province of ideological legitimation and the systematic simulation of existing
power configurations. The German Romantics' insistence on wit, in other
words, added a specific temperamental environment—and procedure—to
the *critique* of naively idealist and rationalist platforms of cultural valuation
implemented through strategic fragmentation.

From the outset, irony also occurred to the early Romantics as an affect-
ive accompaniment to the plays of fragmentation. Like wit, it is a widely
accessible, indeed inevitable cultural experience. Whereas wit characterizes
the temporality and emotive luster of certain moments in texts written in
cognizance of their linguistic features, irony is a phenomenon of the narrative frameworks that texts inevitably form, configure, disrupt, confuse, and
efface. An ironic moment foregrounds a dissonance between multiple

frameworks that have risen with equal necessity as part of narrative scaffolding. The same referent simply seems radically, sometimes comically dissonant according to perspectival frameworks that have proliferated with ease in the text. The perspectival dissonance that texts generate in their multiplicity of viewpoints is the narratological correlative of the doubling that is another Romantic obsession. Rehearsed in such canonical early modern works such as *Don Quixote*, this Romantic doubling assumes several forms, all extreme, including the entertainment of the play of doubles of key characters elsewhere in the narrative, underscoring an irreducible split within the fictive field, and, in the case of poetry, the invocation or even depiction within the text of an idealized interlocutor or double to the poetic persona.

Irony is a splendid instance of a textual phenomenon that Romantic thinkers, including Schlegel and Kierkegaard, set about endowing with a philosophical or systematic significance. Indeed, one of the unusual aspirations of the epigenetic, self-configuring discourse that Romantic philosophy demanded of itself, a project common, in different respects to Kant, Fichte, and Hegel, was that literary epiphenomena—sublimity, imagistic framing, and doubling, in addition to irony—were as much at home within it as the implements and apparatus of logic.

Wit and irony are linked to the overarching Romantic experiment in guerilla discourse or fragmentation not by logical compulsion or determination, but through uncanny and unpredictable elective affinity (justifying the extended chemical rhetoric in the Schlegelian fragments), a spontaneous configuration that Benjamin, in a distant moment, would characterize as a constellation. There is no comprehensive logic that could predict or predicate the coincidence of fragmentation, the image (which can be understood in part as the visual fragment), wit, genre, doubling, and the sublime as a constellation prevailing, if not presiding over Romantic cultural programming and intellectual work. One can plausibly formulate the rationales by which these factors coincided in a common cultural space, yet within the field of discourse, these factors, tantamount to chemical radicals, intersected, combined, and recombined in discontinuous and unpredictable ways. They yielded variegated and often surprising results when, as occasionally happens in the body of the fragments, they were directed toward particular artifacts and cultural phenomena.

It is precisely the open-endedness with which the discourse of fragments, wit, genre, and doubling can generate unpredictable and apt comments regarding very specific artifacts, some ancient and some quite contemporary, that serves as a harbinger of the stance and positionality of the modern critic. Embroidering on Friedrich Richter, a sentimental novelist on whom literary history has not conferred the seal of creative innovation, Schlegel comments: "The man of universal tendency can idolize his arbitrariness or else find great pleasure in those grotesque porcelain figures that his pictorial wit drums together like imperial soldiers. . . . His décor consists in leaden arabesques in the Nuremberg style. . . . His Madonna is a sentimental sexton's wife, and his Christ is cast in the role of an enlightened student of divinity."[7] Although these acerbic observations are judgmental in their thrust, this is not their main thunder. The power of these phrases is in opposite proportion to their marked compression. It inheres largely in the stark contrast between Romantic sublimity and domestic triviality. The Meissen figures dragooned into military ranks prefigure by half a dozen generations the discourse of kitsch developed by the likes of Adorno[8] and Milan Kundera.[9] In this fragment, Schlegel places critical poetry at the service of surreal defamiliarization.

Schlegel's specific "readout" of Richter could not take place in obliviousness to the theoretical elaboration of poetics, wit, and irony serving as the motive and broadest interest of the *Fragments*. One specific payoff, in other words, of conceptual work transpiring at the deep-roots level of the philosophical or theoretical operating system is the nuance, drift, or signature that this work can import to the readouts of specific cultural artifacts. By dint of the Schlegel circle's generative work, this modality of philosophically driven reading was already in place for Hegel and Kierkegaard. The former's reading of Sophocles' *Antigone* as an impasse between natural and civil law prompted by the family's ambiguous status as a protocommunity[10] nonetheless, in important respects, outside communal jurisdiction is an early tour de force in a tradition of exegesis also celebrated by Benjamin's early essay on Goethe's *Elective Affinities*[11] and extending to Derrida's dazzling readings of Plato, Kant, Hegel, Nietzsche, Freud, and Mallarmé, among others, the preeminent feature of which may be that they pivot, literally, on a trope, a turning point or interface between linguistic *and* conceptual articulation.

The theorizing of criticism that Schlegel undertakes in the *Fragments* does not terminate in an edifying program of manners and etiquettes at a remove from contemporary culture. The *Fragments* release writers of the moment from a significant share of the accrued legacy of rationalism, schematism, and a priori formalism. They not only announce an interlocking configuration of attitudes, stances, conceptual revisions, and practical devices that would result in a literarily as well as ideologically radical criticism. In strategic instances, they also get down to the dirty work of addressing the cultural artifacts directly in their purview, of instantiating the readings that emerge from their principles. Indelibly marked by such demonstrations of concentrated critical sabotage, the post-Schlegelian critic emerges as a volatile loner in perpetual readiness to hurry to the scene of cultural action, whether outrageous or commonplace, as a pretext for dispensing a running commentary.

Simply pursuing the guises of the critical sniper unleashed by Schlegel and his fellow Romantics, whose untoward outbursts of gunfire have been orchestrated by the poetics of fragmentation, constitutes a full-time, phantasmagoric calling. Under different auras, this figure is the *flâneur* lifted by Benjamin from the poems of Baudelaire and the urban fiction of Poe and Hoffmann, the modern sexual adventurer, whose halting and clumsy early missteps are traced in *Madame Bovary*, the connoisseur, who between Huyssmans and Proust runs a full gamut from decadence to nobility, or the deluded political radicals of Conrad's *The Secret Agent*.

The *Fragments* stand as an ardent, if incongruous hymn of celebration for a written medium that can extract and mobilize the radical potentials of all genres, that can embody the creativity of poetry as the metadiscourse of creative genius, that can translate the diverse media and scenes of cultural programming into each other's terms, that can shatter moral complacency with the abrupt sidestepping of witticism. Nothing less than messianic hope, revolutionary ardor, is invested—into nothing more substantial than a notation, a script, a technology of writing. In the power that the cultural moment ascribes to this script, it is endowed with Kabbalistic cyphers, whether these are deployed explicitly or not. The *Fragments* initiate an age in which all subsequent writing is perforce fragmentary, in which the critic is both a poet and prophet of aphorism, in which criticism is the poetry of exile and dispossession that might just, in its imagination and inspiration, be able to redeem the cultural mainstream or "inside." They usher in an era in which any writing synthesized under the aura of utopianism, any writing invested with the radical innocence that sustained discourse demands, necessarily reverts back to the *Fragments*.

In this context, then, the avatars of the *Frühromantik* militate for a cultural criticism whose terse irreverence carries over (or transfers) from wit in a prosaic landscape booby-trapped with turns of phrase stunning in their poetic invention and condensation. This running *Kritik*, insist the Schlegels and their compeers, will nonetheless transpire in a milieu maintaining nothing less than philosophical standards of logic and conceptual rigor. With this in mind, August Wilhelm Schlegel contributed a number of precisions on the permeable interface between poetry and philosophy. He insisted that "The poet can learn little from the philosopher, but the philosopher much from the poet," but key here is that under current conditions of cultural production, the two are learning from each other. August Wilhelm highlights Klopstock as a figure situated on this rift or membrane. He is "a grammatical poet and a poetical grammarian." Lest the translatability between poetry and philosophy seem too fast and easy, Friedrich Schlegel explains that "the vagaries of poetry have their value as raw materials and preliminaries for universality, even when they're eccentric and monstrous."[12] A fragment of the philosophical, universality, inheres in the poetic, we might say. The quest for a universal discourse of the forms and genres and cultures of culture bounces back and forth between the fragments of the *other* modes of writing that the genres proper harbor within themselves.

It is crucial to recognize here that poetry, like wit, does not bespeak a recognized and formally constituted literary genre so much as a quality or temperament of script. It is only in this sense that "the poetry of one writer is termed philosophical, of another philological, of a third, rhetorical, etc. But what then is poetical poetry?"[13] At the vertiginous moment of a heteroglossic confluence of the genres into a composite critical discourse that is at once poetic, dramatic, witty, imagistic, and ironic, it becomes as problematical to formulate what is exclusive and proper to poetry alone ("poetical poetry") as it is to do so for any of the generic constituents of the discursive amalgam. It is precisely in the sense of the impossibility of any genre's remaining strictly within its own parameters that, in the famous *Athenaeum* Fragment 252, Schlegel, anticipating Heidegger's *Identity and Difference*, applies a statute of severe limitation to the proposition of identity, $A = A$.[14]

Poetry contributes to a composite medium of cultural inscription, one deriving from and at home with a variety of traditional genres and their histories, because the first outpost of the universal. On its other flank, poetry vibrates sympathetically with immanence and inner sense. As August Wilhelm specifies: "Poetry is music for the inner ear and painting for the inner eye; but faint music, evanescent painting."[15] The early Romantics were militating, then, for a discourse of cultural *Kritik* that opens itself to and accepts certain susceptibilities, the vulnerabilities of indistinctness and ephemerality indicative of a poetic sensibility. To demand that criticism bespeak and enact wit is to project the strong position, the assertive stance implicit in these poetic indeterminacies. The *Fragments*, in keeping with their own stutter-step approach to any particular problematic, offer a variety of scenarios for the wittification of cultural discourse. "A good riddle should be witty; otherwise nothing remains once the answer has been found. And there's a charm in having a witty idea which is enigmatic to the point of needing to be solved."[16] For the Romantics to contemplate the riddle is for them to insist that viable criticism be enigmatic, that it foreground rather than obscure intractable difficulties. The residue or remains left behind by a genuinely witty riddle, as opposed to a blank one, is the stuff of what Heidegger calls thinking. In its role as a dramaturge of the culturally and linguistically radical, wit performs the function of foregrounding, setting into the abyss, furnishing the captivating and self-absorbed image with a frame. "A fragment, like a miniature work of art, has to be entirely isolated from the surrounding world and be complete in itself like a porcupine."[17]

In the latter *Critical Fragments*, Schlegel underscores the density and viscosity constituting the environment of wit: "What's commonly called reason is only a subspecies of it: namely the thin and watery sort. There's also a thick, fiery kind that actually makes wit witty, and gives an electricity and elasticity to a solid style." It is not in the interest of a discourse of strategic fragmentation to bracket reason so much as to upgrade its quality, to ensure that reason bespeaks the same piquancy, yeastiness, and wit as the criticism in which it is deployed. "Wit is its own end, like virtue, like love and art."[18] Wit, then, in the sense in which Schlegel develops it, is not the optional infusion of humor or lightness into cultural inquiry. It is, rather, a highly strategic demolition, specifically of complexes of mutually affirming concepts so pervasive as to be transparent. "A witty idea is a disintegration of spiritual substances which, before being suddenly separated, must have been thoroughly mixed. The imagination must first be sated with all sorts of life before one can electrify it, with the friction of free social intercourse so that the slightest friendly or hostile touch can elicit brilliant sparks and lustrous rays—or smashing thunderbolts."[19]

Electrification, a pivotal Romantic trope for intuition and flashes of the imagination, here effects a precipitation out from each other of ideational elements so interfused as to have become blatant. But electric wit dances as well between the terminals separating individuated intellectual faculties from social relations. The *Fragments* hold up the hope that the freedom and radicality realized in the witty deployment of language will circulate back into the domain of social relationships, effecting a liberation for all under their sway. (It is out of a concern for the public's readiness for the cultural modifications effected by the early Romantics that education becomes a significant, if muted submotif of the *Fragments*.) Hence it is in the above citation that witty formulations shake up not only complacent moralistic truisms, but stultified "social intercourse." The workings of a feedback loop between rhetorical and social conditions still discernible in the writings of Benjamin and other associates of the Institut für Soziale Forschung are at play. The image of electricity joins a rhetoric of chemical precipitation evident throughout the *Fragments* to add the force of physical process and materiality to the shakeup of facile complexes of ideation effected by witty discourse in its Schlegelian sense.

If we allow fragmentation to serve as the umbrella term for a multifaceted strategy of linguistico-conceptual disruption that the early Romantics posed to the field of knowledge that they inherited, then poetics, irony, the image, and precisions regarding genre constitute the major elements in the terminology or vocabulary through which this megacollective project became translated into specific interventions. We might be impelled to infer that at a far later date, deconstruction arose as a similarly multifaceted project of cultural critique and *démontage* and that it, too, is instrumented by a battery or vocabulary of highly sophisticated rhetorico-conceptual devices or tropes. These have been well documented and orchestrated by Rodolphe Gasché.[20] It may well be precisely the serious philosophical implications ensuing from tropes whose cultural home base is literary, whether wit, poetry, irony, *différance*, the architrace, or the re-mark, that impelled Philippe Lacoue-Labarthe and Jean-Luc Nancy to devote a study of their own, *The Literary Absolute*,[21] to German Romanticism early in the collective experiment of deconstruction. The centrality of the work on genre performed by the Schlegels and their associates is not lost on Lacoue-Labarthe and

Nancy. They understand fully that the obsessive and sometimes remorseless refinements of genre parameters performed by the *Frühromantik* was ultimately in the service of precipitating—chemically—a medium of inscription indebted to all rigorously practiced genres and that operates free and clear, in the Enlightenment sense of freedom, of any of them.

The pivotal rhetoric of the genres in the *Fragments* doubles, then, as a meticulous strategy in the elaboration of the aesthetics of script and as a free-for-all, a demolition derby of genres set on a collision course with each other. On impact, their preconceived boundaries dissolve. This mélange of generic parameters becomes explicit in *Critical Fragments* 53: "In respect to their unity, most modern poems are allegories (mysteries, moralities) or novellas (adventures, intrigues), or a mixture or dilution of these."[22] If by this point in time modern poetry has become qualified by fiction and allegorical representation, "Novels are the Socratic dialogues of our times. And this free form has become the refuge of common sense in its flight from pedantry."[23] This pointed comment alone at least begins a respectable response to the formidable enigma of how Kierkegaard could synthesize such texts as *Repetition*, "The Immediate Stages of the Erotic," and "The Diary of a Seducer" in critical reaction to the dialectical momentum and overarching systematic comprehensiveness driving the Hegelian philosophy. The field for the free-wheeling, open-ended deliberation on the truth, argues Schlegel, has been resituated in the modern novel, itself a hybrid genre, a genre of genres. The inherently literary polymorphous perversity of the novel fits it out to serve as the dramatic scene of Socratic irony:

> Socratic irony is the only involuntary and yet completely deliberate dissimulation. It is equally impossible to feign it or divulge it. To a person who hasn't got it, it will remain a riddle even after it is openly confessed. It is meant to deceive no one except those who find it a deception and who either take pleasure in the roguery of making fools of the whole world or else become angry when they get an inkling they themselves might be included. In this sort of irony, everything should be playful and serious, guilelessly open and deeply hidden. It originates in the union of *savoir vivre* and scientific spirit, in the conjunction of a perfectly instinctive and a perfectly conscious philosophy. It contains and arouses a feeling of indissoluble antagonism between the absolute and the relative, between the impossibility and the necessity of complete communication. It is the freest of all licenses.[24]

Socratic irony, in its service as a go-between between deception and frankness, playfulness and deliberation, feigning and self-deception, assumes the role of fickle, hovering paradox that Kant ascribes to beauty in *The Critique of Judgment*.[25]

When Schlegel makes the novel the particular province of Socratic irony, the field, that is, in which the effects on systematic thought wrought by an entire complex of textual epiphenomena—among them representation in general, narrative double vision, poetic condensation, witty modulation, imagistic framing, and ironic disqualification—he ushers in the age of the philosophical novel, a cue he himself has taken in his own *Lucinde* and to which, in different ways, Kierkegaard, Nietzsche, Proust, Musil, Sartre, and Blanchot, would be acutely responsive. From *Thus Spoke Zarathustra* to *Thomas the Obscure* and beyond, a perverse subset of the novel would release the uncanny elective affinity between conceptual programming and novelistic invention that Schlegel announces in the *Fragments*.

This particular generic amalgamation would set the stage for Kierkegaard's casting of Socrates, in *The Concept of Irony*, as a master seducer of his students, but whose enticements and dissimulations, not unlike the ones that Schlegel outlines in *Critical Fragments* 108, prevail at the level of rhetoric, rather than of sexual performance.

> His position was altogether too personally isolated, every relation contracted too loosely conjoined to be anything more than a significant contact. He stood outside every relationship, and the law governing it was a perpetual attraction and repulsion. His connection with a particular individual was only momentary, while high above this he hovered in ironic satisfaction. . . . The ironic freedom he enjoyed, for as no relationship had sufficient strength to hold him he constantly felt freely above it.[26]

Under the aura of Romantic fragmentation, Socrates, the initiator of dispassionate Western philosophical inquiry, literally becomes a cipher and a figure of irony, detachment, free play, and interpersonal, if not yet sexual promiscuity, and the open-ended expenditure of erotic tension and attraction. This modus operandi and this way of understanding the tenor of Socratic deliberations, the Socratic imprint on philosophy, carries over from the figure of Socrates to his relations with all who would aspire to learn from him:

> In this sense one might possibly call him a seducer, for he deceived the youth and possibly awakened longings which he never satisfied, allowed them to become inflamed by the subtle pleasures of anticipation yet never gave them nour-

ishing food. He deceived them all in the same way as he deceived Alcibiades. . . .
Then he was gone, the enchantment was over, then they felt the deep pangs of
unrequited love, felt that they had been deceived and that it was not Socrates
who loved them but they who loved Socrates. . . . His relation to his students
was therefore stimulating, to be sure but at all personal in a positive sense. What
restrained him in this regard was once again his irony.[27]

Against the backdrop of the play of genres in the discourse of Romanticism—whose ultimate product is the terse, duplicitous, and devastating medium of criticism—Socrates emerges as the all-time hero of the
philosophical novel, of the tradition of philosophy recast as a heteroglossic
novel of the ages.

As esteemed as the position that Schlegel accords the novel as a theater
of Socratic wit and irony, this genre remained merely one of several formal
traditions that Schlegel addressed in the enterprise of distilling a discourse
of general writing out of an admixture of genres. His project entails not so
much a Goethean witches' brew of *all* the genres so much as a collision
into the nuclei of the *other* script modalities that the genres retain within
themselves. "All genres are good, says Voltaire, except the one that's boring.
But what is the boring genre? It may be bigger than all the rest."[28] The
genres under the specific purview of the *Fragments* number not only lyrical
poetry and philosophy, but also drama, satire, painting, history, and even
music. It is on the hard lines and borders between the traditional genres
that a metadiscourse of culture begins to emerge: "A dialogue is a chain or
garland of fragments. An exchange of letters is a dialogue on a larger scale,
and memoirs constitute a system of fragments. But as yet no genre exists
that is fragmentary both in form and content." "Viewed subjectively, philosophy, like epic poetry, always begins in medias res."[29]

At the conceptual horizon of Schlegel's painstaking sifting and sorting
through the traditional genres and the subjection of his own formulations to
considerable poetic standards of wit and piquancy (as introduced in *Critical
Fragments* 97), the metadiscourse of culture, a genre of genres, if you will,
eventfully emerges. And it has a name, this language culled from features of
all the operative literary forms and traditions, but exercising a freedom, in
an Enlightenment sense, to address any phenomenon of art, sociopsychological formation, and culture.

The name of this genre of genres is criticism itself. Criticism names the
discursive material and technology by which a free, disinterested, unencum-

bered, unimpeded commentary on the prevailing conditions of art, intellectual work, and cultural enfranchisement may be delivered. It is, as suggested above, nothing more formidable than a medium of notation, but it is one in which a considerable sum of Romantic hope and messianic zeal have been invested.

Schlegel is as wary of criticism in its formal sense and performance, to be sure, as of any isolated genre. To the degree that it is judgmental, established criticism is an agent of the overall social repression that would become an ongoing target of the Nietzschean philosophy:

> They have a habit of calling themselves Criticism. They write coldly, superficially, pretentiously, and beyond all measure vapidly. Nature, feeling, nobility, and greatness of spirit simply don't exist for them, and yet they act as if they could summon these things to appear before their judgment-stools. . . . For them correctness is equivalent to virtue. Taste is their idol: a fetish that can only be worshipped joylessly. Who doesn't recognize in this portrait the priest of the temple of *belles lettres* who have the same sex as those of *Cybele*?[30]

The established guild or brotherhood of critics acts as an agent, above all, of a detachment in the experience and evaluation of art resulting here, according to August Wilhelm, in a distinctive vapidity, coldness, and superficiality of interpretation. The potential vitality of exegesis is measured against the intimacy of the aesthetic experience and the free play of the spirit. The calibration of taste and the setting of the parameters of correctness is no work for authentic people of letters. Nor is the self-righteous and self-aggrandizing commerce in domesticated conceptual paradigms. Through this Romantic intervention, the guild of critics learns that it has been gelded. The temple of culture where the critics worship turns out to be the salon frequented by the self-unmanned priests of Cybele.

So much for establishment, card-carrying criticism and the moral rectitude that, in any age, offers itself in place of the vexed calls and agonized uncertainties reached by hard-nosed and free-wheeling intellectual deliberation. On some deeper stratum closer to the cultural engine room, a location rarely frequented by the celebrities and the crowds, who may find it objectionable and repugnant, the *Fragments* have done nothing but embody and perform the broader work of Criticism in the age of modernity. On the basis of the full panoply of cultural forms and conventions, they have synthesized a medium of inscription, passionate in its disinterest, capable of gravitating to any locus of cultural work and inscribing it with the legend of illumination. The interventions of this critical notation are perforce limited in their scope, achievement, and consequence. They are abrupt and inconsequential in the style of their provocation and their emergence. They raise more questions and doubts than they resolve. In their free-wheeling style, they leave in their wake a kaleidoscopic tangle of the traditions and cultural examples that they have invoked. Yet in the programmatic imperfection of their calling and design, the *Fragments* furnish a format and a model for cultural responsiveness and responsibility amid battle conditions, amid the lifestyle of a cosmopolitan modernity that is itself discontinuous, inconsequential, and overdetermined by a thick overlay of prescriptions and responsibilities, themselves often mutually contradictory.

As the unindicted coconspirators identified with early Romanticism comprehensively demonstrated, criticism is a feature of existence under a broader modernity. It is a sensibility available to and indeed incumbent upon the citizens of this configuration. The modalities of this intellectual work and cultural participation are embedded, inconsistently, throughout the *Fragments* themselves. It does Friedrich Schlegel and his collaborators an injustice to furnish any prescription for critical work more specific and deterministic than an example, one highlighting criticism's license to alight on a vast array of cultural artifacts from a broad panorama of conceptual oversight combined with its obligation to go in close, to bring the full resources of fragmentation, poetics, wit, and irony to bear in reaching precise formulations that initiate thinking in their ability to *shock*.

Within two pages of the *Athenaeum Fragments*, we read a meditation on the cultural and stylistic values of historical writing that begins like this:

> The French Revolution, Fichte's philosophy, and Goethe's *Meister* are the greatest tendencies of the age. Whoever is offended by this juxtaposition, whoever cannot take any revolution seriously that isn't noisy and materialistic, hasn't yet achieved a lofty, broad perspective on the history of mankind. Even in our shabby histories of civilization, which usually resemble a collection of variants accompanied by a running commentary for which the original classical text has been lost; even there many a little book, almost unnoticed by the rabble of the time, plays a role greater than anything they did.[31]

This is a passage extolling a brief Chinese encyclopedia of mixed phenomena whose meaning and significance may be lost from time and memory, whose revolutionary potential may subside into oblivion. It is first of all incumbent on any vibrant criticism to recognize and select the cultural productions capable of reprogramming the existing field of knowledge, in this case a constellation of historical events and outcomes in France, the conceptual work of Fichte, and a novel by Goethe. The above citation knows that in accounting for a sea change in epistemological conditions, it has been confident and wide ranging enough to juxtapose two different discursive genres with a very tangible set of societal, governmental, and communal events and changes. We infer from the passage that it is criticism's duty to distinguish the revolutionary potential, that is to say, the radical conceptual, cognitive, and experiential modifications effected through these artifacts, from the conventional "running commentary" issued by the "shabby histories of civilization" whose tedium buries any vitality that might have inhered in the "original classic text."

Quite understandably, the next fragment theorizes what it would take to enact in criticism, the revolution that its immediate predecessor has chronicled. Criticism expands, in other words, into a context-specific theorization of the conditions for its own formulations, which are intimately tied to, but not identical with the theoretical parameters of several related and adjacent, if you will, genres.

> Archaism of the words, novelty in their placement, compelling brevity and digressive fullness, reproducing even the inexplicable features of the individuals it delineates: these are the essential characteristics of the historical style. Most essential of all are nobility, splendor, dignity. The historical style is distinguished by the homogeneity and purity of its naïve words of true ancestry, and by the selection of the most significant, weighty, and precious words; by a notably outlined—rather too rigidly than not clearly enough—articulated periodic structure, like that of Thucidides; by spare solidity, august alacrity, and superb joviality of tone and color after the manner of Caesar; but particularly by that innate and exalted cultivation of Tacitus, which poetizes, civilizes, and philosophizes the dry facts of pure empiricism, refines and generalizes them so that they seem to have been apprehended and variously sifted by someone who is at once a perfect thinker, artist, and hero, who has achieved this without allowing raw poetry, pure philosophy, or isolated wit to disturb the harmony of the whole at any point. All this must be blended into history.[32]

It is with nothing less than breathtaking rapidity that a swath of discourse bookmarking for posterity the radicality shared by Fichte and Goethe and the events of the French Revolution and noting well the lessons to be learned from a careful reading of Thucidides, Caesar, and Tacitus develops into a prolegomena for historical annotation in general. There is indeed in the passage a radical succession, if not simultaneity, with which Tacitus's positivizing, civilizing, and philosophizing of "the dry facts of pure empiricism" morphs into an explicit theory of historical discourse, an annotation whose worth is defined by its shock and beauty.

Criticism thus demonstrates in these adjacent Schlegelian fragments that it marks closely the particular values and features of specific texts; that it comprehends in several senses the confluence between different genres and cultural media, including the "hard facts" or the actual events; that it conceptualizes the status of representation and discourse in culture, and especially the role and constitution of criticism itself. Criticism performs all these roles while gathering and marshalling itself in a performance of the constitutive genres and discourses of culture—and of itself. It assumes this considerable archival and judgmental burden while imposing upon itself a demand for creative and generative freshness and unpredictability. It can achieve these demanding design parameters only on the basis of an erudition that is at once broad and deep, yet it assumes full responsibility for its fragmentariness, that is, for the abruptness, incompletion, and calculated violence of its exegetical forays.

If there is any relevance to the above formulations, authentic criticism, as it is both configured and bequeathed to Modernity by the *Frühromantik*, entails a vast, almost impossible array of specifications. So complex are the parameters surrounding a criticism that rises to the challenges and quandaries of modern conditions that in certain unavoidable respects, the discourse cancels itself out. This may in part explain the attraction and aura surrounding the script of the cultural critics who most reactively rose to the challenge posed by Schlegel and his coterie: Kierkegaard, Nietzsche, Benjamin, Adorno, Bataille, Barthes, Foucault, Derrida, and Miller. Criticism, in its occasional nature, breadth, shock, fluency, selective close-up detail, and its proclivity for simultaneous self-performance, is the cultural discourse with the greatest proclivity to self-effacement. Perhaps this is why it is the genre with the weakest definition, the tendency to prompt the greatest overuse in the discursive division of labor. An at times bewildering proliferation of roles and functions characterizes the discursive legacy of the *Frühromantik*. This may help to explain why criticism has so few advocates per se, why its discursive partners deriving from the traditions of poetics, philosophy, religion, and exegesis speak louder, if not more clearly and distinctly.

1. See I. A. Richards, *Practical Criticism: A Study of Literary Judgment* (New York: Harcourt, Brace & World, 1929), pp. 3–16.

2. See William Empson, *7 Types of Ambiguity* (New York: New Directions, 1966), pp. 1–47.

3. Walter Benjamin's messianic aspirations for cultural criticism were authentic even while he was fully aware of the ironies attending this wish. Perhaps more than any writer, Benjamin established the set of bearings that will accrue to the critic over the following essays: a mixture of resolute affirmation and commitment to the processes of intellectual synthesis and cultural inscription, a stoic and quasi-empirical engagement with whatever emerges on the critic's "sights," and the *flâneur's* compulsive forays and interactions within the field of cultural production, with its attendant, ultimately wearing detachment and alienation. Some of Benjamin's most stirring formulations of this critical credo are to be found in Convolute N of *The Arcades Project*, ed. Howard Eiland and Kevin McLaughlin (Cambridge, Mass.: Harvard University Press, 1999), pp. 456–63, 473–75; and "On the Concept of History," in Walter Benjamin, *Selected Writings*, ed. Marcus Bullock, Howard Eiland, and Gary Smith, 4 vols. (Cambridge, Mass.: Harvard University Press, 1996–2003), 4:389–400.

4. Walter Benjamin, *The Origin of German Tragic Drama*, trans. John Osborne (London: New Left Books, 1977).

5. I attempt to deal with this materiality in *High Resolution: Critical Theory and the Problem of Literacy* (Oxford: Oxford University Press, 1989), pp. 128–31.

6. I am referring here not only to the literal fashion in which Georges Bataille hid and saved the manuscript of Benjamin's *Arcades Project* for the duration of World War II, but to a constellation of Frankfurt School interests, concerns, bearings, and approaches that were sustained during and after the war by a broad range of French writers and cultural critics along with Bataille. This body of work is, of course, characterized by its openness to popular artifacts as well as to "high art," by its high philosophical aspirations and criteria for criticism,

and by the sweep it recurrently orchestrates between individual (or personal) psychology and "mass psychology." No French cultural critic exemplifies the continuation of the Benjaminian discourse and approach to the world better than Roland Barthes, who, with the addition of formal linguistic discourse and paradigms, seems to pick up right where Benjamin left off.

7. See Jacques Derrida, "The Law of Genre," in *Acts of Literature*, ed. Derek Attridge (New York: Routledge, 1992), pp. 221–52.

8. Citations from the *Athenaeum* and *Philosophical Fragments* derive from *Friedrich Schlegel's Lucinde and Fragments*, trans. Peter Firchow (Minneapolis: University of Minnesota Press, 1971).

9. Walter Benjamin, "On Some Motifs in Baudelaire," in *Selected Writings*, 4:319–20.

10. Jacques Derrida, "Plato's Pharmacy," in *Dissemination*, trans, Barbara Johnson (Chicago: University of Chicago Press, 1981), pp. 169–70.

11. See Immanuel Kant, *Critique of Judgment*, trans. J. H. Bernard (New York: Hafner, 1951), sections 44–53, 147–75.

12. See Martin Heidegger, "The Origin of the Work of Art" and "What are Poets For?" in *Poetry, Language, Thought*, trans. Albert Hofstadter (New York: Harper & Row, 1971), pp. 37–39, 70–71, 74, 103–7, 137–39.

13. Walter Benjamin, "On the Image of Proust, in *Selected Writings*, 2:237.

14. Ibid.

15. Walter Benjamin, "Franz Kafka: On the Tenth Anniversary of His Death," in *Selected Writings*, 2:799.

16. Ibid., p. 802.

17. Ibid., p. 809.

18. Immanuel Kant, *Critique of Pure Reason*, trans. Paul Guyer and Alan W. Wood (Cambridge: Cambridge University Press, 1998), pp. 459–67.

19. Ibid. p. 224.

20. Ibid.

21. Ibid., p. 226.

22. Heidegger, of course, pushes hard on the notion of "the open." See "The Origin of the Work of Art" and "What are Poets For?" in *Poetry, Language Thought*, pp. 49, 55, 60–64, 69, 70, 73–74, 106–07, 132.

23. Some of Derrida's most compelling remarks relating deconstruction to what has been previously deemed impossible and linking it to the unforeseen event are to be found in his *Specters of Marx*, trans. Peggy Kamuf (New York: Routledge, 1994), pp. 65–66, 167–70. Also see in this regard "Hostipitality," in *Acts of Religion*, ed. Gil Anidjar (New York: Routledge, 2002), pp. 364, 386–87.

24. Slavoj Žižek, for example, has maintained an unwavering incredulity toward what he sees as misguided attempts to think beyond the inevitable structures and outcomes of the psychoanalytical drive, with all the defenses, repressions, and distortions that it provokes, and somehow to circumvent the inevitabilities of the Lacanian Real. Žižek assembles an odd assortment of shirk-

ers of the Real, including wishy-washy liberalism, Buddhism, and deconstruction, as ongoing targets of his skepticism, which is often engaging and witty even where it abdicates the experiment of disclosing systematic limitations. See his *The Fragile Absolute* (London: Verso, 2000), pp. 3–4, 6–10, 15–18, 23, 46–47, 73–75, 98–99, 108–09; also, *The Ticklish Subject* (London: Verso, 1999), pp. 52–58, 92–95, 105, 160–61, 186–87, 196, 337.

25. See Roland Barthes, *The Rustle of Language*, trans. Richard Howard (New York: Hill & Wang, 1986), pp. 9–10, 17–21, 38–46, 76–79, 106–110, 321–22, 350–58.

26. See Anthony Wilden, *System and Structure* (London: Tavistock, 1972), pp. 164–74, 188–90, 202–25, 351–61, 400–6.

27. Werner Hamacher, *Premises: Essays on Philosophy and Literature from Kant to Celan*, trans. Peter Fenves (Cambridge: Harvard University Press, 1996).

28. Cynthia Chase, *Decomposing Figures: Rhetorical Readings in the Romantic Tradition* (Baltimore: Johns Hopkins University Press, 1986).

29. Of particular relevance to the present study is Jacobs's *In the Language of Walter Benjamin* (Baltimore; Johns Hopkins University Press, 1999). But since *The Dissimulating Harmony* (Baltimore: Johns Hopkins University Press, 1978), the unit of her thought and writing has been the critical essay, which reaches out to the broader methodological and ethical questions of the moment only by way of meticulous readings, often of the marginal productions by the authors in question, rather than of their canonical works.

30. Jacques Derrida, *The Gift of Death*, trans. David Wills (Chicago: University of Chicago Press, 1995), pp. 42, 43.

31. Ibid., pp. 29, 90, 91,

32. Ibid., p. 9.

33. I have devised a preliminary reading of this figure in *Afterimages of Modernity* (Baltimore: Johns Hopkins University Press, 1990), pp. 3–7, 17–18.

34. For the notion of the performative in literature and criticism, see J. Hillis Miller, *Speech Acts in Literature* (Stanford: Stanford University Press, 2001). Also see Paul de Man, *Allegories of Reading* (New Haven: Yale University Press, 1979), pp. 8–10, 23, 46, 56, 122–29, 131; Jacques Derrida, "Signature Event Context," in *Glyph 1: Johns Hopkins Textual Studies*, ed. Samuel Weber and Henry Sussman (Baltimore: Johns Hopkins University Press, 1977), pp. 181, 186–93; "Limited Inc abc . . .," in *Glyph 2: Johns Hopkins Textual Studies*, ed. Samuel Weber and Henry Sussman (Baltimore: Johns Hopkins University Press, 1977), pp. 163, 174, 196–97, 228–33, 242–43; "An Interview with Jacques Derrida," in *Acts of Literature*, pp. 51, 60, 69, 74; "The Law of Genre," pp. 239–41; and "Ulysses Gramophone: Hear Say Yes in Joyce," in *Acts of Literature*, pp. 298–300.

35. Maurice Blanchot, *The Space of Literature*, trans. Ann Smock (Lincoln: University of Nebraska Press, 1989), pp. 52, 62.

36. G. W. F. Hegel, "Independence and Dependence of Self-Consciousness: Lordship and Bondage," in *Hegel's Phenomenology of Spirit*, trans. A. V. Miller (Oxford: Oxford University Press, 1977), p. 117.

37. Walter Benjamin, "Notes for a Study of the Beauty of Colored Illustrations in Children's Books," in *Selected Writings*, 1:264–66.

38. Walter Benjamin, "Hashish in Marseilles," in *Selected Writings*, 3:673–79.

39. Walter Benjamin, *The Arcades Project*, pp. 456–57, 460, 467–68, 473.

40. J. Hillis Miller, *Topographies* (Stanford: Stanford University Press, 1995).

41. Ibid., p. 4.

42. J. Hillis Miller and Manuel Asensi, *Black Holes: Or, Boustrophedonic Reading* (Stanford: Stanford University Press, 1999).

43. Ibid., pp. 349–51.

44. Ibid., pp. 359, 361–63.

45. Maurice Blanchot, *The Infinite Conversation*, trans. Susan Hanson (Minneapolis: University of Minnesota Press, 1993), pp. 202–4.

46. Ibid., pp. 222–29, 162–68, 258–62.

47. Ibid., p. 205.

2. PROLEGOMENA TO ANY PRESENT AND FUTURE LANGUAGE POETRY

I was introduced to language poetry by Linda Reinfeld, author of *Language Poetry: Writing as Rescue* (Baton Rouge: Louisiana State University Press, 1992), a notable poet and translator in her own right, during the early 1990s, when she completed her graduate studies in English at Buffalo. I'm deeply grateful for this introduction, as for her ongoing instruction, friendship, and support.

1. Franz Kafka, "The Cares of as Family Man," in *The Complete Stories of Franz Kafka*, ed. Nahum N. Glatzer (New York: Schocken Books, 1976), pp. 427–29.

2. Michel Foucault, *The Order of Things*, trans. Richard Howard (New York: Vintage, 1994), pp. 17–42.

3. Charles Bernstein, "Thought's Measure," in *Content's Dream* (Los Angeles: Sun and Moon, 1986), p. 63.

4. I discuss the parallelism between discursive styles and philosophical projects in twentieth-century discourse at length in "Kafka and Modern Philosophy: Wittgenstein, Deconstruction, and the Cuisine of the Imaginary," in *Afterimages of Modernity: Structure and Indifference in Twentieth-Century Literature* (Baltimore: Johns Hopkins University Press, 1990), pp. 58–94.

5. Bruce Andrews, Charles Bernstein, Ray di Palma, Steve McCaffery, and Ron Silliman, *LEGEND* (New York: L=A=N=G=U=A=G=E/Segue, 1980).

6. These motifs combine to brilliant effect in Benjamin's epochal essay, "On Some Motifs in Baudelaire," in Walter Benjamin, *Selected Writings*, ed. Marcus

Bullock, Howard Eiland, and Gary Smith, 4 vols. (Cambridge, Mass.: Harvard University Press, 2003), 4:318–21, 324, 327–32.

7. Charles Bernstein, *Controlling Interests* (New York: Roof Books, 1986).

8. Charles Bernstein, "The Blue Divide," in *Controlling Interests*, 55.

9. Charles Bernstein, "Artifice of Absorption," in *A Poetics* (Cambridge, Mass.: Harvard University Press, 1992), p. 30.

10. Ibid., pp. 9, 30.

11. I introduce this term in the sense that psychoanalysts, mostly of the object-relations school, deploy it: as an expression emerging from the raw and undigested extreme of language, deriving from the inception of life, what Lacan calls the "pre-Oedipal," which persists in our later parlance and disproportionately colors our attitudes toward ourselves and the other. For seminal passages on introjections in this sense, see Otto Kernberg, "Structural Derivatives of Object Relations," in *Essential Papers on Object Relations*, ed. Peter Buckley (New York: New York University Press, 1986), pp. 359–65; Heinz Kohut, *The Analysis of the Self* (Madison, Conn.: International Universities Press, 1989), pp. 210–20, 278–83.

12. James Joyce, *Ulysses, The Corrected Text*, ed. Hans Walter Gabler (New York: Random House, 1986), p. 144.

13. Charles Bernstein, "The Next Available Place," in *Controlling Interests*, p. 31.

14. Walter Benjamin, "Franz Kafka," in *Selected Writings*, 2:814.

15. Charles Bernstein, "Standing Target," in *Controlling Interests*, pp. 39, 45.

16. Ibid., pp. 41, 43.

17. Charles Bernstein, *The Sophist* (Los Angeles: Sun and Moon, 1987).

18. Charles Bernstein, "Amblyopia," in *The Sophist*, pp. 112, 121, 126, 118.

19. Ibid., p. 124.

20. Charles Bernstein, "Ministry of Psychological Science," in *The Sophist*, pp. 114–15.

21. Charles Bernstein, "Amblyopia," in *The Sophist*, pp. 128–29.

22. Ibid., p. 122.

23. I have elsewhere argued that the histories of art, criticism, and intellectual work in general can be well understood as a series of contracts going in and out of effect according to their value in addressing pressing epistemological questions and in satisfying temporary considerations of design. See *The Aesthetic Contract* (Stanford: Stanford University Press, 1997), pp. 137–205.

3. WALTER, THE CRITIC

1. No one of late has observed this disjunction between culture and textuality more trenchantly than Tom Cohen in *Ideology and Inscription* (Cambridge: Cambridge University Press, 1999).

2. For a discussion of iterability, a pivotal construct of speech-act theory, see Jacques Derrida, "Signature Event Context" in *Glyph 1: Johns Hopkins Textual*

Studies, ed. Samuel Weber and Henry Sussman (Baltimore: Johns Hopkins University Press, 1977), pp. 186–97; also his "Limited Inc abc . . .," *in Glyph 2: Johns Hopkins Textual Studies*, ed. Samuel Weber and Henry Sussman (Baltimore: Johns Hopkins University Press, 1977), pp. 175, 183–85, 197–201, 209–10, 212, 217–19, 223–24, 226, 242–45, 249.

3. Walter Benjamin, "The Concept of Criticism in German Romanticism," in *Selected Writings*, ed. Marcus Bullock, Howard Eiland, and Gary Smith, 4 vols. (Cambridge, Mass.: Harvard University Press, 1996–2003), 1:116–200.

4. Walter Benjamin, "Goethe's *Elective Affinities*," in *Selected Writings*, 1:297–360.

5. Walter Benjamin, *The Origins of German Tragic Drama*, trans. John Osborne (London: New Left Books, 1977).

6. Walter Benjamin, "The Work of Art in the Age of Its Technological Reproducibility," in *Selected Writings*, 3:101–33

7. Walter Benjamin, *One-Way Street*, in *Selected Writings*, 1:444–488.

8. Walter Benjamin, *Moscow Diary*, trans. Richard Sieburth (Cambridge, Mass.: Harvard University Press, 1986).

9. Walter Benjamin, *Berlin Chronicle*, and *Berlin Childhood around 1900*, in *Selected Writings*, 3:344–414.

10. Walter Benjamin, "The Concept of Criticism in German Romanticism," pp. 129–30.

11. Ibid., p. 135.

12. Ibid., p. 138.

13. Ibid., p. 139.

14. Ibid., p. 147.

15. Ibid., p. 146.

16. Ibid., p. 148.

17. Ibid.

18. Ibid., p. 151.

19. Ibid., p. 153–54.

20. Ibid.

21. Ibid., p. 159. In his call for an immanent criticism, Benjamin is anticipating the terrain of subsequent thinkers who would infuse textual multiplicity and indeterminacy into systematic elaborations of sociopolitical relations. In such as text as Adorno's *Minima Moralia*, his Frankfurt School colleagues joined him in this enterprise. But in relation to this particular aspect of Benjamin's notion of criticism, I think more specifically of Derrida's treatments of religion and politics and of Laclau's contingency-motivated political theory. In all of these instances, discourse pulls back from its systematic dimensions and aspirations by opening itself to contingency.

22. Jorge Luis Borges, *Ficciones* (New York: Grove Press, 1962), p. 96.

23. Benjamin, "The Concept of Criticism in German Romanticism," p. 167.

24. Ibid., p. 173. The mandate for a poetic prose, like the isolation of a trope for fragmentation in parabasis, mentioned a few lines below in my text, derives

directly from the canonical works of the *Frühromantik*, notably from the *Athenaeum* and *Critical Fragments* by the Schlegels and their close cohorts, which Benjamin had obviously read with intense and loving care. I follow Benjamin directly back to these sources in my Afterword, "Fragmentary Romantic Script as the Enabling Legislation for Contemporary Criticism."

25. Heinz Kohut stepped into the breech as the poet of this notion of psychological integration. Lacan was aware of the integrationist tendencies of American psychiatry since early in the *Seminars*. I attempted to merge the varieties of assimilation or integration that one encounters both in the therapeutic situation and in critical encounters with cultural artifacts in *Psyche and Text* (Albany: SUNY Press, 1993). In the intervening years since that project, I have come to apprehend the skew between these cognitive registers with increasing clarity.

26. Benjamin, "The Concept of Criticism in German Romanticism," p. 175.

27. Ibid., p. 175.

28. Walter Benjamin, "Goethe's *Elective Affinities*," in *Selected Writings*, 1:333–34.

29. Ibid., pp. 297, 299, 300; 304–5; 305–6.

30. Ibid., p. 334.

31. Ibid.

32. Ibid., p. 342.

33. Ibid., p. 332, 355.

34. Ibid., p. 355.

35. Walter Benjamin, "Announcement of the Journal *Angelus Novus*," in *Selected Writings*, 1:293.

36. Ibid., p. 292.

37. Ibid., p. 296.

38. Walter Benjamin, "Program for Literary Criticism," in *Selected Writings*, 2:290.

39. Walter Benjamin, "The Lisbon Earthquake," in *Selected Writings*, 2:536.

40. In Walter Benjamin, "On Some Motifs in Baudelaire," in *Selected Writings*, 4:313–55.

41. Walter Benjamin, "On the Concept of History," in *Selected Writings*, 4;389–400.

42. Walter Benjamin, *One-Way Street*, in *Selected Writings*, 1:444, 474.

43. Ibid., pp. 444–45.

44. Ibid., p. 445.

45. Ibid., 445–46.

46. I think here above all of Faust's visit, in *Faust II*, to the Upper Peneios.

47. See John Murray Cuddihy, *The Ordeal of Civility* (New York: Dell, 1974), p. 4:

Thus, Jewish emancipation, assimilation, and modernization constitute a single, total, phenomenon. The secularizing Jewish intellectual, as the avant-garde of his decolonized people, suffered in his own person the trauma of this culture shock. Unable to turn back, unable completely to acculturate, caught between "his own" whom he had left behind and the Gentile "host culture" where he felt ill at ease and alienated, intellectual Jews and Jewish intellectuals experienced cultural shame and awkwardness, guilt, and "the guilt of shame." The focus of their concern, often unacknowledged, was the public behavior of their fellow Jews, the *Ostjuden*.

48. Walter Benjamin, "German Men and Women: A Sequence of Letters Selected and edited by Detlev Holz," in *Selected Writings*, 3:167–235.

49. Walter Benjamin, "Franz Kafka: On the Tenth Anniversary of His Death," in *Selected Writings*, 2:812.

50. Benjamin, *One-Way Street*, p. 446.

51. I unpack my own version of Freud's transition from a "linguist of consciousness" to the canonical and instituting/institutional founder of psychoanalysis in "The Subject of the Nerves: Philosophy and Freud," in *The Hegelian Aftermath* (Baltimore: Johns Hopkins University Press, 1982), pp. 164–77, 184–202.

52. Benjamin, *One-Way Street*, p. 455.

53. Ibid., p. 471.

54. Ibid., pp. 449–50.

55. Ibid., p. 450.

56. Ibid., p. 463–66.

57. Ibid., p. 463.

58. Ibid., p. 96.

59. For an account of Benjamin's thwarted attempt to attain the degree and rank conferred upon acceptance of his *Habilitationsschrift*, see, among other sources, Bernd Witte, *Walter Benjamin: An Intellectual Biography*, trans. James Rolleston (Detroit: Wayne State University Press, 1991), pp. 76–86.

60. Benjamin, *One-Way Street*, p. 465.

61. James Joyce, *A Portrait of the Artist as a Young Man* (New York: Penguin, 1986), pp. 50–59.

62. Benjamin, *One-Way Street*, p. 462

63. Ibid., p. 461.

64. Ibid., pp. 486, 447, 447.

65. Ibid., pp. 473, 474.

66. Ibid., pp. 474–75.

67. Ibid., pp. 450.

68. Ibid., pp. 450–55.

69. Ibid., p. 452.

70. Ibid., p. 453.

71. Ibid., pp. 453–54.

72. Of the object-relations thinkers in psychoanalysis, three who have done the most to theorize people's relations to things invested with (good or bad)

"aura" to them are W. R. D. Fairbairn, John Bowlby, and D. W. Winnicott. Fundamental writings by all three authors are included in *Essential Papers on Object Relations*, ed. Peter Buckley (New York: New York University Press, 1986). See Fairbairn, "A Revised Psychopathology of the Psychoses and Psychoneuroses" and "The Repression and Return of Bad Objects (with Special Reference to the 'War Neuroses')," pp. 71–126; Bowlby, "The Nature of the Child's Tie to his Mother," pp. 153–199; and Winnicott, "Transitional Objects and Transitional Phenomena," pp. 254–71.

73. Benjamin indeed does encounter Adrienne Monnier, Léon-Paul Fargue, Léon-Pierre Quint, Albert Le Cuziat, and Félix Bertaux, among other personal acquaintances of Proust, as well as Joyce in his 1930 "Paris Diary," in *Selected Writings*, 2:327–54. In this piece, Fargue reports on the famous meeting, or rather non-encounter, between Joyce and Proust at a dinner he gave (pp. 338–39).

74. Benjamin, *One-Way Street*, p. 458.

75. Ibid., p. 457.

76. See my *Aesthetic Contract*, 23–70, 209–15.

77. Benjamin, *One-Way Street*, p. 456.

78. Ibid., p. 486.

79. For some of Claude Lévi-Strauss's key formulations concerning structural analysis, as well as those invoking the figure of the index card as an instrument of this procedure, see his "The Structural Study of Myth," in *Structural Anthropology*, trans. Claire Jacobson and Brooke Grundfest Schoepf (New York: Penguin, 1979), pp. 206–31.

80. Benjamin, *One-Way Street*, p. 456.

81. Immanuel Kant, *Critique of Pure Reason*, trans. Paul Guyer and Alan W. Wood (Cambridge: Cambridge University Press, 1998), pp. 459–95.

82. Benjamin, *One-Way Street*, p. 459

83. Ibid., pp. 460–61.

4. BETWEEN THE REGISTERS: *THE ARCADES PROJECT*, THE TALMUD, AND *GLAS*

1. For the notion of thrownness, see Martin Heidegger, *Being and Time*, trans. Joan Stambaugh (Albany: State University of New York Press, 1996), pp. 122, 135–37, 139, 144–45, 148, 161, 167, 181, 183, 188–89, 195–96, 251–52, 276–77, 284–87, 328–29, 339–40, 342–45, 347–48, 364–66, 382–83, 385–86, 410–12.

2. Franz Kafka, "The Cares of a Family Man," in *The Complete Stories*, ed. Nahum N. Glatzer (New York: Schocken, 1976), pp. 428.

3. See "Pierre Menard, Author of Don Quixote" in Jorge Luis Borges, *Ficciones* (New York: Grove Press, 1962), pp. 45–56.

4. See Marshall McLuhan, *The Mechanical Bride* (Boston: Beacon Press, 1967), pp. 2–7.

5. Given that this important visual artist and cultural figure's name was Jean-Ignace-Isidore-Gérard Grandville, it may be well understandable why posterity remembers him simply as "Grandville."

6. Walter Benjamin, *The Arcades Project*, trans. Howard Eiland and Kevin McLaughlin (Cambridge, Mass.: Harvard University Press, 1999), p. 473 [N9,7]. Page references are keyed both to this edition and to Benjamin's original convolutes and notebooks.

7. See Maurice Blanchot, *The Space of Literature*, trans. Ann Smock (Lincoln: University of Nebraska Press, 1989), pp. 44–48, 51–56, 81, 87, 93, 136–38, 153–57.

8. Benjamin, *The Arcades Project*, pp. 456–57 [N1,4] and p. 460 [N1a8].

9. Ibid., p. 3.

10. Walter Benjamin, "On Some Motifs in Baudelaire," in *Selected Writings*, ed. Marcus Bullock, Howard Eiland, and Gary Smith, 4 vols. (Cambridge, Mass.: Harvard University Press, 1996–2003), 4:327–31, 334–35.

11. Benjamin, *The Arcades Project*, p. 9.

12. See, among many possible passages, James Joyce, *Finnegans Wake* (New York: Viking, 1986), pp. 107–24, 182–83.

13. Genesis 22:1–19. Also see Søren Kierkegaard, *Fear and Trembling / Repetition*, trans. and ed. Howard V. Hong and Edna H. Hong (Princeton: Princeton University Press, 1983), vol. 6 of *Kierkegaard's Writings*, trans. and ed. Howard V. Hong and Edna H. Hong (Princeton: Princeton University Press, 1978–), pp. 15–38, 48–53, 59–63.

14. Walter Benjamin, *The Arcades Project*, pp. 248 [J11,8], 250 [J12a,5], 272 [J24,3], 461 [N2a,1], 558 [S8a,5].

15. Benjamin, *The Arcades Project*, p. 93 [C5a,1].

16. Ibid., p. 85 [C1a,4].

17. Ibid., p. 170 [F8a].

18. Louis Aragon, *Paris Pesant*, trans. Simon Watson Taylor (Boston: Exact Change, 1994), p. 15.

19. It is important to remember that *The Arcades Project*, to the degree that it heralds a new art form, is above all a work of citation and text display. In Convolute N, [N1a,8], p. 460, Benjamin characterizes this work as "literary montage." Throughout the *Project*, Benjamin remains attentive to the supplemental rapport between prostitution and gambling and the "mainstream" capitalist economy in goods, services, and trade expanding exponentially throughout the nineteenth century. In Benjamin's choreography of textual materials, prostitution and gambling are supplemental to the "official" economy and they are supplemental to each other (in the sense that "soft" funds not siphoned off to one pursuit often end up expended in the other). Benjamin's showcasing of these symbiotic and supplemental economic relations in nineteenth-century Paris reaches a climax in Convolute O of *The Arcades Project*, "Prostitution and Gambling." Within the framework of the materials that make

up this segment, Benjamin orchestrates a swerving dialectic in which the materials and discourse of prostitution repeatedly morph into those of gambling and vice versa. What is particularly notable here is that Benjamin, through the apt selection of materials and minute attention to their sequence, can have the textual fragments do all his speaking for him. Particularly in the age of cybernetic Web sites, we need further aesthetic studies of this artwork of citation and text display. For some of Benjamin's most telling segues between prostitution and gambling, see Convolute O in *The Arcades Project*, pp. 494 [O2,4; O2,5; O2a,1], 500 [O5a,3, O6,1], 502 [O7,3, O7,4], 509 [O10a,1, O10a,2, O10a,3], 511 [O11a,2, O11a,2], 512 [O12,2, O12,3], 513 [O13,3, O13,4].

20. Aragon, *Paris Passant*, p. 17.

21. Adin Steinsaltz, in *The Talmud: The Steinsaltz Edition. A Reference Guide*, ed. and trans. Israel V. Berman, vol. 2, *Tractate Bava Mezia*, part 2 (New York: Random House, 1989), pp. 11–36, provides a comprehensive overview to this history.

22. J. Hillis Miller and Manuel Asensi, *Black Holes: Or, Boustrophedonic Reading* (Stanford: Stanford University Press, 1999), pp. 333–35, 349–55, 359–61.

23. Ibid., p. 359.

24. Adin Steinsaltz, in *A Reference Guide*, pp. 48–59, identifies the multiple registers and units of the Talmudic page. A similar schematic is provided by Robert Goldenberg in his fine overview, "Talmud," in *Back to the Sources: Reading the Classic Jewish Texts*, ed. Barry Holtz (New York: Simon & Schuster, 1984), pp. 140–43. The frontispiece of the present chapter is the first page of chapter 3 of *Tractate Bava Mezia*, known by its first word, "Hamafkid," concerning the status of animals and other property left under supervision, compensated and uncompensated. The reproduced page, from Munich Hebrew Codex 95, written in Paris between 1340 and 1370, does not conform to the standard page whose layout I characterize in my elucidation. It was the Bomberg edition of the Talmud, published in Venice between 1520 and 1523, that established the modern page composition, to which my remarks address themselves. See Steinsaltz, *A Reference Guide*, p. 49. I am grateful to the staff at the Beinecke Library, Yale University, for the clarification regarding the provenance of Munich Hebrew Codex 95.

25. The geometric thrust and bearing of Islamic visual decoration over and against a Hindu reach toward sublimity through algebraic multiplication was one of the many treasures revealed to me and my fellow students at Brandeis University during the 1960s in the art history courses offered by Leo Bronstein.

26. As Derrida specified at a May 25–26, 2001 conference in Kolding, Denmark, devoted to a collective reprise of *Glas* (trans. John P. Leavy, Jr. and Richard Rand [Lincoln: University of Nebraska Press, 1986]), one can quickly go astray in linking his 1974 work, pivoting as it does on the hinge between socioideological conventionality and its not totally inverse Other, to a religious canon that, albeit typographically radical, does not shy away from predicating

behavior and the terms of social tolerance and exclusion. The rapport between deconstruction and theology will never be an easy one, to whatever extent both discourses verge toward the limits of metaphysical and ideological systematization. The author of the current hypotheses received a sorely needed refresher course in the complexity and difficulty of these matters amid an atmosphere of lucid discussion in Kolding.

27. Avital Ronell's *The Telephone Book: Technology, Schizophrenia, Electric Speech* (Lincoln: University of Nebraska Press, 1989) not only engages in a profound and original meditation on the philosophical operating system underlying her chosen phenomena, it brings the book medium to some of its foregone conclusions. It contains the most systematic deployment of typography, textual registers, and page composition, as allegories of textual dynamics, to have emerged thus far in the theoretical field. The briefest and most incomplete list of her innovations in this regard would have to include the placement of her notes in a "Classified" and saffron (if not yellow) pages section; pagination by a graphic "thumb index" system; inscribing the pages in a section on Heidegger and schizophrenia with wavering blank rifts or schizzes (pp. 139–54); tending to set Heidegger's text in attenuated columns, underscoring both their current fetishistic status and arbitrariness; reverse typesetting that transforms the page into the simulacrum of an inscribed pane of translucent material (e.g., pp. 18, 48); and setting certain sections of text at a skew and exploiting every opportunity for headlines, characters, and charts to underscore significant happenings in her own glosses on the effect of graphic technology on contemporary culture. This work "dissolves" the genre of the academic treatise while preparing the way for something else emerging on the horizon but not yet fully realized.

28. Citations of the Talmudic passage at hand derive from Steinsaltz, *Tractate Bava Metzia*, pp. 207–67. The specific citation at hand is to be found on pp. 207–8.

29. Ibid., p, 209.

30. Ibid., pp. 217–18.

31. For Derrida's virtuoso performance of *glas* as concantenation, of the repetition and cascading of subrational elements (e.g. *gl*) speaking more to the composition of language than more definitive components, see his *Glas*, pp. 47–53, 119–21, 139–62, 210–12, 222, 235–36, 253. Note that within the framework of the present chapter, italicized page references refer to the Hegel (left-hand) columns on the pages of *Glas*, while unitalicized citations go back to the right-hand column devoted to Genet.

32. *Tractate Bava Mezia*, p. 219.

33. Ibid., p. 207.

34. Ibid., pp. 218–19.

35. See Jacques Lacan, "Kant with Sade," trans. James B. Swenson, Jr., *October* 51 (1989): 55–75.

36. Derrida, *Glas*, pp. *181*, 160.

37. Ibid., pp. *166–84*, 147–64.

38. Ibid., pp. *178–79*, 158–59.

39. Ibid., pp. *174–79*, 153–58.

40. Ibid., pp. *251*, 225.

41. Ibid., pp. *208*, 185; *142*, 124.

42. Typographical epiphenomena in *Glas* that could easily be called Talmudic in their effect are to be found in Derrida, *Glas*, pp. *13–14, 48–49, 68, 78, 96–97, 186–87, 253, 275*; 7–8, 39–40, 57, 66–67, 82–83, 165–66, 226–27, 247–48. I have commented at length on the supplemental interplay between the readings of Hegel and Genet constituting the architecture of *Glas* in "Hegel, *Glas*, and the Broader Modernity," in *Hegel after Derrida*, ed. Stuart Barnett (New York: Routledge, 1998), pp. 260–92.

43. Joyce, *Finnegans Wake*, pp. 260–308.

44. Derrida, *Glas*, pp. *214–19*, 192–96.

45. Ibid., pp. *218*, 194.

46. Ibid., pp. *258–59*, 231–33.

47. Joyce, *Finnegans Wake*, pp. 107, 114, 117, 121.

48. See Gilles Deleuze and Félix Guattari, *A Thousand Plateaus: Capitalism and Schizophrenia*, trans. Brian Massumi (Minneapolis: University of Minnesota Press, 1989), pp. 139–42, 148; also *Anti-Oedipus*, trans. Robert Hurley, Mark Seem, and Helen R. Lane (Minneapolis: University of Minnesota Press, 1983), pp. 140–42. I have attempted to formulate the status of these outmoded political formations that are nonetheless somehow always lurking beneath the surface of social space in Chapter 5 of the present book.

5. DETERRITORIALIZING THE TEXT: FLOW THEORY AND DECONSTRUCTION

1. All citations from this text refer to Gilles Deleuze and Félix Guattari, *A Thousand Plateaus: Capitalism and Schizophrenia*, trans. Brian Massumi (Minneapolis: University of Minnesota Press, 1989).

2. Jorge Luis Borges, "Death and the Compass," in *Ficciones* (New York: Grove Press, 1962), p. 137.

3. For the figure of faciality, see Deleuze and Guattari, *A Thousand Plateaus*, pp. 62–63, 115–17, 168–70, 174–91, 301.

4. Deleuze and Guattari, *A Thousand Plateaus*, pp. 238–39.

5. Ibid., p. 213

6. Ibid.

7. See, for example, Karl Marx, *Capital: A Critique of Political Economy*, vol. 1, trans. Ben Fowkes (London: Penguin, 1996), pp. 273, 349–50, 367–69, 377, 611–14, 620–21, 790–97, 818–19.

8. Deleuze and Guattari, *A Thousand Plateaus*, pp. 4, 9, 15, 24, 34, 36–37, 76, 97–98, 122–23, 132, 153–54, 158, 169, 214, 225, 243–44, 253–54, 256–57, 260–61, 268, 306, 346, 355–56, 378, 381, 400, 482, 507.

9. Jacques Lacan, *The Seminar of Jacques Lacan III: The Psychoses, 1955–56,* trans. Russell Grigg (New York: W.W. Norton, 1993), p. 92.

10. Lacan, *Seminar III: The Psychoses,* pp. 141–42.

11. Gilles Deleuze and Félix Guattari, *Anti-Oedipus: Capitalism and Schizophrenia,* trans. Robert Hurley, Mark Seem. and Helen R. Lane (Minneapolis: University of Minnesota Press, 1996), pp. 141–42.

12. In different respects, both the notion of the rhizome and that of the assemblage may claim enormous relevance to the modality of criticism as an element in the wider discursive division of labor whose parameters are being elaborated throughout the present volume. Deleuze and Guattari's rhizomatic imagery underscores their preference for visualizing the cultural, social, biological, and physical phenomena of the world as a text, even though they repeatedly, under certain rhetorical conditions, fall back from this apprehension (i.e., relapse into a positivistic posture vis à vis certain phenomena). In this context, it proves worthwhile to imagine the incremental body of one's readings as an "assemblage," a term that Deleuze and Guattari appropriate from Marx characterizing a superstructure of sociopolitical organization or a configuration of cultural conditions. To think of the assemblage as textually constituted accords with their overarching sense of the world as a rhizomatic organization and disequilibrium.

13. Deleuze and Guattari, *A Thousand Plateaus,* p. 50.

14. Ibid., pp. 53–54.

15. See Marcel Griaule, *Conversations with Ogotemmêli: An Introduction to Dogon Religious Ideas* (London: Oxford University Press, 1965).

16. Deleuze and Guattari, *A Thousand Plateaus,* p. 267.

17. See Marcel Proust, *A la recherche du temps perdu,* ed. Pierre Clarac and André Ferré, 3 vols. (Paris: Pleiade, 1954), 1:326; 2:835–40. Also see Italo Calvino, "The Aquatic Uncle," in *Cosmicomics,* trans. William Weaver (New York: Collier, 1970), pp. 81–96.

18. Deleuze and Guattari, *A Thousand Plateaus,* p. 371.

19. Ibid., p. 153.

20. Ibid., pp. 153–54.

21. Ibid., pp. 132–33.

22. Deleuze and Guattari, *Anti-Oedipus,* pp. 132–33.

23. Deleuze and Guattari, *A Thousand Plateaus,* pp. 139–41.

24. Ibid.

25. Ibid.

26. Ibid., pp. 141, 142.

27. Ibid., pp. 135, 136–37.

28. Ibid., p. 148

29. See, for example, Jacques Derrida, *Dissemination,* trans. Barbara Johnson (Chicago: University of Chicago Press, 1981), pp. 167–71, 209–22, 227–31, 251–52, 318–23.

30. Deleuze and Guattari, *A Thousand Plateaus,* pp. 206–07, 209, 211–12, 216–17, 222–25, 228.

6. DERRIDA AS CRITIC: A JOYCEAN ODYSSEY

1. Jacques Derrida, "Ulysses Gramophone: Hear Say Yes in Joyce," in *Acts of Literature*, ed. Derek Attridge (New York: Routledge, 1994), p. 257.

2. Ibid., pp. 268, 284.

3. Ibid., p. 279.

4. Ibid., pp. 268, 281.

5. Jacques Derrida, *The Post Card*, trans. Alan Bass (Chicago: University of Chicago Press, 1987); "Des Tours de Babel," in *Acts of Religion*, ed. Gil Anidjar (New York: Routledge, 2002), pp. 102–34; "The Eyes of Language: The Abyss and the Volcano," in *Acts of Religion*, pp. 189–227; *Archive Fever: A Freudian Impression*, trans. Eric Prenowitz (Chicago: University of Chicago Press, 1995).

6. Jean-Luc Nancy, for example, an early and ongoing contributor to deconstruction's atelier, may be said to have raised and dealt with political constructs and issues in a more pragmatic fashion than Derrida, even while holding true to the broader parameters of deconstruction's ongoing project. See Nancy's *The Inoperative Community*, ed. Peter Connor, trans. Peter Conner et al. (Minneapolis: University of Minnesota Press, 1991); also, *A Finite Thinking*, ed. Simon Sparks (Stanford: Stanford University Press, 2003), pp. 277–307.

7. Henry Sussman, *The Aesthetic Contract* (Stanford: Stanford University Press, 1997), pp. 165–77.

8. "The deconstruction sets out to show that this is not necessarily the case." Paul de Man, *Allegories of Reading* (New Haven: Yale University Press, 1979), p. 122.

9. Ibid., p. 125.

10. Sussman, *The Aesthetic Contract*, pp. 286–87.

11. Jacques Derrida, "Plato's Pharmacy," in *Dissemination*, pp. 95–117, 142–71.

12. Jacques Derrida, *Of Grammatology*, trans. Guyatri C. Spivak (Baltimore: Johns Hopkins University Press, 1976), pp. 108–12, 125–32; *Dissemination*, pp. 75–76, 94, 98–99, 118, 122, 124.

13. Jacques Derrida, "The Double Session," in *Dissemination*, pp. 216, 258, 261, 285; also, *Glas*, trans. John P. Leavey, Jr. and Richard Rand (Lincoln: University of Nebraska Press, 1986), pp. 128–29, 240.

14. Jacques Derrida, "White Mythology," in *Margins of Philosophy* trans. Alan Bass (Chicago: University of Chicago Press, 1982), pp. 209, 232–38, 242–54, 260–71.

15. Derrida, *Glas*, pp. 3, 8, 12, 15, 23, 42, 86–87, 146–62, 196, 220, 246–53.

16. Jacques Derrida, *The Truth in Painting*, trans. Geoff Bennington and Ian McLeod (Chicago: University of Chicago Press, 1987), pp. 1, 11–12, 42–45, 60–64, 67–79, 97–100, 301–04, 320–22, 341–45.

17. Jacques Derrida, *Specters of Marx*, trans. Peggy Kamuf (New York: Routledge, 1994), pp. 28, 59, 62–66, 69–70, 73, 101, 104, 169.

18. Henry Sussman, "The Court as Text: Inversion, Supplanting, and Derangement in Kafka's *Der Prozeß*," *PMLA* 92 (1977): 41–55.

19. Jacques Derrida, "Before the Law," in *Acts of Literature*, pp. 181–220.

20. It could well be argued that each one of Derrida's major books effects a significant rearrangement and reconfiguration of the issues and artifacts open to deconstruction. Matters of technology, particularly that involved in communications and representation, achieved a new centrality in his *La carte postale* (Paris: Flammarion, 1980), from which he never retreated. See Derrida, *The Post Card*, pp. 3, 13, 23, 27, 29, 30–32, 43–44, 46–50, 54, 58, 62, 66–70, 82, 93, 138–44, 159, 162, 175–79, 185–87, 338, 346, 373, 395–404. Also see Avital Ronell, *The Telephone Book* (Lincoln: University of Nebraska Press, 1989).

21. See Sigmund Freud, "Jokes and their Relation to the Unconscious," in *The Standard Edition of the Complete Psychological Writings of Sigmund Freud*, ed. and trans. James Strachey, 24 vols. (London: Hogarth Press, 1953–74), 8:147–49, 159–80, 181–87.

22. Jacques Derrida, "La parole soufflée" and "The Theater of Cruelty and the Closure of Representation," in *Writing and Difference*, trans. Alan Bass (Chicago: University of Chicago Press, 1978), pp. 169–95, 232–50.

23. Jacques Derrida, *Signeponge = Signsponge*, trans. Richard Rand (New York: Columbia University Press, 1984).

24. Above all, Jacques Derrida, "The Law of Genre," in *Acts of Literature*.

25. Jacques Derrida, *Shibboleth pour Paul Celan* (Paris: Galilée, 1986).

26. Derrida, "Ulysses Gramophone: Hear Say Yes in Joyce," originally published as *Ulysse gramophone* (Paris: Galilée, 1987).

27. Jacques Derrida, *The Ear of the Other: Otobiographie, Transference, Translation*, trans. Peggy Kamuf (New York: Schocken, 1985).

28. Derrida, "Ulysses Gramophone," p. 267.

29. Ibid., pp. 264, 284, 259.

30. Ibid., pp. 257–58.

31. Walter Benjamin, "The Task of the Translator," in *Selected Writings*, ed. Marcus Bullock, Howard Eiland, and Gary Smith, 4 vols. 1:253–66; also see Carol Jacobs, "The Monstrosity of Translation, in *In the Language of Walter Benjamin* (Baltimore: Johns Hopkins University Press, 1999), pp. 75–90.

32. For example, in Jacques Derrida, *Speech and Phenomena and Other Essays on Husserl's Theory of Signs*, trans. David B. Allison (Evanston: Northwestern University Press, 1973), pp. 68, 78–80, 82–86.

33. Jacques Derrida, *Adieu to Emmanuel Levinas* (Stanford: Stanford University Press, 1999); also, "Violence and Metaphysics: An Essay on the Thought of Emmanuel Levinas," in *Writing and Difference*, pp. 79–153.

34. Jacques Derrida, "Différance" and "*Ousia* and *Grammē*: Note on a Note from *Being and Time*," in *Margins of Philosophy*, pp. 1–68.

35. Jacques Derrida, "Edmond Jabès and the Question of the Book," in *Writing and Difference*, pp. 64–78.

36. Derrida, "Ulysses Gramophone," pp. 277–78.

37. Ibid.

38. Ibid., pp. 284–85.

39. Ibid., p. 281.

40. This is the running textual register written by Jacques Derrida in Geoffrey Bennington and Jacques Derrida, *Jacques Derrida*, trans. Geoff Bennington (Chicago: University of Chicago Press, 1999); a translation of Geoffrey Bennington and Jacques Derrida, *Jacques Derrida* (Paris: Seuil, 1991).

41. Derrida, "Ulysses Gramophone," p. 268.

42. Jacques Derrida, "Hostipitality," in *Acts of Religion*, pp. 356–420.

43. Derrida, "Ulysses Gramophone," pp. 280, 283.

44. Ibid., pp. 282–84.

45. Ibid., pp. 264, 284.

46. Stuart Gilbert, *James Joyce's "Ulysses"* (New York: Vintage, 1952).

47. Frank Budgen, *James Joyce and the Making of "Ulysses"* (Bloomington: Indiana University Press, 1960).

48. Derrida, "Ulysses Gramophone," p. 280.

49. See Richard Ellmann, *James Joyce* (Oxford: Oxford University Press, 1966), pp. 206–07, 212, 227, 234–35, 265, 273, 277, 297, 299, 331–32, 338, 363–63, 402, 414–19, 426–29, 470–71, 290–94, 569–70, 646–47.

50. James Joyce, *Ulysses: The Corrected Text*, ed. Hans Walter Gabler (New York: Random House, 1986), pp. 69, 96, 110–11, 122, 134, 239, 401, 446–48, 450, 502, 513, 521, 590.

51. Sussman, *The Aesthetic Contract*, pp. 157–77.

52. Derek Attridge, "This Strange Institution Called Literature: An Interview with Jacques Derrida," in *Acts of Literature*, pp. 33–75.

53. See Derrida, *Archive Fever*, pp. 1–5, 12, 18–20, 26–29, 38–43, 57.

54. Derrida, *Acts of Literature*, p. 53.

55. Henry Sussman, *High Resolution: Critical Theory and the Problem of Literacy* (New York: Oxford University Press, 1989), pp. 15–24.

56. Andzrej Warminski is so bold as to formulate the parameters of a de Manian "rhetorical reading." See his "'As the Poets Do It': On the Material Sublime," in *Material Events: Paul de Man and the Afterlife of Theory*, ed. Tom Cohen, et. al. (Minneapolis: University of Minnesota Press, 2001), pp. 3–31.

57. Derrida, *Of Grammatology*, pp. 97–102, 105–06, 118–20, 141–316.

58. Jacques Derrida, *The Truth in Painting*.

59. Jacques Derrida, "The Pit and the Pyramid: An Introduction to Hegel's Semiology," in *Writing and Difference*, pp. 69–108. Also, *Glas*, pp. 6–150.

7. THE FOURTH ABRAHAMIC RELIGION?

1. Hent de Vries, *Philosophy and the Turn to Religion* (Baltimore: Johns Hopkins University Press, 1999).

2. For example, see Rodolphe Gasché, "God, for Example," in *Inventions of Difference* (Cambridge: Harvard University Press, 1994), pp. 150–70.

3. This issue has been raised, with respect to Derrida's *The Gift of Death*, trans. David Wills (Chicago: University of Chicago Press, 1995).

4. See Jacques Derrida, "On Forgiveness," in *On Cosmopolitanism and Forgiveness*, trans. Mark Dooley and Michael Hughes (London: Routledge, 2001), pp. 27–60.

5. *The Meaning of the Glorious Koran*, trans. Marmaduke Pickthall, Everyman's Library (New York: Alfred A. Knopf, 1992), pp. 120–21.

6. Jacques Derrida, "Hostipitality," in *Acts of Religion*, ed. Gil Anidjar (New York: Routledge, 2002), 356–420.

7. Behind Derrida's philosophically rigorous work on difference stands the backdrop of Saussure's linguistic-cultural understanding of the differential nature of the entire field of signifiers. "Everything that has been said up to this point," he writes in his *Course in General Linguistics* (trans. Wade Baskin [New York: McGraw Hill, 1966]), "boils down to this: in language there are only differences" (p. 120). This is a phenomenon also known in the field of child language development: signifiers don't mean by virtue of an inborn linguistic essence, they attach to different elements of the referential and linguistic worlds through their difference from one another and through the diversity and coverage that this difference allows. One observes a parallel phenomenon in the field of "world religions": the respective religions adjudicate various matters less by virtue of an inherent and essential truth than by claiming a specific and hence differentiated location on religion's "global" map.

8. We are indebted to Louis Marin for his seminal work on the semiological implications of the sacrament of Communion. See his *La critique du discours* (Paris: Minuit, 1975), pp. 51–77, 92–100, 134–46, 245–50, 327–39.

9. See Adin Steinsaltz, in *The Talmud: The Steinsaltz Edition. A Reference Guide*, ed. and trans. Israel V. Berman, vol. 2, *Tractate Bava Mezia*, part 2 (New York: Random House, 1989), pp. 53–54.

10. Hent de Vries, *Philosophy and the Turn to Religion*, p. 50.

11. Jacques Derrida, *Speech and Phenomena and Other Essays on Husserl's Theory of Signs*, trans. David B. Allison (Evanston: Northwestern University Press, 1973), p. 6.

12. Jacques Derrida, "Faith and Knowledge, in" *Acts of Religion*, pp. 54–55.

13. Derrida most fully explores the notion of the address both as a destination for writing and as the bearing of the writer in *The Post Card*, pp. 25, 33; also see *Acts of Religion*, pp. 337, 343–45.

14. Avital Ronell, *Stupidity* (Lincoln: University of Nebraska Press, 2001).

15. Jacques Derrida, "Interpretations at War," in *Acts of Religion*, p. 165.

16. Jacques Derrida, "The Eyes of Language: The Abyss and the Volcano," in *Acts of Religion*, pp. 189–227.

17. Jacques Derrida," "Force of Law," in *Acts of Religion*, pp. 228–98.

18. Walter Benjamin, "Critique of Violence," in *Selected Writings*, ed. Marcus Bullock, Howard Eiland, and Gary Smith, 4 vols. (Cambridge, Mass.: Harvard University Press, 1996–2003), 1:241.

19. See Jacques Derrida, "Before the Law," in *Acts of Literature*, pp. 185, 187–92, 194–97, 199–212, 214–20.

20. Derrida," "Force of Law," pp. 251–55.

21. Ibid., p. 253.

22. See especially Jacques Derrida, *Specters of Marx*, trans. Peggy Kamuf (New York: Routledge, 1994), pp. 35, 65, 167–69. Also see "The Eyes of Language," p. 215, and Hostipitality," pp. 364, 386–87.

23. Ibid., p. 254.

24. Ibid., p. 242

25. Ibid., p. 240.

26. Jacques Derrida, "Hostipitality," in *Acts of Religion*, p. 364.

27. Ibid., p. 362.

28. Ibid., pp. 369. 363, 365.

29. Ibid., p. 365.

30. Ibid., p. 408.

31. Derrida, "Hostipitality, p. 396.

32. Sigmund Freud, "Three Essays on the Theory of Sexuality," in *The Standard Edition of the Complete Psychological Writings of Sigmund Freud*, ed. and trans. James Strachey, 24 vols. (London: Hogarth Press, 1953–74), 11:28, 36, 78, 80–81, 97, 122–23, 132–36.

33. Derrida's apology for the limitations, primarily in terms of space and attention, of his own elucidations becomes one of the characteristic gestures of the essays, emanating from many different stages and contexts in his work assembled in *Acts of Religion*, pp. 2, 44, 72, 77, 83, 236, 245, 260, 414.

34. John Donne, "Divine Poems," in *Poetical Works*, ed. Herbert Grierson (Oxford: Oxford University Press, 1966), pp. 266–338.

35. George Herbert, "The Church-Porch," "The Reprisall," "Easter," "Affliction (I)," "Prayer (II)," "Home," "The Collar," "The Glimpse," "The Search," and "The Flower" in *The Poems of George Herbert*, ed. Helen Gardner (London: Oxford University Press, 1961), pp. 3–20, 30, 31, 35–36, 39–53, 93–94, 97–99, 143–45, 152–54, 156–57.

36. Richard Crashaw, "Sacred Poems in One English Version" and "Sacred Poems in Two English Versions," in *The Complete Poetry of Richard Crashaw*, ed. George Walton Williams (New York: New York University Press, 1972), pp. 3–154.

37. Derrida's French phrase for *On the Name*, ed. Thomas Dutoit, trans. David Wood, John P. Leavy, Jr., and Ian McLeod (Stanford: Stanford University Press, 1995), p. 27. I have been invaluably guided and informed on certain pivotal points by my conversations with Outi Pasanen, a commentator on and translator of Derrida from the University of Helsinki with a remarkable over-

view of the project and literature of deconstruction. Both in conversation and in forthcoming work, she consolidates some of Derrida's specific psychoanalytical, theological, ethical, and literary interventions with his foundational work, above all on Husserl, on the transcendental psychology and the parameters of phenomenology. Pasanen's insights have clarified my prior understandings of deconstruction's critique of purity, its call for exegetical events bearing the full surprise of what cannot be anticipated, and its possibilities for community.

38. Jacques Derrida, "*Khōra*," in *On the Name*, trans. Thomas Dutoit (Stanford: Stanford University Press, 1995), p. 89.

39. See in particular Jacques Derrida, "Plato's Pharmacy," in *Dissemination*, trans, Barbara Johnson (Chicago: University of Chicago Press, 1981), pp. 128–55.

40. Derrida, "*Khōra*," pp. 95–96.

41. Derrida elaborates on *khōra's* refusal to furnish support on pp. 95–96:

She [*khōra*] "is" nothing other than the sum or the process of what has just been inscribed "on" her, on her subject, right against her subject, but she is not the *subject* or the *present support* of all these interpretations. . . . This absence of support, which cannot be translated to absent support or into absence as support, provokes and resists any binary or dialectical determination, any inspection of a philosophical *type*, or lest us say, more rigorously, of an *ontological* type.

42. Ibid., p. 92.

43. Ibid., p. 103.

44. Ibid., p. 104.

45. Ibid., p. 111.

46. Ibid., pp. 116–17.

47. Ibid., p. 120.

48. Immanuel Kant, *Critique of Judgment*, trans. J. H. Bernard (New York: Hafner Press, 1951), pp. 196–98.

49. Derrida, "*Khōra*," p. 126.

50. Jacques Derrida, *Glas*, trans. John P. Leavey, Jr. and Richard Rand (Lincoln: University of Nebraska Press, 1986), pp. 240–42.

51. Jacques Derrida, "A Silkworm of One's Own (Points of View Stitched on the Other Veil)," in *Acts of Religion*, pp. 309–55.

52. Also see Jacques Derrida, *The Ear of the Other: Otobiography, Transference, Translation*, trans. Peggy Kamuf (New York: Schocken Books, 1985).

53. Needless to say, equality and tolerance are imperative operating principles of any modern system of governance and administration. I'm simply pointing to the fact that since each of us emerges from a site of particularity on the map of a multicultural society, we as individuals cannot be assumed to espouse these indispensable ideals on any significant level of meaningfulness or profundity until we have taken into account or been afforded the possibility of working through our particular heritage (or baggage). To take the achievement of the

values of equality and tolerance as a foregone conclusion is to foreclose the difficult process of the enunciation and processing of singularity and difference in whose absence their espousal amounts to a vapid endorsement. Such public consideration of differences toward the end of disseminating a Levinasian sense of alterity may well constitute one of the most laudable purposes toward which general education, whether at the secondary of university levels, can be put. Needless to say as well: This education in the articulate reading and interpretation of differences cannot begin early enough.

54. Derrida, "A Silkworm of One's Own," p. 350.

55. Kant, *Critique of Judgment*, pp. 182–202.

56. Ludwig Wittgenstein, *On Certainty*, ed. G. E. M. Anscombe and G. H. von Wright (New York: Harper & Row, 1969), pp. 2–5e, 9–9e, 16–18e, 41–46e, 87–90e.

57. Jacques Derrida, "Interpretations at War: Kant, the Jew, the German," in *Acts of Religion*, pp. 166, 168.

58. Jacques Derrida, "Taking a Stand for Algeria," in *Acts of Religion*, pp. 299–308.

59. Derrida, "Interpretations at War," p. 138.

60. Derrida, "Hostipitality," p. 399.

61. Ibid., p. 402.

62. Derrida, "A Silkworm of One's Own," pp. 311–12.

63. Ibid., p. 312.

64. See Jacques Derrida, "The Double Session," in *Dissemination*, pp. 251–54, 257–65.

65. Derrida, "A Silkworm of One's Own," pp. 323–24.

66. Ibid., pp. 327–28.

67. Franz Kafka, *The Complete Stories*, ed. Nahum N. Glatzer (New York: Schocken Books, 1976), p. 427.

68. Jacques Derrida, "The Eyes of Language," pp. 195, 198.

69. Ibid., p. 196.

70. Ibid., p. 193.

71. Ibid., p. 198.

72. Ibid.

73. Although in conjunction with *The Cantos of Ezra Pound* I detected a modernist gravitation toward putative sites of pure poetic utterance, I was initially apprised of the full conceptual and tactical extent of a rigorous critique of purity in the project of deconstruction by Marcus Coelen, currently of the University of Munich, who, during his student years at Buffalo produced a seminar paper entitled "*Verpassen*: On the Motif of Purity in Plato's *Phaedo*." The notion of purity and its implications have received an important recent update by Outi Pasanen in her "Gasché on De Man and Derrida: Forgetting the Moment of Crisis," in *Deconstruction: Critical Concepts on Literary and Cultural Studies*, ed. Jonathan Culler (London: Routledge, 2003), pp. 349–51, 357–64.

74. Derrida, "The Eyes of Language," p. 217.

75. Ibid.

76. Ibid., p. 218.

77. Jacques Derrida, "Faith and Knowledge: The Two Sources of' 'Religion' at the Limits of Reason Alone," in *Acts of Religion*, p. 68.

78. *Assurance*, is, of course, also the word for "insurance" in French.

79. Derrida, "Faith and Knowledge," pp. 73–74.

80. Ibid., p. 72.

81. Regarding the moral imperative, see Immanuel Kant, *Critique of Pure Reason*, trans. Paul Guyer and Alan W. Wood (Cambridge: Cambridge University Press, 1998), pp. 403–05, 678–81; with respect to the *sensus communis*, see *Critique of Judgment*, pp. 135–40, 151–63.

82. Derrida, "The Force of Law," pp. 248–49.

83. This strand of Derrida's ongoing interest is already evident in his "Freud and the Scene of Writing," in *Writing and Difference*, trans. Alan Bass (Chicago: University of Chicago Press, 1978), pp. 196–277.

84. Derrida, "The Eyes of Language," pp. 218–19.

85. Derrida, "The Law of Genre," in *Acts of Literature*, p. 225.

86. "Address" is Derrida's equivalent to what I here term "bearing." For Derrida's elaboration of this term, above all see his "Force of Law," in *Acts of Religion*, pp. 237, 243–45.

87. See Rodolphe Gasché, *Of Minimal Things* (Stanford: Stanford University Press, 1999), pp. 3–27.

88. Jacques Derrida, *Specters of Marx: The State of the Debt, the Work of Mourning, and the New International*, trans. Peggy Kamuf (New York: Routledge, 1994), pp. 60–61.

89. Jacques Derrida, *The Politics of Friendship*, trans. George Collins (London: Verso, 1994), p. 54.

90. See, above all, Jean-Luc Nancy, *The Inoperative Community*, ed. Peter Conner, trans. Peter Connor, et. al. (Minneapolis: University of Minnesota Press, 1991), pp. 1–42, 71–81; Giorgio Agamben, *The Coming Community*, trans. Michael Hardt (Minneapolis: University of Minnesota Press, 2001), pp. 1–22, 39–46, 67–88.

91. On the notion of packs, see Gilles Deleuze and Félix Guattari, *A Thousand Plateaus: Capitalism and Schizophrenia*, trans. Brian Massumi (Minneapolis: University of Minnesota Press, 1989), pp. 29, 32, 35–37, 233–239, 241–48, 262–63.

92. Jorge Luis Borges, "Tlön, Uqbar, Orbis Tertius," in *Ficciones* (New York: Grove Press, 1962), 31.

93. Deleuze and Guattari, *A Thousand Plateaus*, p. 21.

94. Ibid., p. 9.

95. Derrida, "The Law of Genre," p. 224.

96. Jacques Derrida, *Glas*, 240–42.

97. While Derrida goes to considerable lengths to temper the fashion in which Western culture memorializes and canonizes itself with little sensitivity to the metaphysics that it mobilizes in performing these functions, there is a strong current of his work dedicated to marking and re-marking significant developments in and contributions to thinking. This strand of his thought reaches a high point in a series of addresses and/or articles composed on the occasion of the deaths of his compatriots in the intellectual and academic worlds whose work he values. Deconstruction is not resistant to assistance at funerals. It has worked hard to reconfigure what they might mean and what function they might serve. See Jacques Derrida, *The Work of Mourning* (Chicago: University of Chicago Press, 2002).

98. J. Hillis Miller, *Speech Acts in Literature* (Stanford: Stanford University Press, 2001), p. 63.

99. Ibid., p. 112.

100. Ibid., p. 127.

101. Jacques Derrida, *Specters of Marx*, pp. 65–66.

102. Martin Heidegger, "What are Poets For?" in *Poetry Language, Thought*, trans. Albert Hofstadter (New York: Harper & Row, 1971), pp. 89–142.

103. Ibid., p. 132.

104. Ibid., p. 94.

105. Ibid., p. 96.

106. For example, "Willing has in it the character of command; for purposeful self-assertion is a mode in which the attitude of the producing, and the objective character of the world, concentrate into an unconditional and therefore unity. In this self-concentration, the command character of the will announces itself" ("What are Poets For?", 111).

107. Ibid., p. 105.

108. For Heidegger's work on the notion of the *Riß* or poetic trait/outline so essential to the endeavor of art as inscription, see "The Origin of the Work of Art," in his *Poetry, Language, Thought*, pp. 63–64, 68–74.

109. Heidegger, "What are Poets For?" p. 116.

110. Ibid., p. 95.

111. Jorge Luis Borges, "Death and the Compass," in *Ficciones* (New York: Grove Press, 1962), p. 141.

112. Ibid., p. 129.

AFTERWORD. FRAGMENTARY SCRIPT AS THE ENABLING LEGISLATION FOR MODERN CRITICISM

1. See Søren Kierkegaard, *Fear and Trembling/Repetition*, trans. and ed. Howard V. Hong and Edna H. Hong (Princeton: Princeton University Press, 1983), vol. 6 of *Kierkegaard's Writings*, trans. and ed. Howard V. Hong and Edna H. Hong (Princeton: Princeton University Press, 1978–), pp. 1:133–34, 148–53, 158, 170–76, 179–87, 220–31, 275, 283–98, 300–15.

2. For the notion of eternal recurrence, see, among other locations, Friedrich Nietzsche, *Thus Spoke Zarathustra*, trans. Walter Kaufmann (New York: Penguin, 1966), pp. 217–19, 228–31, 323–24; *The Gay Science*, trans. Josefine Nauckhoff (Cambridge: Cambridge University Press, 2001), pp. 161–62, 194–95, and trans. Walter Kaufmann and R. J. Hollingdale (New York: Random House, 1967), pp. 35–36, 255, 330–31, 417, 536–37, 539–40, 544–50.

3. For some of the seminal and characteristic passages in which Freud elaborates the division of labor between such intrapsychic agencies as the id, the ego, and the superego and in which he characterizes the play between the different strata of consciousness, see Sigmund Freud, *The Standard Edition of the Complete Psychological Writings of Sigmund Freud*, ed. and trans. James Strachey, 24 vols. (London: Hogarth Press, 1953–74), 2:288–92, 298–301; 4:122–28; 5:506–7, 516, 535–47, 573–74; 8:160–70; 18:19–20; 19:13–39, 48–66.

4. See Søren Kierkegaard, *Either/Or*, trans. Howard V. and Edna H. Hong (Princeton: Princeton University Press, 1987), vols. 2 and 3 of *Kierkegaard's Writings*, trans. and ed. Howard V. Hong and Edna H. Hong (Princeton: Princeton University Press, 1978–), 2:306–08, 325–28, 336, 341– 367, 375–82, 384–86, 391, 398–407, 429–39.

5. For a splendid exegetical ballet accounting for Freud's appropriation of E. T. A. Hoffmann's tale and suggesting alternate Lacanian and deconstructive interpretations of the story and its key figures, see Samuel Weber, "The Sideshow: Or Notes on a Canny Moment," *MLN* 88: 1102–33.

6. For the temporal reversal or metalepsis in which the joke is fulfilled in laughter before it is rationally understood, see Sigmund Freud, "The Joke in its Relation to the Unconscious," in *The Standard Edition*, 8:12–14, 28–29, 41–44, 74, 94–107, 146–53, 167–71, 174–80.

7. *Friedrich Schlegel's Lucinde and Fragments*, trans. Peter Firchow (Minneapolis: University of Minnesota Press, 1971), *Athenaeum*, no. 424, p. 233.

8. Theodor Adorno, *Minima Moralia*, trans. E. F. N. Jephcott (London: Verso, 1984), pp. 25, 43, 50–51, 55, 118, 147, 203, 206, 226.

9. Milan Kundera, *The Unbearable Lightness of Being*, trans. Michael Henry Heim (New York: Harper & Row, 1984), pp. 12, 96–97, 248, 251–57, 278.

10. G. W. F. Hegel, "The Ethical Order," in *Hegel's Phenomenology of Spirit*, trans. A. V. Miller (Oxford: Oxford University Press, 1977), pp. 266–94.

11. The interface between philosophical figures such as the pivotal *Schein* and critical engagement in this pivotal essay by Benjamin has of course been discussed in Chapter 3 above.

12. *Lucinde and Fragments*, *Athenaeum Fragments* 131, 127, 139, pp. 178–89.

13. Ibid., *Critical Fragments* 100, p. 154.

14. See Martin Heidegger, *Identity and Difference*, trans. Joan Stambaugh (New York: Harper & Row, 1969), pp. 23–42, 85–106.

15. *Lucinde and Fragments*, *Athenaeum Fragments* 174, p. 184

16. Ibid., *Critical Fragments* 96, p. 154.

17. Ibid. *Athenaeum Fragments* 206, p. 154

18. Ibid., *Critical Fragments* 104, 97, 59, pp. 189, 153, 150

19. Ibid., *Critical Fragments* 34, p. 146.

20. See Rodolphe Gasché, *The Tain of the Mirror: Derrida and the Philosophy of Reflection* (Cambridge, Mass.: Harvard University Press, 1986), pp. 185–251.

21. See Philippe Lacoue-Labarthe and Jean-Luc Nancy, *The Literary Absolute*, trans. Philip Barnard and Cheryl Lester (Albany: SUNY Press, 1988), pp. 39–58, 101–19.

22. *Lucinde and Fragments, Critical Fragments* 53, p. 149.

23. Ibid., *Critical Fragments* 26, p. 145.

24. Ibid., *Critical Fragments* 108, p. 155–56.

25. Immanuel Kant, *Critique of Judgment*, trans. J. H. Bernard (New York: Hafner, 1951), pp. 52–54, 61, 69, 73, 79–81.

26. Søren Kierkegaard, *The Concept of Irony*, trans. Lee M. Capel (Bloomington: Indiana University Press, 1968), p. 207.

27. Ibid., pp. 212–13.

28. *Lucinde and Fragments, Athenaeum Fragments* 324, p. 209.

29. Ibid., *Athenaeum Fragments* 77, 84, pp. 170, 171.

30. Ibid., *Athenaeum Fragments* 205, p. 189.

31. Ibid., *Athenaeum Fragments* 216, p. 190.

32. Ibid., *Athenaeum Fragments* 217, p. 191.